CLEAN FOOD

FLAVOR IS TRUMP

By

ERIKA G. CENCI

Chef, Author of

The Original
A Touch of Europe® Cookbooks

Order this book online at www.trafford.com/07-1417
or email orders@trafford.com

Most Trafford titles are also available at major online book retailers.

For information, contact the publisher, the author, or her designated representative.

"A Touch of Europe", a trademark of Erika G. Cenci (1986 – 20--)

Created and Written by Erika G. Cenci

Recipes and Food Styling by Erika G. Cenci

Editing and Contributor James (Jim) A. Cenci

Photographs, typography, formatting, displays and Covers – Design and Photographs by James A. Cenci

Note for Librarians: A cataloguing record for this book is available from Library
and Archives Canada at www.collectionscanada.ca/amicus/index-e.html

Printed in Victoria, BC, Canada.

ISBN: 978-1-4251-3623-9

*We at Trafford believe that it is the responsibility of us all, as both individuals
and corporations, to make choices that are environmentally and socially sound.
You, in turn, are supporting this responsible conduct each time you purchase a
Trafford book, or make use of our publishing services. To find out how you are
helping, please visit www.trafford.com/responsiblepublishing.html*

*Our mission is to efficiently provide the world's finest, most comprehensive
book publishing service, enabling every author to experience success.
To find out how to publish your book, your way, and have it available
worldwide, visit us online at www.trafford.com/10510*

www.trafford.com

North America & international
toll-free: 1 888 232 4444 (USA & Canada)
phone: 250 383 6864 ♦ fax: 250 383 6804
email: info@trafford.com

The United Kingdom & Europe
phone: +44 (0)1865 722 113 ♦ local rate: 0845 230 9601
facsimile: +44 (0)1865 722 868 ♦ email: info.uk@trafford.com

10 9 8 7 6 5 4 3

Contents

DEDICATION

In memory,
I dedicate this
cookbook to my mother.

ACKNOWLEDGEMENTS

A special thanks to my husband, Jim, for his genuine high level of interest, support of, and professional assistance rendered in achieving my book writing objectives.

FOREWORD

Ever wish to cook like another admired? You can! Or, ever wish you didn't need to spend so much time preparing for and cooking flavorful meals? You don't have to! Or, have you ever disregarded trying a recipe because it looks too difficult, too time consuming, or because it is unfamiliar?

Then this user-friendly cookbook might help overcome skepticism, reign-in assertiveness or achieve aspirations. And, you'll love results of your efforts. I've assembled some of many of my eclectic creations from my files and transformed them into easy to follow, comprehensive instructions so the dishes will turn out as you hope they would, and many recipes won't take all day to prepare.

You'll find "one of a kind" recipes for quick (everyday) meals as well as recipes for Sunday meals and special occasions. Plus, you'll find an array of extraordinary dessert recipes alive with natural flavor without the level of difficulty one might expect in yielding desserts of such high quality.

It all begins with knowing more about compatibility of food combinations that yield balanced, tantalizing, palate lingering flavors and unyielding presentations that are natural and appealing - without falling short on flavor. Remember my motto, "Flavor is Trump" that's "my style of cooking", noticeable in recipes you'll find in this cookbook. Be aware of what you are eating, consider making my style, your style – with seasonally fresh, "CLEAN FOOD."

Next step is controlling purchasing processed food, meanwhile, establishing a regimen that becomes routine in determining freshness and quality of natural foodstuffs, such purchases don't have to be an expense beyond one's means to buy quality fresh products. The quality of finished preparations can also determine the ultimate level of quality. For example a consumer can buy best rated paint money can buy but, if the work is not quality, at this point, the rating of the paint is irrelevant. Quality (neat) application, detailing, and doing the best with what you've got to work with is my point and the quality (durability) of paint will speak for itself over time - the paint _job_ will first be judged. The same philosophy applies to food, the pleasing quality and flavor of table ready foods should create desire to repeat whenever possible. Regarding prices, you might ask, how is it possible to have control over prices? The answer is, you don't, but you do have personal control over your purchasing choices.

It is surprising the number of consumers who don't know what to do with celery root, rutabaga, or even what to do with unfamiliar varieties of potatoes. Simply stated just prepare, process and cook purple potatoes the same way you would white potatoes. There are time limitations when cooking vegetables, which should be adhered to for best flavor and texture. I'm always asked questions about this and that while food shopping, so I've included a compilation of tips and recipes in my cookbook that could be of help in expanding use of money saving, more flavorful fresh ingredients that can provide greater flexibility in use and yield for the money. Do a cost "comparison and benefit" test for yourself so you can conclude what is best for you and your family.

To summarize up to this point: "The big pluses are that fresh (pure organic, to whatever extent possible in today's environment) ingredients are more flavorful when properly cooked and they most always cost less." I believe that, "by exploring reality in the fact that inexpensive, seasonally fresh ingredients can become gourmet dishes in a matter of minutes with a little routine planning - like pre-measuring ingredients, using recommended cooking times, methods and techniques - plus, you'll know exactly the composition of the subsistence (no additives) you've prepared for yourself, your family and friends." I know, because I do this at home, and professionally, every day!

Throughout this cookbook I focus on simplicity and easily adaptable methods in preparing, processing and cooking seasonally available fruits, produce and vegetables as well as meats, fowl, seafood and fish, for example, so that menu planning is easier. Food shopping, an essential part of life, can be fun and less expensive. Round up and expose the family and possibly friends, to new supply sources - like purchasing seasonal produce and fruits at the local farmer's market or buy directly from orchards and farms.

The most fun-filled bargain of them all is, when being fortunate enough to find an orchard or farm that boasts a "you pick" program. To stretch the penny even more, consider preserving fruits and vegetables "by canning." A day or two used canning tomatoes simply means that a few pounds of tomatoes have been stretched into several meals and when a recipe calls for tomatoes, without delay you've retrieved a jar stored on your pantry shelf – to make a flavorful marinara sauce for serving over rigatoni or another favorite pasta, a casserole or other preparations in minutes without leaving the house. Absolutely delicious, and convenient!

While browsing through this cookbook, imagine putting together a wholesome variety of one course or multi- course menus that fit in with a tight, loose or leisure schedule, budget and lifestyle – because "natural flavors are right under your nose, the "how-to" is in your hands, and the fresh ingredients to let you create those flavors are at your fingertips". Anytime is a good time to take advantage of the season! "Happy Cooking & Enjoy"

Erika

AFFLUENT and INFLUENTIAL CUISINES of EUROPE

Many countries have created regional versions of dumplings in various shapes, sizes, texture – some filled, some are not. Some are solid, round, flat, elongated, oval, and square to highlight a few of many. These examples illustrate how commonplace dumplings have become through generations. Boiled, they can be regarded as a whole meal with some sort of sauce or as an accompaniment to main dish ingredients, and used in soups and stews. Dumplings, all with different names, shapes and fillings, but all are similarly processed and cooked. The commonality is that many consist of some sort of dough and potatoes, rolled and shaped accordingly, and some are filled, boiled, baked or steamed. Dumplings, such as Poland's famed Pierogi, Italy's Gnocchi, Germany's Potato Dumplings and even America's Chicken and Dumplings meal, these are only a few of many that were selected simply to highlight commonalities stemming from the dumpling's originator and just how widespread the popularity and variances of the "dumpling" and other foods has become over centuries.

A few tidbits, far from being all inclusive, but rather a continuation revisiting places from where came some of the world's greatest cuisines - countries such as Italy with its white sauces to the North and red sauces to its South sharing a notable blend of both in between including green, the color of the great flavorful basil pesto. Then there is Greece with specialties like lamb kabobs and its succulent garlic sauce; Spain's traditional, popular paella, and France's cassoulet and bouillabaisse - all of those most familiar, traditional delicacies spring to the forefront of my mind among Eastern European fare, which is oftentimes erroneously associated with dull, starchy dishes with mounds of bland cabbage – farthest from fact, and without getting too fancy - in Hungary – it's their flavorful goulash; in Germany – it's the bratwurst, schnitzel and its lesser known rind (beef) rouladen and sauerbraten; in Russia – it's their borscht and piroshki, and in Poland – it's their pierogi. To venture further, this time into understated Ostpreusen, where grand flavors in roast goose are found and served with delectable kielke, which are small sausage-shape raw dumplings, all of which, rank among many other countries within the world's most familiar of many culinary treasures – wholesome, unprocessed and palate satisfying - most certainly not heavy, starchy or bland as some people may imagine. Only those who've been fortunate enough to experience the flavors of food specialties traditional to countries visited know and can taste the difference between original and imitations.

The unique flavors of Hungarian or East German, Austrian or Balkan cuisine also derived from influxes of influential, diverse cultures nestled between all four directions that link with and produce harmonizing effects in food with that of the heartiness of Northern European fair with that of spices of the South. The latter, prompted me to initially think of paprika symbolically linked with Hungary - synonymous with Hungarian goulash (gulyás). But, not all goulashes are distinctly Hungarian except for its more pungent flavor than that of Austria's less pungent version.

Interestingly enough the introduction of paprika in Hungarian cuisine was brought about by Turks when paprika was originally known as Hungarian sweet pepper, a blend of dried red-skinned chilies possessing pungency levels ranging from mild to hot and a color range from red-orange to deep red. Hungarian cuisine is delightfully as rich, but not particularly high in fat content and calories, in its vegetables and noodle dishes as it is in its meat dishes, and they all are quite easy to prepare - adding it all up it seems all that is needed for most meals there are three pots, a large bowl, one knife, dishes, flatware, and a strainer of sufficient size to accommodate the size of individual families and lifestyle. If that is all it takes for them to yield such pleasing flavor, no obstructions should prevail in preparing a wonderful family meal at home.

Could it be that Italy introduced veal scaloppini through Austria into Germany - inspiring the creation of veal schnitzel, (wiener schnitzel), made world famous by Austria, even though the basic process for preparing veal for both scaloppina and schnitzel is similar, the sauces are the exception. For example, in Italy two of its most commonly known sauces are a red (tomato base) sauce predominantly enjoyed in Southern-most parts opposite to the lemon-caper sauce (white sauces) most commonly enjoyed in the Northern-most parts.

Whereas in Germany, pork is consumed more than veal, however, veal is often enjoyed in other types of preparations-dishes. The well known pork schnitzel - German translation: swine schnitzel is accompanied by any number of delectable sauces, such as: a squeeze of lemon (zitrone schnitzel); a cream sauce (rahm or sahne schnitzel); a paprika sauce (synonymous); a bell peppers sauce (gypsy schnitzel); a mushroom sauce (pilz or jager schnitzel); a mushroom-onion sauce (pilz-zwiebel schnitzel); onion sauce (zwiebel schnitzel), and the Holsteiner Schnitzel, which is topped with egg and other ingredients .

So to distinguish one schnitzel from another, as you may have noticed in the aforementioned, the type of sauce determined the names of schnitzels. So the heavier sauces, such as mushrooms, over schnitzel are actually toppings from which the sauce becomes the bi-product of any given topping harmonized with other appropriate flavor balancing herbs and spices that yield flavorful liquids.

HERBS and USES – IN BALANCE

You may be cooking gourmet meals without realizing it! Cooking with fresh herbs not only adds flavor to concoctions, but also increases nutritional values in preparations, and using herbs in appropriate quantities reduces need for salt, or less of it and eliminating other sodium based ingredients, like baking soda in baked goods. Liberally using salt as a dramatization overstates the value and necessity of salt in foodstuffs to reach the highest level of flavor of the main ingredient in a dish. Substituting excessive use of salt with fresh herbs add variable, interesting, savory flavor to even the simplest of foods, which I firmly believe is a much healthier alternative. Commercially processed foods containing familiar and unfamiliar additives are listed on labels, unfortunately though, labels aren't always read or noticed by consumers. As a consumer and professional, I personally like knowing what all I'm eating, so I habitually read labels even though I prefer fresh over all else. By cooking from scratch, I know exactly the ingredients, and amounts of which, I've put into my preparations.

There are two familiar ingredients that seem to be in everything, and they individually seem to be constant subjects to debate - one hand says salt and sugar, in varying amounts, are good for us while the other hand says they aren't. I, of course, use both but with what I perceive as in appropriate, compromising amounts. Consumption-wise, I think the main issue is over what amount is too much and what amount is too little in terms of making healthy dietary choices - though there is natural sugar in many fresh foods, even in potatoes. That is why I believe it is worth (health-wise) adding up stated sugar and salt values of processed foods. In particular, determining estimated amounts a person might consume in one day might be enlightening and reveal that adjustments may or may not be necessary to remain within suggested individual dietary health safety margins. The complexity, and pros and cons of such issues are huge, but the decision to indulge or not indulge in anything rest with every individual.

As awareness of health benefits and widespread use of other varieties of fresh herbs reaches certain levels of demand, hopefully a wider selection of herbal varieties may become routinely stocked in produce departments of supermarkets. There are, however, roadside stands and growers at farmer's markets who specialize in growing, harvesting and showcasing both uncommon (not generally available) and commonly known (generally available) fresh herbs. You might even want to consider growing herbs in your personal home garden. Some varieties can be grown together in planters, or among bedded flowers and even around landscape plants, but avoid treating them with harmful chemicals, to keep their growing space organic. In my opinion, health benefits of natural fresh herbs and accompanying fresh (organic) ingredients far out-weight any nutritional benefits certain commercially processed foods can ever offer, whether fortified or un-fortified.

As you may be aware, herbs are best when harvested in the morning just after dew has evaporated, but before warmed by the sun. Handling herbs very gently avoids bruising, so they'll stay picture perfect for use as garnishing or in cooking without losing little, if any flavor. Select and scissor-snip only enough herbs the same day as planned to use, or for drying or freezing. Spread out or fan herbs on a large flat basket or tray rather than in a pile, or keep them loosely wrapped in moistened paper towel and refrigerated, or snip stem ends and fully submerge herbs in a clean sink or container of cold water – to revive and retain freshness. Herbs should look fresh and clean, be free of disease, pesticides and not be discolored or bruised. Always, gently rinse herbs under cool running water and paper towel dry them before use.

Experiment cooking with fresh herbs: For best results, avoid mixing two very strong herbs together in preparations and avoid overuse of any single herb variety in concoctions except for illustrative purposes. But, how can overuse be detected? You'll know, for example, when the flavor of oregano is paramount when taste testing the preparation and you wonder where the balancing affect of garlic-tomato flavor went – to fix it this time, add more liquid and other ingredients to taste. The next time, simply use less oregano. Opposite example, when balanced herbs and other ingredients complement each other the flavor will be more appealing, and further, it should be more difficult to single out a specific herb in this preparation during a taste test. Also, altering the original balanced preparation by omitting one herb variety without altering anything else will certainly reveal a noticeable diminished flavor quality. More than likely the balancing affect of the removed herb gave way to others - the strongest of which remaining will most likely become the dominating, identifiable flavor. Just remember that a bumpy ride results when spokes in a wheel are missing.

In my view, it's very important to use herbs sparingly at first when experimenting because a small amount goes a long way toward adding desirable flavor to a dish – in affect the herb should be the enhancer rather than the dominating flavor in your finished preparation. Fresh herbs are like tasting or cooking with wine, it takes a combination of knowing a bit about herb strength levels and what foods will they complement, factoring in compatibility (pairing), experimenting, experiencing and adjusting results of your tests until you've got control over the basics and reach expected flavor of the yield. For example, dried herbs are stronger than fresh herbs. Powdered herbs are stronger than crumbled. _Consider this rule of thumb – it's helpful just knowing that a difference does exist between the two: One-fourth teaspoon of powdered herbs equals ¾ to 1-teaspoon of fresh, and crumbled herbs are equal to about 2-teaspoons of fresh herbs._

For best results, _know when is the right moment to or not to introduce herbs to a preparation_ and then _use them sparingly_ until familiarity is gained with their individual strengths. Here are two examples: When making vinaigrette, add finely chopped herbs about _one hour before serving._ In sauces and casseroles, _add finely chopped herbs_ _directly to the mixture._

SAMPLING OF HERBS & EXAMPLE USES

Anise: Is of the parsley family, it has a mild licorice flavor, use with chicken, fish, stews, salads, beverages, stewed fruits, fruit soups. Dried Anise seeds can be used in baked goods and liqueurs.

Basil: Is of the mint family, excellent with tomatoes, tomato sauces, vinegars, rice, and meats, such as, chicken, veal, pork, rabbit, or fish, salads, soups and pasta. Different varieties of basil possess different sensory qualities, so it's a decision to choose between basil with a strong, peppery flavor, or other varieties with flavors similar to cinnamon, garlic or lemon.

Bay Leaves: Are leaves from a small tree, native to Asia, imparting a lemon-nutmeg flavor - widely used in stuffing, stews, sauces, soups and in fish dishes to mention a few, however, in most preparations bay leaves are removed before serving Bay leaves have different strengths, depending where they are cultivated. For the most part, bay leaves cultivated in the US are milder than Turkish bay leaves, which are more aromatic and strength level is nearly doubled, about 2 to 1 ratio.

Borage: A mild flavor herb, use leaves in salads and soups. Finely chop borage just before adding to what is cooking.

Chives: Is of the onion family, use in salads, stews, appetizers, butters, yogurt, sour cream and cream sauces or chicken, egg and fish preparations. The slender, hollow green stems of one variety have a mild onion-like flavor and the Garlic Chives with broader and flatter stems have a garlic-like flavor.

Coriander: An herb originally found in Egypt. Coriander seeds are used in pickling spices and curry powder. The leaves, known as cilantro or Chinese parsley, are found in many Indian and Mexican dishes.

Dill: Is a member of the parsley family, use with fish and fish sauces, or with beets, eggs, chicken, salads, breads, cucumber soup, veal, prawns, salad dressings and butter. Dill leaves have a parsley-like flavor with a hint of anise while dill seeds have slightly bitter flavor with also a hint of anise.

Marjoram: Is a member of the mint family. Use in stews, soups, meats, such as, pork, lamb, wild game, breads, tomato sauces, peas and white beans. Flavor is similar to thyme and oregano as well as similar strong aroma.

Mint: Aroma of mint leaves is comparable to lemon-lime. Use in salads, fruit dishes, teas, sherbet, lamb, puddings, custards, peas, fruit soups and candies.

Oregano: Use in Italian and Greek dishes, in tomato sauces, soups, pork, veal, Italian cheese, such as mascarpone and ricotta, in salad dressings, breads, butter, cream sauces, fish, chicken and rabbit. Oregano has a strong peppery flavor and because of its strength, prudent doses are recommended

Parsley: Has a rather peppery, tangy fresh flavor in its curly, dark green leaves. The flavor in its stalks is stronger and those are generally used in bouquet garni. Use leaves in tomato sauces, fish, meats, soups, stews, vegetables, salad dressings, butter, and potatoes.   The flavor in flat, dark leaves of Italian parsley is stronger and coarser than the curly variety.

Rosemary: Use with lamb, pork, poultry, vegetables, bread, butter, marinades, rabbit, and potatoes. Rosemary has a strong flavor like that of lemon and pine and its aroma is camphor-like.

Sage: Use with fish, meats, stuffing for poultry, soups, stews, marinades, tomatoes, and butter. Sage has a strong, slightly bitter-musty flavor.

Savory: Summer Savory is milder than Winter Savory, which has a bitter, stronger flavor similar to that of thyme and rosemary. Use with pork, fish, beans, chicken, goose, and duck.

Tarragon - Estragon: French, German, Norwegian, Spanish and Swedish for tarragon. Use with meats, marinades, soup, stews, fish, beans, salad dressings, and vinegar. Tarragon has an anis-like flavor with a hint of sage and strong aroma.

Estragon - French, German, Norwegian, Spanish and Swedish for tarragon.

Thyme: Use in stews, fish, chowders, poultry, stuffing, breads, and butter. The leaves of thyme have a strong, slightly lemony flavor and aroma.

BASIC USES OF ROOT VEGETABLES

Beet (Beet Root): Has a sweet, tangy, musty flavor; after peeled, it can be chopped, diced, grated and puréed and in any of these forms beet can be sautéed, boiled, grilled, baked and pickled or shredded for salad; use in soups, stews and cooked for use as an accompaniment.

Bok Choy: Is a member of the cabbage family; it has a mild flavor and can be eaten raw; it can be chopped, diced, julienne and used in salads, as an ingredient in soups, stews or any other preparation where a very mild flavor of cabbage is desired; it can be eaten sautéed, steamed or cooked to serve as an accompaniment.

Celeriac (Celery Root): Has flavor similar to celery and parsley, it can be eaten raw after peeling; it can be chopped or diced for use in salads with apples and pears; it can be pickled, cooked, or mashed with potatoes or diced and used as an flavor enhancing ingredient in soups and stews.

Fennel: Has flavor and aroma similar to anise; use as flavoring in baked goods and in Italian or other European dishes; can also be used in alcoholic beverages and in any other preparation, in which licorice flavor of anise is desired like in soups, stews or making fennel tea.

Kohlrabi: Although not a root vegetable, it is cooked the same way root vegetables are cooked and used; it has flavor of turnip, but milder and sweeter.

Parsley Root: Is a member of the parsley family, its flavor is similar to celery and carrot; use as a flavoring in soups, stews and preparations, in which this natural flavoring is desired.

Parsnip: Has a sweet flavor similar to carrot; after peeled, it can be diced, chopped, grated and puréed, and in any of those forms, it can be an ingredient in soups, stews, gulashes, or it can be mashed in with potatoes.

Radish, Daikon: Is native to Asia. It has a sweet, slightly spicy flavor similar, but slightly milder than the American red radish with white flesh. After peeled, it can be eaten raw or cooked; it can be chunked, sliced, chopped for use as an ingredient or shredded for use in mixed salads.

Rutabaga: Is a member of the cabbage family; raw and after peeled, it has a slightly sweet flavor; it can be diced, chopped, grated and puréed, and in any of those forms it can be sautéed, boiled, grilled and baked; it can be cooked and served singularly, mashed or in with a mix of other vegetables, including potatoes; it can be used as an accompaniment, as an ingredient in soups, stews and goulashes.

Turnip: Is from the turnip plant; the fresher the turnip, the milder is its flavor; after peeled, it can be processed and used the same as rutabaga.

GARLIC

Garlic, a member of the onion family rich in vitamins, such as, amino acids, calcium, iron, potassium, vitamin C, B6 and it's said to have many protective health benefits, plus an excellent food enhancer.

A craving for garlic in all sorts of concoctions seems to be on the rise, whether in trendy or in mimicked dishes commonplace in countries like Italy, Greece, Turkey, Spain and others where garlic is typically used more frequently than not. Then there are other countries like the Netherlands where its usage is moderate, except where there are large populations of immigrants from countries where garlic is widely used, or in restaurants where ethnic foods are on menus. But years ago, use of garlic in Germany by upper class Germans in particular was considered improper because of its "so called" offensive smell, and therefore restrained themselves to eat very little of it, or abstained from eating it or even avoiding being in close proximity of it -including distancing themselves from people who've been eating it - until it became known that chewing on a sprig of parsley would erase or reduce the offensive smell of garlic.

I have always loved the smell of garlic and the element of flavor it adds to domestic and wild game, fish, seafood concoctions and a myriad of sauces. I believe that realization of garlic's potential health and flavoring benefits has become more apparent, because demand for garlic, as aforementioned, seems to be on the rise even in unlikely places like Germany. Use of Garlic in today's food world has intensified, especially among the younger generation of Germans. I'm sure the influx of immigrants from Turkey, Yugoslavia and Middle Eastern regions, introducing their style of cooking, invariably had some influence. I found this to be particularly noticeable during the 1950's and even more so today because some of the favorite "Sunny" vacation spots frequented by Germans are in countries where ethnic foods routinely consist of garlic. These vacationers didn't have many other choices, unless the host vacation spot exclusively catered to vacationer's home country food preparations. Perhaps "garlic brings out the sun in people" or is it that "sun brings out the garlic in people and parsley is the overcast!" Whichever, I always have and still love garlic, and I'm even German - from the old country!

Authentic Italian, Greek, Yugoslavian and Turkish restaurants, for example, became very popular in Germany during the early 60's and we frequently enjoyed all of them - garlic dishes galore. The only difficulty we experienced was deciding on whether to try a different entrée or choose the same one we've before ordered. We ordered the same one - how could another entrée possibly taste as good, we concluded! We eventually weakened. This time, at a Yugoslavian restaurant in Rüsselsheim, Germany, we ordered what they called "Balkan Platter". It was also phenomenal! It consisted of a bed of tomato rice, skewered, grilled lamb, bell peppers and onions, grilled sliced bacon, sautéed lamb patties-loaded with garlic, roasted vegetables and garnished with a couple of skewered, double-hot red peppers with bread accompaniments. Then after being introduced to lamb kabobs enjoyed with five extra aromatic servings of garlic sauce devoured at a Greek restaurant in Schalksmühle, Germany meant the hour and half drive at breakneck speeds on the Autobahn to get there was worth every minute of the treacherous drive. Within or outside of Italy, arguably everyone knows the simplicity and flavor in the full spectrum of Italian food is some of the greatest food on earth. Regardless of ethnicity specifics, there are personal favorites everywhere in the world and I particularly enjoy the variety and authenticity in flavors in all of them – within reason.

Reminiscently speaking of typical German hospitality, my friends invited me to accompany them to a fine restaurant in Mülheim, Germany for dinner during a winter vacation. I accepted the invitation! The Chechen Chef and owner of the restaurant, being a long time friend of my friends and escorts, exited his kitchen to welcome us and exchange greetings. Noticing that I wasn't feeling up to par because a head-cold had gotten a grip on me during this most recent excursion to my homeland, the chef and friends insisted that I drink a garlic schnapps they said would help relieve congestion and help build up my immune system. Not being on any medication and not one to even drink a one-ounce shot of anything pure, over 35% in that of a wonderful rare liqueur, I reluctantly, but obligingly, downed the vodka-garlic schnapps. Expecting to react breathlessly after swallowing it, I instead felt instant improvement from the unexpected soothing flavor of this combination. Amazingly, after a second schnapps, my congestion was relieved enough to enjoy the flavors of a very traditional, house specialty dinner of roast pork, dumplings and sour kraut. The alcohol was simply identified as the booster to get garlic into the bloodstream quicker.

They say garlic everyday fortifies our immune system, but simply omit alcohol if you prefer garlic on its own. You might want to offer the rest of the household a clove also or have some fresh parsley handy to chew on afterwards. And, if on some heavy medications, there may even be an incompatibility issue with certain dosages of a harmless herb like "garlic" so you probably already know from your doctor about any restricted dietary issues associated with your condition. Another alternative is to make my Garlic-Egg drop soup.

To your health and long life, I'm sharing that simple recipe as my friends did for me. See index for Garlic-Egg drop soup. As winter approaches, just in case, we personally store a freshly prepared bottle of good quality garlic-vodka in the refrigerator or in the freezer to have available over winter month's to fortify our immune system whenever one of us feel like a cold coming on. We have always avoided using any type of medication, but one-ounce of garlic-vodka before bedtime on such occasions has helped us ward off cold symptoms for quite a number of years. <u>But even so, it is not intended to be promoted as a medication or cure for anything and may not work for all, or be for everyone.</u>

A word of caution though - do not consume when any medications have been used, or use in conjunction with any type of medications, or when any conditions, health or otherwise would be at risk to you or anyone else of any age or condition or when good judgment and reasoning is or could be impaired, and as well as we all know this and all types of alcohol must be kept out of reach of children.

You need 1 bottle of good quality vodka and 1 large bulb of organic garlic (preferred). Pour out 3-4 ounces of vodka into a clean container, reserved. Insert a funnel into the neck opening of the bottle, and using a garlic press, press at least 10 cloves to, at least, 1 bulb of pressed garlic directly into the funnel adding enough to fill the cavity almost up to its neck. Do not fill the neck. Replace - secure lid and store prepared vodka in the refrigerator or freezer for at least 2-3 days to marinate before drinking- shake bottle periodically. Expect the vodka to become slightly cloudy. Shake and let garlic settle to the bottom before pouring for drinking. Pour slowly so that garlic remains in the bottle. Best when kept in the refrigerator or freezer. Prost, Toast, Salute, Cheerio, and to good health. *Note: See recipe below and Index for other wholesome, excellent recipes containing garlic. For illustrative purposes, this recipe is duplicated.*

GARLIC CUSTARD

Excellent as a first course, served with baby spinach leaves drizzled lightly with extra virgin olive oil and a sprinkling of Parmesan cheese, sea salt and cracked black pepper.

Serves: 4-6

14 large cloves garlic, peeled (Organic preferred)
¼ cup extra virgin olive oil
1 cup of chicken stock
2 cups whipping cream
4 eggs
1/8 teaspoon of sugar
½ teaspoon white pepper, freshly ground
Sea salt
Natural cooking spray, preferably Pam

Preheat oven to 350°F

Place garlic cloves and oil in a medium ovenproof dish, toss until well coated and bake for 25-30 minutes. Strain garlic and discard oil. In a medium saucepan, add stock, garlic and 1-cup of cream. Bring to a boil, and reduce heat to simmer to reduce mixture to 1-cup, and purée mixture until smooth and thick. In a bowl, whisk together eggs, remaining 1-cup of cream and garlic purée, and season to taste with sugar, pepper and salt. Coat 4-6 custard cups (6-ounce size ramekins) with cooking spray, and fill each with garlic mixture. Place ramekins in a large ovenproof dish, pour hot water a third of the way up the ramekins and bake for 35-40 minutes. Remove ramekins from oven, let cool slightly. Run a thin knife blade around the edge to loosen custard from ramekins. Center a warm plate over each ramekin, flip over and un-mold custards onto plates. *Enjoy "Garlic Custard" warm with crusty French bread or Italian crostini.*

FATTY ACIDS DEFINED
(Source: Webster's Dictionary)

<u>Trans-fatty acids</u> are unusually shared fatty acids that can arise when polyunsaturated oils are hydrogenated. <u>Hydrogenated fat</u> means a process that when a usually bland, white semisolid saturated fat, such as hard margarine, is made from unsaturated liquid oil.

<u>Fatty acid (unit)</u> is a group of water-insoluble organic acids found in animals and certain plants that combine with glycerol to form triglycerides: they are classified as saturated or unsaturated (monounsaturated or polyunsaturated) based on the number of hydrogen atoms attached to the fatty acid; carbon chain (which has oxygen atoms at the end). Food additives used as lubricants, binders and components of other food additives. <u>Triglycerides</u>, are a major class of lipids including fats and oils and each triglyceride consist of one glycerol unit and three fatty acid units.

<u>Glycerol</u> is an organic alcohol that combines with three fatty acids to produce a triglyceride, aka glycerin - a food additive derived from fats used as a sweetener, solvent and/or <u>humectant</u> in processed foods such as confections and candies. Also, it is a sweet, clear syrup-like liquid, a by-product of the fermentation of wine - its presence enhances wine fattiness and softness. <u>Humectant</u> is a type of food additive that has hygroscopic abilities (to absorbing or attracting moisture from the air) and used to promote moisture retention in a processed food to maintain or improve its texture and shelf life – also known as a moisture-retention agent.

<u>Unsaturated fat:</u> A triglyceride composed of monounsaturated or polyunsaturated fatty acids and believed to help reduce the amount of cholesterol in the blood; generally, it comes from plants and is liquid (an oil) at room temperature. Unsaturated fatty acid has one or more points of un-saturation. <u>Monounsaturated fat:</u> Is a triglyceride composed of monounsaturated fatty acid: generally, it comes from plants like olive, peanut and cottonseed oils, which are high in monounsaturated fats, and is liquid (an oil) at room temperature. Monounsaturated fatty acid has one point of un-saturation.

<u>Lipids</u> are a class of nutrients consisting of fats or fatlike substances insoluble in water, but soluble in organic solvents such as alcohol; includes triglycerides (fats and oils), phospholipids and sterols. <u>Sterols:</u> Is any of a group of lipids found in plants and animals.

<u>Phospholipids</u> are any of a group of lipids, similar to triglycerides, composed of two fatty acids, a phosphorus-containing acid and glycerol such as lecithin.

OLIVE & OTHER HEALTHY OILS

Olives and olive oil have a long, rich heritage dating back to the beginning of historical times. We all know about the branch of an olive tree and the dove. Since then the olive branch has been used as a symbol of life and peace. Ancient civilizations used olive oil for makeup, perfume, shampoo and even as a medicinal aid for ailments. Around 1,000 BC, Greeks and Romans discovered the culinary aspects of olive oil and centuries later in the 1700s it is said that Americans were first exposed to olive oil when the Franciscan missionaries introduced olive trees while settling in California. Then in the mid 1800s European immigrants began incorporating olive oil into American cooking. Said also, Mediterranean cuisine, introduced about 100 years ago to America, had become quite popular because of claimed health benefits. Experts believe substituting saturated fats with olive oil, combined with a diet rich in fruits, vegetables and grains, may play a key role in helping prevent some diseases. Olive oil is free of cholesterol.

Olives are small tree fruit, native to the Mediterranean region, which have a single pit and high oil content. Unripe varieties are green. There, however, are ripe green and black varieties – both have very bitter flavor when eaten raw, but highly consumable after washing, soaking and pickling them, or pressed for producing oil.

Olive oil is highlighted because of its oily finish and most significant is the method used for processing it is different than other oils. More specifically, juice extraction is conducted by a mechanical process called "cold pressing" rather than by methods exposing juice to extremely high temperatures, or chemical refining processes. And so, it is the characteristic of olive oil that places it in the "cooking oil" category.

Though, there is one processing exception applicable only to "Extra Light" olive oil, which is however chemically processed for reason - to improve flavor in lesser quality olives perhaps used in this variety of olive oil. Reading labels oftentimes takes the guesswork out of determining nutritional values and benefits of this and any other consumable product.

For many years I've substituted saturated fat with an appropriately adjusted amount of olive oil in my style of cooking, a noticeable listed ingredient in my breads and other recipes that, for me, yield amazingly moist, lower fat, and healthier results. I don't profess to be a health expert but rather basing knowledge on my personal experience, and as with anything, reasonable dosages are always recommended.

Furthermore, pressed tree-ripened olives produces oil that possess distinctive fruity-olive flavor and it's graded according to the degree of acidity, and mostly used as a cooking medium, flavoring and ingredient.

"Cold pressing" is a method used to extract juice without use of heat, usually regarded as the "first pressing" such as is used to yield "Extra Virgin" Olive Oil.

Bitterness or sweetness of finished oil depends on the variety of fruit used in the production process, a characteristic normality, which should be considered when choosing a variety to use in preparations. For example, choose regional olive oil especially when preparing a dish originated from a specific region of the world or using it as a flavor enhancer to ingredients possessing bland flavor. In choosing, think of it as a wine tasting event and being a bit creatively adventurous and trusting your senses exploring the nutritional world of olive oils. <u>Notice low level of acidity in these varieties.</u>

<u>Extra Virgin Olive Oil</u>: Produced from the <u>first cold pressing,</u> the finest and fruitiest; it has a pale straw to bright green color and it has no more than <u>1% acid.</u>

<u>Light Olive Oil</u>: Produced from the <u>last pressing</u>; it has a very mild flavor, light color, high smoke point and up to 3% acid.

<u>Pure Olive Oil</u>: This variety has been cleaned, filtered and stripped of much of its flavor and color by using heat and mechanical devices during the refining process; it has up to 3% acid.

<u>Virgin Olive Oil</u>: An olive oil with 2% acid; it has a less fruity flavor than extra virgin olive oil and a pale yellow to medium yellow-green color.

<u>Considerations</u>: A Greek salad with feta and a rich texture olive oil; a fresh mozzarella, basil and tomato salad paired with a lighter fruit and herb flavored oil, or consider antipasti complimented with very tangy oil which stands up amidst strong flavored meats and vegetables. I might add that the price of olive oil is not necessarily a true reflection of its degree of quality – there are great tasting, less expensive oils in today's market, but for me, <u>organic is most preferred.</u>

<u>Organic Virgin Coconut Oil</u>: Is made from organic, fresh coconuts and processed without the use of chemicals or high heat. The extraction method used is referenced as "wet-milling" - a cold-process that produces oil naturally rich in lauric acid; contains no trans-fatty acids, and it's considered a functional food source. Use it when a lighter multi-purpose oil is desired, such as with fish, seafood and chicken. Coconut oil solidifies below 76°F in this state, it is excellent used as a cream or butter substitute, it does not require refrigeration, it does, however, have an expiration date.

OTHER HEALTHY OILS

<u>Macadamia Nut Oil</u>: Flavor intensifies during baking or roasting. Excellent drizzled over pasta and vegetables. Use with green salads, fruit salads, seafood, sauces, breads and cakes.

Grape-Seed Oil: Has lowest levels of saturated fats compared to any vegetable oil, and perfect for cooking or baking at high temperatures.

Walnut Oil: Topaz is the color of walnut oil, characteristic of good quality oil; it should possess a rich nutty flavor, and its label should state that walnuts used have been roasted. Once <u>any</u> nut oil container is opened, it should thereafter be stored in a cool dark place. Some sources recommend refrigeration after opened to prevent rancidness, but I personally prefer to not refrigerate any type of oil because refrigeration causes cloudiness, thickening and loss of full aroma. Instead, I recommend buying smaller quantities that most likely will be used up within a month or two. The effects of **Walnut oil,** as well as <u>Hazelnut</u> and <u>Almond oils</u> are best when used as an ingredient in salad dressings; drizzled over pasta dishes, tossed over vegetables, and used in breads, cakes and cookies.

Pumpkin Seed Oil: This oil is produced from a unique variety of pumpkin grown in the Styria region of Austria. The skinless pumpkin seeds, when carefully roasted and crushed produces thick, dark green oil that boasts a toasted aroma and nutty flavor. This rare oil contains a high amount of unsaturated fats and essential vitamins, including vitamin "E". It is excellent drizzled over vegetables; use it in breads, cakes and cookies; use it as an ingredient in salad dressings and marinades, or drizzle it over soups.

Avocado oil: Avocado oil is the elite oil among cooking oils claimed to have the highest smoke point of all vegetable oils, 520°F, when refined. It possesses numerous health benefits - good nutritional value, low trans fatty acids, and "cold pressed" avocado is rich in vitamin B, C and E, plus several minerals. Even though avocado pulp contains a lot of oil, it sets itself apart from other oils because it contains only a small amount of saturated fats when most other oils contain 9 calories per gram, 255 calories per ounce. Avocado oil has a unique, mild flavor and tastes great as an ingredient in salad dressings, in soups, dips, and marinades. And, it's also great for baking, roasting, grilling and high temperature cooking. Avocado is grown in Mexico, USA, Israel, South Africa, Spain, Australia and New Zealand.

Apricot kernel oil: is obtained by removing the pit from apricots and cracking the pit shells to access the kernel within, which is pressed to extract its oil. This oil is high in monounsaturated fat and contains no trans-fatty acids. Use it for high-heat cooking, such as sautéing and pan frying. Its mild flavor adds a bit of sweetness to salad dressings, sweet soups and desserts. Use it also for other cooking styles and baking.

Try this simple, flavorful avocado snack: Peel and cut a ripe avocado in half, remove pit, drizzle with 2-teaspoons of fresh limejuice, lemon juice or orange juice, finishing with a sprinkling of fine sea salt and freshly ground pepper. Simply delicious!

SALT

TOO LITTLE SALT????   *NOT ENOUGH SALT????*   *TOO MUCH SALT????*

WHAT'S THE RIGHT ANSWER????

To illustrate, here is a little conversational scenario to think about: Arguably, some people might say, when asked about use of salted verses unsalted butter:

(Response) -"I like salted butter on my bread"!
(Comment) – Do you know that you are combining that amount of salt with the salt content in the bread?

(Response) - "No, but I don't mind that"!
(Comment) - That's ok, but now you're combining salt in butter and salt in the bread along with salt in a slice of ham.

(Response) - "Oh"! "But, I don't mind that either, I like ham"!
(Comment) - That's ok too, but now consider that more salt is added to your diet with a slice of cheese, plus don't overlook the fact that commercial mayonnaise contains salt too and we yet haven't topped it all with the final slice of commercial bread invariably containing salt. But wait, there is more!

Comments: Adding up all of this, the sodium chloride count will amaze you - all of that salt in one sandwich, and adding to that the amount of salt in processed lunch, dinner and snacks, if you snack. Salt consumption in one day could be off the chart as they say in some journals - too much salt is unhealthy while other sources express salt's nutritional benefits. But yet, this mineral, with its historic significance, is widely used, and understandably so, as a <u>preservative and purifier in processed foods;</u> it is used industrially, and it's used for many other purposes too numerous to mention in this book.

So, what daily amount provides the proper nutritional dosage for humans and what amount is considered excessive? From a technical standpoint, and my opinion only, I believe daily dosage of salt depends on each and every individual, basing this evaluation on perceived activity levels - when less active, one may desire, or consume, more salt (snacks) that's not needed and not expended.

Contrastingly, when most active, the desire for, or consumption of salt may be less, but needed to replenish loss of it due to the physical level of the activity. *I'm emphasizing less use of salt (sodium) in cooking and more frequent use of fresh herbs, advancing the level of nutrition and broader range of benefits.*

Regardless which view is most supported, *I personally like both salt and butter, but most importantly, I also like being in control over the amount of this nutrient, called salt, I ingest.* I regard salt as a flavor enhancer, and a pinch of salt is a pinch rather than considered as a teaspoonful, or adding sprinklings of specialty salts for dramatization. *Those are all reasons why I prefer using only fresh ingredients, that way, I know what I'm eating and by my having control over that, I can regulate the amount of necessary ingredients used in preparations, and I can keep as many unwanted chemicals, as much as possible, out of food freshly prepared for myself, family and patron consumption.* Something to think about and reading labels is always a wise thing to do!

Sea salts from the Mediterranean Sea, the North Sea, or the Atlantic Ocean are favored. While browsing through my cookbook, it's clearly noticeable that I prefer the clean flavor of Sea Salt in my recipes; it is unrefined when directly collected from ocean or sea; it is evaporated naturally by the sun and wind; refined to retain traces of proprietary minerals, such as iron, magnesium, calcium, potassium, manganese, zinc and iodine, and it is considered healthier and more flavorful. Fine grind is most preferred.

Italian Sea Salt (or Sicilian Sea Salt) is most favored for its lower sodium chloride content; it is rich in minerals, and no further refining takes place once water has evaporated and the salt is crushed and ground. Fine grind is most preferred.

Organic Salt is another preferred salt: Organic Salt is gauged by standards based on the purity of the water from where salt was harvested; cleanliness of harvesting and the stringent control over processing and packaging at processing plants like those in France, New Zealand and Wales. Fine grind is most preferred.

Salt, a preservative, which, adds texture and strength to bread dough, for example; it acts as a binder – to hold ingredients together; it controls fermentation - holding fermentation in check and helps produce product consistency, and its considered as a color developer, and as a enhancer, in processed meats. Salt, I find, is most useful in marinades, brines, pickling etc., and as an ingredient in processed foods, that which is processed and meant for storing - to extend the life of products well beyond product's normal life span whether product is displayed, encased, canned, or used on raw products, like fish, being transported - products that are intended for commerce is a typical, but not all inclusive example of uses of salt.

However, for over 30 years, in my Dessert, Tortes and Cakes recipes, salt has been, and still is, intentionally omitted to allow the intended delicacy of listed

ingredients to integrate flavors among themselves without adding salt. Salt retards, and interferes with, the development of such results in my desserts.
Where ever salt is not listed in my recipes, the assumption should be made that it was intentionally omitted. Baking soda is not at all used in any of my recipes. Of course, salt is used in other recipes, however, as appropriate, and in reasonable amounts for the number of servings.

CONDIMENTS - SEASONINGS

Capers: European supply sources are Spain (Almeria and Balearic Islands), France (Province), Italy, especially Sicily and the Aeolian Island of Salina, the Mediteranean Island of Pantelleria. Capers also are cultivated in Dalmatia and Greece, in other geographical regions like Algeria, Egypt, Morocco, Tunisia, Cyprus and the Levant, the Coastal areas of the Black sea and Iran. Areas with intensive caper cultivation production include Spain and Italy. Culinary uses: Capers of commerce are immature flower buds pickled in vinegar or preserved in granular salt. Semi-mature fruits (caper berries) and round shoots with small leaves may also be pickled for use as a condiment. Capers possess a sharp piquant flavor adding pungency, peculiar aroma and saltiness to foods such as pasta, sauces, pica, fish, meat and sometimes salads. There is similarity in flavor to that of mustard and black pepper. Capers make an important contribution to "the one" of classic flavor among others, including olives and rucola - also known as arugula or garden rocket. Tender young shoots, including immature small leaves, may also be eaten as a vegetable or pickled. The ash from burned caper roots can be used as a source of salt. The brine in capers is very salty so draining it is very important before adding only a moderate amount of capers to your preparation.

Aioli: Is a provincial garlic mayonnaise traditionally served with steamed fish, hardboiled eggs, cooked vegetables, grilled meat kebobs, and with chicken.

Allspice: Is made from berries of the Jamaica peppertree, dried and ground which tastes like a combination of cloves, nutmeg and cinnamon used in sweet and savory cooking and baking.

Apricot glaze: Is a warm-strained apricot jam that is spreadable onto cakes, such as Sacher torte or glazing over fruits.

Consommé: Is a rich broth resulting from long simmering of meat or vegetables, or a combination of both, made clear by removing any particles and sediment, and used as a stock base or in soups.

Coulis: Is a sauce made from puréed fruits and vegetables or thickened juice of meat.

Crostini: Is Italian for small, thin slices of toasted bread, usually brushed with olive oil. Serve with soups or salads, or topped with a spread or other flavorful topping.

Croutons: Are toasted or roasted, diced breads used for garnishing soups or salads, and often browned in butter, garlic and herbs or grilled.

Gazpacho: Is a chilled vegetable soup, of Spanish origin, which is traditionally made with sun-ripened tomatoes, red peppers, cucumbers, Spanish olive oil, garlic and fresh herbs.

Genoise (zhen-waahz): Is a type of sponge cake in which whole eggs are beaten with sugar until light and foamy before flour and finely ground nuts or other ingredients are folded in.

Marzipan: Is a paste-like blend of finely ground almonds, sugar or confectioner sugar in which egg whites are oftentimes included. Raw, readymade, packaged marzipan is generally available in most supermarket baking sections.

Quark: Is a soft, easy to spread, un-ripened cheese extremely popular in Germany, Austria and Switzerland. Quark possesses flavor similar to cottage cheese and its texture is similar to that of sour cream. It is unsalted, milder and less rich than Italy's mascarpone dessert cheese. Customary uses: In cheesecakes, in desserts, or simply spread it on dark bread topped with jams, or eaten with fruits. Fresh cheese is best consumed within a short time period after purchase. Usually both whole milk and skim milk quark are available in European Delis and some supermarkets. For best results, strain quark overnight in the refrigerator and discard liquid if it is to be used in cakes or desserts.

Remoulade: Is a sauce, essentially an herb mayonnaise and mustard blend seasoned with chopped fresh chervil, parsley, chives, gherkin pickles, capers, oftentimes accompanied with cold meats and fish.

Truffles: Two most common varieties are black and the white truffles. Truffles are a fungus (sometimes referred to as mushrooms), a delicacy harvested from underground around the rooting system of oak and chestnut trees during Fall with either the use of "so-called" truffle pigs or trained dogs. Using pigs to hunt truffles is a natural, because truffles are part of their natural diet.   The rare and most flavorful "black truffle" is considered the most luxurious, most expensive ingredient used in French and Italian cooking.

<u>Vanilla sugar</u>: Is sugar that is fused with vanilla beans, a process producing its distinctive vanilla fragrance. To produce this at home, slice down side of bean with the back of a knife to scrape seeds into a glass jar filled with superfine sugar, available in supermarkets baking section. After a week, sugar should be permeated with the aroma of vanilla – leave sliced beans buried in sugar. Use vanilla sugar to flavor cakes, puddings, fruits and whipped cream. Store tightly sealed in a dry place.

<u>Vinaigrette</u>: Is a dressing for salads - a combination of vinegar and oil often incorporated with fresh herbs deepened with mustard and seasoned with fine sea salt, white or black pepper and a pinch of sugar or a teaspoon of honey.

<u>Zabaglione</u>: Is an extremely light, frothy custard consisting of egg yolk (preferably organic) superfine sugar, sweet wine or champagne whisked together in the top half of a double boiler and served warm or cold with pudding, cakes and fruits.

ACCESSABLE PRODUCTS & SUPPLY SOURCES

*Dried Pasta, DeCecco or Barilla Brands, available in most supermarkets
*Rossi Pasta, Specialty pastas, 114 Green Street, P.O. Box 759, Marietta, Ohio 45750
(800) 227-6774
*Italian Macaroni Products – Olive Tree Marketing Intl. Inc.,
Miami Beach, FL. 33141 (305) 788-3093
*Sea Salt, La Baleine or Hain Iodized sea salt, available in most supermarkets
*Purcell Mountain Farms, rice, beans, lentils & nuts
1-208-267-0627
*Baker's sugar, available in most supermarkets
*Bob's Red Mill, 5209 SE International Way, Milwaukie, Oregon 97222
(503) 654-3215, available in some supermarkets
*Bavarian Meat Products, 2934 Western Ave., Seattle, WA. 98121
(206) 448-3540 – Fax (206) 956-0526
*Jahr's European Sausages, 160 Ranchette Lane. Selah, WA. 98942
(509) 697-8904
*D,Artagnan, Inc. – Specialties, Game Meats, Fowl, Truffles & more – (800) 327-8246
www.dartagnan.com
*Cheeses - Igourmet Cheeses – (877) 446-8763 and
*Valley Game & Gourmet
(800) 521-2156 – www.valleygame.com
*Cleanest Chicken – www.smartchicken.com - available in some supermarkets
*Ghirardelli, Chocolates, available in Supermarkets
*Guittard Chocolate Company – (800) 468-2462

SPICES & SEASONINGS used in RECIPES & THEN SOME

WHERE TO GET THEM - LEGEND

Supermarket (s)   Specialty Food Stores (sfs)   Internet (i)

DRIED	LIQUID–PERISHABLE
Active dry yeast (s)	Almond oil (s) (sfs) (i)
	Apricot oil (s) (sfs) (i)
Baking powder (s)	Avocado oil (s) (sfs) (i)
Bay leaves, dried (s)	
	Capers, Spanish (s) (sfs)
Caraway seeds (s) (i)	Chile sauce (s)
Cardamom (s) (i)	Curry paste (sfs)
Cayenne pepper (s)	
Chili powder (s)	Grape-seed oil (s) (sfs)
Cinnamon (s)	
Confectioner sugar (s)	Hazel nut oil (s) (sfs)
Coriander (s) (i)	
Cumin (s) (i)	Mustard, Dijon (s)
Curry powder, hot (s)	Macadamia nut oil (s) (sfs) (i)
Curry powder, mild (s)	
	Olive oil, extra virgin (s) (sfs)
Dash, Mrs. original (s)	Olive oil, light (s)
Juniper berries (sfs) (i)	Pumpkin seed oil (sfs) (i)
Paprika (s)	Specialty Salts (s) (sfs) (i)
Pepper, black (s)	
Pepper flakes, hot (s)	Vanilla Extract (s)
Peppercorn, mélange (s)	Vinegars,
Peppercorn, white (s)	Balsamic, white (s) (sfs)
	Balsamic, dark (s) (sfs)
Sage, dried (s)	Bavarian beer (i)
Sea salt, fine ground (s) (i)	Champagne (s) (sfs)
Sea salt, course (s) (i)	Pear (s) (sfs)
Saffron (s) (sfs) (i)	Red wine (s)
	Sherry (sfs)
Tea, green (s)	
Turmeric (s) (sfs)	Walnut oil (s) (sfs)

TIPS

Drying bread crumbs: Oven-dry fresh bread and process for a uniform, smoother and denser coating of crumbs on foods. Process fresh bread while still fresh in a food processor, when softer, less dense coating on foods is preferred. For best results: Use only white unseasoned bread, crust removed, for drying or fresh bread processing.

Soaking fish and shrimp, in salt water overnight in the refrigerator to preserve plumpness - cod, halibut, sea bass, or shrimp, soak 24 hours in 1-2 tablespoons of coarse sea salt for 1-2 pounds of fish or peeled, divined prawns. Cover with water and soak overnight. When ready, drain, pat dry with paper towels and proceed with recipe.

To make au gratin, is to sprinkle cooked preparations with breadcrumbs, cheese, nuts or butter and bake at high heat allowing a crust to form.

To baste is to moisten, roast meats, such as roast duck, roast beef, roast veal, roast pork, roast turkey and roast chicken with their own juices - promotes juiciness and skin crispiness.

To simmer, is cooking ingredients in liquid just below the boiling point.

To skim, is the process of removing fat, using a skimming spoon, from surface of a broth or liquid intended for soups and sauces.

To strain, is to pass ingredients, mostly liquid, through a sieve – a technique used for clarifying sauces and stocks.

To sweat, is to cook vegetables such as onions in fat over low heat to a point when they are softened and glistening, removing them from heat before turning brown.

To marinate: is when meats, fish, poultry, vegetables and fruits are coated and let stand in a mixture for a period of time – a typical mixture may consist of vinegar, lime, lemon and orange juices enhanced with herbs and spices to effect flavoring and tenderizing introduced product. Marinating also reduces time cooking, grilling, roasting or sautéing. Marinate fresh or dried fruits in alcohol or liqueur until they take on the flavor of the marinade.

To knead, is to combine thoroughly and work components of a dough either manually with both hands, or more quickly with an electric mixer equipped with a dough hook, until dough becomes smooth and elastic.

To flambé, is the pouring of liqueur over finished desserts or food while cooking - igniting the alcohol to dramatize a dish, or enhance flavor and aroma.

To flavor, is to add spices, fresh or dried herbs, extracts or alcohol to foods to yield a particular taste.

To fold or blend, means to combine a light airy mixture (often beaten egg whites) with another mixture which is heavier. This process begins with the lighter mixture on top of the heavier one, then cutting through both with a spatula followed by gently scraping along the bottom and up the sides of the bowl - rotating the bowl slightly and repeating previous step until mixtures are thoroughly blended. Exercise care when folding to avoid collapsing the lighter mixture or losing its volume. This application is commonly used when making sponge cakes.

To clarify, is making a cloudy liquid clear, such as a soup or sauce, by stirring-in a slightly whisked egg white and carefully heating, cooling and straining liquid through a sieve or cheesecloth. Egg whites attract the sediment.

To deglaze, is to stir a liquid, such as wine, spirits, water or stock, to dissolve food particles and/or caramelized drippings left in a pan after cooked food has been removed. The liquid yield or, otherwise, pan juices from such process is usually used as a base for sauce.

To bake, is to bake foods in an enclosure and surrounded by dry heat, such as in an oven.

To bake blind, is to bake pastry shells or tart shells without filling. Prick bottom crust to release steam with a fork then the bottom is covered with baking paper and filled with dried beans or dried peas and baked completely to retain shape before being filled.

To caramelize, is to heat sugar to high temperature until browned thus altering its normal flavor to richly intensified and its useful purpose is to enhance flavor and appearance of foods.

To chocolate coat, is known in Europe by its French name, "couverture." A very high quality chocolate with at least 32% cocoa butter makes it particularly suitable for applying a thin, shiny chocolate glaze (or coating) over tortes such as Sacher torte, truffles and other pastries and candies. Chocolate of this quality is usually obtainable at specialty chocolate shops, European supply stores and mail order outlets. To preserve chocolate without diminishing its quality and dark-shiny appearance, store it in a cool, dry place. When stored improperly, chocolate becomes dull and appears powdery. This condition is called "bloom."

P U M P K I N

<u>*How to prepare it:*</u> *First, wash and dry the pumpkin before setting it on a sanitized cutting board. Begin cutting through the tough pumpkin rind as shown in steps 1 and 2 below. If having difficulty, try slightly rocking the pumpkin back and forth with one hand while with a seesawing motion and applying downward pressure of the knife with the other hand - rather than a back and forth slicing motion, to reduce resistance. Steps 3 through 7 always cut and slice with flat side down!*

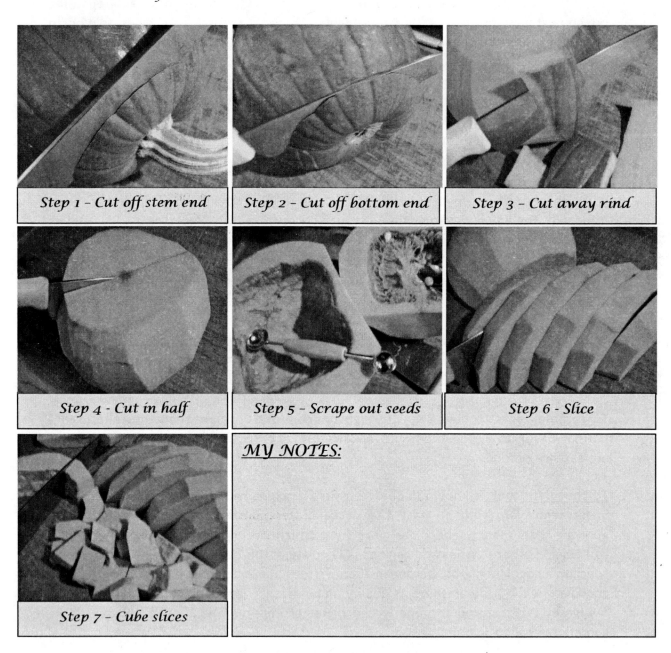

Step 1 - Cut off stem end

Step 2 - Cut off bottom end

Step 3 - Cut away rind

Step 4 - Cut in half

Step 5 - Scrape out seeds

Step 6 - Slice

Step 7 - Cube slices

<u>MY NOTES:</u>

BUTTERNUT SQUASH

How to prepare it: *First, wash and dry it before setting it on a sanitized cutting board. Cut, to separate the solid flesh piece and the seeded bulb-like end, as shown in Step1. The halved bulb-like piece as shown in Steps 2 and 3 is to be scraped out with a melon baler or a spoon. Edible seeds can be dried and roasted. Cut the solid piece in half after slicing away its rind as shown in Step 3 then slice and cube as shown in Step 4.*

Step 1 – Cut off ends

Step 2 – Separate

Step 3 – Cut away rind

Step 4 – Cube slices

MY NOTES:

L. Parsnip – R. Celeriac

Parsnip-peeled-sliced-diced

Both parsnip and celeriac (celery root) are among other root vegetables listed and described in the "Root Vegetable" section. Processing them is similar to butternut squash, and their foliage is often chopped and used in soups and stocks.

LOW FAT CONSOMMÉ

"Heart Healthy"

Makes about 1 quart

CONSOMMÉ

1 onion, coarsely chopped
1 carrot, peeled, coarsely chopped
1 parsnip, peeled, coarsely chopped
½ bulb of fennel, coarsely chopped
½ cup celery root, peeled, coarsely chopped
1 leek, coarsely chopped
2 cloves of garlic, halved
½ teaspoon white peppercorns
1-2 teaspoons sea salt

1 bouquet garni (*see instructions below*)

½ cup each of julienne leeks-white parts only, carrots, celery stalk and chopped wild mushrooms, such as shiitake or chanterelle
¼ cup each of fresh parsley, watercress or chives, chopped, for garnish

Prepare bouquet garni: Loosely wrap the green part of a leek around a bay leaf, a sprig of thyme, some of the celery leaves and a few stems of parsley and tie with household string. *Prepare ahead.*

To make consommé: Place chopped vegetables in a large saucepan with 8 cups of water. Add garlic, peppercorns, salt and the bouquet of garni. Bring to a boil, cover and reduce heat - to simmer gently for 1 hour. Let stock cool slightly, press stock through a fine strainer and discard the vegetables and bouquet garni.

Transfer strained consommé to a clean saucepan, bring to a slow boil, add julienne vegetables and mushrooms, turn heat to simmer and cook gently for 5-6 minutes. Ladle into serving bowls and sprinkle each with parsley, watercress or chives.

Note: To freeze, allow stock to cool, transfer to small freezer containers. Consommé can be kept frozen for up to 4 months tightly sealed.

Photo Left, Leeks - - Right, carrots Center, whole fennel bulb

STOCKS

LOW FAT CONSOMMÉ

BROWN STOCK

CHICKEN STOCK

FISH STOCK

TURKEY STOCK

ONION CONFIT

BROWN STOCK

Roasted bones produce excellent flavor and color to "stock" based foods, and the simmering process enables opportunity to easily remove excess fat.

Makes about 6-8 cups

In a 400°F oven, roast 1½ pounds each of beef and veal bones 35-45 minutes, or until golden brown on all sides, turning bones once during roasting using long tongs, adding:

1 onion, quartered
2 carrots, peeled and chopped
1 leek, cleaned and chopped
1 celery stalk, chopped
½ celery root, peeled and chopped

Transfer substance to a clean stockpot, and add:

4 quarts of water
1 bouquet of Garni *(see adjacent Note)*
6 peppercorns
2 teaspoons sea salt
1 bay leaf
2 sprigs of flat-leaf parsley

Simmer 3-4 hours. Skim off any impurities rising to the surface with a flat strainer.

Ladle the stock in batches into a fine strainer over a large, heat-proofed bowl, and gently press solids against the side of the bowl with the ladle to extract all liquid – discard meat, bones and vegetables.

Refrigerate for several hours and then remove solidified fat from the surface, and discard.

Note: Bouquet garni is a bundled combination of fresh herbs and vegetables used to flavor soups and stocks and discarded after use. A typical example would be the tying of sprigs of parsley, thyme, leeks, a small carrot, celery leaves and bay leaves enclosed in a piece of cheesecloth or simply just tied together with household string.

Chef's note: Portion-freeze stock in pint-size freezer containers when stock is not intended for immediate use. Use within 4-months.

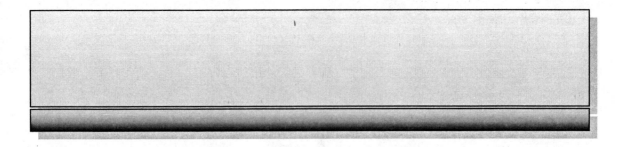

FISH STOCK

Makes about 6 cups

Soak 3-4 pounds of chopped fish bones and trimmings in lightly salted water for 10-minutes, drain, discard fish bones and trimmings, transfer liquid to a clean stockpot and add the following ingredients:

2½ quarts of cold water
2 tablespoons crushed peppercorns
2 bay leaves
2 chopped celery stalks
1 chopped onion
2 sprigs of fresh flat leaf parsley
2 sprigs fresh thyme
1/3 cup of fresh lemon juice

Simmer for 35-minutes skimming off any impurities rising to the surface with a flat strainer.

Ladle stock in batches through a fine strainer into a clean heat-proofed, large bowl, and gently press solids against sides of bowl with the ladle to extract all liquid and discard vegetables.

Chef's note: If not made for immediate use, portion-freeze stock in pint-size freezer containers for future use. Stock frozen is best when used within 4-months.

CHICKEN STOCK

Makes about 2½ quarts

12 cups of water
2 pounds chicken parts such as, wings, thighs or drumsticks
1 large onion, peeled and cut into quarters
1 large carrot, peeled and sliced
1 large parsnip, peeled and cut into cubes
¼ cup of leeks, trimmed, washed and cut into rings
2 garlic cloves
2 parsley sprigs
2 teaspoons sea salt
1 teaspoon of peppercorns

In a large pot bring water to a boil, add chicken parts and boil 10 minutes.

Skim-off foam and discard, add onion, carrots, parsnip, leeks, garlic, parsley, salt and peppercorns.

Reduce heat to moderate-low, cover partially and simmer stock for 3 hours. Strain stock and discard chicken parts and vegetables.

Refrigerate stock for 2-3 hours, remove and discard fat from the surface. Stock can be kept refrigerated up to 3 days, or frozen up to 4 months.

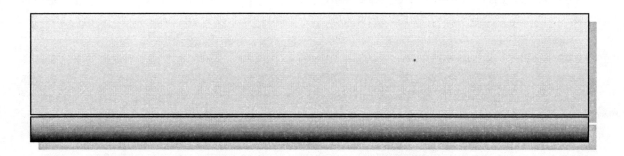

TURKEY STOCK

Makes 2 Quarts

12 cups water
2 pounds turkey wings
1 onion, peeled and quartered
1 large carrot, peeled, sliced
1 large celery stalk, sliced
1 clove garlic
¼ cup of leeks, cut into rings
¼ cup rutabaga, peeled, cut into cubes
¼ cup parsnip, peeled, cut into cubes
2 teaspoons sea salt
1 teaspoon of peppercorns
1 teaspoon fresh thyme, chopped

In a large pot, bring water to a boil, add turkey wings, cook 10-minutes, skim-off foam and discard, add onion, carrot, celery, garlic, leeks, rutabaga, parsnip, salt, peppercorns and thyme. Reduce heat to moderate-low, cover partially, and simmer the stock for 2½ to 3-hours. Strain stock, discard wings and vegetables, and skim-off fat before using. Stock can be refrigerated for up to 3-days, or kept frozen up to 4-months.

ONION CONFIT (Kohn-FEE)

Makes: about 2 cups

2 tablespoons unsalted butter
1 teaspoon of extra virgin olive oil
2 pounds of red, sweet onions, peeled and thinly sliced
1 teaspoon of sugar or orange honey
½ teaspoon fine sea salt
1 teaspoon white pepper, freshly ground
1/3 cup of fresh orange juice, or more, if needed
1/3 cup Zinfandel wine
1 tablespoon black currant vinegar or red raspberry vinegar (Avail. in Supermarkets)

Heat butter and oil over medium-high heat in a large, deep skillet and add onions, sugar or honey, salt and pepper stirring often. Cook uncovered for about 10-15 minutes. As juice from onions release and reabsorbs it, stir and turn onions frequently to avoid burning (any burnt onion will bitterly taint all onions in the pan).

Cover and cook for another 10-minutes on medium heat. Add orange juice, wine, vinegar, and cook covered for 10-15 minutes stirring often, and season again with salt, sugar or honey and pepper if necessary. Mixture should be thick resembling a loose marmalade.

Chef's note: The perfect onion confit has the right balance of salt, sugar, pepper and orange juice, wine and vinegar resulting in a sweet tartness and be soft but not mushy. Serve warm or at room temperature. Walla Walla sweet onions are an excellent alternative to red onions - add a splash of white balsamic vinegar if white onions are used. White Balsamic vinegar is generally available in most supermarkets.

CHILLED & HOT

SOUPS & STEWS

MEATLESS & MEAT

Top Left – Chilled Watermelon Soup, see recipe on Page 42 with Watermelon-Peach

Top Right – Chilled Watermelon Soup, see recipe on Page 41, with Crab-Watercress Coulis

Bottom Right – Hot Butternut Squash-Celery Soup, see Page 58

*Top Left –
Purple Potato,
see Page 49*

*Center Left –
Green
Asparagus, see
Page 51*

*Bottom Left –
Butternut
Squash, see
Page 58*

*Top Right –
Tomato-Gin,
see Page 62*

*Center Right
– White
Asparagus,
see Page 51*

*Bottom
Right –
Pumpkin-
Savoy-Pasta,
see Page 57*

CHILLED SOUPS

Enjoy these few of many varieties of chilled soups I've created over the years. Chilled soups are traditional, seasonal delicacies of Germany, particularly found in regions nearest to where the main ingredient is harvested. From there, the idea of succulent chilled soups spread throughout Germany and other parts of the world by food industry persons within, and from other countries near and distant.

Introduction, and acceptance, of my vast array of chilled seasonal soups by ever-willing, trusting patrons of my former restaurant in Western Washington was as easy as if offering them a bowl of ice cream.

Sundays were "travel days to Yakima Valley, Eastern Washington to shop for fresh fruits, berries and produce to use in my former restaurant in Tacoma, Washington. Even though round trip travel time consumed five hours plus, it was worth it to experience the sight of restaurant patron's expressions on Mondays when the ever-changing menu listed unheard of combinations, such as the Chilled Watermelon-Peach Soup recipe found on Page 42. Never disappointed, patrons returned regularly to experience adventuresome entrées nowhere else to be found before then, except in Europe or perhaps rarely in very upscale metropolitan restaurants. This and some of many other chilled soups I've beforehand introduced and now sharing some of those recipes for your enjoyment at home. Chilled soups have natural, pleasing flavors that seem to neutralize the heat of summer, especially with accompaniments like a light salad and fresh baked bread – for a great tasting light summer lunch or snack, along with a glass of your favorite Fume Blanc.

WATERMELON

Native to Africa, a mix of both bitter and sweet watermelon with identical exterior features grow wild in the same locality, and to determine the difference between the two, natives punctured them to taste their juice before harvesting sweet ones for food, and for drinking, especially during dry periods. For centuries, watermelon is also grown in the warmer parts of Russia, Asia Minor, the Near East and Middle East. Apparently watermelon was introduced to China about a century ago. According to European botanists of the 16th and 17th centuries, a wide range of sizes and shapes, rind, seed and flesh colors existed.

Currently, shapes, sizes and colors most familiar to us have yellow flesh; seedless melons with red flesh; the most common red watermelon with speckled seeds; those with white, red, brown and black seeds, and the green seeded variety. The watermelon plant was doubtlessly known centuries ago in most European countries where growing conditions were accommodating, and European colonists apparently brought watermelon seeds with them to Massachusetts during the mid 1600s. American watermelon flesh is generally consumed fresh and well chilled and the rind can be made into preserves or pickled and the seeds used for planting. In certain regions of Russia, beer is made from watermelon juice. Also, juice is boiled down to reduce it to heavy syrup for its sugar. Seeds are oftentimes roasted with or without salting and eaten by hand.

MUSKMELON

Muskmelon, native to Persia, is an important food source and garden crop. Translated, musk means a "kind of perfume", because of its fragrant flesh. One of the most popular of melons in America is the small oval, heavily netted variety called cantaloupe or those with smooth rind called casaba and honeydew.

Interestingly though, cantaloupe are muskmelon, but muskmelon are not cantaloupe - this is because muskmelon will not cross with watermelon, cucumber, pumpkin or squash, but varieties within the species intercross freely, which perhaps is the reason for differences in appearance of rinds and colors. "Melon" is French translation and spin-off from the Latin word melopepo meaning apple shaped melon derived from Greek words of similar meaning.

It is said that the Spaniards introduced cantaloupe to North America. And it's believed that the English colonies in Virginia and Massachusetts grew cantaloupe from seed, as did the North American Indians. Indian Tribes in Florida; the Middle West and in New England, grew melon of various sizes, shapes and colors like those we today are most familiar with.

Improvements have been made in developing uniformity among varieties regarding size and shapes, especially involving thickness and quality of flesh. Melons of all varieties are of the gourd family, and for various purposes, special strains of melons are being produced and genetically altered, engineered to resist a disease called powdery mildew.

Although, 20 years ago, I seem to remember the flesh of melons were fruitier tasting, had less water content and their rind seemed thinner. Nonetheless, enjoy my Chilled Watermelon Soup recipes on the following pages.

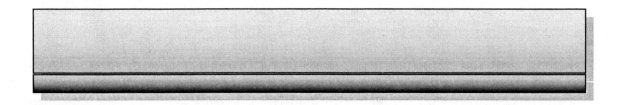

CHILLED YELLOW WATERMELON SOUP
With
CRAB and WATERCRESS COULIS

"Signature-1993 – A highly praised, popular entrée at our multi-course Winemaker's dinners – Photo displays soup garnished with crème fraiche, red bell peppers and sautéed tiger prawn, another of several signature versions"

Serves: 4 - 6

SOUP

6 cups yellow watermelon, peeled, halved, seeded and coarsely chopped
¼ cup Walla Walla sweet onions, finely chopped
2 cloves garlic, minced
2 tablespoons fresh limejuice
2 tablespoons Aqvavit (Avail, in Liquor Stores)
1 tablespoon of extra virgin olive oil
½ teaspoon sea salt
¼ teaspoon white pepper, freshly ground

Purée watermelon, onion and garlic in a blender, or food processor, until smooth and transfer purée to a large glass bowl, and stir-in limejuice, aqvavit, oil, salt and pepper.

Chill soup uncovered about 2-hours - season soup with more salt and pepper if desired.

CRAB

2 cups jumbo cooked crabmeat, picked over
¼ cup watercress leaves, chopped
1 teaspoon of extra virgin olive oil
1 teaspoon Aqvavit
¼ teaspoon sea salt
¼ teaspoon white pepper, freshly ground

In a medium bowl, toss crabmeat with chopped watercress, 1-teaspoon of oil, 1-teaspoon Aqvavit, ¼ teaspoon salt, ¼ teaspoon pepper and refrigerate covered until ready to use.

COULIS

Leaves from 2-bunches of watercress, washed
1½ teaspoons extra virgin olive oil
2-3 teaspoons filtered water
Pinch of sea salt

In a food processor or blender, purée watercress leaves with 1½ teaspoons oil and 2-teaspoons of water.

Strain into a small bowl to remove any course bits, add remaining 1-teaspoon of water as needed to obtain a creamy consistency and season with salt.

Ladle soup into 4 chilled serving bowls, top each with ¼ cup of crab mixture, drizzle each with watercress coulis and enjoy.

Photo left: Chilled Watermelon Soup - Prawn garnishing. See Chilled Watermelon Soup with Crab -Watercress Coulis on previous page.
Photo right: Shows Signature Chilled Watermelon Soup - blueberries garnishing, another of several signature versions. See Watermelon-Peach recipe, below.

CHILLED WATERMELON-PEACH SOUP

"Heart Healthy" - "Cooking with Erika"
Created and demonstrated this on local, weekly TV Segment, aired during year 2001.

Serves: 8

10 cups of seedless watermelon, peeled, (4-5 pounds) and cut into 1-inch pieces)

4 medium ripe peaches, halved, pitted, peeled, and cut into 1-inch pieces
½ cup of fresh orange juice
4 tablespoons cornstarch

1/3 cup orange honey, (Avail. in health food stores)
8 tablespoons low-fat vanilla ice cream (optional), or
Frozen low-fat yogurt, for garnish

Fresh mint leaves, for garnish
16 peach slices, for garnish

Purée watermelon and peaches in batches and transfer purée to a large saucepan. In a small bowl, combine orange juice and cornstarch. Bring watermelon soup to a slow boil, reduce heat to medium-low and whisk-in the cornstarch mixture, stir-in honey and cook 3-5 minutes, or until slightly thickened. Cool to room temperature and transfer to a large glass bowl, cover and chill overnight.

Ladle chilled soup into 8 bowls, top with vanilla ice cream or frozen yogurt, mint leaves and sliced peaches.

YAKIMA VALLEY CHILLED "ELEGANT LADY" PEACH SOUP
"Signature 1993"

Serves: 6

SOUP

8 large ripe peaches, peeled, pitted and puréed (such as Elegant or Summer Lady)
1 cup of late harvest Riesling wine
2 cups bottled natural spring water
½ teaspoon freshly grated ginger
1½ cups fine sugar
1/3 cup orange juice, freshly squeezed
4 tablespoons lemon juice, freshly squeezed
3 tablespoons cornstarch

ORANGE CREAM

1 cup whipping cream
1 tablespoon orange juice, freshly squeezed
2 tablespoons confectioner sugar
Mint leaves, for garnish

For the soup: In a large saucepan, combine puréed peaches, wine, water, ginger, sugar and orange juice. In a small bowl, combine lemon juice and cornstarch, stir cornstarch mixture into peach mixture, bring peach soup to a slow boil, reduce heat to medium-low and cook until slightly thickened, about 3-5 minutes.

Transfer peach soup to a large heatproof glass bowl, chill for at least 4-6 hours, stirring occasionally.

For the Orange Cream: Beat cream, 1-tablespoon of orange juice and confectioner sugar in a medium bowl until stiff peaks form and refrigerate until ready to serve.

To serve: Ladle chilled peach soup into 6-pre-chilled glass bowls, top each with a dollop of cream and garnish with mint leaves. Serve with chilled Late Harvest Riesling.

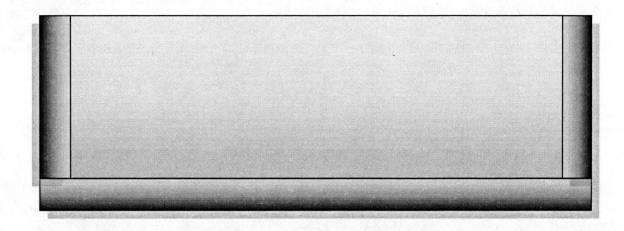

43

CHILLED APRICOT SOUP
With
BLACKBERRY CREAM
"Signature"

Serves: 4

4 cups ripe apricots, halved, pits removed, chopped
1 cup Late Harvest Riesling wine
1 cup of water
½ cup sugar, plus 2-tablespoons
1 teaspoon of fresh lemon juice
3½ tablespoons Lemon vodka
4 tablespoons cornstarch

In a medium saucepan, combine apricots, wine, water, sugar, and lemon juice.

Bring to a boil, reduce heat to medium-low and simmer for 10-minutes. Let soup cool, transfer to a blender and purée until smooth. Return to clean saucepan.

In a small bowl, combine Lemon Vodka and cornstarch, whisk cornstarch mixture into apricot soup, and cook 2-minutes or until slightly thickened.

Transfer puréed soup to a large glass bowl, cover with plastic wrap and refrigerate until cold – at least 4-hours or overnight.

BLACKBERRY CREAM

1 cup of whipping cream
2 tablespoons confectioner sugar
1 teaspoon Lemon vodka
1½ cups ripe blackberries

Using an electric mixer, beat cream in a small bowl until soft peaks form, then add the confectioner sugar and vodka - beat until stiff peaks form.

Gently fold 1-cup of blackberries into whipped cream, ladle soup into serving bowls, top each with a dollop of blackberry cream and garnish each serving with the remaining blackberries. Enjoy chilled.

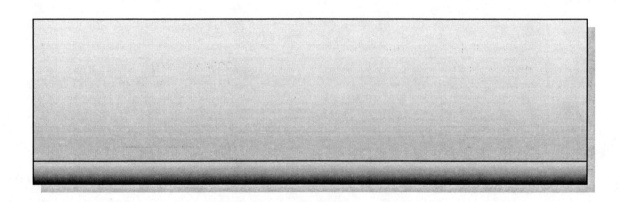

CHILLED BLUEBERRY SOUP
With
LEMON ICE CREAM
"Signature"

Serves: 4

4½ cups blueberries, washed, stems removed
1 cup Port wine, plus 3½-tablespoons
1 cup of water
½ cup sugar
4 tablespoons cornstarch

4 scoops lemon ice cream, store bought
2 tablespoons lemon zest, finely grated

In a medium saucepan combine 4-cups blueberries, 1-cup Port wine, water and sugar. Bring to a boil, reduce heat to medium-low and simmer for 6-minutes.

Let soup cool, transfer to a blender - purée until smooth – return to a clean saucepan.

In a small bowl, combine remaining 3½-tablespoons Port wine with cornstarch, whisk cornstarch mixture into blueberry soup, cook for 2-minutes or until slightly thickened.

Transfer puréed blueberry soup to a heatproof glass bowl, cover with plastic wrap and refrigerate for at least 4-hours or overnight.

Ladle soup into serving bowls, top each with a scoop of lemon ice cream, garnish each with remaining ½ cup of blueberries and sprinkle each serving with lemon zest, enjoy chilled.

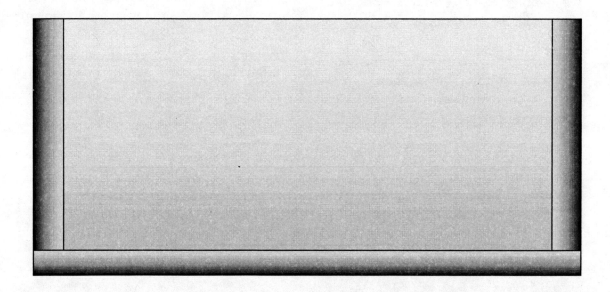

CHILLED YELLOW BELL PEPPER SOUP
With
CRÈME FRAÎCHE and CUCUMBERS
"Signature"

Serves: 4-6

SOUP

2 tablespoons extra virgin olive oil
7 large sweet yellow peppers, seeded and coarsely chopped
1 medium-sweet onion, chopped
1 tablespoon minced garlic
1 cup of water
½ cup dry Chardonnay or Riesling wine
Sea salt
White pepper, freshly ground
¼ cup watercress leaves, chopped
1 cup of cucumber, peeled, seeded and coarsely chopped

Heat oil over medium heat in a large saucepan, and add peppers and onion - cook 5-10 minutes, or until peppers are just beginning to soften, stirring occasionally. Add garlic, water and wine, bring to boil, reduce heat, and simmer for 5-10 minutes.

Remove from heat, cool slightly, and season with salt and pepper. In a blender container, or food processor bowl, blend mixture one-half at a time until smooth – to purée. Transfer puréed pepper soup to a large glass bowl and chill overnight in refrigerator.

CRÈME FRAÎCHE

½ cup whipping cream
½ cup sour cream

In a small mixing bowl, stir together, whipping cream and sour cream - cover with plastic wrap and let it stand at room temperature for 2-5 hours, or until mixture thickens. When thickened, chill in the refrigerator until serving time. Stir before serving – yields about 1-cup.

To serve: Ladle pepper soup into individual bowls, top each with a dollop of crème fraîche, sprinkle with watercress and chopped cucumbers. Enjoy with grilled French bread slices and dry or medium-dry Riesling wine.

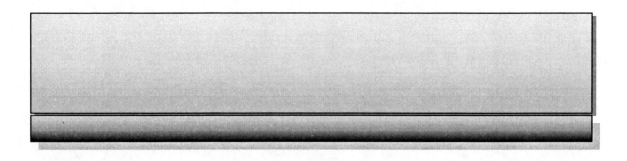

CHILLED ASPARAGUS-SPINACH SOUP
With
CRÈME FRAÎCHE
"Signature"

"Cooking with Erika"
Created and demonstrated this on local, weekly TV Segment, aired July 2, 2002.

Serves: 4

1½ tablespoons extra virgin olive oil
2 leeks, white and light-green parts only, finely chopped
2½ cups vegetable stock or water
1½ pounds of fresh asparagus, tips cut into
 1-inch pieces, stems chopped discarding woody ends
2 cups baby spinach leaves, stems removed
4 lemon slices for garnish
Sea salt
White pepper, freshly ground
4 teaspoons crème fraîche (see Recipe on facing page)
Lemon slices, for garnish

Heat oil in a medium saucepan, add leeks and cook over low heat, stirring often - about 2-minutes. Add stock or water and bring to a boil. Add asparagus stems and cook over medium-low heat until tender, about 2-3 minutes. Add spinach, cook for 1-minute - season to taste with salt and pepper.

In batches, purée soup in a blender and transfer soup to a large glass bowl, cover and refrigerate until chilled, at least 2-hours. Cook asparagus tips in a medium saucepan of boiling, salted water until barely tender, about 2-3 minutes. Drain.

Plunge asparagus tips into a bowl of ice water. Drain again and pat dry.

Ladle chilled soup into bowls and garnish with crème fraîche, asparagus tips and lemon slices. *Enjoy.*

CHILLED YELLOW TOMATO SOUP
With
BASIL OIL and AVOCADO
"Signature"

"Cooking with Erika"
Created and demonstrated this on local, weekly TV Segment, aired during year 2002

Serves: 4

SOUP

1¾ pounds yellow tomatoes, halved
1 cup cucumber, peeled, seeded and chopped
1 cup yellow bell pepper, seeded and chopped
½ cup Walla-Walla sweet onion, finely chopped
2 tablespoons fresh lemon juice
1 tablespoon of fresh limejuice
3 tablespoons extra virgin olive oil
1 tablespoon champagne vinegar or dry Riesling wine
Pinch of sugar
Sea salt
White pepper, finely ground
1 tablespoon of garlic, minced
1 medium jalapeno chili, seeded, chopped
1 avocado, halved, pit removed, peeled and chopped for garnish
2 tablespoons Italian parsley, chopped for garnish

Chop tomatoes and set aside ½ cup chopped tomatoes, ¼ cup cucumber and ¼ cup bell pepper.

Combine remaining tomatoes, cucumbers and bell peppers in a food processor, add onion, lemon juice, limejuice, oil, vinegar or wine, garlic, jalapeno chili - process until smooth - season with sugar, salt and pepper.

Transfer soup to a large bowl, and add reserved vegetables. Cover and chill overnight.

BASIL OIL

Makes about 1 cup

2 cups fresh basil leaves, coarsely chopped
¾ cup extra virgin olive oil
2 green onions, chopped
1 medium jalapeno chili, seeded, chopped
1 tablespoon of garlic, minced
¼ cup of water

Combine all ingredients, except water, in food processor and purée until almost smooth. Transfer purée to fine strainer set over a bowl. Using a rubber spatula, press on solids to extract as much liquid as possible - discard solids in strainer. Whisk ¼ cup water into mixture in bowl, season to taste with salt and pepper, cover and refrigerate. Whisk before using.

Divide soup among 4-bowls, drizzle with basil oil and garnish with avocado and parsley. Enjoy with crusty Italian bread and crisp white wine.

CREAM OF PURPLE POTATO SOUP

"Signature" – Original, among other identified recipes in this cookbook created for, and personally demonstrated this recipe for the Washington State Potato Seed Commission at the Washington State University Exploratory Laboratory, November 17, 2006)

Serves 4-6

2 tablespoons extra virgin olive oil
1 tablespoon unsalted butter
3 large purple potatoes, peeled, cut into cubes
½ cup onions, peeled, chopped
3 garlic cloves, peeled, chopped
1 medium parsnip, trimmed, peeled, chopped
½ of a small celery root, trimmed, peeled, chopped
6 cups of water
1-2 teaspoons sea salt
¼ cup whipping cream
½ teaspoon mélange peppercorns, freshly ground
4-6 teaspoons crème fraîche, for garnish
Italian parsley, chopped, for garnish

1 tablespoon of unsalted butter
1 teaspoon of extra virgin olive oil
12 ounces, fresh shiitake mushrooms, trimmed, thinly sliced
Pinch of sugar
Sea salt
Mélange peppercorn, freshly ground

To prepare soup: Heat 2 tablespoons of oil and 1 tablespoon of butter in a large saucepan over medium heat – add potatoes, onion, garlic, parsnip and celery root - cook for 3-5 minutes, stirring while pouring in 6 cups of water – add 1 teaspoon salt and bring to a boil. Reduce heat and simmer partially covered for about 30-minutes or until vegetables are soft - let soup cool slightly. Purée soup in batches in a blender or food processor and transfer to a clean large saucepan, add cream and cook over low heat for 10-minutes stirring occasionally – keep warm, and season with salt and pepper, if needed.

To prepare mushrooms: In a large skillet heat 1-tablespoon of butter and 1 tablespoon of oil over medium-high heat, add mushrooms and sugar, cook until light brown, about 6-8 minutes, stirring occasionally – season with salt and pepper.

To serve: Ladle soup into soup bowls, garnish each with a teaspoon of crème fraîche, sprinkle with parsley and top each with mushrooms and serve with toasted crostini.

Note: All food specimens in photos throughout this cookbook were styled by the author, prepared table ready, unaltered and enjoyed naturally.

H
O
T

S
O
U
P
S

Top Left –
Purple
Potato,
previous
Page

Center Left
– Green
Asparagus,
next Page

Bottom
Left –
Butternut
Squash,
Page 58

Top Right
– Tomato-
Gin, Page
62

Center
Right
White
Asparagus,
next Page

Pumpkin-
Savoy-
Pasta,
Page 57

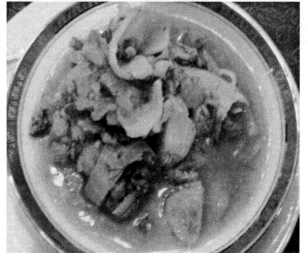

CREAM of GREEN or WHITE ASPARAGUS SOUP

Serves: 4

2 pounds asparagus green or white
2 cups chicken stock or asparagus water
1 cup of whipping cream
Pinch of sugar
5 teaspoons cornstarch
2-3 tablespoons whole milk
¼ teaspoon nutmeg, freshly ground
Sea salt
White pepper, freshly ground
4 teaspoons crème fraîche, (See Index) for garnish
4 tablespoons watercress, chopped (optional)
1 cup of fresh cooked crabmeat, for garnish (optional)

Peel and discard tough skin from asparagus. Trim bottom thick ends - wash, drain, cut-off 1¼-inches of tips and set aside. Slice spears crosswise into thin discs.

Bring a saucepan of water to a boil, add salt and asparagus tips, and simmer for 2-3 minutes.

Drain, reserving 2-cups of asparagus water and place asparagus tips in a bowl of iced water to stop further cooking, drain and set aside.

Add chicken stock or the asparagus water and whipping cream to a medium saucepan with sugar - bring to a boil.

Add sliced asparagus to the saucepan and cook gently for 10-minutes and let asparagus mixture cool slightly. Purée asparagus in a food processor or blender, and return mixture to a clean saucepan and heat again.

In a small bowl, mix cornstarch with milk until it forms a smooth paste. Pour a small amount of hot asparagus mixture into the paste and blend.

Return paste to the saucepan and bring to a boil, stirring constantly, until slightly thickened. Turn off heat, add nutmeg and season to taste with salt and pepper.

Pour soup into 4 large bowls, swirl 1-teaspoon of crème fraîche in the center of each, sprinkle each with watercress, arrange some asparagus tips on top and garnish servings with crabmeat.

Enjoy with your favorite cooled, crisp white wine.

Green Asparagus Soup   *White Asparagus Soup*

TIPS

Handling green asparagus: Break-off tough ends of asparagus stalks with fingers, or cut stalks to uniform lengths and peel stalks with a vegetable peeler. The latter method is more appealing to the eye, but the first is easier. Whichever method used, proper cooking technique is the key to yielding perfectly cooked asparagus.

Advantage of bundling: Tying asparagus in small bundles before cooking keeps spears all facing the same direction and makes lifting bundles out of the boiling water much easier without damaging tender spears.

Avoid overcrowding: Using a large, deep enough pot to avoid overcrowding and allow spears to be positioned upright, to steam, while the thicker submerged base stems simmer in the water.

Specialty cookers: These are oblong-shaped pans which have an inner trivet with handles for tying asparagus – designed for easier lowering and lifting asparagus into and out of boiling water.

Cooking asparagus: Whatever method used, use a generous amount of boiling water, and a good pinch of salt. Cover and cook spears about 3-6 minutes, depending on their girth. You will know they are done when just crisp tender, but not mushy. Remove asparagus from water, drain well and top with your favorite toppings or enjoy asparagus as a side dish. *(See Recipe Index for other delicious recipes containing asparagus).*

52

VEGETABLE CANNELLINI SOUP

Serves: 6-8

1 cup dried cannellini (white kidney beans), soaked in cold water to cover at least 12-hours or overnight, drain.

10 cups water
4 tablespoons extra virgin olive oil
1 large onion, chopped
3 cloves garlic, chopped
2 cups Yukon Gold potatoes, peeled and diced
2 medium carrots, trimmed on both ends, peeled and diced
2 medium zucchini, diced
1 medium parsnip, peeled and diced
1½ cups tomatoes, peeled, seeded, diced
2 leeks (white and pale green parts only), thinly sliced
4 fresh thyme sprigs
1 bay leaf
1 cup of cooked bow tie pasta
1-2 teaspoons sea salt
1 teaspoon pepper, freshly ground
½ cup Italian parsley, chopped

Place drained beans in a large saucepan, add 6-cups of water, bring to a boil, reduce heat to medium-low, partially cover and cook, about 1-hour or until beans are almost tender – stir occasionally. Drain beans, reserve liquid and set aside.

In another large saucepan, heat oil over medium heat and when hot, add onion – sauté them until soft – add garlic, potatoes, carrots, zucchini, parsnip, tomatoes, and leeks - sauté stirring, about 2 minutes. Add 4 cups of water, the thyme, bay leaf and 1½ teaspoons of salt.

Bring to a boil, cover partially, turn heat to medium-low and cook 15-20 minutes, or until vegetables are almost tender.

Add cooked beans and 1-cup of bean liquid and cook on medium-low heat 15-20 minutes or until vegetables and beans are tender.

Discard thyme sprigs and bay leaf, add cooked bow tie pasta, season with salt and pepper, stir-in parsley and ladle soup into serving bowls.

Enjoy with crusty Italian bread.

Note: Add reserved bean liquid or water to thin soup, if needed, and simmer 5-10 minutes.

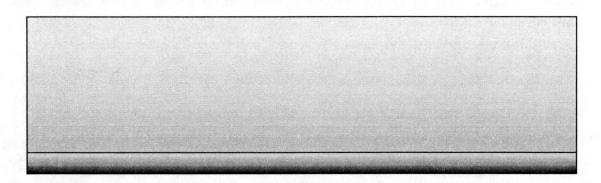

BARLEY-POTATO SOUP
"Signature"

Serves: 4-6

8 ounces of pearl barley
4 cups of beef or chicken stock
4 cups vegetable stock or water

2 tablespoons of extra virgin olive oil
1 medium onion, chopped
¼ cup of leeks, whites only, crosscut into thin rings
1 cup of Yukon gold potatoes, peeled, diced
1 cup of carrots, peeled, diced
1 cup of celery root, peeled, diced
1 tablespoon of fresh marjoram, finely chopped
Pinch of saffron threads or ¼ teaspoon turmeric
Sea salt
Pepper, freshly ground
Parsley, chopped for garnish
¼ cup Parmesan cheese, freshly grated

Soak barley for about 30 minutes in cold water, drain and transfer to a large pot, add 4 cups of beef or chicken stock and 4 cups of vegetable stock or water. Bring to boil, turn heat to low and simmer for 1-hour, 15-minutes. Heat oil in a large saucepan over medium heat, and add onions, leeks, potatoes, carrots and celery root. Sauté until almost soft - add vegetable mixture to the barley and cook on medium-low heat for about 15-20 minutes. Stir in marjoram and the saffron or turmeric - season to taste with salt and pepper. Ladle into soup bowls, garnish with parsley, sprinkle with the grated Parmesan cheese.

BRANDIED ONION SOUP
"Signature"

Serves: 6

3 tablespoons unsalted butter
2½ pounds onions, preferably sweet onions, thinly sliced
Pinch of sugar
8 cups chicken stock or beef stock
¾ cup dry white wine
1-2 tablespoons brandy
Sea salt
Pepper, freshly ground

12 slices of buttered French bread baguette
½ - 1 cup Black Forest Ham, coarsely chopped
2 cups Swiss cheese, grated

Melt butter in a heavy-large pot over medium high heat. Add onions and sauté until golden brown, about 10-minutes, stirring occasionally. Add sugar, sauté 5-more minutes, add stock and wine, and bring to a boil. Reduce heat to medium-low and simmer until flavors blend, about 15-20 minutes. Add brandy to taste and simmer 5-more minutes. Season soup with salt and pepper, and keep warm.

Preheat broiler

Arrange bread on baking sheet, broil until beginning to color, about 1-minute. Mount ham and cheese on bread, and broil until cheese melts, about 2-minutes. Ladle soup into large bowls, top each bowl with 2 slices of bread and serve immediately.

BRUSSELS SPROUTS-CARROT-LEEK SOUP
"Signature"

Serves: 6-8

2 tablespoons of unsalted butter
1 pound Brussels sprouts, trimmed, cut in half
2 cups of Yukon gold potatoes, peeled, diced
2 cups of carrots, peeled, diced
2 cups of leeks, white part only, cut into rings
1 cup of parsnip, peeled, diced
8 cups of hot chicken stock, vegetable stock or water
Sea salt
Mélange pepper, freshly ground
1 clove of garlic, minced
¼ teaspoon of nutmeg, freshly ground
2 tablespoons Italian parsley, freshly chopped
1 loaf baguette
Olive oil for brushing
½ cup of Grana Padano or Parmesan cheese, freshly grated

In a large saucepan melt butter over medium heat, add vegetables and cook for 6-8 minutes, or until vegetables begin to soften stirring often. Add stock or water, bring to a full boil, and turn heat to medium-low to cook uncovered about 20 minutes, season with salt if needed, and add mélange pepper, garlic, nutmeg and parsley. Keep warm.

Preheat oven to 350°F

Cut the baguette into 1-inch slices, arrange slices on a large baking sheet - brush slices with oil, sprinkle with 1 teaspoon of cheese and toast slices until golden. Ladle soup into soup bowls and enjoy along with toasted baguette slices on the side.

LEEK-POTATO SOUP
"Signature"

"Cooking with Erika"
Created for demonstration on local, weekly TV Segment, aired during year 2001

Serves: 6

2 tablespoons extra virgin olive oil
1 tablespoon unsalted butter
2 cups leeks, white parts only, cut into rings
1 small onion, diced
2 cups Yukon gold potatoes peeled and diced
4-5 cups chicken, vegetable stock or water
1 sprig of fresh thyme
1 teaspoon garlic, chopped
¼ teaspoon saffron
Sea salt
Pepper, freshly ground

Crème fraîche or sour cream for garnish
2 tablespoons fresh Italian parsley, minced

In a large saucepan, heat the olive oil and butter over medium heat. Add leeks and onions sauté until leeks and onions are soft, about 1 minute. Add potatoes, and sauté 2-more minutes. Add stock or water, thyme and garlic. Bring to a boil, turn heat to medium-low and cook covered until potatoes are tender, about 20 minutes.

Discard thyme sprig. In batches, purée soup, in a blender or food processor until smooth. Return soup to saucepan, add saffron and cook 1-more minute on medium-low heat. Season with salt and pepper, and ladle soup into bowls, garnish with crème fraîche or sour cream and parsley. *Enjoy* with crusty French bread.

CREAMY LEEK SOUP
With
GARLIC TOASTED BREAD CUBES
"Signature"

"Cooking with Erika"
Created for demonstration on local, weekly TV Segment, aired during year 2001

Serves: 6

1 tablespoon of unsalted butter
2½ cups leeks, crosscut into thin rings, white and pale green parts only
2 large shallots, minced
1½ pounds parsnip, peeled, coarsely chopped, about 3½ cups
4 cups vegetable stock or water
Sea salt
2 tablespoons of half and half, optimal
¼ teaspoon nutmeg, freshly ground
¼ teaspoon of white pepper, freshly ground
6 white bread slices
1 tablespoon of extra virgin olive oil or Grape-seed oil
1 teaspoon of garlic, minced
6 tablespoons of fresh parsley, chopped

Melt butter in a large saucepan, over medium heat, and add next 3 ingredients and sauté until vegetables are almost tender, about 5-minutes, turn heat to low – stir-in stock, or water, bring to a boil and simmer for 15-20 minutes, season with salt and pepper, if needed, cool slightly.

Working in batches, purée the vegetables in a blender until smooth, and pour purée into a clean, large saucepan, cook gently for 2 minutes on medium heat, add half and half, nutmeg and white pepper. Keep warm.

Meanwhile, cut bread into small cubes, heat oil in a medium skillet, and add bread cubes and garlic - sauté until bread cubes are golden in color, stirring often. Ladle soup into soup bowls, sprinkle with parsley and top with bread cubes.

<u>Chef's note:</u> Save any vegetable stock produced after cooking carrots, cauliflower or any root vegetable for use in soups and sauces. Vegetable stock can also be frozen for future use. *Enjoy!*

PUMPKIN-APPLE SOUP
"Signature"

"Cooking with Erika"
Created during 1992, menu item in my
former restaurant in Tacoma, W.A.
Demonstrated on local, weekly TV
segment, aired during year 2001

Serves: 6

1 teaspoon of extra virgin olive oil
1 small onion, finely chopped
1 pumpkin, about 2 pounds, peeled,
seeded and cut into 1 inch cubes
½ cup of celery root, peeled and cut into 1
inch cubes
4-5 cups chicken stock or vegetable stock
1-2 teaspoon of sea salt
1/8 teaspoon white pepper, freshly ground
1/8 teaspoon nutmeg, freshly ground
2 teaspoons curry powder
¼ cup of dry Riesling wine
4 tablespoons of whipping cream
1 large apple, such as golden or red
delicious, peeled, cored and finely grated
1 small apple, cored and sliced for garnish
6 teaspoons of sour cream, organic
preferred
Watercress or parsley, chopped for garnish

Heat oil in a large saucepan over medium heat - add onion and cook until soft, stirring often, about 5-10 minutes. Add pumpkin, celery root, and 4½-cups of chicken stock or vegetable stock and 1-teaspoon of salt. Bring to a boil, reduce heat, cover and simmer until pumpkin and celery root are tender, about 30 minutes – let cool slightly.

In batches, purée pumpkin mixture and cooking liquid together in a blender or food processor until smooth. Return puréed mixture to saucepan. Stir in pepper, nutmeg, curry powder, wine, whipping cream, grated apple and simmer 15 more minutes, and if necessary, thin soup with remaining stock. Ladle soup into 6 soup bowls and garnish with apple slices, sour cream, watercress or parsley. *Enjoy!*

PUMPKIN-SAVOY-ANISE SOUP
With
PASTA SEA SHELLS

Serves: 6

¼ cup extra virgin olive oil or grape seed oil
3 cups pumpkin, peeled, seeded and cut
into small chunks
2 cups anise bulb, trimmed and coarsely
chopped
1 cup sweet onions, chopped
2 cups savoy cabbage, coarsely shredded
8 cups of water
2 teaspoons of sea salt
1 tablespoon of ground turmeric
Pepper, freshly round
¼ pound of large, cooked pasta seashells,
halved
¼ cup Italian parsley, chopped
¼ cup fresh chives, chopped

Heat oil in a large saucepan over medium heat, add pumpkin, anise, onion and cabbage – sauté 6-minutes, add water and salt and bring to a boil – reduce heat to medium-low, partially cover saucepan with lid and cook for 30-40 minutes or until vegetables are tender. Reduce heat to low, stir-in turmeric, pepper, seashells, parsley and chives – adjust seasoning, if needed. Ladle soup into soup bowls and serve with crostini.

BUTTERNUT SQUASH-CELERY ROOT SOUP
"Signature"

Serves: 6

¼ cup extra virgin olive oil
2 cups butternut squash, peeled, seeded and cut into small chunks
2 cups carrots, peeled and cut into rounds
2 cups celery (celeriac) root, trimmed on both ends, peeled and cut into small chunks
1 cup fennel bulb, trimmed and coarsely chopped

2 cups sweet onions, peeled, chopped
3 cloves garlic, peeled, chopped
8 cups of water
2 teaspoons of sea salt
1 tablespoon of ground turmeric
1 teaspoon mélange peppercorns, freshly ground
¼ cup Italian parsley, chopped
¼ cut watercress leaves, chopped

Pumpkin-Savoy-Anise Soup with Pasta Sea Shells, see recipe on previous page

This page, opposite recipe, Butternut Squash / Celery Root Soup - bottom photo

Heat oil in a large saucepan over medium heat, add the next 5 ingredients, and sauté vegetables over medium-low heat until almost soft, about 6-8 minutes. Add onions and garlic, sauté 2 more minutes, add water and salt – bring to a boil, reduce heat to medium-low, partially cover with lid and cook for 30 minutes or until vegetables are tender, stirring occasionally. Stir-in the turmeric and pepper, season with salt, if needed—add parsley and watercress. Turn off heat. Ladle into soup bowls and serve with crusty French bread slices. *Note:* If pressed for time, prepare vegetables, except potatoes, a day ahead and store them in plastic bags - refrigerate until ready to use.

GARLIC-EGGDROP SOUP
"Signature - 1987"

"Cooking with Erika:
One of many food demonstrations on weekly, local TV segment, aired during year 2001.

Serves: 6

STOCK

2 chicken backs or ½ pound of chicken wings
10-12 cups of cold water
½ teaspoon of sea salt
1 carrot, peeled, chopped
1 parsnip, peeled, chopped
1 celery top, chopped
¼ teaspoon black peppercorn

Rinse chicken and cover with cold water in a large saucepan. Bring to a boil. Skim off foam. Add salt, vegetables and peppercorn. Cover and simmer 1-2 hours, checking periodically, and strain chicken stock into a clean large saucepan. Discard chicken and vegetables. Keep strained stock on medium-low heat.

SOUP

½ teaspoon of sea salt
¼ teaspoon pepper, freshly ground
1-2 tablespoons fresh garlic, minced
2 eggs, lightly beaten
1 tablespoon of all-purpose flour
¼ teaspoon nutmeg, freshly grated
1 teaspoon fresh chives, chopped
2 teaspoons fresh parsley, finely chopped

Mix salt, pepper, garlic, eggs and flour together, in a small bowl, until well blended. Drop into simmering chicken stock - turn off heat - add nutmeg, chives, and parsley. If desired, add more garlic and salt. Ladle into soup bowls and enjoy with rye or French bread and butter.

Chef's note: I believe it's noteworthy to mention that the natural combination of hot chicken stock and garlic is one of the most soothing flavors to enjoy anytime, but it's especially uplifting during wintertime. We enjoy this soup often.

Front clockwise Golden & Orange Carrots Cauliflower Cucumber

Rear Clockwise Shallots Garlic Cucumber

CHESTNUT-PARSNIP-CELERY SOUP

Serves: 6

6 tablespoons extra virgin olive oil
2 cups parsnip, peeled, cut into small cubes
2 cups celery root, peeled, cut into small cubes
Sea salt
½ cup leeks, white parts only, cut into rings
½ cup white onion, diced
¾ pound vacuum packed, cooked and peeled chestnut (Avail. in Specialty Food Stores)
10 cups chicken stock, vegetable stock, or water
½ teaspoon of freshly ground white pepper
¼ teaspoon freshly ground nutmeg
1 tablespoon whipping cream
Parsley for garnish

Preheat oven to 375°F

Arrange parsnip and celery in a baking pan, toss with 4 tablespoons olive oil and sprinkle with salt.   Roast 25 minutes, or until vegetables are almost tender.   Transfer vegetables to a bowl and set aside.

Heat remaining 2 tablespoons of olive oil in a large saucepan over medium heat - add leeks, onions and sauté until tender, about 5 minutes.

Add chestnuts, parsnip and celery root, sauté 1 minute more, minute, stirring often and then add 8 cups of stock or water bringing it to a boil, lower heat and simmer 10-15 minutes – turn off heat, and let soup cool slightly to purée it in batches in a food processor or blender until smooth - return puréed soup to a clean saucepan.

Add more stock to thin soup if necessary.

Cook soup gently 1-2 more minutes, season with salt, pepper, nutmeg, and stir-in the cream.   Ladle into serving bowls, sprinkle with parsley and *enjoy* while hot.

Left

Parsnip

Right

Celery Root

RUTABAGA-PARSNIP SOUP
With
GRILLED BREAD SLICES
"Signature"

"Cooking with Erika"
Created and demonstrated this on local, weekly TV segment, aired during year 2001

Serves: 6

3 tablespoons unsalted butter
1¾ pounds rutabaga, peeled, chopped
(about 3 cups)
1 large parsnip, peeled, chopped
1 cup onion, peeled, chopped
2 cloves of garlic, peeled, chopped
2 medium Yukon gold potatoes, peeled,
chopped
5 fresh thyme sprigs
6-7 cups of chicken stock or vegetable
stock
Sea salt and Pepper, freshly ground

4 tablespoons fresh Italian parsley, minced
4 tablespoons watercress, chopped
4 tablespoons unsalted butter
2 cloves of garlic, minced
6 slices French bread, ½-inch thick

In a large saucepan, melt butter over medium heat and add rutabaga, parsnip, onion, garlic and potatoes. Sauté, stir often, until vegetables are almost soft, about 10 minutes. Add thyme and 6½ cups of stock, and bring to boil - reduce heat and simmer partially covered for 30 minutes or until vegetables are very tender, discard thyme sprigs, and working in batches, purée vegetables in a blender until smooth.

Transfer to a large saucepan, simmer soup 6-minutes, season with salt and pepper, stir-in 2-tablespoons of parsley and 2-tablespoons of watercress – keep warm.

Preheat oven to broil

In a small bowl, combine remaining 2-tablespoons parsley and 2-tablespoons watercress with 4 tablespoons of butter and minced garlic. Place bread slices on a baking sheet and spread butter-herb mixture on top of each slice. Grill bread slices until golden in color. Ladle soup into bowls and place one slice of grilled bread on top of soup and enjoy.

<u>Chef's note:</u> To thin soup, if desired, add about ¼ - ½ cup of chicken or vegetable stock.

CREAM of TOMATO-GIN SOUP
With
MEDALLION of MONTRACHET
"Signature"

Serves 4-6

2 tablespoons of extra virgin olive oil
1 onion, chopped (preferably Wall Walla sweet onions)
2 cloves garlic, chopped
1/3 cup of fresh basil leaves
1 sprig of fresh thyme
2 sprigs of flat-leaf fresh parsley
1½ tablespoons of tomato paste
1 pound very ripe red tomatoes, quartered
1 pound very ripe yellow tomatoes, quartered
Pinch of sugar
Sea salt
Pepper, freshly ground
2 cups of chicken stock or water
2 tablespoons of Gin
6 tablespoons of crème fraîche
Watercress leaves, for garnish
½ pound goat cheese, such as Montrachet (goat cheese)

Heat oil in a large saucepan and gently cook the onion for 3-5 minutes or until soft and translucent. Add garlic, basil, thyme, parsley, tomato paste, add red and yellow tomatoes and season with sugar, salt and pepper. Pour in chicken stock or water and bring to a boil, reduce heat, cover and simmer for 15-20 minutes – discard thyme sprig. Purée soup in a blender or food processor, return soup to the saucepan and stir in gin and reheat gently without boiling. Adjust seasoning if needed. Ladle soup into warmed soup bowls, top each with 1-tablespoon crème fraîche and garnish each with watercress leaves and the medallion of goat cheese. *Enjoy!*

Prepare Montrachet medallions:
Slice cheese into 4-6, 1-inch thick medallions, coat each slice of cheese with 1 beaten egg, and coat them with finely ground dry breadcrumbs. Heat light olive oil, about 1-cup, in a large, deep skillet over medium-high heat. When hot, add prepared medallions and fry them until golden brown on each side – turning once, about 1-minute per side.

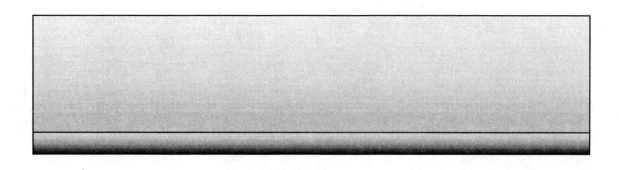

GREEN TOMATO SOUP
With
CRÈME FRAÎCHE and ROASTED PINE NUTS
"Signature"

Serves: 6

SOUP

4 tablespoons extra virgin olive oil
1 cup of onion, chopped, preferably sweet onion
Pinch of sugar
8-10 cups ripe "green zebra" tomatoes
4 cups water
2 teaspoons sea salt
1 teaspoon white pepper, freshly ground
1/3 cup of garlic, minced
1 cup of dry white wine
1 tablespoon arugula leaves, chopped
1 tablespoon fresh Italian Parsley, chopped

Preparing Green Tomato Soup: Over medium heat, heat olive oil in a large saucepan, add onions, pinch of sugar, sauté onions until they are soft, about 2-minutes, stirring often. Add tomatoes and sauté 5-more minutes, add water, sea salt, pepper, garlic, and cook for 20-minutes on medium-low heat – let cool slightly - transfer tomato mixture to food processor, and purée in batches. Return tomato mixture to same saucepan, add wine and simmer 2-more minutes. Stir-in arugula and parsley – season with salt and pepper if needed, and keep warm until ready to serve.

PINE NUTS

¼ teaspoon extra virgin olive oil
1 cup of pine nuts

Preparing pine nuts: In a small skillet, heat ¼ teaspoon of olive oil over medium-low heat, add pine nuts and sauté them until golden, stirring often. Transfer pine nuts to a small bowl, ladle soup into soup bowls, top with a dollop of crème fraîche, sprinkle with pine nuts, and enjoy with crusty French bread slices.

CRÈME FRAÎCHE

1 cup of heavy cream (not ultra-pasteurized)
1 tablespoon of buttermilk

Crème Fraîche can be prepared ahead: In a jar, combine cream and buttermilk, cover tightly and shake mixture for at least 1-minute. Let stand at room temperature for at least 8-hours, or until thick. *Note:* Crème fraîche can be kept up to 1-week when covered and refrigerated.

ZUCCHINI-CUCUMBER SOUP
With
PARMESAN CROUTONS
"Signature"

Serves: 6

CROUTONS

2 tablespoons unsalted butter
4 slices (½-inch thick) country bread, cut into ½-inch cubes
Sea salt
Pepper, freshly ground
1/3 cup Italian parsley, finely chopped
2 teaspoons freshly grated Parmesan cheese

Croutons can be made ahead: In a large skillet, melt butter over moderately high heat, add bread cubes, toss to coat with butter, and season with salt and pepper.

Stir in parsley, sauté stirring for about 3-minutes or until bread cubes are lightly toasted and crispy.

Transfer to a large plate or bowl, sprinkle with Parmesan cheese and toss again lightly.

SOUP

1 tablespoon unsalted butter
1 tablespoon of extra virgin olive oil
½ cup Walla-Walla sweet onions, chopped
2 pounds small zucchini, both ends trimmed, cut into ½-inch pieces

2 cups cucumbers, both ends trimmed, peeled, seeded, and cut into ½-inch pieces
4 cups vegetable stock or water
Sea salt
White pepper, freshly ground
6 tablespoons crème fraîche or sour cream
Basil leaves, for garnish

In a large-heavy saucepan, heat butter and olive oil. Add onion and cook over medium heat, stirring occasionally, until the onion is soft, about 1-minute. Increase heat to medium-high and add zucchini, and cucumber - sauté 1-minute.

Add stock, or water, bring to a boil, turn heat to medium-low, and simmer until zucchini and cucumbers are soft, about 15-minutes.

Let cool slightly working in batches, purée soup in a blender or food processor until smooth. Return soup to the saucepan, reheat gently, and season with salt and pepper.

Ladle soup into serving bowls and top each with a dollop of crème fraîche or sour cream, top with croutons and garnish with basil leaves. Enjoy with your favorite Chardonnay.

PORK and LAMB BUTTERNUT SQUASH WINTER STEW

"Cooking with Erika"
Created and demonstrated this on weekly, local TV Segment, aired during year 2002.
(Version I)

Serves: 6

½ pound boneless lamb, cut into ½ inch cubes
½ pound boneless pork loin, cut into ½ inch cubes
2 tablespoons all-purpose flour
1 tablespoon unsalted butter
2 tablespoons extra virgin olive oil
Sea salt
Pepper, freshly ground
½ cup onions, peeled, chopped
1½ cups Yukon gold potatoes, peeled, chopped
1 cup of parsnip, peeled, chopped
1 cup of turnips, peeled, chopped
4 cups butternut squash or pumpkin, peeled, seeded, cubed
1 tablespoon of fresh thyme leaves
6-7 cups hot water
Sea salt
Pepper, freshly ground
2 tablespoons fresh parsley, finely chopped

Dust lamb and pork with flour, heat butter and oil in a large heavy saucepan, brown meat in batches on all sides, about 10-minutes, and season meat with salt and pepper - add onion, potatoes, parsnip, turnips and sauté for 10-minutes, stirring constantly. Add squash or pumpkin, sauté 2-more minutes – add thyme leaves and 5-cups of water, bring to a boil, stir one more time, cover and simmer 45-minutes, or until meat is tender.

Remove from heat and season to taste with salt and pepper, stir-in parsley. Ladle stew into deep soup bowls and serve hot with crusty French bread.

<u>*Note:*</u> If a thinner stew is desired, add remaining 1-cup of water and cook on low heat 5-10 minutes longer.

Foreground

Butternut Squash

CLASSIC RAISIN-MANGO-BEEF STEW

Serves: 6

1 tablespoon of grape-seed oil
1 tablespoon unsalted butter
2 pounds beef tenderloin, cut into 1-inch cubes
Sea salt
Pepper, freshly ground
1½ cups sweet onions, peeled and chopped
2 garlic cloves, chopped
2 tablespoons sweet paprika
½ teaspoon ground cinnamon
1 teaspoon of ground cardamom
½ cup port wine
1 cup of water
½ cup golden raisins
1½ cups mango, peeled, cubed, *see instructions, right column*
1 teaspoon finely grated lemon peel, organic lemon preferred
¼ cup cilantro, freshly chopped

Heat oil and butter in a heavy, large saucepan over medium-high heat, and working in batches, add the beef and brown it on all sides, about 3-5 minutes per batch.

Transfer browned beef to a warm large dish, sprinkle beef lightly with salt and pepper. Cover with foil to keep warm.

Turn heat to medium - add onions to saucepan and cook until soft, about 1-2 minutes. Add garlic - stirring frequently - add paprika, cinnamon and cardamom.

Add wine, water, raisins and mango, bring to a boil - turn heat to medium-low, and cook until juices thicken, about 5-10 minutes. Stirring occasionally, add lemon peel, cooked beef, and any accumulated meat juices.

Stir until heated through, about 3-5 minutes and season with salt and pepper, if needed. Stir-in cilantro, spoon beef stew into a large warm serving dish.

Enjoy with basmati rice, couscous or polenta.

To prepare mango, cut off both ends of the fruit and set the fruit vertically on end. About ¼ inch from top center, slice down the fruit on one side closest to the pit and set that slice aside. Repeat this on 3 remaining sides. With flesh side up, slice through the flesh, avoid cutting through the peel, in a checker board pattern to form cubes. Repeat process with remaining sides. With a thumb positioned on each end of a side, slide fingers under fruit, in a scooping manner, press down on ends with thumbs while pressing the underside upward with fingertips to separate cubes. Scoop cubes away from peel with a spoon and repeat process on 3 remaining sides. Discard peel.

APRICOT-ALMOND-LAMB STEW

Serves: 4 - 6

2 pounds boneless lamb or mutton, trim any excess fat, cut meat into ¾ inch cubes
1 teaspoon of sea salt
2 tablespoons grape seed oil
1/3 cup blanched whole almonds
¼ cup sugar
1 cinnamon stick, 3-inch stick
1 cup of water
4 tablespoons fresh orange juice
1½ cups of dried prunes, pitted and halved
1 cup dried apricots, coarsely chopped

Sprinkle lamb or mutton (*see Note*) with salt. Heat oil in a large saucepan over medium-high heat, and working in batches, add lamb or mutton. Stirring constantly, cook lamb or mutton until lightly browned. Turn heat to medium.

Remove browned meat from pan. Add almonds, sugar and cinnamon stick to pan drippings, stirring constantly, add water and orange juice.

Bring to a boil, while stirring, add browned meat, cover and simmer on medium-low heat - about 1-hour or until meat is tender.

Stir-in prunes and apricots 10-minutes before cooking time ends, and before serving, remove the cinnamon stick.

Serve with hot couscous or basmati rice.

Chef's note: To tone down strong flavor of mutton, trim excess fat, use very little oil to brown it and then discard the oil. Use new oil (fats) to cook any onions or vegetables.

Middle Eastern countries often use ghee to brown meats and vegetables.

Ghee (gee) is a form of clarified butter – pure unsalted butter fat, and because milk solids are allowed to brown, ghee imparts a nutty-caramel-like flavor, plus it can be heated to high temperatures without burning.

Adding dried or fresh fruits and nuts gives mutton dishes finishing touches to yield sweeter, fruitier flavor.

WILD MUSHROOM GOULASH with FETTUCCINE
"Signature"

Serves: 6

GOULASH

2 tablespoons extra virgin olive oil, plus extra as needed
2 tablespoons unsalted butter, plus extra as needed
½ pound fresh portabella mushrooms, chopped
½ pound fresh button mushrooms, chopped, or chopped oyster mushrooms
½ pound fresh shiitake mushrooms, chopped
½ pound fresh chanterelle mushrooms, chopped
½ pound of fresh inokie mushrooms or lion mushrooms, chopped
2 cups onions, chopped
Pinch of sugar
2 cups tomatoes, peeled, seeded and chopped
1 tablespoon of garlic, chopped
¼ cup whipping cream
Sea salt
Pepper, freshly ground
2 tablespoons sweet paprika
¼ cup sour cream
2 tablespoons watercress, chopped
1 tablespoon parsley, chopped

In a large saucepan, heat 1-teaspoon oil and 1-teaspoon butter over medium-high heat, add portabella mushrooms and sauté until golden brown on all sides. Transfer portabella mushrooms to a warmed large dish, cover with foil, set aside and keep warm.

Repeat entire process with remaining mushrooms, adding more oil and butter as needed. In same saucepan, add onions, sugar, and sauté over medium heat until golden brown, about 10-minutes.

Add tomatoes, garlic, and cook 10-minutes or until sauce is slightly thickened. Stir-in whipping cream and cook 2-more minutes.

Return mushroom to saucepan and season with salt and pepper – stir-in the paprika. Stir-in sour cream, watercress and parsley – keep warm on low heat until ready to serve.

FETTUCCINE

6 quarts of water
2 teaspoons of sea salt
1 pound of fettuccine
1 tablespoon unsalted butter, melted, or
1 tablespoon extra virgin olive oil

In a large pot, bring water and salt to a boil, add fettuccine and cook until al dente, about 10-12 minutes. Drain and transfer pasta to a large, warmed serving bowl, drizzle with butter and toss lightly. Divide fettuccine among 6 large warmed serving plates, and top each with mushroom-goulash.

AQUATICS - FISH

L. Codfish-Red Onion Confit, Page 72   ///   R. Codfish-Champagne-Squash , Page 76

L. Crab Stuffed Filet of Salmon, Page 91 ///   R. Sea Scallops, Page 116

L. Filet of Dover Sole, Page 85   ///   R. Lobster-Saffron Pernod, Page 114

CODFISH

There are several varieties of Codfish in this large family of saltwater fish, and while some have slight variations in size, texture and flavor, all are generally mild flavored, lean, flaky and delectable whether poached, steamed, grilled or baked - probably one of the most widely distributed and consumed fish variety in the marketplace. That is, perhaps, because of abundance, availability and enjoyableness. Some details follow:

Of all members of the codfish family the Pacific Cod, which has the softest texture, is harvested from the Northern Atlantic Ocean among other varieties like haddock, Pollock, whiting and hake. The degree of difference between the texture of fresh Pacific cod and fresh haddock's delicate texture and stronger flavor, is insignificant during the cooking process, except that both require less time to cook than other varieties that have firmer flesh. Also compensation must be made during the cooking process for thickness of cuts (center or end cuts); the cooking method used, as well as the variety of cod to be cooked - usually a vigilant adjustment of one minute or two will do. Haddock is also found in the North Atlantic Ocean from Cape Cod to Newfoundland.

Throughout the U.S. varieties of cod are known by different names like whiting, which is found in the Atlantic Ocean from New England to Virginia and along the European coast - it's also referred to as hake and silver perch. Hake is also found from Southern Canada to North Carolina. There are other varieties of hake, like the familiar Lingcod among black hake, Boston hake, king hake, mud hake and white hake. From Alaskan waters is harvested the Alaskan Pollock, which is used for making imitation shellfish products, and which is often referred to as Pacific Pollock, Walleye Pollock and Snow Cod. Then, from the Atlantic Ocean from Nova Scotia to Virginia is found the American Pollock, often referred to as Boston bluefish and blue cod, also used to make imitation shellfish products among other uses.

Like most fish, cod is high in protein, low in fat and calories. When shopping let your nose, fingers and eyes determine freshness - check to ensure the fish has a clean briny scent; that its flesh is moist and firm and that its color is bright with no hint of browning - fresh cod should be snow white.

As always, it is best to check the "use by", "sell by" date for the freshest delivery and if possible purchase fresh fish the same day you intend to use it. If there is no other choice but to purchase frozen fish you'll need to consider the moisture factor, texture and flavor variances associated with frozen products in comparison to fresh products - especially fish because its flesh is much more delicate than are meat products. Avoid using microwave to thaw because both quality and flavor will most certainly be adversely affected. For best results, place desired portions of frozen cod in a flat, glass container, cover and let fish *thaw in the refrigerator (on bottom shelf) overnight if necessary or thaw under consistent cold running water, although for resource conservation purposes, I prefer refrigerator thawing - it only takes a little planning ahead. Whichever process you choose, wash and dry fish thoroughly with paper towels before proceeding with your favorite recipe.*

FILLET of PACIFIC WILD CODFISH
With
RED ONION CONFIT and BRUISED SPINACH
"Signature"

Serves: 4

MARINATE CODFISH

2 pounds cod fillet, cut into four portions
Coarse sea salt, about 1½ ounces
4 tablespoons limejuice, freshly squeezed

Rinse cod, pat dry with paper towel and place it in a shallow glass dish – sprinkle with coarse sea salt and limejuice – cover with plastic wrap and refrigerate 24-hours. _Chef's note:_ Because of the delicacy of codfish, pre-assemble and pre-measure recipe ingredients and begin the cooking process with ingredients that require longer cooking times, those which can be cooked ahead and set aside, such as the sequence of actions below illustrate.

ONION CONFIT (kohn-FEE)

2 tablespoons of light olive oil
2 cups red onions, half-moon sliced, each slice about 1/8-1/4 inch thick
Fine sea salt
White pepper, freshly ground
¼ cup orange juice, freshly squeezed
Pinch of sugar

To cook onions: Heat a large skillet over medium-high heat for 1-minute. Pour-in 2- tablespoons of olive oil and Swirl to coat pan. As soon as oil is simmering, but not smoking, add onions in an even layer then sprinkle them lightly with fine sea salt and pepper letting them cook undisturbed until they begin to soften, about 2-3 minutes.

Turn heat to medium, add orange juice and sugar – cook 20-30 more minutes or until onions are very soft and slightly thickened. Again, season with fine sea salt and white pepper if needed and remove onions with a slotted spoon - discard oil. Place cooked onions in a warm shallow dish, cover - keep warm – reheat if necessary, but do not cook.

CODFISH FILLET

Marinated codfish
Mélange peppercorns, coarsely ground
2 tablespoons unsalted butter

ACCOMPANIMENTS

2 tablespoons unsalted butter
3 cups baby spinach leaves, loosely packed
Fine sea salt and mélange peppercorn,
finely ground

Tomato wedges, for garnish
Lemon slices, for garnish

To cook codfish: Remove cod from refrigerator and pat dry with paper towel and sprinkle lightly with mélange pepper. Heat 2-tablespoons of butter in a large non-stick skillet over medium-high heat and cook one side of cod until nicely colored – turn over and cook until golden brown and opaque in the center, about 2-minutes per side.

Place a fillet in the center of each pre-warmed dinner plate, spoon some pan dripping over each serving, and cover with foil to keep warm.

To prepare servings: Using the same skillet turn heat to medium-high and add 2-tablespoons of butter. Pinch spinach to bruise and toss leaves in the skillet, turn off heat, again toss spinach and sprinkle lightly with salt and pepper. Remove spinach from the skillet and arrange it alongside each fillet, spoon warm confit over each fillet and garnish with tomato wedges and lemon slices.

Enjoy with a glass of your favorite Semillon, Pinot Gris, Sauvignon Blanc, or perhaps a Viognier.

Notes

LING COD SOUP
With
RED BELL PEPPERS-GARLIC ROUELLE

Serves: 6-8

SOUP

2 tablespoons extra virgin olive oil
1 medium onion, finely chopped
1 fennel bulb, coarsely chopped
8 cups fish stock or 6-cups water and
2-cups bottled clam juice
3 pounds ripe tomatoes, peeled, seeded
and coarsely chopped
4 medium-size Yukon gold potatoes,
peeled, cut into ¼ inch thick pieces
¼ teaspoon of saffron threads, or
½ teaspoon turmeric
2½ pounds ling cod fillets, cut into 1½-inch
pieces, refrigerate until ready to use
1 cup fresh Italian parsley, chopped

Heat oil in a large saucepan over medium heat, add onion and sauté until onion is translucent, about 2-minutes, add fennel and stock and bring to a boil.

Reduce heat, cover and simmer until fennel is almost tender, about 5-minutes. Add tomatoes and potatoes.

Partially cover and simmer until potatoes are tender, about 10-15 minutes, stir-in saffron or turmeric and keep soup warm.

RED BELL PEPPERS-GARLIC ROUILLE

1 roasted red bell pepper, cut into strips
1 large potato, peeled, cooked and diced
6 tablespoons extra virgin olive oil
3 garlic cloves
Sea salt and freshly ground pepper
¼ teaspoon of sweet paprika
1 French bread baguette, cut into ¼ inch
thick rounds

Transfer bell peppers and potatoes to food processor and add 2-tablespoons of oil and the garlic. Process mixture until smooth and, with the machine running, gradually blend-in the remaining 4 tablespoons of oil and season with paprika, salt and pepper.

Bring soup to simmer, add fish to soup-base and simmer until fish is just opaque in center, about 5-10 minutes and stir in parsley. _Note:_ While soup is simmering, heat up the broiler, arrange bread rounds on a baking sheet and broil until crisp, about 2-minutes. Ladle soup into soup bowls, top each with 2 toasted rounds top-coated with rouille. Pass around remaining toasts along with pepper-garlic rouille, and prepare yourself to enjoy a very special treat.

Fillet of Pacific Wild Cod - Red Onion Confit, see Page 72

Filet of Codfish – Champagne-Butternut Squash Sauce, see next Page

FILLET of CODFISH
With
CHAMPAGNE-BUTTERNUT SQUASH SAUCE
"Signature"

Serves: 4

4 codfish fillet, 6-ounces each – prepared ahead
Coarse sea salt
½ cup of dry champagne

Preparing codfish: Wash and pat dry codfish with paper towels and place fillets in a shallow dish. Sprinkle each fillet lightly with coarse sea salt and pour ½ cup of champagne over them. Cover dish with plastic wrap and refrigerate 24-hours.

Cooking codfish: Remove cod from refrigerator, pat fish dry with paper towels and lightly sprinkle fish on both sides with pepper. Heat 2-tablespoons of butter in a large skillet over medium-high heat, add cod and cook until nicely colored on one side, turn fish over and cook until golden brown and opaque in the center, about 1-2 minutes per side. Transfer fish to 4 pre-warmed dinner plates, spoon some of the pan dripping over each fillet and cover with foil to keep warm.

CHAMPAGNE-BUTTERNUT SQUASH SAUCE

Pink peppercorns, coarsely ground, (Avail. in Supermarkets and Specialty Stores)
3 tablespoons of unsalted butter
¼ cup shallots, peeled and minced
1½ cups of dry champagne
1 cup of whipping cream
1 cup butternut squash, cooked and puréed
Fine sea salt
Italian parsley, finely chopped, for garnish
Lime wedges, for garnish

Making the sauce: Turn heat to medium, add the remaining 1½-cups of champagne to the skillet, and the add shallots - cook until sauce liquid is reduced to almost half, about 3-5 minutes. Add cream and squash, cook 2-more minutes, season with salt and pepper, and stir-in the remaining 1-tablespoon of butter – turn off heat.

To serve: Spoon Champagne-butternut squash sauce around each fillet, sprinkle with parsley, and garnish with lime wedges. Enjoy with risotto, petite green beans, and a glass of your favorite Semillon, Sauvignon Blanc, dry Riesling or Chardonnay.

BAKED SPINACH-GOAT CHEESE
Stuffed
FILLET of SALMON
"Signature"

Serves: 4

4 center-cut salmon fillets, about 6 ounces each
Sea salt
Pepper, freshly ground
½ tablespoon unsalted butter
½ cup of shallots, chopped
1 cup of spinach leaves, tough stems removed, washed, dried and chopped
¼ cup watercress leaves, chopped
1 cup goat cheese, crumbled
½ teaspoon sweet paprika
Sea salt
Pepper, freshly ground
2 tablespoons crème fraîche or sour cream
1/3 cup of extra virgin olive oil
Pinch of saffron
½ cup of dry white wine

Cut a slit half the depth of the salmon fillet, and slide the tip of the knife flat just under each side of the slit to form a pocket.

Sprinkle salmon fillet lightly with salt and pepper. Cover with plastic wrap and refrigerate until ready to stuff.

Heat butter in a medium skillet over medium heat. Add shallots and cook 1-2 minutes, or until soft but not colored. Transfer to a bowl, and add spinach, watercress, goat cheese and paprika, and season lightly with salt and pepper. Stir in the crème fraîche or sour cream.

Preheat oven to 400°F

Spoon equal amounts of filling into each pocket of the salmon. Spoon any leftover filling onto a heatproof baking dish, place salmon on top of filling, and drizzle olive oil over each fillet. In a small bowl, combine saffron with wine and pour over salmon and bake for 15-20 minutes, or until the salmon is opaque and feels firm to the touch.

Carefully remove salmon from the baking dish and place a serving of salmon on each of 4 warm plates, spoon filling alongside salmon, and drizzle wine dripping over each serving.

Note: All finished food specimens in photos throughout this cookbook were styled by the author, prepared table ready, unaltered and enjoyed naturally.

PAN SEARED SALMON
With
LEMON-CAPER SAUCE and POLENTA
"Signature-1991"

"Cooking with Erika"
Demonstrated menu on local, weekly TV segment, aired during 2002.

Serves: 4

4 tablespoons unsalted butter
4 salmon-fillets (6-ounces each), skinned
1 teaspoon of sea salt
1 teaspoon pepper, freshly ground
2 shallots, finely chopped
¼ teaspoon sugar
½ cup whipping cream
2 tablespoons fresh lemon juice
2 tablespoons capers, drained (Avail. in supermarket spice section)
2 tablespoons fresh parsley, chopped
2 tablespoons fresh watercress, chopped
Baby spinach leaves, chopped for garnish
Lemon wedges for garnish

Polenta (see Recipe Index)

Heat 3-tablespoons butter in a heavy-large skillet over medium-high heat. Add salmon fillet to skillet. Sprinkle each with salt and pepper, sear 4-5 minutes on each side, depending on thickness of salmon, or until cooked through.

Remove salmon from skillet and keep warm. Turn heat to medium, add shallots and sugar to skillet and sauté until shallots are soft and golden in color, about 1-2 minutes. Turn heat to medium-low, stir-in cream and cook 1-minute. Add lemon juice, capers, parsley and watercress. Stir-in remaining 1-tablespoon butter, return salmon to sauce and heat through.

Spoon equal amounts of polenta onto warmed plates, and top each serving with a salmon fillet and spoon sauce over salmon, garnish with chopped spinach and lemon wedges. Enjoy with your favorite Riesling, Pinot Gris or Viognier wine.

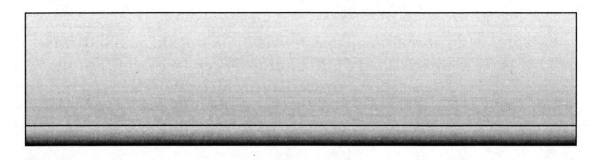

SMOKED SALMON and VODKA-CAVIAR SAUCE
Over
SAFFRON PASTA
"Signature"

Serves: 4

SAUCE

1 tablespoon of unsalted butter
½ cup of leeks, white part only, thinly sliced
1 cup whipping cream
2 tablespoons of Vodka
6 ounces mild-smoked salmon, diced
2 tablespoons black caviar, drained
¼ cup watercress leaves, chopped
Sea salt
Pepper, freshly ground

Melt butter in a large saucepan over medium heat, add leeks and sauté them until soft, about 2 minutes. Add cream, vodka, and cook 5 minutes.

Turn heat to low, stir in salmon, caviar and watercress, season with salt and pepper, if needed. Keep warm.

PASTA

1 pound of linguine or fettuccini
1 teaspoon of sea salt
¼ teaspoon saffron
2 tablespoons of unsalted butter, melted

Crusty French bread slices

Bring a large saucepan of salted water to a boil. Cook pasta according to instruction on the package. Drain pasta.

In a large warmed bowl, combine saffron and butter, add pasta and toss to combine. Divide pasta among 4 warm serving plates, spoon salmon mixture over pasta and enjoy with crusty French bread slices, iced vodka or your favorite dry Riesling wine.

SMOKED SALMON ROULADE with BLINI And DANDELION-WATERCRESS GREENS

Serves: 8

8 ounces cream cheese, softened at room temperature
8 ounces mascarpone cheese
2 ounces Aquavit (Avail. in Liquor Stores)
½ cup dill, freshly chopped
¼ cup chives, freshly chopped
Sea salt
Pepper, freshly ground
16 thin slices of smoked salmon, about 1-pound
4 eggs, hardboiled and halved for garnish
1 cup salmon roe (caviar)

In a mixer bowl, blend cream cheese, mascarpone and Aqvavit until smooth – stir-in dill and chives, and season with salt and pepper. Lay a piece of plastic wrap on a cutting board and place 1-slice of salmon on plastic wrap, evenly spread 2-tablespoons of cheese mixture on salmon and roll salmon into a log. Transfer salmon to a large platter, loosely cover with plastic wrap to retain freshness and repeat process for remaining roulade. Cover with plastic wrap and refrigerate until ready to serve.

BLINI (blee-nee)

(blini-plural/blin-singular)

1 cup of buckwheat flour
½ cup all-purpose flour
½ teaspoon baking powder
½ teaspoon sea salt
2 large eggs, slightly beaten
3 tablespoons unsalted butter, melted
1½ cups whole milk
8 teaspoons unsalted butter, for cooking pancakes

In a medium bowl, stir together buckwheat and all-purpose flour, stir-in baking powder and salt, add eggs, butter and milk – stir until smooth, let rest 10-15 minutes. Cooking time for blini is about ½ minute per side.

Heat a large skillet over medium-high heat, add 1-teaspoon butter and when butter starts to sizzle, turn heat to medium and pour ¼ cup of batter into skillet. Lift edge of blin(i) to check - and when bottom is golden brown, turn over – cook for about ½ minute - transfer blini to a warmed large plate. Using the same skillet, repeat process with 1-teaspoon of butter and ¼ cup batter until all batter is used.

DANDELION SALAD

¼ cup extra virgin olive oil
¼ cup lemon juice, freshly squeezed
¼ cup orange juice, freshly squeezed
¼ cup sweet onions, minced
2-3 tablespoons honey
8 cups tender dandelion greens
2 bunches watercress leaves
Sea salt
Pepper, freshly ground

In a large bowl, mix together oil, lemon juice, orange juice, onions and honey. Add dandelion and watercress and toss. Divide dandelion salad onto 8 serving plates, place a blin (bleen) on top of salad, arrange 2-salmon roulade on top of blin, garnish each with 1 egg half, top each egg half with a dollop of salmon roe (caviar). Enjoy with iced Aqvavit or with your favorite well chilled Sauvignon Blanc, Semillon or Pinot Gris.

SMOKED SALMON
On a Bed of
FRESH ASPARAGUS
"Signature"

"Cooking with Erika"
Created and demonstrated this on local,
weekly TV segment, aired July 2, 2002.

Serves: 4

4 ounces baby greens, washed and dried
2 pounds green, cooked asparagus spears
½ pound white, cooked asparagus spears
4 ounces smoked salmon fillet
4 hard-boiled eggs, peeled and cut into quarters
Fresh dill sprigs for garnish

VINAIGRETTE

1 large shallot, peeled and minced
6 tablespoons white balsamic vinegar
Pinch of sugar
¼ teaspoon pepper, freshly ground
¼ teaspoon sea salt
4 tablespoons extra virgin olive oil
3 tablespoons arugula leaves, chopped

In a small bowl, combine shallots, vinegar, sugar, salt, pepper and olive oil. Adjust seasoning to taste, stir-in arugula. In a medium bowl, toss greens with enough vinaigrette to cover lightly, transfer to a large serving platter, arrange green and white asparagus on top of greens, drizzle asparagus with remaining vinaigrette, garnish with salmon, eggs and dill. *Enjoy with grilled French bread slices and a glass of fine Riesling or Chardonnay!*

Also, created and demonstrated the "King Salmon-Spinach Penne Rigote" recipe (right column) on local TV segment, aired during March, 2003

KING SALMON with
SPINACH PENNE RIGOTE

Serves: 4

2-3 tablespoons of extra virgin olive oil
1/3 cup of shallots, peeled, chopped
1/3 cup of leeks, white part only, cut into rings
2 pounds of fresh King Salmon fillet, boned, skin removed, cut into ½ inch cubes
Sea salt
Mélange peppercorns, freshly ground
1 cup of crème fraîche, or ½ cup of whipping cream and ¼ cup sour cream
2 teaspoons of fresh limejuice
2 tablespoons fresh parsley, chopped
Lemon slices for garnish

1 pound of spinach penne rigote
Water
2 teaspoons of sea salt
1 tablespoon of extra virgin olive oil
1 teaspoon of fresh limejuice

In a large nonstick skillet, heat 2 tablespoons of oil over medium heat add shallots and leeks - sauté until soft, about 2-3 minutes. Add salmon and cook until lightly browned, about 2-3 minutes. Season with salt and pepper, stir in crème fraîche, or the whipping cream and sour cream, and simmer 1-2 minutes. Turn heat to low and stir in 2-teaspoons limejuice and parsley. Keep warm until ready to serve. In a large saucepan, bring 6 quarts of water to a boil, add the salt and pasta, and cook for 10-12 minutes or until al dente. Drain well, transfer to a large bowl, drizzle with 1 tablespoon of oil and limejuice, toss to combine, and divide the pasta among 4 large warmed serving plates. Spoon equal amounts of salmon over each plate and garnish with lemon slices.

SALMON-MASCARPONE
With
BLACK (SQUID INK) FETTUCCINE and FRESH ASPARAGUS
"Signature-1987"

Served as the main course of the five course "sit-down" dinner prepared for 140 guests at the combined "1999" Asparagus Festival and Spring Barrel Tasting, event, Yakima Valley, Sunnyside, Washington State. (April 24, 1999)

Serves: 4-6

SALMON-MASCARPONE

1 teaspoon unsalted butter
1 tablespoon of shallots, chopped
½ cup of heavy cream
1 cup of mascarpone cheese
¼ cup of sour cream, organic preferred
4 tablespoons of dry white wine
2 tablespoons Pernod (Available in Liquor Store)
2 pounds of fresh salmon fillet, skin removed, cut into 1 inch cubes
Sea salt
Black pepper, freshly ground
1 tablespoon fresh chives, chopped
1 tablespoon of watercress, chopped

Heat butter in a medium saucepan, add shallots and cook stirring until softened, about 1-minute. Stir in heavy cream, mascarpone, sour cream, wine, and pernod. Whisk continuously until smooth, and simmer on low heat for 10 minutes. Add salmon and simmer gently for 5 more minutes, avoid overcooking to retain texture and cube shape. Season with salt and pepper, stir in chives and watercress, and keep warm *Note:* While fettuccine is cooking, cook asparagus to save time.

FETTUCCINE

1 pound of black fettuccine
6 quarts of water
½ teaspoon of sea salt

In a large saucepan, bring water to a boil, and add salt. Drop in the fettuccine and stir. Cook for 7 minutes or until al dente. Drain well.

ASPARAGUS

1½-2 pounds of fresh green asparagus, woody ends trimmed, peeled and cut to uniform lengths
2 tablespoons of unsalted butter
1 tablespoon of fresh lemon juice
1 large bunch of watercress leaves, coarsely chopped
Sea salt
Pepper, freshly ground
Lemon wedges for garnish

Bring a large saucepan of salted water to a boil. Add asparagus and cook until tender, about 3-4 minutes.

Drain and pat dry. Melt butter in a medium skillet, and add lemon juice, watercress and season with salt and pepper. Add asparagus and toss gently.

To enjoy, arrange fettuccine on four pre-warmed plates, spoon salmon mixture over fettuccine, arrange asparagus alongside, and garnish with lemon wedges.

SPANISH TUNA
And
OLIVE TAPENADE
CROSTINI

Makes: 12 servings

12 slices French baguette, 1-inch thick
1 cup Spanish olive oil, for brushing bread
slices, plus 2-tablespoons
16 ounces canned, Spanish tuna,
drained (imported)
Sea salt
Pepper, freshly ground
1 cup Spanish olives, drained and pitted
1½ Spanish anchovy fillets, drained
3 cloves garlic

Preheat oven to 350

Spanish tuna is available at Euro. Pacific Imports, at La Tienda, 1-800-710-4304, and through product suppliers via Internet.

The provisioning of products supplier and contact information for product above is furnished as a convenience and does not necessarily carry my endorsement.

Opposite photo - Fillet of Dover Sole, see Recipe on Page 85

Place bread slices on a large baking sheet and lightly brush both sides of each slice with olive oil, and bake until crispy and slightly golden brown, about 6-minutes.

Remove crostini from oven and place on a large platter. Place drained tuna in a large bowl, season lightly with salt and pepper and set aside.

In a food processor, combine olives, anchovy fillets, garlic and remaining 2-tablespoons of oil – purée 15-20 seconds or until mixture is smooth.

Transfer mixture to bowl containing tuna and mix until combined. Top each crostini slice with 1 to 2-tablespoon of tuna mixture and enjoy with your favorite Lemberger or a Spanish red table wine.

SOLE

Briefly, "sole" is a saltwater flatfish member of the flounder family. There are many species of flounder, and because some flounder are dubbed as sole, I believe it is interesting and helpful to shoppers to know a little about origins, weight ranges, texture and differences in flavor intensity.

To highlight, "true Dover sole", is considered possessing the sweetest-most flavorful and firmest-whitest flesh of all - its average market weight is generally between 1- 2 pounds. In comparison to other member species of the flounder family with some exceptions, generally ranging in weight between 2 - 6 pounds while some may have pinkish-white flesh rather than white.

"True Dover sole" is harvested from both the English Channel and the North Sea, and if you happen to travel in Ireland, you'll find the same variety of sole harvested from those waters under the name of black sole and known by other names in other parts of Europe - but menus most likely will state from which waters the featured fish were harvested. Then from Northwest Pacific and Alaskan waters come the larger "Dover Sole" with an average market weight within the 2 - 6 pounds range and the "English sole" also known as "California Dover sole" and "Lemon sole" is harvested off U.S. Coastal waters – its average market weight is about ¾ pound. The average market weight of East Coast "Lemon sole", also known as winter flounder, is about 2- pounds, which has fine texture and sweet flavor.

Some varieties of flounder are labeled and marketed as sole in retail outlets, all of which have a mild flavor, but the degree of texture firmness and flavor are most prominent and pleasant in that of "true Dover sole". I'm guessing that such labeling practices may have developed because of so many varieties of flounder to label individually, thus making labeling simpler – using the one word symbolizing the best generic description for flavor, "sole". But, this practice can be confusing when shopping for the highest quality of sole, and the uninformed looking forward to cooking an elegant meal using the same guidelines as for fish having fairly consistent firmness of flesh could have less than desirable results if differences aren't known.

The flavor in all flounder is good, but knowing differences means applying better approaches to cooking the very delicate flesh of this species, basing the cooking process on origin of harvest and variety, which should help overcome disappointing results. Precise cooking time is crucial, even one-half minute off on either side will either make a winner or loser, undercooked or "mushy" overcooked dish.

FILLET of DOVER SOLE
With
MASCARPONE, COCTAIL SHRIMP
And
STEAMED CLAMS
"Signature"

Serves: 4

4 fillet of Dover sole (2½-3 pounds), skinned, rinsed and patted dry with paper towels
Sea salt
White peppercorns, freshly ground
8 ounces of mascarpone cheese
¼ cup watercress leaves, chopped
½ cup shallots, peeled, minced
2 cups dry Riesling wine
¼ teaspoon sea salt
1½ dozen little neck clams or another species, washed in 3-4 changes of water
1 cup whipping cream
8 ounces, small cooked cocktail shrimp
¼ cup crème fraîche
2 cups bamboo (green) rice, cooked and kept warm, or
2 cups basmati rice, cooked and flavored with turmeric or saffron
Fresh chives, chopped, for garnish

Place sole on a flat surface and lightly sprinkle with salt and pepper. In a small bowl, combine mascarpone, watercress and ¼ cup of shallots – season lightly with salt and pepper, top each fillet with 2-3 tablespoons of mascarpone mixture and carefully roll up fillet starting at the widest end.

Secure each rolled fillet with small wooden skewers, cover with plastic wrap and chill them until ready to use.

In a large saucepan bring the wine, ¼ teaspoon of salt with remaining ¼ cup of shallots to a boil – turn heat to medium-low and simmer for 5-8 minutes, add clams, cover them and cook 3-4 minutes. Discard any clams that do not open - Strain and reserve the cooking liquid and set clams aside.

In a large saucepan, add reserved cooking liquid and cook liquid over medium heat until reduced by almost half, about 3-5 minutes. Add cream and cook for 3-minutes, add the rolled sole and simmer covered over low heat for about 6-8 minutes. Add shrimp, stir-in the crème fraîche and heat for 1-minute – season with salt and pepper, if needed.

Arrange 1 serving of sole on each of 4 pre-warmed dinner plates, spoon some of the shrimp sauce over each serving and cover each plate with foil to keep warm. Add cooked clams to sauce and simmer over low heat until heated through, about 1-2 minutes. Arrange clams around sole, spoon remaining sauce over clams and the sole, garnish each plate with chives, and serve hot rice separately.

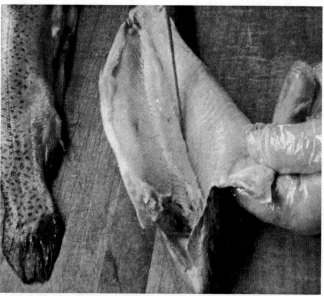

| Photo #1
Rainbow Trout | Photo #2 – Boning, butter-flying fillet, for stuffing, see photo #3, below |

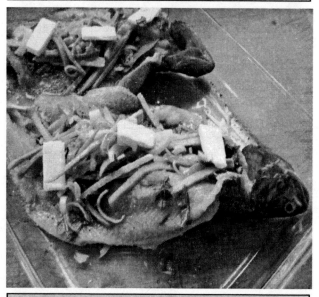

| Photo #3 - Boned-butterflied trout topped with filling - ready for folding over to resemble whole fish - see opposite photo | Photo #4
Riesling Poached Rainbow Trout – Stuffed
See Recipe on next Page |

Note: Secure the filled cavity with wooden picks and remove them before serving. Lifting the poached trout from the roasting pan, in one piece, is easier when using two large metal spatulas inserted under each end of the fish and placing it on the serving dish or platter. Spoon pan dripping or parsley sauce over the fish, add boiled baby potatoes to the dish, serve and enjoy.

RIESLING-POACHED RAINBOW TROUT
With
BOILED BABY POTATOES
And
PARSLEY SAUCE
"Signature"

Serves: 4

5 tablespoons chilled unsalted butter
2 large leeks (white and pale-green parts only), thinly sliced
2 carrots, peeled, cut into julienne strips
4 whole fresh trout, boned and butter-flied
4 teaspoons watercress leaves, chopped
2 bay leaves, torn in half
1½ cups Johannisberg Riesling
½ cup heavy cream
4 teaspoons fresh parsley, chopped
Sea salt
Pepper, freshly ground
12 whole baby potatoes, cooked, peeled and kept warm

Preheat oven to 400°F

Melt 1-tablespoon of butter in a heavy, large skillet, over medium heat, and add sliced leeks and carrot strips, sauté until crisp-tender, about 2-minutes. Open fish flat and arrange skin-side down in a large roasting pan. Sprinkle fish with salt, pepper and watercress. Top with leek, carrot mixture and the bay leaves. Dot with 3-tablespoons butter, pour Riesling over fish, and bake until just opaque in center, about 15-20 minutes. Transfer fish and vegetables to warmed serving plates, and tent with foil to keep warm.

Strain pan juices into a medium saucepan, discard bay leaves and boil until reduced to half, about 3-5 minutes.

Add cream and cook 2-minutes, turn off heat and add 1 remaining tablespoon of butter and whisk until butter is melted, stir-in parsley, season to taste with salt and pepper, add potatoes and heat gently.

Pour sauce over the fish and place 3 potatoes on each plate, and enjoy.

Chef's note: See trout illustration photos 1 – 4, on previous page.

FRESH TUNA STEAKS
With
GARLIC, TOMATOES, CAPERS and GIN
"Signature"

"Cooking with Erika"
Created and demonstrated this on local, weekly TV segment, aired during year 2001

Serves: 4

6 tablespoons extra virgin olive oil
2 cups onions, chopped
2 cloves garlic, minced
1 pound red tomatoes, coarsely chopped
½ pound yellow tomatoes, coarsely chopped
1 cup fresh basil leaves, loosely packed, chopped
1½ tablespoons capers, drained
2 tablespoons gin

4 fresh Ahi tuna steaks, 5-6 ounces each – see note below

Sea salt
Pepper, freshly ground

Heat 3-tablespoons olive oil in a heavy, medium saucepan over medium heat. Add onions, sauté until tender, about 5-minutes. Add garlic, stir-in red and yellow tomatoes, simmer uncovered until mixture thickens, stirring occasionally, about 15-20 minutes-add basil, capers and gin, cook 2 more minutes, season with salt and pepper if needed, and keep warm.

Heat remaining 3-tablespoons of oil in a large skillet over medium-high heat, and sprinkle tuna with salt and pepper.

Add tuna to skillet and cook until edges are light brown, but pink in center, about 3 minutes per side.

Stir-in the tomato mixture and simmer, about 1-2 minutes longer.

Enjoy with your favorite pasta or basmati rice, toasted French bread, a hearty salad, and a glass of your favorite dry white wine.

<u>*Chef's note:*</u> If planning to use frozen tuna, thaw it overnight in the refrigerator and pat dry with paper towels.

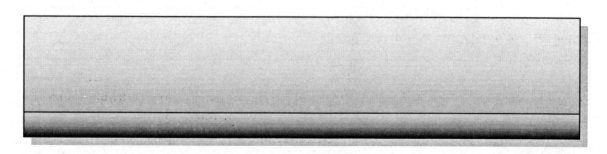

FISH – SEAFOOD
COMBINATIONS

SICILIAN STYLE SEAFOOD SOUP
"Signature-1976" Recreated for demonstration on weekly-local TV Segment, 2002

Serves: 6

3 tablespoons extra virgin olive oil
½ cup onions, diced
1 cup of tomatoes, diced
2 tablespoons garlic, minced
1 cup of water
1 cup bottled clam juice
1 cup of dry white wine
1 cup of clams, drained, chopped
½ pound sea scallops
½ teaspoon saffron or ground turmeric
1 cup cooked orzo pasta
1 cup cooked medium-size shrimp
¼ teaspoon dried, crushed red pepper
1 tablespoon fresh basil, chopped
1 tablespoon fresh Italian parsley, chopped
½ cup baby spinach leaves

Sea salt
Pepper

Heat oil in a heavy, large saucepan over medium heat, add onions, sauté until tender, about 2-minutes, add tomatoes and garlic, sauté 1-more minute, add water, clam juice and wine. Cook on medium-low heat for 15-minutes, add clams and scallops, cook 5-minutes, turn heat to low, add saffron, orzo, shrimp, dried pepper, basil, parsley, spinach, and season to taste with salt and pepper.

SEA SCALLOPS - RIESLING-WATERCRESS SAUCE
"Signature"

Serves: 4

SCALLOPS

8 large sea scallops, rinsed and patted dry with paper towel
1-2 teaspoons fine sea salt
1-2 teaspoons mélange peppercorns, freshly ground

SAUCE

1 teaspoon unsalted butter
2 teaspoons extra virgin olive oil
¼ cup Late Harvest Riesling wine
1¼ cups whipping cream
Fine sea salt
Mélange peppercorns, freshly ground
½ cup watercress leaves, chopped

Sprinkle scallops lightly with salt and pepper on both sides. In a large non-stick skillet, heat butter and oil over medium-high heat. When hot, add scallops and cook on one side for 1-2 minutes. Turn and cook 1-2 minutes more. Transfer scallops to a warm platter, cover with foil to keep warm.

Add cream to hot skillet, stirring constantly, cook over medium heat 1-minute, stir in wine and cook 1-more minute. Turn off heat, season with salt and pepper, stir in watercress. Arrange scallops on warmed serving plates and spoon sauce around them, or spoon sauce on plates and arrange scallops on top of sauce, and serve with toasted French bread slices and a well-chilled glass of Dry Riesling wine. Enjoy!

CRAB STUFFED SALMON FILLETS
With
PURÉED LEEK SAUCE
"Signature"

Serves: 4

SALMON and CRAB-TURMERIC STUFFING

½ pound of fresh cooked King or
Dungeness crab, picked over
½ cup of watercress leaves, washed, dried
and chopped
2 shallots, chopped
Sea salt
Pepper, freshly ground
¼ teaspoon of ground turmeric

2 thick center cuts of salmon fillet, ¾
pounds each, skin removed
Extra virgin olive oil
2 tablespoons of unsalted butter, melted
Parsley, minced for garnish

Preheat oven to 400°F

Place crabmeat watercress and shallots in a medium bowl, season with salt and pepper, add turmeric, and mix thoroughly.

Cut pockets into thick sides of the salmon filets and stuff crab mixture into pockets. Line a baking dish with oiled parchment paper, place stuffed salmon on the parchment paper, brush each fillet with melted butter and bake for about 15 minutes, or until cooked through.

PURÉED LEEK SAUCE

(Save time, while salmon is baking, prepare sauce)

1 tablespoon of unsalted butter
2 cups of leeks, white and light green parts
only, washed and chopped
Sea salt
Pepper, freshly ground
½ cup of whipping cream
1/3 cup of dry white wine
1 tablespoon of unsalted butter
1 tablespoon fresh parsley, minced

Heat 1-tablespoon of butter in a small saucepan over medium heat, add leeks, sauté 1 minute, sprinkle lightly with salt and pepper, and add cream and wine.

Cook 2 minutes and let cool slightly, transfer to a food processor or blender, purée until smooth, transfer puréed leeks to a small saucepan, turn heat to medium-low stir in 1 tablespoon of butter, season to taste with salt and pepper. Stir in parsley. Keep warm.

Slice each fillet into 2 pieces, sprinkle with parsley. Transfer salmon to 4 warmed serving plates, spoon puréed leek sauce over fillets, and *enjoy with parsley new potatoes - see Recipe Index.*

GRITS SOUFFLÉ
With
FRESH CRAB and PRAWNS AQVAVIT
"Signature"

Recipe demonstrated live on local Public Television

Serves: 6

1¾ cups homemade chicken stock, vegetable stock, or water
2 tablespoons unsalted butter, plus extra for greasing
1 garlic clove, minced
¾ cup plus 2-tablespoons quick cooking hominy grits
½ cup whipping cream
3 large eggs, slightly beaten
¼ teaspoon sea salt
½ teaspoon black pepper, freshly ground
¼ cup white cheddar cheese, freshly grated
¼ cup soft, fresh goat cheese, crumbled
1 tablespoon fresh Italian parsley, chopped

½ pound "picked over" fresh Dungeness crabmeat, coarsely chopped
2 tablespoons extra virgin olive oil
6 large prawns, shelled and divined
Sea salt
Black pepper, freshly ground
½ cup whipping cream
4 tablespoons Aqvavit
1 tablespoon fresh Italian parsley, chopped
Lemon slices for garnish
Watercress for garnish
1 red Yakima sweet bell pepper, seeded and cut into ¼ inch strips for garnish
1 yellow or gold Yakima sweet bell pepper seeded, and cut into ¼ inch strips for garnish

Preheat oven to 350ºF
Generously butter 6-7 ounce ramekins or custard cups

Bring stock or water, butter and garlic to a boil in a heavy medium saucepan, gradually whisk-in grits, and return mixture to boil, whisking occasionally. Reduce heat to medium-low, cover and simmer until grits is thick and all stock or water is absorbed — whisking frequently, about 4-5 minutes. Whisk-in ½ cup cream and simmer 3-minutes, whisking occasionally. *Transfer grits* mixture to a bowl, and let it cool, add eggs, salt, pepper, cheddar cheese, goat cheese, and parsley. Spoon half of the grits mixture in prepared ramekins, sprinkle each with crabmeat, and spoon remaining grits mixture on top of crabmeat. *Transfer ramekins* to 13x9x2 inch heatproof glass dish, or metal baking pan. Pour enough hot water into a glass dish, or pan, to cover the bottom half of ramekins. *Bake grits soufflé* until set and golden brown on top, about 35 to 40 minutes. Cool grits in pan, about 15 minutes.

Meanwhile prepare prawns: Heat oil in a heavy-large skillet and sauté prawns over medium-high heat, until they begin to lose their raw, grayish color, about 1-2 minutes per side. Sprinkle prawns with salt and pepper, turn heat to medium, add cream and Aqvavit, cook 1-more minute, stir-in parsley and keep warm. *Using a small knife,* cut around soufflé to loosen, invert each soufflé onto individual plates, place 1-prawn on top of each serving, garnish with lemon slices and watercress. Spoon small amount of sauce around each serving and garnish with red and yellow or gold bell peppers - *enjoy with a glass of Yakima Valley Viognier, Dry Riesling or Chardonnay.*

BAKED NORTHWEST KING SALMON
With
DUNGENESS CRAB
And
SALMON ROE-CHIVE SAUCE
"Signature"

Serves: 4

SALMON

4-6 ounces each of fresh salmon fillet, skinned and boned
Sea salt
Pink peppercorns, freshly ground
1/3 cup of extra virgin olive oil
½ pound fresh dungeness crab meat, picked over
½ cup mascarpone cheese
¼ cup soft goat cheese, such as Montrachet cheese
2 shallots, finely chopped
1/3 cup watercress leaves, chopped
4 tablespoons Aqvavit liqueur

SAUCE

½ cup Viognier wine
1½ cups whipping cream
1/3 cup chives, chopped
¼ cup pink salmon roe
2 cups spinach leaves, for garnish
Lemon wedges, for garnish

Place salmon fillet in a medium oven proof glass dish, sprinkle each lightly with salt and pepper and drizzle oil over each fillet.

Preheat oven to 400°F

In a medium bowl, combine crab, mascarpone and goat cheese, shallots, watercress, Aqvavit and season with salt and pepper. Spread crab mixture evenly over each prepared salmon fillet. Bake for 8-10 minutes – turn heat to 380ºF and bake 3-5-more minutes or until topping is golden and bubbly. While salmon is baking, make sauce.

Prepare sauce: In a small saucepan, bring wine to a boil, turn heat to medium-low - cook 5-minutes. Add cream, cook 5-10 minutes, turn off heat and add chives and salmon roe - Season with salt and pepper, if needed. Arrange salmon fillet on 4-warmed serving plates, spoon sauce around each fillet and garnish with spinach leaves and lemon wedges.

CRAB and SHRIMP
Over
BLACK (SQUID INK) PASTA
With
SAUTÉED CHANTERELLE MUSROOMS
"Signature"

Serves 4-6:

3 tablespoons light olive oil
2 shallots, minced
¼ teaspoon sugar
½ pound chanterelle mushrooms, scrubbed and diced
1 garlic clove, minced
Sea salt
Pepper, freshly ground
1 cup of dry-white wine
2 teaspoons fresh thyme, chopped
¼ teaspoon saffron
1 cup of heavy cream
1 pound of fresh cooked crabmeat, picked over
1 pound cooked, shelled shrimp
2 tablespoons fresh watercress, chopped
Lemon wedges, for garnish

1 pound black, squid-ink linguine or fettuccine
½ teaspoon sea salt
2 tablespoons unsalted butter
Lemon wedges, for garnish

In a large skillet over medium heat, heat olive oil, add shallots, sprinkle with sugar, sauté 1-minute, turn heat to medium-high and add mushrooms.

Cook 10-minutes, add garlic and cook 1-minute longer. Season with salt and pepper and keep warm.

In a medium saucepan, heat wine over medium heat, add thyme and cook until reduced by half, about 5-minutes.

Add saffron and cream, turn heat to medium-low and cook 10-more minutes or until reduced again by half.

Reduce heat to low, stir-in crab, shrimp and watercress, and season with salt and pepper. Keep warm.

Bring 6 quarts of water to a boil, add salt and pasta, cook until al-dente, about 8-10 minutes, and drain.

Transfer to the skillet with the chanterelles, add butter and toss lightly.

Transfer pasta to a large, warmed, deep serving platter and spoon crab and shrimp mixture over pasta, and garnish with lemon wedges.

BOUILLABAISSE
"Signature"

Serves: 6-8

1 pound of fresh mussels or clams
Water
Sea salt
3½ pounds of fresh flounder, monkfish,
bass, haddock or red snapper
2 tablespoons of fresh lemon juice
5 garlic cloves
½ cup of extra virgin olive oil
1 onion, finely chopped
1 each peeled carrot, bulb fennel and leek-
white part only, cut into julienne strips
¼ celery stalk, diced
2 potatoes, peeled, diced
2 cups of dry white wine
1 bay leaf
1 bouquet garni, *see Index*
3 medium tomatoes, seeded, chopped
Pinch of saffron threads or ¼ teaspoon
turmeric
Pepper, freshly ground
12 large cooked, shelled shrimp, peeled
Fresh basil, chopped for garnish
8 slices of French bread

Soak mussels or clams 2 hours in several changes of salted, cold water. Wash and clean fish, remove heads, tails; fins and skin, reserving heads, tails and trimmings for stock, except discard fins and skin. Pat fish dry with paper towels. Cut fish into 2-3 inch pieces. Sprinkle with lemon juice, cover and let stand 20 minutes in the refrigerator.

To make stock: Pour 8 cups of water into a large saucepan. Add trimmings, 1 teaspoon of salt, bring water to a boil and cook uncovered for 15 minutes.

Strain fish stock, discard trimmings and pour fish stock back into the pan and bring to a boil. Scrape clean, the soaked clamshells or mussels, pull out and cut off beards. Add mussels or clams to fish stock, boil 10 minutes or until shells open. Discard any mussels or clams that do not open. Remove mussels or clams from liquid and refrigerate until ready to use.

Strain fish stock again, set aside. Set 1-garlic clove aside, crush remaining 4 garlic cloves. Heat 1/3 cup of oil in a large saucepan, add crushed garlic, onion, carrot fennel, leek, celery and potatoes, sauté over medium heat for 5 minutes. Add wine, reserved fish stock, the bay leaf, bouquet garni, tomatoes, saffron or turmeric, and bring to a boil, cook 10-minutes uncovered over medium-high heat. Add trimmed fish, cook 5-6 more minutes and discard bay leaf and garni. Turn heat to medium-low, add cooked mussels or clams and shrimp, heat through, season with salt and pepper, and keep warm until ready to serve.

Meanwhile finely chop reserved garlic, combine with remaining oil and use to coat both sides of bread. Brown the bread in a large skillet on both sides until golden in color and keep it warm in a covered breadbasket. Pour soup into a tureen, sprinkle with basil and enjoy!

SEAFOOD STEW - (Halibut, Snapper & Shrimp)
"Signature-1990"

Serves 4-6

4 tablespoons extra virgin olive oil
½ cup onion, chopped
½ cup leeks, white part only, cut into rings
1 pound tomatoes, peeled, seeded, chopped
¼ cup fennel root, chopped
1 carrot, peeled, diced
1 red bell pepper, seeded, diced
½ cup of water
½ cup of dry white wine
1 bay leaf
1 bottle clam juice
1 pound of halibut fillet, cut into small cubes
1 pound of snapper, cut into small cubes
1 pound of fresh or frozen cooked, medium-size, shelled shrimp (See Note, below)
1 tablespoon fresh thyme, chopped
¼ teaspoon of saffron, or turmeric
Sea salt
Black pepper, freshly ground
2 tablespoons of fresh Italian parsley, for garnish

Note: If using frozen shrimp, thaw shrimp in the refrigerator, rinse shrimp in cold water, pat dry, and keep refrigerated until ready to use.

Heat oil in a heavy-large saucepan over medium-high heat, add onion and leeks, sauté until tender, about 5-minutes, add tomatoes, fennel, carrot and bell peppers, and sauté 6-more minutes, stirring constantly. Add water, wine, bay leaf, clam juice, bring to a boil, turn heat to medium-low, and cook 20-minutes, stirring occasionally. Add halibut and snapper, and cook gently 5-more minutes, add shrimp, thyme, saffron or turmeric and add salt and pepper-to taste. Cook fish soup gently 1-more minute, discard bay leaf, ladle into large soup bowls, and sprinkle with parsley. *Enjoy stew's excellent flavor with crusty French bread slices and your favorite Sangiovese or Pinot Noir.*

Curried Prawns with Black (Squid Ink) Pasta, Page 103

BIVALVES & CRUSTACEANS

Bouillabaisse, Page 95

Sea Scallops in Irish Cream-Coffee Sauce, Page 116

Medallions of Lobster Tail with Saffron-Pernod Sauce, Page 114

BAKED OYSTERS
With
GORGONZOLA, CARAMELIZED ONIONS
And
WATERCRESS SALAD

Serves: 4

OYSTERS

Rock salt
20 oysters on half-shell
Sea salt
Pepper, freshly ground
6 ounces of gorgonzola cheese
2 tablespoons garlic, minced
½ cup fresh breadcrumbs
4 tablespoons unsalted butter, softened
2 tablespoons Italian parsley, chopped

Preheat oven to 400°F

Place enough rock salt in a shallow baking dish to keep oyster shells from tipping over.

Position oysters on rock salt and lightly sprinkle oysters with sea salt and pepper.

In a small bowl, combine gorgonzola cheese, garlic, breadcrumbs, butter and the parsley. Mix well and spoon gorgonzola cheese mixture over oysters.

Bake 10-15 minutes or until cheese is melted and bubbly. While oysters are baking, prepare onions and salad.

ONIONS

2 tablespoons light olive oil
2 cups onions, thinly sliced
¼ teaspoon sugar
¼ teaspoon sea salt
½ teaspoon pepper, freshly ground

In a large skillet, heat oil over medium-high heat, and add onions, sugar, salt and pepper. Cook until onions are golden in color, about 10-minutes, stirring often. Keep warm.

SALAD & DRESSING

2 tablespoons of extra virgin olive oil
4 tablespoons white balsamic vinegar
½ teaspoon sugar
Sea salt
Pepper, freshly ground
4 cups watercress leaves

In a small bowl, blend oil, vinegar, sugar, and season to taste with salt and pepper.

To enjoy: Divide watercress on 4-large, warmed plates, drizzle dressing over the watercress, then spoon caramelized onions on top of watercress, arrange 5-oysters on top of onions, and serve with buttered French bread slices, and your favorite chilled Chardonnay or Riesling Wine.

CRAB CAKES with AVOCADO SALAD
And
RASPBERRY MOUSSE DESSERT
"Signature-1991"

DINNER for TWO

CRAB CAKES

3 tablespoons extra virgin olive oil
¼ tablespoon unsalted butter
1 cup red onions, chopped
¼ teaspoon garlic, minced
½ teaspoon ground cumin
¼ teaspoon ground turmeric
½ cup tomatoes, peeled, seeded, chopped
12 ounces jumbo lump crabmeat, picked over
1½ cups dry-plain breadcrumbs
4 tablespoons fresh cilantro, chopped
3 teaspoons fresh lime juice
1 tablespoon fresh chives, minced
1 teaspoon lime zest, finely grated
¼ teaspoon cayenne pepper
1 egg, beaten to blend
Sea salt
Pepper, freshly ground

Heat 1-tablespoon of oil in a heavy, small skillet over medium heat, add ¾ cup onions and garlic and sauté 5-minutes, add cumin and turmeric, then add ¼ cup tomato - sauté 1-minute more and transfer to a medium-size bowl - let cool for about 15-minutes.

Add crab, ½ cup breadcrumbs, 2-tablespoons cilantro, 1- teaspoon limejuice, chives, ½ teaspoon lime zest and cayenne pepper to onion mixture, mix-in the egg, season with salt and pepper and form crab mixture into 4 equal size patties.

Place remaining 1-cup of breadcrumbs on a large plate, coat crab cakes with crumbs pressing to adhere. Transfer to another large plate. Can be made 6-hours ahead, covered and chilled.

AVOCADO SALAD

2 small avocados, peeled, pitted, diced
1 tablespoon extra virgin olive oil
Sea salt
Pepper, freshly ground
Pinch of sugar
1 bunch watercress leaves, for garnish
Tomato wedges, for garnish

Mix remaining ¼ cup of onions, ¼ cup tomatoes, 2-tablespoons cilantro, 2-teaspoons limejuice and ½ teaspoon lime zest in a medium bowl. Add avocado, olive oil, season with salt, pepper and sugar, toss to coat, cover, and chill up to 2-hours.

To prepare crab cakes: Heat remaining 2-tablespoons olive oil and butter in a large nonstick skillet over medium-high heat. Add crab cakes, cook until golden brown, about 2-3-minutes per side.

To prepare salad: Divide avocado salad among 2-large dinner plates. Place 2-crab cakes alongside of salad

100

and garnish with watercress and tomato wedges.

RASPBERRY MOUSSE

1-8 ounce package of frozen unsweetened raspberries, thawed, drained
8 ounces cream cheese, room temperature
¾ cup sugar, plus 2-tablespoons
½ cup chilled whipping cream

½ cup water
¼ cup fresh orange juice
20 champagne biscuits, (Crisp Lady finger-style cookies, preferably imported, or homemade)
Fresh raspberries, for garnish
Fresh mint leaves, or shaved chocolate, for garnish

Purée thawed raspberries in food processor until smooth. Strain raspberries into a medium-size bowl and press down on solids to extract as much liquid as possible and discard seeds.

Using an electric mixer, beat cream cheese and ½ cup sugar in a medium bowl until it is smooth. Beat chilled whipping cream in another bowl until stiff peaks form.

Gently fold whipped cream into cream cheese mixture. Add puréed raspberries and fold just until combined.

Bring remaining ¼ cup plus 2-tablespoons sugar, ½ cup water and orange juice to boil in a small saucepan, stir and boil 1-minute. Remove from heat-cool slightly. Dip biscuit briefly into orange syrup turning to coat. Place biscuit, flat side up, on the bottom of a medium-size glass bowl. Repeat with enough biscuits to cover bottom of the glass bowl, trimming biscuits to fit if necessary.

Spread 1/3 of raspberry cream cheese mixture over biscuits in the glass bowl.

Dip more biscuits into orange syrup and arrange them over the top of the raspberry cream cheese mixture in the bowl. Top with another layer of dipped biscuits trimmed to fit if necessary. Repeat layering with more raspberry cream and biscuits. Cover and refrigerate until set – at least 3-hours or up to 1-day.

Garnish with fresh raspberries and fresh mint, or shaved chocolate, and enjoy.

TURMERIC SHRIMP TAPAS

Serves: 4-6

1 pound uncooked large shrimp, peeled and divined
3 tablespoons Spanish olive oil
4 cloves garlic, chopped
1 teaspoon of sea salt
½ teaspoon pepper, freshly ground
1 tablespoon of ground turmeric
½ teaspoon black caraway seeds
Sea salt
¼ cup parsley, freshly chopped for garnish

In a large bowl, combine shrimp with 1-tablespoon oil, garlic, 1-teaspoon salt, ½ teaspoon pepper, turmeric and caraway seeds. Heat remaining 2-tablespoons oil in a large skillet over medium-high heat, add shrimp mixture and stir until cooked through (opaque) and still crunchy tender - about 2-minutes. Be careful not to overcook.

Transfer cooked shrimp to a pre-warmed oval, large bowl or platter, season with salt, if needed, garnish with parsley and enjoy with French bread slices, wine or sherry.

Note: If using frozen shrimp, defrost overnight in refrigerator, drain and pat dry with paper towels.

SHRIMP STUFFED EGG HALVES

Makes: 16 egg halves

8 large hard-boiled eggs, peeled
3 tablespoons mayonnaise
½ tablespoon hot curry powder
1 teaspoon Brandy
1 tablespoon minced shallots
½ cup cooked shrimp meat, plus extra for garnish
Sea salt
Pepper, freshly ground
Watercress, for garnish
Lemon wedges, for garnish

Cut eggs in half, lengthwise, scoop-out yolks, and place yolks in a medium-size bowl. Mash yolks with a fork, mix-in mayonnaise, curry powder, brandy, and shallots.

Chop shrimp meat, add to yolk mixture, and season with salt and pepper.

Mound shrimp mixture in cavity of each egg white half, about 1-tablespoon for each.

Place watercress on large platter, place shrimp stuffed egg halves on top of watercress, garnish with remaining shrimp meat and lemon wedges.

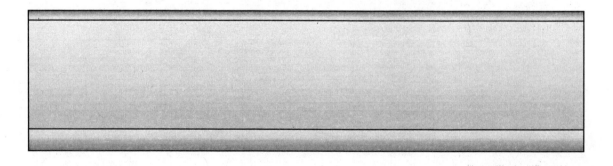

CURRIED PRAWNS
With
BLACK (SQUID INK) FETTUCCINE
"Signature-1990"

Serves: 4-6

PRAWNS

2 tablespoons unsalted butter
1 tablespoon of extra virgin olive oil
1 pound of large raw prawns, peeled and divined, tail intact
1½ teaspoons of sea salt
2½ tablespoons hot curry powder
1 teaspoon of ground turmeric
1-2 teaspoon mélange peppercorns, freshly ground

SAUCE

1½ cups whipping cream
1 teaspoon tomato paste, preferably imported organic Italian brand
¼ cup chicken stock
2 tablespoons brandy
Parmesan cheese, freshly grated (optional)

PASTA

1 pound of squid ink fettuccine
1 teaspoon of sea salt
2 teaspoons extra virgin olive oil

To cook prawns: Heat butter and 1 tablespoon of oil in a large skillet over medium-high heat. Add prawns and sprinkle with salt, 1 tablespoon of curry, turmeric, and 1-teaspoon of pepper.

Cook prawns 1-2 minutes per side, or until they turn pink. Transfer prawns from skillet to a hot serving platter, spoon pan drippings over prawns and cover with foil to keep warm.

To cook sauce: Add to the same skillet, the cream, tomato paste, chicken stock and the brandy – bring to a boil, reduce heat to medium-low – add remaining 1½ -tablespoons of curry, the remaining teaspoon of pepper - salt to taste and cook for 2-3 minutes or until slightly thickened. Keep warm on low heat.

To cook pasta: Bring a large pot of water to a boil, add 1-teaspoon of salt, add fettuccine and cook 8-10 minutes, drain pasta, transfer to a large bowl, sprinkle with 2-teaspoons of olive oil and toss.

To enjoy: Divide fettuccine onto 4 large, warmed serving plates, spoon some warm sauce over each serving, arrange prawns on top of sauce and sprinkle with cheese if desired. Enjoy with Pinot Noir, a light Zinfandel Pinot Gris or dry Chardonnay.

SEARED SCALLOPS
With
BLACK THAI RICE and DIJON DRESSING
"Signature"

"Cooking with Erika"
Created and demonstrated this on local, weekly TV segment, aired during year 2001

Serves: 4

DRESSING

1 lemon
1 tablespoon of Dijon mustard
2 tablespoons heavy cream
3 tablespoons extra virgin olive oil
Pinch sugar
Sea salt
Pepper, freshly ground

Grate the zest from the lemon and reserve. Squeeze juice from half the lemon into a small bowl, and add mustard and cream, whisking to blend. Slowly add the olive oil whisking until thickened. Season with sugar, salt and pepper and set aside.

BLACK TAI RICE

1 cup of black Tai rice
Water
2 teaspoons of extra virgin olive oil
Sea salt
Pepper, freshly ground

Rinse rice well, place 1 cup rice and 1½ cups of unsalted water in a saucepan. Bring to a boil, cover and simmer on low heat 25 minutes. Remove from heat, stir in oil, let stand 10 minutes, fluff with fork and keep warm. *Chef's note: For best results, season with salt and pepper to taste after rice is cooked. This rice is available in specialty* food shops and some mail order outlets.

SCALLOPS

16 large sea scallops, patted dry and seasoned lightly with salt and pepper
1 tablespoon of light olive oil
1 tablespoon unsalted butter
1 cup dry white wine or dry white vermouth
Sea salt
Pepper, freshly ground
1 large bunch watercress, trimmed, rinsed and dried
2 tablespoons of fresh chives, finely chopped for garnish

In a large nonstick skillet over medium-high heat, heat 1-teaspoon oil and 1-teaspoon butter and add 6-8 scallops leaving a bit of space between them. Sear the scallops without moving them around, and when well browned at the bottom edges (about 1-2 minutes), turn to brown the other side, about 1-minute or so more.

Remove scallops from skillet, transfer them to a warm-large plate and cover loosely with foil to keep warm. Repeat with remaining oil, butter and scallops. Pour off fat, return skillet to medium heat, add the reserved lemon zest, the wine or vermouth to deglaze, scraping off any bits stuck to the bottom of the skillet. Strain wine mixture into a clean, small saucepan and cook until wine is reduced to a syrupy glaze, about 3-5 minutes, remove from heat, add watercress and Dijon dressing - toss to coat watercress and, if needed, season with salt and pepper. _To serve:_ Divide Watercress-Dijon dressing onto 4 dinner plates. Arrange 4-scallops on top of watercress dressing, garnish scallops with chives, arrange Thai rice around scallops and enjoy with your favorite Riesling or Chardonnay.

PENNE and AQVAVIT-SORREL MUSSELS
"Signature"

Created and demonstrated this recipe on local, weekly TV segment, during year 2001 – "Cooking with Erika"

Serves: 4-6

PASTA

1 pound of Penne, or any other type pasta such as Ziti
6 quarts water
2 teaspoons sea salt
2 teaspoons of extra virgin olive oil

Cook pasta in rapidly boiling, salted water until al-dente, about 10-12 minutes. Drain and place pasta in a large serving dish, drizzle with oil, toss and keep warm. _Note:_ While pasta is boiling, prepare sauce and mussels.

SAUCE

1 tablespoon unsalted butter
¼ cup shallots, chopped
1½ cups heavy cream
2 tablespoons Aqvavit
3 tablespoons dry white wine
¼ teaspoon turmeric, (Avail. in supermarket spice section)

Sea salt
Pepper, freshly ground

MUSSELS

2 pounds New Zealand green-shell mussels on the half shell, defrosted in refrigerator overnight
2 tablespoons fresh sorrel, chopped (Avail. in supermarket produce section)
Lemon wedges, for garnish

Heat butter in a large skillet over medium heat, and add shallots and sauté 3-5 minutes. Add cream, Aqvavit and wine. Simmer until reduced to almost half, about 6-minutes, add turmeric, salt and pepper (to taste) and then add mussels.

Cover and cook gently for 3-4 minutes and stir-in sorrel. Arrange mussels on top of penne pasta, and drizzle sauce from pan over mussels and penne and serve immediately.

NEW ZEALAND MUSSELS
With
LINGUINE

Serves: 4-6

1 teaspoon unsalted butter
1/3 cup shallots, peeled, minced
3 cloves garlic, minced
½ cup bottled clam juice
¼ cup dry white wine
½ cup heavy cream
¼ teaspoon pepper, freshly ground
2 pounds frozen green shell mussels-on the half shell, thawed
1/3 cup extra virgin olive oil
Sea salt
Pepper, freshly ground

LINGUINE

6 quarts of water
2 teaspoons of sea salt
1 pound of linguine
2 teaspoons of extra virgin olive oil

Heat butter in a deep, 12-inch skillet over medium-high heat until hot, reduce heat to medium and sauté shallots and garlic for about 2 minutes. Stir-in clam juice, wine and heavy cream. Add ¼ teaspoon of pepper — cook on medium-low heat, stirring occasionally, about 6 minutes. Keep sauce warm. Meanwhile, cook pasta until al-dente, about 10-12 minutes, drain and transfer to a large platter, drizzle with oil and toss lightly. Cover with foil to keep warm.

Preheat oven to broil

While pasta is boiling, prepare mussels.

Place thawed mussels on a large baking sheet, drizzle each with olive oil and sprinkle with salt and pepper - broil mussels 5-6 minutes. Remove from oven and arrange mussels on top of pasta, spoon warm sauce over mussels and pasta. Enjoy with a crisp salad, French bread slices and your favorite Sauvignon Blanc or Sémillon.

Curried Prawns with Black (Squid Ink) Fettuccine, see recipe on Page 103.

Chef's comments: It is not uncommon to find curry dishes on Italian menus in Italy because Indian spices are so readily available and apparently used to add exotic twists to sauces served over pasta, fish, poultry and red meat dishes.

BEER MARINATED GRILLED TIGER PRAWNS

MARINADE

1 bottle (12 ounces) light beer
3 cloves garlic, minced
1 teaspoon of sweet paprika
1 teaspoon of ground turmeric
½ teaspoon fine sea salt
¼ teaspoon pepper, freshly ground
3 tablespoons Dijon mustard
3 tablespoons extra virgin olive oil
¼ teaspoon black caraway seeds
1 bunch watercress, for garnish
Lime wedges, for garnish

16 tiger prawns (shelled and divined, tail intact)
4 wood skewers (10-inch) soaked in warm water for 30-minutes. If using metal skewers, brush them with oil.

In a large bowl, combine all marinade ingredients, add prawns, mix to coat prawns, cover with plastic wrap and marinate for at least 4-6 hours.

Remove prawns from marinade, discard marinade, and thread 4 prawns onto each skewer. Place skewered prawns on preheated grill, about 4 inches from heat source. Cook about 3-5 minutes per side or until pink and light browned – do not overcook.

Place cooked prawns on a large warmed serving platter, garnish with watercress leaves and lime wedges. *Enjoy!*

CRAB and SHRIMP AVOCADO BOATS

This signature dish was demonstrated on local weekly TV segment, aired April 13, 2001

Serves: 4

2 ripe avocados, halved and pitted
2 teaspoons of fresh limejuice
¾ cup of mayonnaise
2 tablespoons chili sauce
1 tablespoon Aqvavit
1 tablespoon of mild curry powder
2 tablespoons green onions, minced
2 tablespoons watercress, chopped
1 tablespoon of fresh parsley, chopped
¼ cup ripe mango, peeled and chopped
8 ounces fresh cooked crabmeat
8 ounces chopped, cooked shrimp meat

Sea salt
Pepper, freshly ground
Lemon and lime wedges, for garnish

Brush avocados with limejuice and place them on a large serving platter. In a medium bowl, stir together mayonnaise, chili sauce, Aqvavit, curry powder, green onions, watercress parsley and mango. Gently stir in crab and shrimp, season with salt and pepper, and top each avocado with a dollop of crab-shrimp mixture. Garnish with lemon and lime wedges and enjoy with crusty French bread along with your favorite Riesling or Chardonnay.

Chef's note: Defrost frozen shrimp overnight in refrigerator and pat-dry shrimp with paper towels before using.

MARINATED PRAWNS-BASMATI RICE
In
TEA-LEMON-VODKA SAUCE
"Signature"

Serves: 4

MARINADE

2 tablespoons extra virgin olive oil
1 teaspoon of sea salt
1 teaspoon mélange peppercorns, freshly ground
½ cup lemon vodka (Avail. in Liquor stores)
1/3 cup medium strength green tea, freshly brewed and chilled
1 pound of large raw prawns, peeled and divined, tail intact

SAUCE

2 tablespoons of unsalted butter
Sea salt
Mélange peppercorns, freshly ground
1/3 cup medium strength hot green tea, freshly brewed
¾ cup of whipping cream
2 tablespoons lemon vodka

4 cups cooked white basmati rice, kept warm

Watercress leaves, for garnish
Lemon wedges, for garnish

To make marinade: Combine oil, salt, pepper, ½ cup of lemon vodka and 1/3 cup chilled tea in a large bowl and mix well. Add prawns and stir to coat evenly, refrigerate for at least 1-hour.

Drain prawns, pat dry with paper towels and discard marinade.

Heat butter in a large skillet over medium-high heat, add drained prawns and cook until pink, about 1-2 minutes per side.

Remove prawns to a hot serving platter, spoon pan drippings over prawns, cover with foil to keep warm.

In the same pan, add 1/3 cup of hot tea, cream and 2 tablespoons of vodka - bring to a boil.

Reduce heat to medium-low and cook stirring until sauce thickens slightly, about 3-5 minutes, and season to taste with salt and pepper.

Equally mound rice onto 4 warmed plates and arrange prawns on top of rice, spoon sauce over prawns, garnish with watercress leaves and lemon wedges.

Enjoy with a glass of chilled Fumé or Sauvignon Blanc or your favorite Sémillon.

MELON-PRAWNS
In
DILL SAUCE
"Signature"

Serves: 4

MELON-PRAWNS

1 small honeydew melon
1 pound of cooked, shelled prawns, tail off, rinsed and patted dry with paper towel.
Juice of ½ of lemon

DILL SAUCE

½ cup cream cheese, softened
6-8 tablespoons buttermilk
Sea salt
Pepper, freshly ground
1 teaspoon of white balsamic vinegar, or white wine vinegar
2½ tablespoons fresh dill, chopped

Prepare melon: Slice melon in half, scoop out seeds and discard – then carefully scoop out the flesh and dice.

Place diced melon flesh in a large glass bowl and add prawns. Sprinkle with the lemon juice and toss lightly.

Dill sauce: Mix cream cheese in a blender or food processor with 2 tablespoons buttermilk, adding up to 6 tablespoons of buttermilk until the mixture reaches the consistency of medium-thick cream.

The quantity of buttermilk needed will depend on the consistency of the cream cheese.

Add salt and pepper to taste, the vinegar and 2-tablespoons of the chopped dill, reserving the rest for garnish.

Mix the dill sauce with the prawns and melon, and chill for 1-hour before serving.

Toss again just before serving. Sprinkle with remaining dill.

Note: If using frozen, cooked prawns, thaw in refrigerator overnight and pat dry with paper towels.

Enjoy with your favorite Dry Riesling, Viognier, or Pinot Gris.

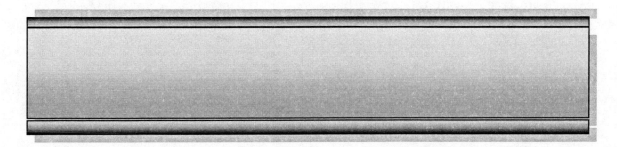

PASTA SHELLS
With
SHRIMP, CHICKEN and MUSSELS
"Signature"

Serves: 4-6

1 pound of pasta shells
2 teaspoons of sea salt
2 teaspoons of extra virgin olive oil

1 tablespoon of extra virgin olive oil
2 shallots, minced
½ pound chicken breast, boned, skinned, diced
1¼ cup of whipping cream
2 tablespoons of Brandy
1/8 teaspoon of saffron threads or ¼ teaspoon of ground turmeric
½ pound of cooked, shelled shrimp with tail on
½ pound mussels, cooked and shelled
Sea salt
Pepper, freshly ground
3 tablespoons of watercress, chopped

Bring 6-8 quarts of water in a large pot to boil, add salt and pasta. Cook until al dente, about 10-12 minutes. Drain, transfer to a large bowl, drizzle with 1-teaspoon of oil, toss lightly and set aside.

Meanwhile, heat 1-tablespoon of oil in a large, deep skillet over medium heat, add shallots, and sauté for 1-2 second, or until soft.

Turn heat to medium-high, add chicken and sauté until just golden, about 2-minutes, stir in cream and brandy, add saffron or turmeric and allow the sauce to simmer for about 6-8 minutes.

Add the cooked shrimp, mussels and pasta, heat through for 1-minute over low heat, turn off the heat, season with salt and pepper, stir-in watercress. Enjoy!

Shrimp verses the Prawn, and commonalities: Shrimp varieties vary in size, from very tiny, miniature, small, medium, large, jumbo and colossal. The number of shrimp per pound is determined by size. For example, there are about 10-count or less per pound of colossal shrimp and, give or take, around 39-count per pound of small shrimp. **Shrimp** are found in fresh waters worldwide. **Prawns** are shrimp-like crustaceans with a narrower body and longer legs, their average market size is usually around 3-4 inches - they are salt and freshwater dwellers that migrate from one body of water to the other to spawn. Categorically, both shrimp and prawn are in the crustacean (shelled) family and both are decapods, because they each possess five pairs of arms, two of which are pinchers.

SAUTÉED VODKA SHRIMP

Serves: 8

2 tablespoons of extra virgin olive oil
2 pounds of large cooked, shelled shrimp, fresh or frozen (if frozen, thaw overnight in the refrigerator and pat dry with paper towels before cooking- do not use microwave)
2 tablespoons of garlic, minced
1 teaspoon of sea salt
½ teaspoon pepper, freshly ground
¼ cup of fresh limejuice
4 tablespoons of Vodka
½ teaspoon hot pepper flakes
¼ cup watercress leaves, chopped

In a large skillet, heat 1 tablespoon of oil over medium-high heat, add 1-pound of shrimp and 1-tablespoon of garlic, sauté for 1-2 seconds. Sprinkle shrimp lightly with salt and pepper. Transfer shrimp to a pre-warmed deep platter, cover with foil and keep warm. Repeat with remaining oil, shrimp and garlic - sauté 1-2 seconds and lightly season with salt and pepper and transfer shrimp to a pre-warmed platter. Add limejuice, vodka and pepper flakes to skillet, turn heat to medium, cook 1-more minute, turn off heat and season with salt and pepper, if needed. Stir in watercress, spoon sauce over shrimp and enjoy with grits and a green salad.

Note: **Suggest avoiding microwaving fish, seafood and poultry, to mention a few of other types of food, because this method causes product's texture to become rubbery, or tough to the bite. The flavor in pan sautéed shrimp is worth the extra five minutes to prepare.**

Sautéed Vodka Shrimp

CRAB and SHRIMP STUFFED CABBAGE LEAVES
With
POTATO CAKE and RIESLING WINE SAUCE
"Signature"

Serves: 8

CABBAGE-CRAB-SHRIMP STUFFING

1 medium head of green cabbage
½ cup finely chopped onions
½ cup fresh breadcrumbs
1 pound cooked shrimp meat, coarsely chopped
1 pound of white crab meat, fresh (preferred) or frozen
½ teaspoon of sea salt
¼ teaspoon white pepper, freshly ground
2 eggs, slightly beaten
2 tablespoons organic sour cream
½ teaspoon of sweet paprika
2 tablespoons fresh parsley, chopped
1 small red bell pepper, halved, seeded, and cut into fine dice
¼ cup Parmesan cheese, freshly grated
3 tablespoons of unsalted butter

1 cup of dry Riesling wine
2 cups of whipping cream
Sea salt
Pepper, freshly ground
¼ cup watercress leaves, chopped

Bring a large saucepan of salted water to a boil, plunge cabbage into boiling water, and boil for 10 minutes turning several times. Remove cabbage carefully from boiling water and set into ice water to peel off limp outer leaves. Repeat process until all leaves have been removed, drain leaves and set aside.

In a large bowl, combine onions, breadcrumbs, shrimp meat, crabmeat, salt, pepper, eggs, sour cream, paprika, parsley, bell pepper, and Parmesan cheese.

Divide shrimp mixture into 8 portions. Working with 2 cabbage leaves at a time, roll or pound them gently to soften its ribs.

Place leaves 1 inside the other, and spread 1 portion of shrimp mixture on the center surface and neatly roll up edges of leaves into a small package and secure with household string. Repeat with remaining cabbage leaves and shrimp mixture.

Heat butter in 2 large, deep skillets, or saucepans, over medium-high heat. Add 4 cabbage rolls to each skillet, or saucepan, sauté for 5 minutes, turning once, turn heat to medium-low, add ½ cup of wine and 1 cup of cream to each skillet. Cover and cook gently for 10 minutes, or until cabbage leaves are soft. Adjust seasoning and keep warm until ready to serve. Place cabbage rolls on a heated platter, cut string and discard, spoon sauce over cabbage rolls, sprinkle with watercress and enjoy with potato cake.

112

POTATO CAKE

8 medium Yukon gold potatoes
1 cup of clarified butter (See Page 339)
Sea salt
Pepper, freshly ground
2 tablespoons fresh thyme leaves, chopped

Preheat oven to 400°F

Prepare Potatoes: Peel, thinly slice potatoes and place in cold water until ready to cook. Drain potatoes and pat dry on paper towels. Heat ¼ cup of clarified butter in a large nonstick skillet over medium heat.

Add just enough potatoes to the skillet to allow them to move around easily and to roll them in the butter for a few minutes until well coated and hot.

Strain potatoes and return the excess butter to the pan and repeat in batches until all potato slices are done. Set aside to cool slightly.

Coat the bottom of a flameproof skillet with ¼ cup of the butter leaving the skillet over low heat, and add a portion of potato slices, arranging them in slightly overlapping circles, using a tong.

Season with salt and pepper, sprinkle with thyme leaves, and arrange a second layer of potatoes on top this time overlapping slices in the opposite direction.

Repeat until all potato slices have been used and seasoned after each layer.

Drizzle remaining butter over the top, then transfer to the oven and bake for 30 minutes, or until tender to the point of a sharp knife.

To un-mold, pour off any excess butter, place a large heatproof plate over the skillet and in a single motion – using 2 hot pads - turn it over, cut into serving pieces and enjoy with your favorite medium-dry Riesling or Chardonnay.

Recommendation: Because of its longer cooking time, process potato cake about 20 minutes ahead of cabbage.

Suggestion: Also try the Basmati Rice Soufflé with the Stuffed Cabbage Leaves, please see Index.

Note: If using frozen shrimp meat, defrost overnight in the refrigerator, drain and pat dry with paper towels. If using frozen crabmeat, defrost overnight in the refrigerator and pat dry with paper towels.

LOBSTER TAIL MEDALLIONS
With
SAFFRON PERNOD SAUCE and PARSLEY PASTA
"Signature"

Serves 4 – 6

LOBSTER STOCK

1 medium onion, sliced
1 medium carrot, peeled and thinly sliced
1 celery stalk, thinly sliced
1 bay leaf
1 teaspoon white peppercorn
3 sprigs of fresh thyme
2 cups dry white wine
4 tablespoons sea salt
Water
4 raw lobster tails, about 1 pound each

SAUCE

2 tablespoons unsalted butter
3 shallots, finely chopped
1 cup reserved strained lobster stock
1½ cups whipping cream
2 large pinches of saffron threads
2 tablespoons Pernod (Avail. in Liquor Stores)
Parsley pasta (*See Products Supplier list on Page 26*)
Sea salt
2 tablespoons unsalted butter, melted
Asparagus tips, cooked, for garnish
Watercress leaves, for garnish

To cook stock and lobster: Place vegetables, bay leaf, peppercorn, thyme and wine in a large stockpot and bring to a boil.

Cook for 5-6 minutes over medium-high heat, add salt and 4 quarts of water and return to a boil, add lobster tails – bring to a boil again – cook covered for 8-10 minutes or until the shell turns bright orange.

Carefully remove cooked lobster with tongs, refresh lobster in cold water, pat dry with paper towels and transfer the lobster to a cutting board.

Strain lobster stock into a large bowl, let cool, reserving 1 cup.

Turn over the lobster tail to expose its soft underside, and using a pair of kitchen scissors, cut lengthwise down each side toward the tail end.

Pull off the soft under-shell to expose the meat. Remove tail meat from the lobster shell keeping it in a single piece.

Using a sharp knife, slice the meat crosswise into medallions.

Transfer medallions to a large dish, cover and refrigerate until ready to use.

To make the sauce: In a medium saucepan, heat 2 tablespoons of butter over medium heat, add shallots and cook about 3-4 seconds or until soft.

Add 1 cup of the reserved, strained stock – bring to a boil and cook to reduce by almost half, about 10-minutes.

Add cream, turn heat to medium-low and cook 5 more minutes.

Add saffron and Pernod, turn heat to low, add lobster medallions to the sauce and gently reheat lobster, but do not boil.

Cook pasta according to the manufacturer's instructions, drain well and transfer the pasta to a pre-warmed large bowl – add melted butter and toss gently.

To serve, arrange lobster medallions on 4-6 warmed serving plates, spoon sauce over lobster, divide pasta among serving plates, garnish with asparagus tips and watercress.

Note: Let frozen lobster tails thaw completely in the refrigerator, overnight if necessary, before cooking to preserve tenderness. Do not thaw or cook in the microwave otherwise lobster meat will be tough.

Note: For best results, select Australian or Main lobster

Lobster Medallions with Saffron-Pernod Sauce and Parsley Pasta

SEA SCALLOPS in IRISH CREAM-COFFEE SAUCE
With
BASMATI RICE SOUFFLÉ
And
BRAISED NAPA CABBAGE
"Signature"

Serves: 4

RICE SOUFFLÉ

2 cups basmati rice, cooked and cooled
2 eggs, slightly beaten
½ cup of sweet onion, chopped
½ cup of sour cream, organic preferred
¼ cup of watercress leaves, chopped
Sea salt
Pepper, freshly ground
Butter for greasing

Preheat oven to 350ºF and butter bottom and sides of four 2/3-cup soufflé dishes

Basmatti Rice Soufflé: In a medium bowl, mix together rice, eggs, onions sour cream, watercress and season with salt and pepper. Divide mixture among 4-prepared soufflé dishes – place dishes in a medium roasting pan or a deep medium-size baking dish and pour enough hot water into the roasting pan, or baking dish to cover the bottom half of the soufflé dishes. Bake for 25-30 minutes or until soufflés have slightly risen and are firm to the touch. Remove pan from oven, carefully remove soufflés from the water bath and let cool slightly. Run a small sharp knife around soufflés to loosen from dish and gently un-mold soufflés onto warm serving plates. *Note:* Prepare cabbage and scallops while rice soufflé is baking.

NAPA CABBAGE

2 tablespoons of unsalted butter
2 large heads of Napa cabbage, coarsely chopped, about 8 cups
¼ cup of fresh parsley, chopped
Sea salt
Pepper, freshly ground
¼ teaspoon of sugar

Heat butter in a large saucepan over medium-high heat, reduce heat to medium, adding cabbage and sauté until soft, about 5-minutes stirring often. Add parsley, season with salt and pepper, add sugar, and sauté 1-2 more minutes. Turn heat to low to keep warm until ready to serve.

SEA SCALLOPS & SAUCE

16 large sea scallops, patted dry
Sea salt
Pepper, freshly ground
2 tablespoons grape seed oil
1 tablespoon unsalted butter
2 cups of heavy cream
3-4 teaspoons of European coffee, finely ground
¼ cup of Irish Mist liqueur, (Avail. in Liquor stores)

Lightly sprinkle scallops with salt and

116

pepper. Heat a large skillet over medium-high heat, add oil, and when oil appears to simmer, add butter, and add 8-scallops leaving space between them.

Sear the scallops without moving them around. After about 1-2 minutes, when bottom edges are well browned, turn and brown the other side for about 1-minute.

Remove scallops from skillet, transfer them to a large warmed plate and repeat process with remaining 8-scallops, remove scallops from skillet and pour off the fat.

Return skillet to medium heat, add cream, coffee and Irish mist and cook 1-3 minutes, or until sauce is slightly thickened.

Spoon sauce around each rice soufflé, arrange 4 scallops on top of sauce, spoon cabbage into 4 small, pre-warmed serving bowls and enjoy!

Sea Scallops in Irish Cream-Coffee Sauce, Rice Soufflé & Napa Cabbage

MERLOT BRAISED BEEF SHORTRIBS
"Signature"

Serve: 6

¼ cup diced pancetta (Avail. at Supermarkets and Specialty Deli's)
4 pounds bone-in beef short ribs, rinsed in coldwater and patted dry with paper towel
1 cup of onion, chopped
½ cup carrots, peeled, and chopped
½ cup rutabaga, peeled, chopped
½ cup parsnip, peeled, chopped
2 cloves garlic, chopped
Sea salt
Mélange pepper, freshly ground
½ teaspoon sweet paprika
2 large tomatoes, peeled, seeded and chopped
2 cups merlot wine
1 cup of water
2 thyme sprigs
1 bay leaf
½ cup parsley, freshly chopped

Heat a heavy large pot over medium heat and add pancetta - sauté until crisp. Using slotted spoon, transfer pancetta to a plate lined with paper towels to drain. Working in batches, brown all sides of ribs over medium-high heat in pot drippings, about 6-8 minutes, per batch.

Transfer ribs to a large platter. Place onions, carrots, rutabaga and parsnip in the pot – sauté vegetables over medium heat for 1-minute, while stirring add garlic, return ribs to pot, sprinkle with salt, pepper and paprika, add tomatoes and wine, cook uncovered over medium-high heat until liquid is reduced by half, about 8-minutes - add water, cover pot partially and simmer for 1½ hours. Uncover, add thyme, sprigs and bay leaf and simmer until ribs are tender, stirring occasionally, about 1-hour longer.

Transfer ribs to a warm platter, and discard thyme, sprigs and bay leaf. Strain meat sauce into a clean medium saucepan and press solids in strainer to extract all of the sauce. Discard solids.

Heat sauce on medium-low for 5-minutes, stir-in parsley, spoon some sauce over short ribs, and pour any remaining sauce into a pre-warmed sauceboat - serve with mashed sweet potatoes, *see recipe on page 234.*

MEAT DISHES

Top photo - Lamb Burger with Purple Mashed Potatoes, Page 134

Bottom photo – Ossobucco (Veal Shanks), Page 146

120

Top Photo – Stuffed Pork Loin, Page 140

Bottom Photo – Lamb Kabobs, Page 132

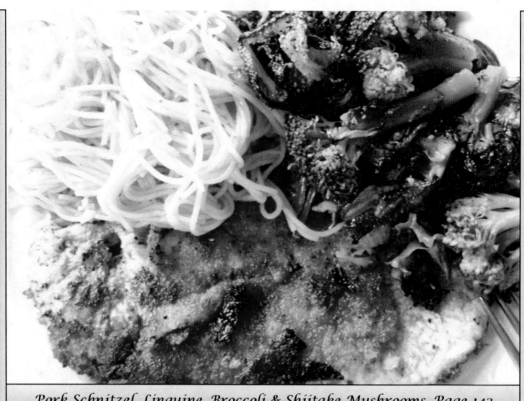

Pork Schnitzel, Linguine, Broccoli & Shiitake Mushrooms, Page 143

Filet Mignon with Coffee-Brandy Sauce, Grilled Mushrooms, Page 123

FILET MIGNON
With
COFFEE-BRANDY SAUCE
"Signature"

Serves: 4

4 filet mignon, center cut, 6-8-ounces each
2 cups strong cold coffee
3 tablespoons port wine
1 tablespoon of extra virgin olive oil
4 tablespoons mélange peppercorn, coarsely ground
Fine sea salt
4 tablespoons unsalted butter
4 tablespoons brandy
2 cups heavy cream
1 tablespoon coffee beans, finely ground
Sea salt
Mélange peppercorn, freshly ground

Rinse filet with cold water, pat dry with paper towels and place them in a deep glass dish. In a small bowl, combine coffee, port wine and oil and pour it over meat. Cover meat with plastic wrap and marinate refrigerated 24-hours, turning meat once.

Remove meat and discard marinade, pat dry with paper towels and thoroughly rub peppercorn over each filet, set aside.

Heat butter in a deep skillet until very hot and add filets to brown for 5-6 minutes on each side – for medium rare.

For well done, 7-8 minutes per side. Lightly sprinkle salt over meat, transfer to a heated platter, spoon pan drippings over each filet, cover with foil, and keep warm.

Wipe skillet clean with paper towels, turn heat to medium-high, add brandy and cook 2 seconds.

Whisk in cream, ground coffee, turn heat to medium-low and cook 3 minutes. Turn off heat, season with salt and pepper.

To enjoy, arrange filet mignon on warmed plates, spoon sauce over each filet and accompany with vino pasta and grilled mushrooms. *See "Rossi Pasta" on supplier list, page 26.*

Chef's note: For best results, use a non-bitter, low acidic, medium bodied coffee. Enjoy an exclusive original!

WINE BRAISED OXTAIL

Serves: 4-6

2 tablespoons light olive oil
6 pounds oxtail, cut into 2-inch thick pieces, excess fat removed
Sea salt
Pepper, freshly ground
2 cloves garlic, chopped
1 cup of onions, chopped
½ cup carrots, peeled, chopped
2 cups red dry wine
2 medium tomatoes, peeled, seeded and chopped
3 cups vegetable stock or water
2 bay leaves
¼ cup Italian parsley, chopped

Heat oil in a heavy large pot over medium-high heat and sprinkle oxtail with salt and pepper.

Working in batches, brown oxtails, about 6-8 minutes per batch and transfer them to a warm, large platter, reduce heat to medium-low, and add garlic, onions and carrots - cook, stirring occasionally, for 1-2 minutes.

Return meat to pot, add wine, return heat to medium and cook uncovered until liquid is reduced to thick and syrupy, about 20-30 minutes.

Add tomatoes, stock or water and bay leaves and stir to deglaze scraping browned bits up from bottom of pot with a wooden spoon.

Cook uncovered on medium-low heat for 1-hour, 40-minutes or until oxtail is fork tender and season with salt and pepper, if needed.

Serve over pasta, basmati rice or mashed potatoes. See recipe Index.

OXTAIL

It is said that oxtail soups and dishes became known during the French revolution when a French Nobel asked for an oxtail, from this, he created oxtail soup. Others say the dish was introduced to England by French refugees, but England claims it was introduced long before the French Revolution. The Huguenots claim they introduced it to England.

Whichever claim is accurate, one thing for certain is that oxtail soup, oxtail broth and oxtail dishes have been among many traditional preparations in Germany and elsewhere in Europe ever since I can remember as a child, raised in West Berlin, Germany. Oxtail is rich in flavor as you'll experience in the recipe, above.

BRAISED RABBIT with PRUNES

Serves: 4

1 pound prunes, pitted
2½ cups Burgundy or other hearty red wine
6 bacon slices, diced
1 rabbit or hare, about 3½ pounds, cut into serving pieces
2 onions, finely chopped
1 teaspoon black peppercorns, crushed
½ teaspoon fresh thyme, chopped
½ teaspoon fresh rosemary, chopped
2 bay-leaves
2 teaspoons sea salt
4 tablespoons brandy
1 apple, peeled, cored and grated
2 tablespoons sour cream
1 tablespoon fresh parsley, chopped

In a medium bowl, combine prunes and wine, cover, and let stand overnight.

Sauté bacon in a large saucepan over medium heat until light brown, add rabbit, and brown evenly on all sides, turning rabbit pieces once or twice.

Add onions, sauté 5-minutes, sprinkle rabbit with crushed peppercorns, thyme, rosemary, and add bay leaves.

Sprinkle rabbit with salt, add prunes, half of marinade, and simmer for 1½-hours on medium-low heat.

Add more marinade to the saucepan if contents become dry. Stir-in brandy, grated apple, and simmer 20-more minutes, adding the remaining marinade or water if needed.

Cook 5-more minutes, stir-in sour cream and parsley, enjoy with potato dumplings, see page 223.

Notes

125

LAMB

Lamb have differences: Differences in breeds, diets, conditions, care, treatment, stress levels, handling, processing, packaging, shipping standards, storage procedures, and differences in methods used for cooking it - to name a few. For example, lamb grown in different regions within any particular state or country may have differing flavors because of varied conditions and of what they are fed. But, what matters from a consumer's standpoint, is likeability of flavor in the plate. Toward that objective, I'll highlight diet, the lamb's diet that is, and some other conditions factored in that make or break a dining experience of delectable lamb! Arguably, the following descriptions of, and differing circumstances, regarding consumption of lamb may have amounted to either a favorable or unfavorable dining experience - there doesn't seem to be an in-between, its either liked or disliked - here is why I think that is:

From the diner's (beneficial) standpoint, I believe everyone would probably love lamb if it's been fed right and cooked right! And, from a nutritional standpoint, consider this: A 3-ounce serving of Australian lamb, for example, has only about 173 calories. Combine that with nutritive benefits such as niacin, zinc and iron, plus it's rich in vitamin b-12.

Ideally, choosing fresh over frozen is always best! But, if storage or sporadic availability of fresh lamb is an issue and you wish store (freeze) portions of lamb for future meals, then I recommend taking advantage of the availability of fresh lamb by purchasing it fresh and vacuum packaging portions to freeze for future use. This simply means that now you know the length of time lamb will have been frozen before using it, secondly, it will taste fresher than lamb purchased already frozen. Certainly fresh is always best, but there are other details to consider to ensure dining experiences consisting of lamb are experiences you wish to repeat.

In view of the aforesaid, and apart from varying cooking methods and use of condiments, I've found Australian lamb to be tastier (sweeter), leaner, juicier and most tender compared to commercially available lamb raised in other parts of the import/export world, including, not all, but many U.S. grown herds. New Zealand Lamb is also on the favorable list. To begin with, favoring Australian lamb stems from traditional care of herds, their free-ranged environment - foraging in large pastures on rye and clover, no growth hormone, antibiotic, or stimulants, therefore produces mildest, natural flavor. Australian and New Zealand lamb have lower meat-to-bone proportion in that of racks of lamb because of regarded maturity at 6-months, rather than the typical 9-12 months for domestic lamb - this extended growth period obviously is the principle reason older lamb yields higher meat-to-bone proportion (larger chops) but, lamb at 3-6 months yield leaner, milder tasting lamb and uncompromised tenderness.

Generally, quality Australian lamb is vacuum packaged to retain freshness, shipped fresh and usually displayed fresh. Although New Zealand's lamb rearing and processing principles and conditions are similar, and based on personal experience, it is mostly displayed in frozen form in some US supermarkets. On the other hand, fresh lamb displayed in a marketplace usually means this place most likely sells its current stock of lamb before reaching the "sell by"-"freeze by" dates. And, requisitioning to replenish stock is generally based on estimated-calculated sales volume per week. However, if lamb is not sold by the "sell-by" date, freezing the product before that date would be the necessary action, or remove the product from the shelf. If the "sell by" date was still indicated on the frozen product and displayed on the shelf, the "sell by" date can be used to estimate how long this product has been frozen. Then, an informed decision can be made to purchase or not to purchase.

Flavor and texture in different breeds, such as Suffolk, Hampshire, Dorset, Columbia or Texel, to name a few - flavor can vary even when two animals of the same breed are fed different diets. Simple factors to consider when purchasing lamb, "Free-range (means plenty of acreage to roam), diet (chemical free) and age (6 months or less). Flavor of one lamb fed with clover and grasses tastes different than another lamb of the same breed feeding on sage, even when following an identical cooking recipe. Texture will vary depending on breed and maturity.

Lamb over 12 months of age is classified as sheep and over 24 months its classification changes to mutton. The meat of older animals is generally tougher with stronger flavor, which is great for making mutton stew. But, knowing it is mutton at the time of purchase is helpful in determining the best cooking method and choosing spices, fruits, sauces and accompaniments that best off-set potential gamy taste and bring flavor into pleasurable balance.

Considerations: Is roaming restricted, verses basically unrestricted free-range; adverse conditions in roaming area and limited grazing-foraging possibilities verses clean roaming area, plentiful grazing-foraging opportunities, and un-stressful environment along with proper handling, packaging, storing, transporting, receiving, storing, preparation and cooking.

For the most part, Australia hasn't entirely strayed away from Organic farming to my knowledge and most of Europe still farms organically. Because organic farming hasn't diminished, pastures there don't need to convert to organic to be certified organic. Instead, they are merely re-certified that organic practices remain within the originally established organic guidelines. Nature's way as it's always been and such conditions should still exist everywhere today, in my opinion. Demand is one thing but reducing quality or modifying nature in meeting demands is unjustifiable and in my opinion unhealthy and wrong. Seasonal is natural and was meant for a purpose.

There are, however, domestic producers of superior, free-range lamb – for example, a lamb herd on a ranch in Utah forages on wild flowers, aspen groves and fed on a blend of corn, alfalfa and all natural grains that never contain animal by-products and their stress level is zero. Another in Colorado feeds their lamb similar grains as well as non-use of growth hormones, therapeutic-hormones or antibiotics. So, there really are domestic sources available that provide excellent natural, lamb. And, choices really are up to the consumer or purchaser of any product, provided the information they use in formulating a decision to purchase or not to purchase is comprehensive enough to make decisions suiting their expectations.

Although not all inclusive, the following information may be of some help to consumers who would like to know more about the product (lamb or any other animal products or by-products for that matter) they have become interested in purchasing: Simply ask supply sources questions, initiating your consumer right in evaluating whether or not you wish to purchase a product based on responses to your questions.

The following are suggested questions to ask providers that may, or may not be, of concern to some consumers but for those who are: Ask where the lamb, or animal product, was grown and processed? What were the grazing conditions for the life of the lamb, free-range or penned? There are differing degrees of free-range verses penned animals – so how much space did the animals have to roam? What did the animal's (diet) food source or foraging area offer during the period of the animal's life, such as: was it fed natural grain, commercially processed grain or meal with additives (a term used very loosely), were growth hormones, steroids (pharmaceuticals) added, or were they fed naturally on grass, clover, sage, wild flowers and other natural mild to strong forage normally found in a free-range environment, taking into account what its winter feed consisted of when clover and the like are not available on the range during winter months. The more information you want to know, inspires the resource provider to find out more about products they are selling.

Was the animal cleaned and tested for disease before slaughter? Are conditions humanely applied before slaughter to keep the animal's stress level as low as possible? How it is slaughtered and how cleanly is it handled from the point of slaughter to the butcher's table? How clean are slaughterhouse conditions, including work habits of people handling and processing products? How clean is the meat packaging plant? Has the meat ever been frozen? If so, the package label should state, "previously frozen" and any other conditions and pertinent information.

But, we as consumers can set product quality standards in the marketplace simply by demanding and buying quality rather than settling for less and possibly paying a little more for it. Ask yourself, what level of product quality are you satisfied with? Are you buying on quality or price? The more in-depth questions you ask, the wiser you become and the better your product will become

- this develops in the form of higher quality products in tune with higher customer satisfaction, <u>based on demand</u>. Get to know more about lamb, it's wonderful, domestic or otherwise - people love it when it's reared, fed, processed, stored, handled and cooked right - naturally.

LAMB with APRICOTS and DATES

Serves: 4 - 6

2 pounds lean, boneless lamb, cubed
2 garlic cloves, minced
½ cup fresh orange juice
4 tablespoons extra virgin olive oil
2 tablespoons parsley, freshly chopped
2 tablespoons mint leaves, freshly chopped
2 teaspoons ground cumin
¼ teaspoon nutmeg, freshly grated
¼ teaspoon ground cinnamon
1 large onion, thinly sliced

1 cup dried apricots, covered and marinated in spring or filtered water overnight - reserve water
½ cup pitted dried dates, coarsely chopped
2 cups vegetable stock or spring water
1-2 teaspoon sea salt
¼ teaspoon pepper, freshly ground

In a large shallow glass dish, mix lamb with garlic, orange juice, 2 tablespoons oil and the herbs and spices. Cover with plastic wrap and refrigerate overnight, stirring occasionally. Drain lamb – reserve marinade.

Heat remaining 2 tablespoons of oil in a large heavy saucepan, add onions and cook over medium heat for 5-minutes. Remove onions and reserve.

Place lamb in saucepan and quickly brown it over medium-high heat on all sides, stirring occasionally.

Add reserved marinade, apricots and reserved soaking liquid, dates, stock or water - add reserved onions, 1-teaspoon salt and the pepper.

Bring to a boil, cover and cook on medium-low heat for 1-hour or until lamb is very tender.

Uncover near the end of cooking time to allow some liquid to evaporate and the sauce to slightly thicken, about 10-15 minutes beforehand, and season with salt and pepper, if needed. Serve over white or brown basmati rice. See Index.

Enjoy!

LAMB MEATBALLS
In
YOGURT-CARDAMOM SAUCE
"Signature"

"Cooking with Erika"
Created for and demonstrated this on local, weekly TV segment,
aired May 3, 2001

Serves: 4

MEATBALLS

1 pound of ground lamb
1 teaspoon fresh ginger root, peeled and minced
1 teaspoon of garlic, minced
1 teaspoon Garam Masala (Avail. middle-Eastern markets)
1 teaspoon of sea salt
½ teaspoon chili powder
1 medium onion, finely chopped
1 fresh green chili, finely chopped
Fresh cilantro leaves
1 tablespoon of gram flour (Avail. middle-Eastern markets)
¼cup of peanut oil or grape seed oil

Place lamb in a large mixing bowl. Add ginger, garlic, Garam Masala, salt, chili powder, onion, green chili, cilantro, the gram flour, and mix well with a fork.

Don food service gloves and using hands shape small meatballs out of the mixture and set aside.

In a large skillet, heat oil over medium-high heat and fry meatballs turning occasionally for 8-10 minutes or until golden. Transfer meatballs to a warm serving platter, cover and keep warm. Meanwhile, prepare sauce.

YOGURT-CARDAMOM SAUCE

2 tablespoons grape seed oil
3 medium onions, finely chopped
2 small cinnamon sticks
2 large black, or green, cardamom, finely ground (Avail. middle-Eastern food markets)
1 teaspoon fresh ginger root, peeled and finely chopped
1 teaspoon of garlic, minced
1 teaspoon of sea salt
4½ tablespoons of unsweetened whole milk yogurt, drained (Drain overnight in a fine strainer, refrigerated – discard liquid)
2/3 cup of water
Fresh cilantro leaves, finely chopped for garnish
1 fresh green chili, finely chopped

In a medium saucepan, heat oil over medium-high heat and sauté onions until golden brown. Add cinnamon sticks and cardamom to the pan, lower heat and stir-fry 5 more minutes. Add ginger, garlic, salt, yogurt and water, and stir to mix well. Remove cinnamon sticks and discard. Transfer sauce to a serving bowl and garnish with chopped cilantro and chilies. Enjoy sauce over meatballs with basmati rice and tomato wedges.

APRICOT-ALMOND LAMB STEW

Serves: 6

2 pounds boneless lamb or mutton, trim
any excess fat, cut meat into ¾ inch cubes
1 teaspoon of sea salt
2 tablespoons grape seed oil
1/3 cup blanched whole almonds
¼ cup sugar
1 cinnamon stick, 3-inch stick
1 cup of water
4 tablespoons fresh orange juice
1½ cups of pitted prunes, halved
1 cup dried apricots, coarsely chopped

Sprinkle lamb or mutton (see note) with salt - heat oil in a large saucepan over medium-high heat and add lamb or mutton in batches, stirring constantly, until lightly browned.

Turn heat to medium. Remove browned meat from pan. Add almonds, sugar and cinnamon stick to pan drippings, stirring constantly, add water and orange juice. Bring to a boil, while stirring add browned meat, cover and simmer on medium-low heat for about 1-hour or until meat is tender. Stir-in prunes and apricots 10-minutes before cooking time ends.

Remove cinnamon stick before serving. Serve with hot couscous or basmati rice.

Note: To tone down strong flavor of mutton, trim excess fat, use very little oil to brown it and then discard the oil. Use new oil (fats) to cook any onions or vegetables, for example. Middle Eastern countries often use ghee to brown meats and vegetables. Ghee (gee) is a form of clarified butter – pure unsalted butter fat, and because milk solids are allowed to brown ghee imparts a nutty-caramel-like flavor, plus it can be heated to high temperatures without burning. Adding dried or fresh fruits and nuts gives mutton dishes the finishing touches to yield sweeter, more pleasant flavor.

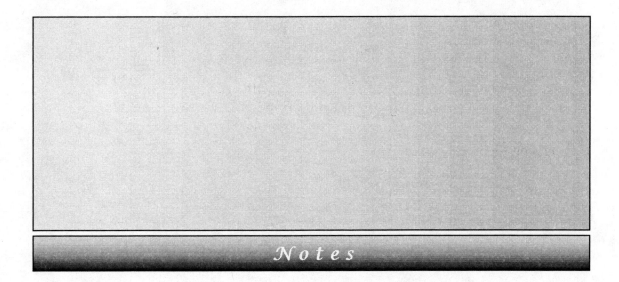

Notes

LAMB KABOB

Serves: 4-6

2¼ pounds of lean, boneless lamb, cut in 1-inch cubes
1 teaspoon of sea salt
½ teaspoon pepper, freshly ground
1 tablespoon of sweet paprika
2 teaspoons zahtar (See Note 2, below-avail. in specialty food stores)
2 red bell peppers, seeded, cut in large squares
2 large yellow bell peppers, seeded, cut into large squares, or
3 large tomatoes cut into wedges
2 medium, sweet onions and cut in thick slices
3-5 tablespoons extra virgin olive oil

Preheat grill or broiler

Season lamb with salt, pepper, paprika and zahtar then slide alternating pieces of seasoned lamb, red peppers tomatoes and onion onto skewers until all ingredients are used. Brush kabobs lightly with oil, grill or broil 15-20 minutes - turning occasionally. Arrange cooked kabobs on a warm serving dish and serve with basmati rice.

Note 1: If using metal skewers, lightly brush each of them with oil. If using bamboo (wood) skewers, soak them in water for at least 30-minutes.

Note 2: Za'atar (Zatar or Zahtar) is a Middle Eastern spice. A blend of powdered herbs, including thyme, marjoram and sumac with salt added. Excellent flavoring sprinkled over breads, meats and vegetables.

Sweet Paprika, Lamb Kabobs

LAMB KORMA

Serves: 6

6 dried red chilies
8 salted cashews
2 medium onions, peeled, chopped
2 garlic cloves, finely chopped
2 teaspoons fresh ginger root, peeled, finely chopped
Water
½ teaspoon ground cumin
2 teaspoons ground coriander
¼ teaspoon ground cardamom
½ teaspoon ground cinnamon
¼ teaspoon ground cloves
½ teaspoon saffron threads
2 tablespoons grape seed oil
2½ pounds of lean, boneless lamb, cut in 1-inch cubes
2 teaspoons sea salt
½ cup plain yogurt (whole milk preferred) drained overnight in refrigerator, discard liquid
1 tablespoon of cilantro, chopped
1 tablespoon of parsley, chopped
2-3 tablespoons coconut (if desired), freshly grated

Using disposable gloves, break open chilies and remove seeds. In a blender or food processor, purée chilies, cashews and ½ of the onions, garlic, ginger root and 3 cups of water (bottled spring water, preferred). Add cumin, coriander, cardamom, cinnamon and cloves. Continue to purée until thick and smooth. In a small bowl, pour 1-2 teaspoon boiling water over saffron threads, set aside to soak.

Heat oil in a large saucepan over medium heat and add remaining onions, sauté until transparent. Stir-in puréed seasoning Cook until oil surfaces. Add 1/3 cup of water and cook until slightly reduced, stir-in lamb, saffron mixture, salt and yogurt. Cover and cook 1-hour or until meat is very tender, season with salt, if needed, and spoon into a large, warm serving dish, sprinkle with cilantro, parsley and coconut, if desired. Serve over hot basmati rice.

Extra TIP - ROASTED BELL PEPPERS

To roast peppers, use tongs held directly over a charcoal grill until all surfaces are evenly blackened, but avoid over-cooking. Remove from heat, rinse under cold running water, peel or scrape off charred skin. Discard skin, seeds and the whitish membranes. Cut peppers into strips, place in a glass dish, cover and refrigerate until ready to use.

Note: If using an electric range, preheat the broiler. Arrange peppers on a cookie sheet and broil until charred on all sides, about 25 minutes, turning every 5 minutes or so. Peel, seed and cut into strips – for use in your preparation.

LAMBURGER – My style
With
MASHED PURPLE POTATOES
"Signature"

Serves: 6

1/3 cup bulgar wheat, (Avail. supermarkets and nutrition shops)
1-2 teaspoons extra virgin olive oil
1½ pounds of ground lamb
1 large sweet onion, peeled, finely chopped
3 cloves of garlic peeled, finely chopped
½ teaspoon of ground cumin
½ teaspoon sweet paprika
1 large egg
½ cup of fresh flat leaf parsley, finely chopped
¼ cup of whole milk yogurt, drained overnight in the refrigerator, discard liquid
1½ teaspoons sea salt
1 teaspoon pepper, freshly ground

Pour 1¼ cups of hot water over bulgar wheat in a medium bowl and let it stand for 15-minutes – drain in a sieve and squeeze out excess moisture and let bulgar cool.

Place bulgar in a large bowl and add the lamb, onion, garlic, cumin, paprika, egg, parsley, yogurt, and salt and pepper. Mix ingredients thoroughly by hand and form the mixture into 6 lamb burgers.

Heat a heavy, large skillet over medium-high heat, add oil, and when hot, add burgers. Cook burgers for about 6-minutes per side or until just cooked at the center. Transfer cooked lamb burgers to warm serving plates, serve with purple mashed potatoes (see recipe on Page 221) and enjoy with your favorite vegetables.

<u>Note:</u> As an alternative to bulgar, use ¼ cup of wheat germ, available in nutrition stores. You can also include about 3-tablespoons of finely chopped mint leaves in the recipe if you wish.

Enjoy!

PORK TENDERLOIN
With
GIN-GORGONZOLA SAUCE-BASMATI RICE and FRESH SORREL
"Signature"

Serves: 4-6

PORK TENDERLOIN

¼ cup Dijon mustard
1 tablespoon of extra virgin olive oil, plus extra
1 tablespoon Gin
1 tablespoon of ground thyme
1 teaspoon unsalted butter
2¾-3 pounds of pork tenderloin
Sea salt
Pepper, freshly ground

Basmati rice, See Index

Preheat oven to 400°F

Lightly oil a medium-rimmed baking sheet, and whisk Dijon mustard, ½ tablespoon oil, 1-tablespoon gin, and thyme in a small bowl to blend. Heat remaining ½ tablespoon oil and 1-teaspoon butter in a large skillet over medium-high heat, sprinkle pork with salt and pepper and place pork in the skillet, sear – turning occasionally - until brown all over, about 8-10 minutes.

Transfer pork to prepared baking sheet, spoon pan dripping over pork and spread Dijon mustard mixture over all sides.

Roast pork until thermometer inserted into thickest part of meat registers 155°F, about 35-minutes. Remove from oven, cover with foil, and allow pork rest 10-minutes.

Photo on Pages 119 & 143 - Shows, pork medallions served with pasta, rather than rice, which also tastes great with the Gorgonzola Sauce. Sauce can be prepared while pork is roasting and resting. Also see another excellent pork medallion recipe on page 142.

GORGONZOLA SAUCE

1 tablespoon unsalted butter
1 teaspoon all-purpose flour
1 cup whipping cream
½ cup dry white wine
2 tablespoons gin
1 cup of Gorgonzola cheese, crumbled
3 cups basmati rice, cooked and kept warm
1 cup fresh sorrel, chopped

Preparing sauce: In a medium saucepan melt 1-tablespoon of butter, over medium heat, add flour - whisk 2-3 seconds, and gradually, whisk-in the cream and white wine. Boil until mixture is slightly thick, add gin, cook 1-minute whisking frequently, turn heat to low, add Gorgonzola, and whisk until cheese is melted and smooth. Keep warm.

To enjoy: Cut pork tenderloin into 1-inch thick slices - transfer to warmed plates, ladle some sauce over pork and serve with extra sauce in a sauce-boat, and the rice in a serving bowl sprinkled with sorrel. Enjoy it family style.

BAKED PORK CHOPS
With
PEAR BRANDY SAUCE and POTATO PURÉE
"Signature"

Serves: 4

1½ cups dry-plain breadcrumbs
1 teaspoon of sea salt
1 teaspoon pepper, freshly ground
1 tablespoon dried, rubbed sage
2 large eggs
1 tablespoon of fresh lemon juice
1 tablespoon of fresh limejuice
¼ cup all-purpose flour
4 bone-in center-cut pork loin chops, each about 1-inch thick
2 tablespoons unsalted butter
2 tablespoons light olive oil

Mix breadcrumbs with salt, pepper and sage in pie dish. Whisk eggs in a small bowl with lemon and limejuices to blend, and pour egg mixture into another pie plate. Place flour on a large plate, coat pork chops on both sides and shake-off excess flour. Dip both sides of chops into egg mixture and coat them on both sides with breadcrumb mixture.

Preheat oven to 360°F

Heat butter with oil in a heavy, large ovenproof skillet over medium-high heat, and add pork chops to the skillet and cook until golden brown, about 2-minutes per side. Transfer to oven and bake until chops are crisp on the outside and the meat thermometer inserted into pork registers 155°F, about 25-30 minutes.

Transfer pork chops to a serving platter and keep warm.

POTATO PURÉE

4 large Yukon gold potatoes, peeled, cut into 2-inch pieces
1 medium onion, peeled, chopped
½ teaspoon sea salt
2 tablespoons unsalted butter
1 tablespoon of sour cream
Sea salt
Pepper, freshly ground
1 tablespoon fresh parsley, chopped

Cook potatoes and onion in a large pot of boiling, salted water until very tender, about 30-minutes. Drain well. Transfer cooked potatoes to a large-warmed bowl, add butter, sour cream and whip until light and fluffy, season with salt and pepper, and stir-in parsley.

PEAR BRANDY SAUCE

1 tablespoon unsalted butter
¼ cup shallots, peeled, chopped
¼ teaspoon sugar
3 large pears, peeled, cored, chopped
¼ cup brandy
1/3 cup Late Harvest Riesling wine
1 cup whipping cream
Sea salt
Pepper, freshly ground
½ teaspoon Mrs. Dash original seasoning
1 tablespoon watercress leaves, chopped
Lemon and lime wedges, for garnish

Melt butter in a medium saucepan over medium heat - add shallots and sugar, and sauté until shallots are soft, about

1-minute. Add pears, cook 3-minutes, stir-in the brandy, wine, and cream. Simmer until flavors blend and sauce thickens slightly, stirring frequently, about 10-minutes.

Season with salt and pepper and add Mrs. Dash seasoning. Stir in the watercress, and keep warm until ready to serve.

Arrange pork chops on warmed serving plates, spoon potato purée along side of pork chops, and then spoon the pear sauce over each pork chop. Garnish with lemon-lime wedges. Enjoy with a glass of your favorite Dry Riesling.

Note: Cook potatoes, and make sauce, while pork chops bake.

YUGOSLAVIAN STYLE VEAL-PORK KABOBS

Serves: 6

1 pound of boneless veal and cut in 1-inch cubes
1 pound lean boneless pork, cut into 1-inch cubes
2 medium, sweet onions and cut into thin rings
6 tablespoons extra virgin olive oil, plus extra
1 teaspoon of sea salt
1 teaspoon of sweet paprika
2 garlic cloves, minced
Tomato wedges, for garnish

Place veal, pork and onions in a large bowl. In a small bowl, combine oil, salt, paprika and garlic - pour oil mixture over meat and onions and toss to combine. Cover with plastic wrap and refrigerate at least 6-hours, stirring occasionally.

Discard onion rings and oil mixture. Thread marinated meat onto 6 metal skewers. Grill or broil until browned and crisp, turning frequently. Serve with tomato wedges.

Note: If using bamboo (wood) skewers, soak in water for at least 30-minutes. Lightly brush metal skewers with oil.

ONION and BACON TARTLETS
With
SPINACH SALAD
"Signature"

Makes 12 servings

CRUST

3 cups all-purpose flour, plus extra
1 teaspoon of sea salt
1 cup of unsalted butter (2-sticks) chilled, cut into ½-inch pieces
6 tablespoons (or more) ice water

FILLING

8 ounces bacon, cut crosswise into ¼-inch strips, or pancetta
1½ pounds onions, chopped
2 tablespoons unsalted butter
3 tablespoons, plus 2-teaspoons all-purpose flour
1¼ cups whole milk
3 large egg yolks
½ teaspoon sea salt
½ teaspoon pepper, freshly ground
1 teaspoon of sweet paprika
1 tablespoon of sour cream
4 tablespoons fresh parsley, finely chopped

4 tablespoons Parmesan cheese, freshly grated

Prepare filling: In a large saucepan, sauté bacon, or pancetta, over medium heat until brown, about 3-5 minutes. Discard all but 2-tablespoons of bacon dripping. Add onions to bacon and sauté until softened, about 5-minutes, remove from heat and let cool.

Blend flour, and salt in a food processor, add butter and pulse until mixture resembles coarse meal. Add 6-tablespoons water and process using pulse until mixture forms moist clumps, adding more water by teaspoonfuls if too dry. Gather dough into a ball-shape and hand roll into a log. Wrap in plastic and chill 1-hour.

Lightly spray, with cooking spray, the sides and bottoms of each of twelve, 4-inch, tartlet spring-form pans with removable bottoms, and set aside. _(Pans are available at most kitchen stores.)_

Cut dough crosswise into 12-equal slices. Rollout each slice on a lightly floured surface to a 6-inch round. Transfer each round to tartlet pan. Press dough onto prepared bottom and up the sides of pan. Trim-off excess dough, pierce bottom with a fork, and refrigerate 10-minutes.

Melt butter in a medium saucepan over medium-low heat, stir in flour and cook 2-minutes (do not brown). Gradually whisk-in milk, and increase heat to medium and cook 2-minutes, whisking constantly. Remove from heat, let cool. Whisk yolks in a large bowl to blend, gradually whisking-in cooled sauce. Mix-in bacon-onion mixture, salt, pepper, paprika, sour cream, parsley and cheese

Preheat oven to 350°F

Spoon filling, about ¼ cup, into each prepared tartlet. Bake until tops begin to brown, about 25-35 minutes. Transfer tartlets to racks and cool slightly before removing from pans.

SPINACH SALAD

12 cups baby spinach leaves, washed, dried thoroughly and transferred to a large glass bowl.

Prepare salad: In a small bowl, mix together 8-tablespoons of extra virgin olive oil, 8-tablespoons white balsamic vinegar, 1-teaspoon salt, 1-teaspoon of pepper, pinch of sugar, 8-tablespoons chopped sweet onions, and 6-tablespoons of chopped fresh parsley. Spoon dressing over spinach and toss lightly.

Place baked tartlets on serving plates and arrange spinach salad alongside tartlets. Enjoy with your favorite chilled crisp white wine.

NOTES:

Notes

ROAST PORK LOIN
Stuffed with
SPINACH, RED BELL PEPPERS and SWEET ONIONS

Serves: 6-8

STUFFING

10 ounces of fresh baby spinach, washed, drained, coarsely chopped
1 large sweet onion, peeled, chopped
2 cloves garlic, peeled, chopped
2 medium red bell peppers, seeded and coarsely chopped
¼ cup fresh Italian parsley, chopped
1 pound oyster mushrooms, cleaned, trimmed, coarsely chopped
1½ cups fresh breadcrumbs
1½ teaspoons sea salt
½ teaspoon sweet paprika
1½ teaspoons black pepper, freshly ground
6 tablespoons of gin
¼ cup extra virgin olive oil
3-4 pounds center cut, boneless pork loin roast, butterflied, _(see Notes 2-3, below)_
Kitchen string

To prepare stuffing: In a large bowl, combine spinach, onions, garlic, peppers, parsley, mushrooms and breadcrumb – mix-in ½ teaspoon of salt, paprika, 1 teaspoon of pepper and 2 tablespoons of gin – set aside.

Preheat oven to 400°F

To butterfly pork: Cut through pork loin lengthwise, to about 1 inch of other side, avoid cutting it in half entirely, lay it out flat, like an open book, on a large sheet of plastic wrap to enclose meat entirely – preventing splatter. With a meat mallet, pound to flatten pork as much as possible, sprinkle with remaining salt and pepper. Spread on the stuffing end to end in an even layer leaving a 2-inch border along the top edge of the lengthiest side. Fold to overlap sides to close and secure with kitchen string to seal in stuffing.

Transfer pork to a flameproof roasting pan, brush pork with olive oil, sprinkle remaining gin over roast, and roast pork on the middle rack of oven for 15-minutes.

Reduce temperature to 325°F and continue roasting for about 1 – 1¼ hours more, or until an instant-read thermometer diagonally inserted at least 2-inches into meat registers 155 - 160ºF. Remove pork from oven and let it rest loosely covered with foil 10-15 minutes.

Transfer pork to a cutting board, cut off string and slice pork into ½-inch slices. Arrange pork slices on a preheated, large platter, spoon pan drippings over slices and enjoy with garlic-roasted potatoes, fresh green beans and carrots.

Note 1: To make sauce, strain pan drippings into a small clean saucepan, turn heat to medium-high and add ½ cup of dry white wine and cook 1-minute. Turn heat to medium-low, add 1-cup of whipping cream, cook 3-5 minutes and season with salt and pepper, if needed. Garnish with chopped watercress leaves or chopped parsley, if desired.

Note 2: Kitchen string, also known as, kitchen twine is available in kitchen supplies shops and some supermarkets.

Note 3: Butter-flying pork loin is probably the easiest method for a busy family to prepare loin roast for stuffing, rather than more complicated, time consuming methods like the spiral cut, which requires a lengthwise, shallow cut, beginning at the removed bone end of the loin to the other end angling the knife as though paring fruit and slicing inward parallel to the cutting surface to continue cutting and unrolling it until the loin is laid out flat to about 1-1½ inches thick.

Roast Pork Loin Stuffed with Spinach, Red Bell Peppers and Sweet Onions

Enjoy!

MEDALLIONS of PORK TENDERLOIN
With
YAKIMA VALLEY APPLES and WALLA WALLA ONIONS
"Signature"

Created for the Washington Fruit Commission and performed the cooking demonstration taped by Taiwanese International Television crews on June 23, 2000 for showing in their home country and several other Regional and International Countries. Also demonstrated this recipe during local, weekly TV segment "Cooking with Erika" promoting Yakima Valley Fruits.

Serves: 4-6

2½-3 pounds of pork tenderloin, crosscut into thick medallions
Sea salt
Pepper, freshly ground
4 teaspoons of ground cumin
4 tablespoons of unsalted butter
4 medium apples, such as golden or red delicious, peeled, cored and sliced
2 medium sweet onions, peeled, cut into thin rings
½ teaspoon of sugar
1 cup of white dry wine, such as Riesling
Sea salt
Pepper, freshly ground
¼ cup of fresh parsley, chopped

Lightly sprinkle the pork medallions on both sides with salt, pepper, plus 2 teaspoons of cumin.

Heat the butter over medium-high heat in a large skillet and sauté medallions in batches in hot sizzling butter on both sides until golden brown, about 6 minutes per side. Remove medallions from skillet and cover to keep warm.

Add apples, onions and sugar to skillet over medium heat, sauté apples and onions until soft and lightly browned, then add wine and the remaining 2 teaspoons of cumin, cook 1-2 minutes.

Season with salt and pepper, and return medallions to the apple onion mixture, cook 1-2 more minutes, turn off heat and stir in the parsley.

Spoon the apple-onion mixture onto warmed serving plates and arrange pork medallions on top of apple-onion mixture and enjoy with basmati rice.

Chef's variation: The apples-onions mixture is also excellent with pork chops. If 4-6 pork chops are used increase cooking time by 30-minutes, or cook until tender.

You may also want to add more apples and onions. Serve with basmati rice, see Index.

Medallions of Pork Tenderloin with pasta. See Tenderloin with Yakima Valley Apples and Walla Walla Onions, recipe on previous Page and a different recipe on Page 135.

PORK SCHNITZEL

Serves: 4

4 pork cutlets, boneless, 4 ounces each
1 teaspoon of sea salt
1 teaspoon pepper, freshly ground
1 teaspoon of paprika
2 eggs
2 tablespoons fresh lemon juice
1¼ cups of dry white breadcrumbs
3 tablespoons extra virgin olive oil
3 tablespoons unsalted butter

Place cutlets between 2-sheets of plastic wrap and pound them with a meat mallet to ¼ inch thickness and lightly sprinkle each with salt, pepper and paprika.

In a shallow bowl, beat together eggs and lemon juice. Dip cutlets in the egg mixture, drain any excess egg from the cutlet, and then coat cutlets with breadcrumbs pressing well with fingers to make crumbs stick.

Heat oil and butter in a large non-stick skillet and cook cutlets in batches for 5-6 minutes until golden brown on both sides. Drain on paper towels, cover and keep them warm. Repeat until all cutlets are cooked.

VEAL CUTLET with OVEN BAKED GRITS, ASPARAGUS TIPS and MUSHROOM-LATE HARVEST RIESLING SAUCE
"Signature"

Serves: 6

GRITS

2 cups of water
1 cup of whipping cream
1 teaspoon of sea salt
2 tablespoons unsalted butter
¾ cup of quick cooking grits
1 teaspoon pepper, freshly ground
½ pound white cheddar cheese, shredded
2 eggs, beaten slightly
Butter for greasing
Parsley for garnish

Preheat oven to 350°F

In a large saucepan, bring water and cream to a boil, and add salt, butter, grits and pepper. Turn heat to medium-low and cook until thick, stirring constantly. Turn off heat, stir in cheese, add eggs and stir rapidly. Pour grits mixture into a large well-buttered heatproof casserole dish. Bake 45 minutes or until set and golden brown. Garnish with parsley.

Note: Grits can be prepared one-day ahead and kept refrigerated for next day baking.

VEAL

6 oval ½-inch thick slices of veal, and cut from the upper leg
2 teaspoons of sea salt
1 teaspoon pepper, freshly ground
All-purpose flour for dusting
6 tablespoons unsalted butter

Prepare Veal: Pound veal, with a meat mallet, to 1/8-inch thickness, lightly sprinkle veal with salt and pepper and dust veal lightly with flour. In a large skillet, heat butter over medium-high heat until light golden. Place veal slices in skillet and quickly brown, about 3 minutes on each side. Reduce heat, cook for about 5 more minutes and transfer veal to a hot serving platter, cover with foil to keep warm.

Note: For best results use 2 skillets to avoid overcrowding cutlets, or sauté cutlets in 2 batches and use 3 tablespoons of butter for each skillet or for each batch.

MUSHROOM-RIESLING SAUCE

½ pound fresh oyster mushrooms, coarsely chopped, or button mushrooms thinly sliced
½ cup of Late Harvest Riesling wine
1 cup whipping cream
Fine sea salt
Pepper, freshly ground

Place mushrooms in the same skillet with the veal pan drippings, and over medium-high heat, sauté mushrooms until golden, about 3-5 minutes. Add wine and cook until the liquid is almost evaporated. Add cream, cook for 2 minutes, season lightly with salt and pepper. Keep warm.

ASPARAGUS

2 pounds of fresh asparagus tips
2 tablespoons of unsalted butter, melted
2 tablespoons of fresh Italian parsley, chopped
Lemon wedges for garnish

In lightly salted water, cook asparagus until just tender, about 2-3 minutes.

Drain and transfer to a shallow bowl, drizzle with 2 tablespoons of butter.

To serve: Place veal on a serving platter or dinner plates, spoon mushroom sauce over the veal, arrange asparagus tips around servings and garnish with parsley and lemon wedges. Enjoy with baked grits and your favorite Riesling wine.

Ossobuco is a specialty of Italy, this dish is best made using shank from the hind leg and the pieces should not be cut any thicker than suggested, to ensure tenderness.

Veal Ossobuco, see Recipe on next Page

VEAL OSSOBUCCO

Serves: 4

4 veal shanks, each 2 inches thick
1 cup all purpose flour seasoned with ½ teaspoon salt and ½ teaspoon freshly ground pepper
3 tablespoons extra virgin olive oil
2 tablespoons of unsalted butter
1 carrot, trimmed on both ends, peeled and sliced
1 stalk of celery, sliced
1 medium sweet onion, peeled, chopped
4 cloves of garlic, peeled, chopped
6 sun ripened red tomatoes, peeled, seeded and chopped
5 sun ripened yellow tomatoes, peeled and chopped
1½ cups of white wine, such as Pinot Grigio or dry Riesling
3½ cups of vegetable stock or water
Sea salt
Pepper, freshly ground

1 bouquet garni – wrap the green part of a small leek loosely around a bay leaf, a sprig of thyme, celery leaves and 3 stems of flat leaf parsley - tie with kitchen string, leaving a long tail of string for easy removal.

Preheat oven to 325°F

Trim meat, lightly coat it with the seasoned flour, and heat oil in a medium skillet over medium heat and brown veal on both sides, about 10-minutes and set aside.

Melt butter over medium heat in a flame proof casserole and cook the carrot, celery and onion for 3-5 minutes. Add garlic and mix well, add tomatoes and cook 5-minutes. Add wine, the browned veal, the stock or water and the bouquet garni, bring to a simmer, season with salt and pepper, cover and bake in a preheated oven for 1½ hours or until veal is tender. Transfer veal to a pre-warmed serving platter, cover with foil and keep warm.

Transfer cooking liquid and vegetables from casserole to a clean medium-size saucepan, discard bouquet garni and bring to a boil, skim off any fat or impurities that rise to the surface and cook for about 15-20 minutes on medium-low heat or until the sauce has thickened and coats the back of a spoon. Stir-in parsley, spoon sauce over veal and serve immediately with polenta or your favorite pasta.

Note: Pork shanks are a nice, less expensive alternative to veal, if preferred. Traditionally, in Italy, this dish is often flavored with orange or lemon zests, which may be added to this recipe if you wish. Citrus fruits claimed to be organic is recommended and thoroughly washed.

WHITE ASPARAGUS BÜTTELBORNER STYLE
With
WATERCRESS and PROSCIUTTO

Serves: 4-6

2-3 pounds fresh white asparagus
1/3 cup of unsalted butter, melted
White pepper, freshly ground
Nutmeg, freshly ground
½ cup watercress leaves, chopped, for garnish
1 cup Prosciutto or Westfälin (Westphalian) ham, coarsely chopped for garnish

Trim asparagus, cutting off woody ends and peeling stems, rinse well. Cook asparagus upright in a special asparagus kettle in salted water to which a pinch of sugar has been added.

Or another method would be to tie asparagus in equal serving bunches with 2 strands of soft string per bunch – to lift cooked asparagus out of the boiling water by snagging string with prongs of a fork without damaging the very tender tips.

Cook asparagus 12-15 minutes depending on size (thickness) and tenderness.

Cover a large plate with paper towel, place cooked asparagus on paper towel and let drain.

Cut string (if used), remove and discard.

Arrange asparagus on a large warmed serving dish, spoon warm, melted butter over asparagus, sprinkle with pepper and nutmeg, and garnish with watercress, prosciutto or Westphalian ham. Enjoy with a cool crisp white wine, such as Semillon, Chardonnay or dry Riesling.

Chef's note: White asparagus is a distinguished favorite in Germany, where much of its population is always looking forward to availability at markets beginning in April - traditionally lasting until June 24th, the feast of Saint John. Traditional accompaniments enjoyed with white asparagus in Germany almost always will be with melted butter, topped with chopped, hardboiled eggs, Westphalian ham and parsley potatoes. Or, with a delicate sauce, such as lemon or orange sauce, a hollandaise sauce topped with cooked shrimp, or with fresh cooked crab.

Also, white asparagus require a longer cooking time than does green asparagus.

DETERMINING QUALITY OF CHICKEN

Have you ever wondered why cuts and types of meat seem to differ in flavor and texture, or wondered why some chicken and some red meats do not brown easily when sautéed, seared, fried or roasted, or ever wondered why flavor of natural pan juices become diluted by the excessive amount of water released from cooked poultry or meat?

For those who don't know the answer to those questions and want to see results for themselves, I suggest performing this simple test: Buy two small packages of fresh boned, skinned chicken breasts - one labeled package containing organic, free-range, hormone-steroid free chicken, plus the other package containing natural; home grown; farm fresh; or makes no stipulation at all. If cost prohibitive purchasing both at the same time, although a least preferred option, then buy one or the other at different shopping times - to spread out the cost, and most importantly, make notes during the cooking process of each specimen based on the process below. Repeat process with the other package whenever you shop again for chicken, note results and compare findings as indicated below.

The testing process: After washing and paper towel drying one (or all) piece of chicken (select similar size piece for testing) from each container and using separate, but identical saucepans, oil, utensils, methods, temperature and procedures, cook chicken simultaneously the same duration until desired doneness. Compare the amount of pan juice in each pan by pouring juices in separate heatproof containers and setting them aside. If juice (water) yield is greater from the non-organic chicken then the results of your test so far, match mine.

Next, compare brownness; the non-organic chicken is more likely to be much lighter in color, and doneness most likely will take longer than the organic chicken. The organic chicken should be golden brown, in less time, using the same cooking conditions. Next, use a very sharp knife to crosscut a bite-size end or middle piece from each breast noting which of the two pieces kind of separate into lengthwise strands (or strings) of meat while cutting. Strands most likely will be the affect of the non-organic piece - while the organic piece stays together and slices look neat, - but continue on with your own testing. Next, test bite each comparing texture and flavor. Make note of which piece of chicken taste pasty and didn't pick up much, if any flavor, from the added flavor enhancing ingredients, and which piece has firmer texture, is juicier and more flavorful. Different brands will have slightly different results, for example, some will yield more water content than others, but the difference between the two types of chicken suggested to use in conducting your own test, will be readily noticeable. Note which type of chicken you would prefer as being healthiest and tastiest for serving to your family and friends. See the difference: Visit: www.smart chicken.com. If you don't see it in your favorite grocery store, ask for it.

Herbed, Oven Roasted Chicken, Page 160

POULTRY

Lemon Chicken Schnitzel with Orzo Pasta, Page 156

Above – Chicken Scaloppina with Eggplant, Page 155

Oven Roasted Game (Guinea) Hen, Page 168

RIESLING CHICKEN
"Signature"

Serves: 4

4 chicken breast halves, boned, skinned
Sea salt
White pepper, freshly ground
3 tablespoons unsalted butter
4 tablespoons cognac
1½ pounds button mushrooms, thinly sliced
2 medium onions, such as Walla-Walla sweets, finely chopped
2 cups of Late Harvest Riesling wine
1 cup whipping cream
2 tablespoons estragon, chopped
2 tablespoons of fresh parsley, chopped

Rinse chicken under cold running water, pat dry with paper towels. Lightly sprinkle chicken pieces with salt and pepper.

Heat 2 tablespoons of butter in a large skillet over medium-high heat and add chicken, sauté until lightly browned on both sides, about 4 minutes per side.

Add brandy and cautiously ignite with a match - to flambé, if desired. Otherwise, just add brandy and proceed with recipe.

Precautionary note: Flambé must be performed by responsible adults only. The very least precaution, in case of emergency, keep a saucepan lid at hand to cover skillet to douse flames if necessary. And, it's recommended to refrain from flambéing in the presence of children. A certified, working condition, fire extinguisher nearby in the kitchen is always cheap insurance.

Transfer chicken to a large warm platter, spoon pan drippings over chicken, cover with foil to keep warm.

Heat the remaining 1-tablespoon of butter in the same skillet, add mushrooms, and sauté over medium-high heat until light golden. Add onions and sauté 3-5 more minutes, stirring often. Add wine and cook 5-minutes on medium-low, add cream, cook 3-more minutes, season with salt and pepper - return chicken to skillet - simmer 2-3 more minutes. Stir-in estragon and parsley and serve with Rice or baby potatoes and green salad.

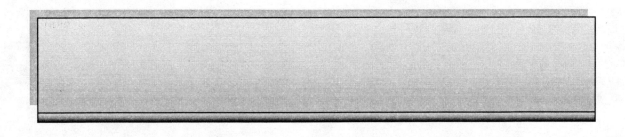

BREAST OF CHICKEN
With
BRANDIED CHERRIES
"Signature"

Created for the Washington Fruit Commission and performed cooking demonstration, taped by Taiwanese International Television Crews on June 23, 2000 to air on TV in their home country.

Serves: 4

2 tablespoons of extra virgin olive oil
1 tablespoon of unsalted butter
4 chicken breast halves, boned, skinned
Sea salt
Pepper, freshly ground
¼ cup shallots, chopped
2 teaspoons of cornstarch
1 cup whipping cream
½ pound fresh Bing cherries, pitted stems, removed, or
2 cups of canned or frozen, (no sugar added) unsweetened cherries, drained
2 tablespoons Port wine
1/3 cup of Brandy
Pinch of sugar

Rinse chicken under cold running water, pat dry with paper towels. Heat oil and butter in a nonstick large skillet over medium heat add chicken, sprinkle lightly with salt and pepper, cook chicken for 5-6 minutes per side or until golden brown on both sides.

Remove chicken, cover and keep warm - in the same skillet, sauté the shallots for 1-minute, or until they are soft.

In a small bowl, blend cornstarch with whipping cream, add to shallots, cook for 1 minute, and add cherries, port wine and brandy - cook 4 more minutes. Season with salt, pepper and sugar - return chicken to cherry sauce. Cook over medium-low heat for 1-2 minutes.

Transfer chicken to serving platter, spoon cherry sauce over chicken, pour remaining cherry sauce in a sauceboat and enjoy with basmati rice.

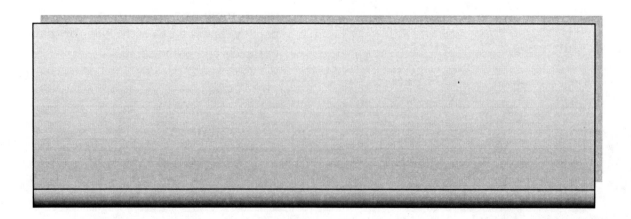

BREAST OF CHICKEN FLORENTINE
(My Version-1984)

Serves: 6

6 chicken breasts halves, boned, skinned
½ cup all-purpose flour
2 teaspoons of sea salt
½ teaspoon white pepper, freshly ground

3 eggs, beaten
½ cup Parmesan cheese, freshly grated
¾ cup plain-dry bread crumbs, preferably homemade, see Index
¾ cup unsalted butter
1 pound button mushrooms, sliced
¼ cup parsley, freshly chopped
2 tablespoons fresh lemon juice
Dash of nutmeg
Pinch of sugar
8 cups fresh baby spinach leaves
Sea salt
Pepper, freshly ground

Rinse chicken under cold running water and pat dry with paper towels and place the chicken between two sheets of plastic wrap. With a meat mallet, pound chicken on each side to ½ inch thick.

Mix together flour, salt and pepper. Dredge the chicken with seasoned flour - shake off excess flour, dip in egg, and combine cheese and breadcrumbs.

Coat with breadcrumb mixture and refrigerate at least 1-hour.

Heat ½ cup of butter in a large skillet over medium-high heat - turn heat to medium and brown chicken on each side, about 6-8 minutes per side.

Cook chicken in batches, allowing space between pieces.

Remove chicken from skillet, transfer to a warm platter and cover to keep warm.

Add mushrooms to drippings in skillet, sauté over medium-high heat until golden, about 5-6 minutes, and season mushrooms with salt and pepper, if needed. Turn heat to low, stir in the parsley and keep warm.

Melt remaining ¼ cup butter in a large saucepan over medium-low heat, add lemon juice, nutmeg, and sugar - add spinach and season with salt and pepper - toss lightly. Arrange chicken on a bed of spinach, topped with mushrooms and enjoy with your favorite dry white wine.

BREAST OF CHICKEN in PEANUT CURRY SAUCE
With
BLACK THAI RICE
"Signature"

Created for and demonstrated this on local, weekly TV segment, aired during year 2001

Serves: 4

CHICKEN

4 chicken breast halves, boned-skinned
1½ teaspoons of sea salt
½ teaspoon of pepper
1 tablespoon of extra virgin olive oil
1 tablespoon of unsalted butter

SAUCE

1 tablespoon of hot curry paste or powder
1 teaspoon of garlic, minced
1 cup canned coconut milk (refrigerate the coconut milk overnight in the can and when ready to use, remove without shaking it and use the thickest cream on top)
2 tablespoons creamy peanut butter, preferably organic
Sea Salt, to taste
Pinch of sugar
½ cup coarsely chopped unsalted cashew nuts
1 teaspoon chopped fresh mint or basil leaves for garnish

BLACK SWEET THAI RICE

Yields 2 cups

1 cup of black rice, rinsed well
1½ cups of water
1 tablespoon of unsalted butter or extra virgin olive oil
¼ teaspoon of sea salt

Preparing rice: Bring water to a boil in a medium saucepan, add the rice and simmer it covered over low heat for 25- minutes. Remove from heat, add butter or oil and salt, let stand 10 minutes and fluff with fork. Keep warm. *Note: If Tai rice is not available, substitute with wild rice and cook according to package instructions.*

Preparing chicken: Rinse chicken under cold running water, pat it dry with paper towels, cut chicken into strips, and salt and pepper strips. Heat oil and butter in a large skillet over medium heat, add chicken stirring until browned evenly and cooked through, about 6-8 minutes.

Transfer chicken strips to a large platter, cover and keep warm.

Preparing sauce: In the same skillet over medium-low heat, add curry paste or powder stirring with a wooden spoon to prevent sticking, about 1-minute. Add garlic, cream of coconut milk and then stir-in the peanut butter. Cook and stir to get a smooth uniform consistency for about 1-2 minutes, season with salt and sugar stirring-in the cashew nuts. Return chicken to the skillet and simmer over low heat until heated through, about 2 minutes. *To serve:* Mound rice in the middle of a large platter and arrange chicken strips around rice, and spoon sauce alongside chicken strips. Sprinkle with mint or basil leaves. Enjoy with your favorite Chardonnay!

CHICKEN SCALOPPINA
With
EGGPLANT

"Cooking with Erika"
Created for and demonstrated this on local, weekly TV segment, aired during year 2001

Serves: 6

1 eggplant, cut into 6 thin slices, lengthwise
2-4 tablespoons extra virgin olive oil
Sea salt
Pepper, freshly ground

6 small chicken breasts, boned, skinned and pounded
½ cup all-purpose flour, for dredging
2 tablespoons of unsalted butter
2 tablespoons of extra virgin olive oil
6 thin slices of whole milk mozzarella
3 large tomatoes, peeled, seeded and chopped
Sea salt
Pepper, freshly ground
½ teaspoon fresh oregano, chopped
½ teaspoon fresh basil, chopped

Brush eggplant slices on both sides with oil and lightly sprinkle with salt and pepper.

Cook eggplant on a hot grill or a ridged steak pan until browned on both sides, turning once. Transfer eggplant to a warmed plate.

Rinse chicken under cold running water, pat dry with paper towels. Dredge chicken in flour and shake off excess.

Melt 2-tablespoons of butter with 1 tablespoon of olive oil in a wide skillet over medium heat and cook chicken in batches.

Cook chicken 3-minutes on one side, turn, season with salt and pepper, and cook 3 more minutes.

Place 1 eggplant slice on each piece of chicken, top with 1 slice of mozzarella, turn heat to medium-low, cover with lid and cook until mozzarella is melted, about 1-2 minutes.

Meanwhile, heat remaining 1 tablespoon of olive oil in another skillet over medium-high heat, add tomatoes, salt and pepper to taste, stir in oregano and basil, cook 3-5 minutes, spoon over chicken and enjoy.

<u>Chef's note:</u> To pound, place chicken breast between 2 sheets of wax paper or plastic wrap, and starting at the thickest part of the breast - pound each side with the smooth side of a meat mallet to flatten to a thickness of about ¼ inch.

LEMON CHICKEN SCHNITZEL

Serves: 4

4 boneless skinless chicken breasts
Sea salt
Mélange peppercorn, freshly ground
2 large eggs
1 tablespoons lemon juice, freshly squeezed
1½ cups fine dry breadcrumbs
3-4 tablespoons of extra virgin olive oil
2 tablespoons unsalted butter
4 tablespoons lemon juice, freshly squeezed
Lemon wedges, for garnish

Pound chicken breasts lightly on both sides between sheets of plastic wrap. Sprinkle each piece of chicken lightly with salt and pepper. In a shallow dish, beat eggs with 1-tablespoon of lemon juice. Dip each piece of chicken in egg mixture, coat with bread crumbs and heat oil and butter in a large skillet over medium-high heat – turn heat to medium – fry chicken until golden brown on both sides, about 5-6 minutes per side. Transfer chicken schnitzel to a pre warmed large platter, cover loosely with foil and set aside. Add 4 tablespoons of lemon juice to pan drippings, cook 2-3 seconds over medium-low heat, drizzle 2-3 teaspoons of pan drippings over each schnitzel, garnish with lemon wedges and serve with orzo pasta, potato salad, green asparagus, peas or carrots.

Lemon -
Chicken
Schnitzel

SAUTÉED BREAST of CHICKEN
With
GOLDEN CAVIAR-VODKA SAUCE
"Signature"

Serves: 4

CHICKEN

4 chicken breast halves, boned, skinned
Sea salt
Pepper, freshly ground
2 tablespoons of unsalted butter

SAUCE

1 tablespoon of shallots, chopped
Pinch of sugar
1 cup of whipping cream
1/3 cup of vodka
1 teaspoon Mrs. Dash original seasoning
Sea salt
Pepper, freshly ground
1/3 cup of golden caviar (Avail.
supermarkets and fish markets)
1/3 cup of fresh watercress, chopped

Preparing chicken: Rinse chicken under cold running water, pat it dry with paper towels, and sprinkle chicken with salt and pepper. Heat butter in a heavy large skillet over medium high heat. Add chicken and cook for 6-8 minutes each side or until cooked through.

Transfer chicken to a warmed platter and cover with foil to keep warm.

Preparing sauce: Add shallots to skillet and sauté until tender. Add sugar, stir in cream and vodka, and bring to a slow boil.

Reduce heat and cook over medium-low heat, about 10 minutes. Add Mrs. Dash and season to taste with salt and pepper.

Return chicken to skillet and heat through. Place chicken breasts on 4 pre-warmed plates, spoon sauce over the chicken, and spoon 1-teaspoon of caviar over each chicken breast, and sprinkle with watercress.

Enjoy with crusty French bread, spinach salad or basmati rice.

ROMANTIC MENU FOR TWO

INDIAN-STYLE CHICKEN with BASMATI RICE

GREEN SALAD with LEMON-HONEY DRESSING

FRUIT COMPOTE with ORANGE COINTREAU

Serves: 2

INDIAN-STYLE BREAST OF CHICKEN with BASMATI RICE

1 tablespoon of extra virgin olive oil
2 medium chicken breast halves, boned and skinned
Sea salt
Pepper, freshly ground
1 small onion, chopped
½ cup dry white wine
1 small apple, peeled, cored and grated
½ teaspoon ginger root, peeled, grated
1 tablespoon of mild curry powder
½ cup heavy cream
½ banana, sliced
Sea salt
Pepper, freshly ground
1 tablespoon of parsley, chopped
1½ cups of basmati rice, cooked and kept warm (See Recipe Index)

Rinse chicken under cold running water, pat dry with paper towel. Heat oil in a medium-size skillet over medium-high heat, sprinkle chicken with salt and pepper, add chicken to hot skillet and sauté until golden brown on each side, about 6-8 minutes per side. Transfer chicken to a warm plate, cover with foil to keep warm, set aside. Add onion to skillet, and sauté until soft about 1-2 minutes, add wine, and cook on medium-low heat 5-more minutes.

Add grated apple, ginger, curry powder, and cream, stir occasionally and cook 2-more minutes. Add banana slices, season with salt and pepper, stir-in parsley, return cooked chicken breasts to skillet and simmer on low heat for about 1-2 minutes to heat chicken through. Keep warm.

SALAD & DRESSING

4 tablespoons fresh lemon juice
1 tablespoon of honey
1 teaspoon fresh parsley, minced
1 teaspoon fresh dill, minced
1 teaspoon fresh chives, minced
Sea salt
Pepper, freshly ground
1 small head of butter lettuce, trimmed, washed and torn into small pieces

In a small bowl, mix together lemon juice, honey, parsley, dill, and chives, season with salt and pepper. Dressing can be made ahead and chilled until ready to use. Divide lettuce onto two salad plates, and drizzle the dressing over lettuce.

FRUIT COMPOTE

1 medium banana, peeled and sliced
1 ripe peach, peeled, halved, pitted and sliced
2 kiwi, peeled and sliced
1 tablespoon of fresh lemon juice
2 tablespoons Orange Cointreau
2 tablespoons honey
1 tablespoon fresh mint, minced
4 tablespoons sweetened whipping cream

Place banana, peach and kiwi in a small glass bowl, drizzle with lemon juice, Orange Liqueur and honey. Sprinkle with mint, toss gently, divide between two dessert plates, and top each with whipped cream and refrigerate until ready to enjoy.

Arrange chicken breast on warmed serving plates, top chicken with sauce and spoon rice alongside of chicken. Enjoy this fabulous menu with your favorite crisp white wine.

SWEET SHERRY MARINATED CHICKEN CUBES
With
SPANISH RICE

Serves: 4-6

¼ cup Spanish olive oil, plus 2 tablespoons
1 cup of sweet Spanish sherry
2 cloves garlic, minced
½ teaspoon ground cumin
½ teaspoon ground coriander
½ teaspoon hot paprika
¼ cup parsley, freshly chopped
1 teaspoon of sea salt
½ teaspoon pepper, freshly ground

Combine above ingredients in a large glass bowl.

2 pounds boneless, skinless chicken breast, cut into small cubes, about ¼ inch

Rinse chicken under cold running water, pat dry with paper towels. Add chicken to combined ingredients, toss to coat, cover with plastic wrap and refrigerate for 6-hours or overnight.

Remove chicken with slotted spoon and transfer to a shallow dish. Discard marinade. Heat remaining 2 tablespoons olive oil in a large skillet over medium-high heat. Add chicken in batches and cook until chicken is golden brown, about 6-minutes. Transfer to a pre-warmed shallow dish and serve with crusty French bread slices or with hot Spanish rice, see recipe below.

SPANISH RICE

3 cups cooked long grain rice, kept warm
2 tablespoons Spanish olive oil (Available at supermarkets internationally)
¼ teaspoon ground saffron

Stir oil and saffron into hot rice, season with salt and pepper, if needed.

HERBED-OVEN ROASTED CHICKEN
"Signature"

"Cooking with Erika"
Created for and demonstrated this on weekly, local TV segment, aired during year 2001.

Serves: 4-5

1 whole 4½ pounds organic chicken, excess fat removed
Fine sea salt
Pepper, freshly ground
2 tablespoons unsalted butter, softened
2 garlic cloves
1 lemon, halved
1 lime, halved
1 cup of dry white wine
½ cup whipping cream
¼ cup fresh basil, chopped
¼ cup fresh Italian parsley, chopped
¼ cup fresh arugula, chopped

Preheat oven to 425°F

Rinse chicken, inside-out, under cold running water and pat dry with paper towel. Place chicken in roasting pan. Season chicken inside-out with salt and pepper, and rub butter into skin over entire chicken. Place garlic cloves, 1-half lemon and 1-lime halve in cavity, and squeeze juice of remaining lemon and lime halves over chicken, and loosely tie legs together to retain shape while roasting.

Roast chicken in middle of oven, 25-minutes. Baste chicken, reduce temperature to 350°F, basting at 7-minute intervals while continuing roasting for 35-45 more minutes, or until chicken is golden and thermometer inserted into fleshy part of a thigh registers 170°F – juices should run clear.

Transfer chicken to a platter, discard string and cover loosely with foil. Transfer pan juices to a small bowl, skim and discard any fat, strain juice into a medium saucepan, add wine and simmer until reduced by half. Stir-in cream, and simmer for 6-more minutes, season to taste with salt and pepper and stir-in fresh herbs.

Cut chicken (*see Note 1*) into serving pieces, spoon herb sauce over chicken and serve with Basmati rice.

Chef's note 1: Removing wishbone from chicken, turkey or any other fowl with full breasts makes carving and slicing easier. To do this, carefully slit neck skin and pull enough skin over the breast to expose the two-prong ends of the wishbone connecting wing joints and the one-prong part connected to the breastbone. Grasp the wishbone at smallest end, pull upward and back just enough to see its outline, cut around outline with the tip of a small, sharp knife and hook a finger under the part of the wishbone connected to the breastbone pulling to separate it from wing joints.

Chef's note 2: Use a dishwasher safe cutting board and disposable gloves when handling poultry, meats, fish, and seafood. Even allocating one side of a cutting board, or the entire board for only processing ingredients considered as having the highest contaminating potential and allocate (label) a second board for cutting, dicing, slicing and general processing of vegetables, herbs and fruits, for example.

Herbed Oven Roasted Chicken presented with Star Fruit, Sweet Peppers, Grapes, Raspberry-Custard Flan and Yakima Valley, Washington Orange Muscat Wine

Notes

OVEN ROASTED TARRAGON CHICKEN
With
YUKON GOLD POTATOES and GREEN BEANS
"Signature"

Created for and demonstrated this on local, weekly TV segment, aired during year 2001.

Serves: 8

1½ pounds of fresh green beans, ends trimmed
1 teaspoon of sea salt

½ cup unsalted butter
1½ cups fresh tarragon, chopped
2 chickens (4-pounds each), rinsed and patted dry
12 garlic cloves, coarsely chopped
Sea salt
Pepper

2 large onions, peeled and quartered (Preferably Walla Walla sweets)
4 pounds medium-size Yukon gold potatoes, peeled and quartered
3 tablespoons extra virgin olive oil
Sea salt
Pepper, freshly ground

2 tablespoons fresh parsley, chopped, for garnish

Cook green beans in a large pot of boiling, salted water until crisp-tender, about 8-10 minutes. Using a strainer, transfer beans to bowl of ice water and cool. Drain beans and set aside.

Position racks in the center and bottom third of oven.

Preheat oven to 400°F

Melt butter in a small saucepan over medium heat, mix-in ½ cup tarragon. Place chicken in a large roasting pan.

Place 6-garlic cloves and ½ cup of tarragon in cavity of each chicken and loosely tie legs together to retain shape while roasting. Brush chicken with some of the tarragon butter, sprinkle each chicken with salt and pepper, position roasting pan on center rack, roast for 30-minutes and baste each chicken occasionally with tarragon butter. Reduce heat to 380°F and continue roasting the chicken for another 30-minutes. Place onions and potatoes on rimmed baking sheet or large heatproof glass dish. Drizzle onions and potatoes with oil, sprinkle with salt and pepper and place on rack below chicken.

Baste chicken occasionally with tarragon butter, turning vegetables occasionally, about 30 minutes or longer. Transfer chicken to a warmed serving platter and tent with foil. Strain pan juices and pour juices into a small saucepan - keep warm.

Place beans in a large skillet over high heat, and add 4-tablespoons pan juices and toss. Season with pepper, toss beans with potatoes and onions, transfer them to another warm platter and sprinkle with parsley. Cut chicken into serving pieces and drizzle chicken with remaining pan juices. Enjoy with vegetables.

BREAST of CHICKEN in AMARETTO SAUCE
"Signature"

Serves: 4

4 chicken breast halves, boned, skinned
Sea salt
Pepper, freshly ground
2 tablespoons unsalted butter
2 shallots, peeled, chopped
2 cups of whipping cream
¼ cup of Amaretto liqueur
Mélange peppercorns, freshly ground
2 tablespoons Italian parsley, chopped for garnish

Sprinkle the chicken lightly with salt and pepper. Heat butter in a large nonstick skillet over medium heat. Add chicken and brown on both sides, about 6 minutes on each side.

Transfer chicken to a warmed platter, cover with foil to keep warm.

In the same skillet over medium heat add shallots and sauté until soft, about 3 minutes. Stir in cream and Amaretto liqueur. Cook gently for 10-minutes or until sauce is slightly thickened, season with salt and mélange pepper, return chicken to the skillet and cook gently 5 more minutes.

Transfer chicken to a warm serving platter, spoon sauce over chicken, sprinkle with parsley. Enjoy with Linguine or Fettuccine.

Notes

SAUTEED BREAST of CHICKEN
With
NECTARINE-RIESLING SAUCE
"Signature"

"Cooking with Erika"
Created for and demonstrated this on local, weekly TV segment, aired August 16, 2001.

Serves: 4

4 large chicken breasts, boned and skinned
2 teaspoons sea salt
2 teaspoons pepper, freshly ground
2 teaspoons Mrs. Dash original seasoning
2 tablespoons unsalted butter
1 tablespoon extra virgin olive oil
¼ cup shallots, chopped
Pinch of sugar
2 cups ripe nectarines, halved, pitted, peeled and chopped
1 cup whipping cream
1 cup of dry Riesling wine
Sea salt
Pepper, freshly ground
1 tablespoon fresh watercress, chopped
2 nectarines, pitted and cut into wedges for garnish
Parsley, chopped for garnish

Rinse chicken under cold running water and pat dry with paper towel. Sprinkle chicken with salt, pepper and Mrs. Dash seasoning. In a large skillet, heat butter and oil, add chicken and sauté over medium heat until golden brown on each side, about 6 minutes per side. Remove chicken and keep warm. Add shallots to the same skillet, sprinkle with a pinch of sugar and sauté shallots for 1-minute, until soft and slightly golden in color - stir often. Add the chopped nectarines, sauté 2 more minutes, add cream and cook for 5 minutes, stirring constantly over medium heat. Stir-in wine, return chicken to the skillet and cook 5-6 more minutes over low heat. Season with salt and pepper, and stir-in the watercress. Arrange chicken on a warm, large platter, spoon sauce over chicken pieces and garnish with nectarine wedges and parsley.

Enjoy with Basmati rice or pasta, such as linguini or fettuccine, and a well-chilled glass of Sun Glow and Nectarine wines, of Eaton Hill Winery, Yakima Valley, WA.

Notes

SAUTÉED CHICKEN BREAST
With
AVOCADO and GREEN PEPPERCORN SAUCE
"Signature"

Created during 1992, a menu item for serving in my former restaurant location, Tacoma, WA.

Serves: 4

4 chicken breasts, boned, skinned
1 teaspoon of sea salt
1 teaspoon white pepper, freshly ground
2 tablespoons unsalted butter
1 teaspoon Mrs. Dash original seasoning

2 avocados, halved, seeds removed,
peeled, and cut into chunks
1 teaspoon, fresh lemon juice
1 cup of half and half
¼ cup whipping cream
¼ cup of dry white wine, such as Riesling
1 teaspoon of green peppercorns, drained
Sea salt
White pepper, freshly ground
Lemon slices for garnish

Rinse chicken under cold running water and pat dry with paper towel. Sprinkle each chicken breast with salt and pepper. Heat butter in a large skillet over medium-high heat, add chicken breasts and sauté until golden brown, about 6 minutes per side. Sprinkle each chicken breast with Mrs. Dash seasoning, transfer chicken to a warm platter and spoon pan-drippings over chicken to keep moist -cover with foil.

Purée avocados with lemon juice and set aside. Add the half and half, whipping cream, wine and peppercorns to the skillet, bring slowly to a boil, reduce heat to simmer, return chicken to the skillet and simmer for 2-more minutes. Arrange chicken on a warm platter, whisk avocado purée into sauce and season to taste with salt and pepper. Spoon warm sauce over chicken, garnish with lemon slices.

Enjoy with basmati rice or pasta, tomato salad, and your favorite dry Riesling, Pinot Gris or Fumé Blanc.

Notes

165

ROAST DUCK
With
MUSCAT GRAPE SAUCE
"Signature"

Serves: 4

1 duck, 8-10 pounds
3 teaspoons of sea salt
2 teaspoons pepper, freshly ground
2 teaspoons fresh sage leaves, chopped
2 sprigs of fresh thyme
1 small onion, chopped
1 cup Muscat grapes, rinsed, stems removed, if present
1 large pear or apple, peeled, cored, chopped
½ cup Muscat wine
½ cup of hot water, mixed with
¼ teaspoon of sea salt for basting

SAUCE

2 cups Muscat grapes, rinsed, stems removed, plus extra for garnish
¼ cup golden raisins
½ cup of cream sherry
1 cup Muscat wine
2 teaspoon of fresh sage leaves, chopped
Sea salt
Pepper, freshly ground

Preheat oven to 400°F

Clean duck, pat dry with paper towels, and sprinkle duck, inside and out, with salt and pepper. In a small bowl, combine herbs onions, grapes, pear or apple and stuff into duck cavity, and truss. Prick duck all over with a fork to release fat during roasting. Place duck, breast-side up in a deep roasting pan and add about ¼ cup of water.

Roast duck for 30 minutes, occasionally basting with a little more hot water during roasting. Reduce heat to 350°F and roast for 1½-hours, or until tender. At this time, siphon out any duck fat and keep basting every 15 minutes with water. Pour Muscat wine over the duck and roast 10 more minutes. Transfer duck to a warm platter and cover with foil to keep warm. Strain pan juices into a medium saucepan, add grapes, raisins, Sherry, wine, and the sage leaves. Cook over medium-low heat for 15 minutes, and season with salt and pepper, if needed. Purée grape mixture in a food mill or food processor and return it to the same saucepan. Keep warm on low heat until ready to serve.

Carve duck into serving pieces, discard filling and arrange pieces on a warm serving platter, drizzle half of grape sauce over duck pieces, and garnish with grape clumps. Ladle remaining sauce into a sauceboat for passing around at your festive table, and enjoy with black Tai rice and carrots.

Note: Siphoned duck fat can be frozen up to 3 months to use in flavoring soups, stews, vegetables and more. Portion packaging is best and when ready to use frozen duck fat, defrost it in the refrigerator.

DUCK CONFIT ROULADE with RED WINE VINAIGRETTE
"Signature"

Serves: 4-6

12 romaine lettuce leaves
1 teaspoon of extra virgin olive oil
¼ cup shallots, minced
2 cups duck confit, cooked and shredded
¾ cup vine ripened tomatoes, chopped
4 tablespoons watercress leaves, chopped

1 cup of red wine vinaigrette
½ cup crumbled Roquefort cheese, or other strong flavored blue cheese
1 tablespoon arugula leaves, chopped
Sea salt
Pepper, freshly ground

Over high heat, bring a large saucepan of water to boil. Add romaine lettuce leaves and cook for 5 seconds or until just blanched. Drain and refresh in ice water bath and pat dry. Trim any hard tips and rough edges. Layout in a single layer on a sheet of wax paper, cover with paper towel and pat down to absorb any remaining moisture.

Heat 1 tablespoon of olive oil in a small sauté pan over medium heat, add shallots, lower heat and allow shallots to cook for about 2 minutes. Scrape into a medium-size bowl, and add duck confit, tomatoes, watercress, 2-tablespoons vinaigrette, season with salt and pepper if needed, toss to blend and set aside.

RED WINE VINAIGRETTE

Makes about ½ cup

1 cup of dry red wine
7 tablespoons of red wine vinegar
3 tablespoons shallots, chopped
2 bay leaves
3 tablespoons Dijon mustard
¼ cup of extra virgin olive oil

Boil wine, 5-tablespoons vinegar, shallots and bay leaves in a small saucepan until liquid is reduced to about ½ cup, stirring occasionally, about 10-minutes. Pour reduction into a small bowl, and cool. Discard bay leaves. Whisk remaining 2 tablespoons vinegar and mustard into reduction. Gradually whisk in ¼ cup olive oil, season with salt and pepper, cover and refrigerate. Let vinaigrette stand 15 minutes at room temperature and whisk before using.

To assemble: Uncover romaine leaves two at a time and lay leaves together with one edge slightly overlapping to make a rather rectangular piece. Place equal portions of duck mixture across the center of the leaves, leaving about 1½ to 2-inch leaf edge all around, fold in the ends and sides to form into a cylindrical shape. Cut each in half crosswise on the diagonal. Place 1-cylinder or 2, on each of six serving plates and warm remaining vinaigrette over very low heat. Whisk in cheese and arugula. Spoon equal portion of warm vinaigrette over salad cylinders and enjoy with French bread slices as a first course along with your favorite, soft Merlot.

GAME (GUINEA) HENS
With
ORANGE JUS and SAUTÉED TOMATO HALVES
"Signature"

Serves: 4

2 game hens, 2-2½ pounds each, rinsed and paper towel dried
Sea salt
White pepper, freshly ground
6 oranges, rinsed and 1-halved
2 fresh rosemary sprigs
5 tablespoons unsalted butter
4 medium leeks, white and tender green parts, wash well and crosscut into 1-inch pieces
½ cup shallots, peeled and roughly chopped
3 juniper berries, crushed
2 bay leaves
1 tablespoon white peppercorns
2 cups orange juice, freshly squeezed
¼ cup dry white wine
1½ pound Roma tomatoes, halved

Preheat oven to 400°F

Sprinkle hens inside and out with salt and pepper, place half of orange with a sprig of rosemary into the cavity of each hen. Tie the legs of each hen together with household string. In a large-deep skillet, heat 3-tablespoons of butter over medium heat and when butter is melted and foamy, add hens breast down and turn to brown evenly on all sides. Place hens in a medium roasting pan, brush hens completely with dripping from skillet, place hens in oven and roast 30 minutes, basting hens every 10-minutes with pan juices.

Meanwhile, peel remaining oranges with a sharp knife, removing all the bitter white pith over a medium bowl to contain juice. Cut between membranes to release orange segments and set aside. Melt 1-tablespoon of butter in a large skillet, over medium-high heat and add half of orange segments, leeks, shallots, juniper berries, bay leaves and peppercorns. Sauté 2-3 minutes, add 1-cup of orange juice and cook on medium heat 5-minutes, season with salt and pepper.

Reduce oven heat to 370°F

Turn hens and roast 15-minutes. Add vegetables and juice from skillet - baste the hens often during roasting for 30-more minutes, or until juice runs clear. Transfer hens to a warmed large platter, cover with foil and keep warm.

Note: Test doneness with a thermometer or pierce the inside of hen's cavity with a carving fork and allow juices to drain. If juices have a pink tinge, rather than clear, roast hens another 5-10 minutes and test again for doneness.

Strain vegetables and pan juices into a small saucepan discarding vegetables. Add remaining 1-cup of orange juice and wine and cook over moderately high heat, about 3-5 minutes – keep warm. Heat remaining 1-tablespoon of butter in a medium skillet over medium-high heat, add tomatoes cut side down, sprinkle them lightly with salt and pepper and sauté with remaining orange segments for 1-2 minutes, turning once - keep warm.

Carving hen - method I: Remove and discard string from legs, cut away the legs and thighs with a sharp knife. For example, slightly twist and pull the leg away from the breast cavity, cut around the bone joint nearest to the breast, carefully twist leg and, if necessary, wedge a knife blade into the joint to separate. Repeat process for wings. Resting hen on its side, or on its back, slice between ribs and flesh to remove half breast in one piece. Repeat process.

Carving hen - method II: With poultry shears, cut around and remove the wishbone, cut through the center of breastbone toward rear. Repeat cutting process through the center of the backbone, or cut through each side of the backbone and discard center.

To serve: Arrange half of a hen, cut side down, on pre-warmed dinner plates, spoon tomato-orange mixture alongside hen, pour orange jus over each serving and serve remaining jus from a sauceboat kept warm at the table. Enjoy with accompaniments such as basmati rice, tiny potato dumplings or couscous along with your favorite white wine – perhaps a dry Riesling, Chardonnay, Pinot Grigio, Semillon, or Sauvignon Blanc.

Game (Guinea) Hen with Orange Jus and Sautéed Tomato Halves

ROAST TURKEY in HERB BUTTER
With
WINE-BRANDY-APPLE-ONION FILLING
"Signature"

Serves: 10-12

TURKEY

1 fresh turkey (16-18 pounds), preferably organic
Sea salt
Pepper, freshly ground
3 cups of chicken stock, or vegetable stock
1 cup of Riesling wine
¼ cup of Brandy
4 tablespoons of all-purpose flour
¼ cup of whipping cream

HERB BUTTER

¾ cup of unsalted butter, softened
3 tablespoons of fresh thyme, chopped, or
1-tablespoon of dried thyme
3 tablespoons of fresh sage, chopped, or 1-tablespoon of dried-rubbed sage
2 teaspoons of sea salt
2 teaspoons pepper, freshly ground

Combine all ingredients in a small bowl and set aside.

APPLE-ONION-FILLING

3 large apples, peeled, cored and cut into small cubes
3 large onions, chopped, about 3-cups
1 teaspoon of fresh thyme, chopped, or ½ teaspoon of dried thyme
½ teaspoon of fresh sage, chopped, or ¼ teaspoon dried-rubbed sage
2 tablespoons Riesling wine
1 tablespoon Brandy

In a medium bowl, mix together apples, onions, Herbs, wine and brandy, and toss well.

Position rack in lowest third of oven and preheat to 400°F

Prepare turkey: Thoroughly rinse turkey with running cold water and pat dry with paper towels. Season turkey cavity with salt and pepper, and slide a hand under skin of turkey breast to loosen to spread half of the herb butter over the breast. Spoon the apple-onion filling into the main cavity.

Place remaining herb butter in a small saucepan, stir over low heat until melted. Brush butter over outside of turkey and loosely tie legs together to retain shape while roasting. Place turkey, breast side up, in a roasting pan, and place in oven to roast for 30 minutes. Reduce heat to 325°F, continue roasting turkey for 1-hour, 30 minutes, basting occasionally with pan drippings. Tent turkey with heavy-duty foil and roast 30 minutes longer. Remove foil and pour 1-cup of chicken stock or vegetable stock, ½ cup of wine and ¼ cup of brandy over turkey. Continue occasional basting with pan drippings and roast uncovered for 1-hour, 45 minutes or until thermometer inserted into thickest part of thigh registers 180°F, or when juices run clear when thickest part of thigh is pierced with a skewer.

Place turkey on a large cutting board or platter, tent with foil - keep warm until ready to carve and enjoy!

Prepare sauce: Strain the pan juices into a large measuring cup. Add enough chicken stock or vegetable stock, and the remaining ½-cup of wine, to pan juices to measure 4-cups. Transfer liquid to a heavy, large saucepan and bring to a boil – turn heat to medium-low - mix flour and whipping cream in a small bowl until smooth paste forms. Whisk paste into hot liquid until smooth, whisking constantly, cook for 7-minutes and season to taste with salt and pepper.

Chef's note: If a thicker sauce is desired, mix 2-3 tablespoons of flour with 6 tablespoons of white wine, whisk into simmering sauce, and cook 2 more minutes.

CURRIED TURKEY
With
APPLE CHUTNEY
"Signature"

Serves: 4

3 tablespoons of unsalted butter
2 pounds of fresh or frozen turkey breast, cut into ¼ inch cubes
1 medium onion, chopped
2 tablespoons of curry powder
½ teaspoon sea salt
¼ teaspoon pepper, freshly ground
2 tablespoons golden raisins
2 tablespoons unsweetened coconut milk
2 tablespoons cream sherry
2 tablespoons cashew nuts, coarsely chopped
½ cup apple chutney (See Recipe Index)
Cilantro for garnish

Rinse turkey under cold running water and pat dry with paper towels. Heat butter in a large saucepan over medium-high heat, add turkey, sauté until golden brown, about 15 minutes, stirring occasionally. Add onions and sauté 5-more minutes, turn heat to medium-low. Season with curry, salt and pepper and add raisins, coconut milk, and sherry. Cook partially covered for 20 minutes, stirring occasionally, stir-in cashews and chutney and simmer 5-minutes. Serve over pasta, such as linguine fettuccine or jasmine rice, and garnish with cilantro.

PERSIMMON STUFFED TURKEY ROLL
With
LATE HARVEST RIESLING SAUCE
"Signature"

Serves: 6

½ cup onion, chopped
4 ripe persimmons (about 1½-cups), peeled, and coarsely chopped
4 tablespoons of watercress, chopped
2 tablespoons of fresh flat leaf parsley, chopped
2 teaspoons of sea salt
2 teaspoons of pepper, freshly ground
1 2½-3 pounds half-breast of boneless turkey, butter-flied, skinned and filet removed
4 tablespoons of unsalted butter, melted

1 cup of Late Harvest Riesling wine, plus 6 tablespoons
1½ cups whipping cream
Sea salt
Pepper, freshly ground
1 tablespoon of watercress, chopped
2 persimmons, peeled sliced for garnish

Preheat oven to 380°F

In a small bowl, combine onion, persimmons, watercress and parsley - season with 1 teaspoon each of salt and pepper. Place turkey breast on work surface, and using a meat mallet, pound turkey to about 1/3 inch thickness. Sprinkle turkey with remaining 1 teaspoon of salt and remaining teaspoon of pepper.

Spread persimmon mixture over turkey leaving ½ inch border on all sides - press to adhere. Tightly roll up (jelly roll-style) the flattened turkey breast into on long roll. Tie turkey roll in 5 places with string to secure. Place a doubled 15-inch square of cheesecloth in a 13x9x2-inch baking pan.

Pour ½ cup of wine over cloth. Place turkey roll on cloth, drizzle turkey roll with butter, wrap tightly with cheesecloth secured, if necessary, with 3 wooden or metal skewers and roast for 1 hour, 15 minutes, or until cooked through and juices run clear when pierced in center.

Let turkey rest for 15 minutes. Remove skewers, if used, the cheesecloth and string - cut turkey roll into ½ inch thick slices, transfer to a warm platter and cover with foil to keep warm.

Meanwhile make sauce. Add remaining ½ cup of wine to the baking pan, scraping up browned bits. Strain pan drippings into a medium saucepan, add cream and bring to a slow boil. Turn heat to medium-low, cook for 6-8 minutes, season with salt and pepper and stir in watercress.

Arrange turkey slices on 6 warmed serving plates, spoon sauce over turkey slices and garnish each with persimmon slices.

SMOKED TURKEY-WATERCRESS SANDWICHES
With
CURRIED APRICOT MAYONNAISE
"Signature"

Serves: 4

TURKEY-WATERCRESS

8 thick slices of French bread slices, or rustic Italian bread
8 teaspoons unsalted butter
1 pound smoked turkey, thinly sliced
2 bunches of watercress, trimmed
8 ripe plum tomatoes, thinly sliced
1 medium, sweet onion, thinly sliced

CURRY-APRICOT MAYONNAISE

1½ cups mayonnaise
¼ cup apricot jam
½ tablespoon mild curry powder

Combine mayonnaise, apricot jam and curry powder in a small bowl.

Note: Mayonnaise can be prepared 2-days ahead, covered and refrigerated.

Preheat broiler

Place bread slices on a large baking sheet and spread 1-teaspoon of butter on each slice of bread. Broil the bread until golden brown, about 2-3 minutes per side, turning once.

Place bread in a napkin-lined basket covered to keep warm. Arrange turkey, watercress, tomatoes and onions on a large platter, place turkey platter on the dining table for self-assembly and enjoyment along with the curried mayonnaise presented in small bowls. Or enjoy lunch out on the patio or deck with a crisp white wine or ice tea.

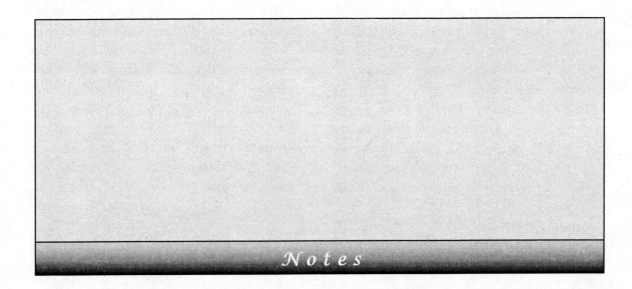

Notes

173

ASPARAGUS PLATTER
With
BEER BATTER PANCAKES
"Signature"

"Cooking with Erika"
Created for and demonstrated on local, weekly TV segment, aired during year 2002.

Serves: 4-6

2 pounds green asparagus, trimmed and peeled, if desired, or
2 pounds of white asparagus, trimmed and peeled
(4 pounds green asparagus if white variety is not available)
2 teaspoons of sea salt
Sugar
4 teaspoons of unsalted butter
1 teaspoon pepper, freshly ground
8 ounces of prosciutto, thinly sliced
1¼ cups of unbleached all-purpose flour
½ cup of light beer
2 eggs, separated
6 tablespoons of extra virgin olive oil
¼ teaspoon of sea salt
½ teaspoon pepper, freshly ground
¼ cup of Italian parsley, chopped

Place green asparagus in a large deep skillet of boiling water, add 1 teaspoon of salt and cook until crisp-tender, about 2-3 minutes. Transfer with tongs to paper towel to drain. Cook white asparagus in another large deep skillet of boiling water, add 1 teaspoon of salt, a pinch of sugar and ¼ teaspoon of butter. Cook until crisp-tender, about 10-minutes and transfer with tongs to paper towels to drain.

In a medium bowl, whisk together flour, beer and egg yolks, season with salt and pepper. Use an electric mixer, beat the egg whites until stiff but not dry. Gently fold egg whites into beer mixture. Heat 2 tablespoons of oil in a large nonstick skillet over medium heat and working in batches, spoon batter into skillet forming 3-inch diameter pancakes equally spaced. Cook until crisp and light brown for about 1 minute per side, turning once.

Arrange green asparagus in the middle of a large-warmed serving platter and arrange white asparagus on top of green asparagus leaving green asparagus partially exposed. Heat the remaining butter in a small skillet until golden in color. Spoon butter over asparagus, sprinkle with parsley, arrange prosciutto on one side of asparagus and arrange pancakes on opposite side. Enjoy with your favorite Riesling wine.

See more vegetarian dishes under separate headings, such as
Fish, Dandelion & Salad

Baked Zita-Dandelion Casserole,
Page 265

Penne-Stuffed Mushroom Caps, Page
196 (Convertible Vegetarian Dish)

VEGETARIAN ENTRÉES

Goat Cheese
Spread, Page 304

The Ultimate
Vegetarian Dish, Page 192

Ricotta-Arugula Dumplings, Page 206

Zucchini Soufflé, Page 204

VEGETARIAN ENTRÉES

Stuffed Zucchini Blossoms,
Page 198

L-Zucchini Fritters, Page 203
R-Zucchini Boats, Page 201

ASPARAGUS in PUFF PASTRY-YAKIMA VALLEY
"Signature"

Created during 1992 in my former restaurant location in Tacoma, and prepared as an hors d'oeuvre for the combined "1999" Asparagus Festival and Spring Barrel tasting, Yakima Valley, Washington State (April 24, 1999)

Serves: 4-6

1 package (10 oz.) of frozen puff pastry
½ cup emmenthaler cheese, grated
4 tablespoons gorgonzola cheese, softened at room temperature
4 tablespoons feta cheese, such as French feta fromage
2 tablespoons whipping cream
1 tablespoon of crème fraîche, (See Index) or organic sour cream
1 tablespoon of parsley, chopped
1 tablespoon aqvavit (Avail. in Liquor Store)
Sea salt
Pepper, freshly ground
2½ pounds of fresh asparagus, trimmed, peeled, and cut in 6 inch lengths
1 teaspoon of sea salt
2 egg yolks
1 teaspoon aqvavit
Lemon wedges for garnish

Layout and thaw puff pastry to room temperature. Meanwhile, prepare cheese filling.

Filling: In a medium bowl, combine emmenthaler, gorgonzola, feta, whipping cream, crème fraîche (or sour cream), parsley and aqvavit. Stir until completely smooth, season with salt and pepper, and set aside.

Bring a large saucepan of water to a boil, and add 1-teaspoon of salt and asparagus, and cook for 2 minutes, drain, pat dry, and set aside.

Preheat oven to 400°F

Roll out sheets of puff pastry on a floured surface into 12-inch squares.

Cut out 4-6 pieces to 6x6 inches each. Spoon equal amounts of filling over each piece of pastry, top each filling with 4 asparagus spears, and roll them up carefully.

Place rolls seam-side down on a lightly oiled baking sheet and tuck ends under to seal.

In a small bowl, whisk together egg yolks with aqvavit, brush each roll with egg yolk mixture and bake on middle rack of oven for 25 minutes, or until golden on top.

Place puff pastry rolls on 4 pre-warmed plates, garnish with remaining asparagus spears, lemon wedges and enjoy!

ASPARAGUS MOUSSE-YAKIMA VALLEY
"Signature"

Created during 1992 in my former restaurant location in Tacoma, and prepared as hors d'oeuvre for the combined "1999" Asparagus Festival and Spring Barrel tasting, Yakima Valley, Washington.

Serves: 8-10

CRUMB MIXTURE

½ cup unsalted butter, melted, plus extra for greasing pan
2¼ cups finely ground savory cracker crumbs
2 tablespoons fresh parsley, chopped
¼ teaspoon sea salt
½ teaspoon pepper, freshly ground

Grease a 10 –12 inch spring form pan

In a large bowl, combine butter, cracker crumbs, parsley, salt and pepper. Press mixture evenly over the bottom of prepared pan. Refrigerate until chilled, about 2 hours.

FILLING

16 ounces cream cheese, softened
¼ pint whipping cream
1 bunch of watercress, large stems removed, chopped
2 tablespoons Parmesan cheese, grated, of good quality
1 tablespoon of mayonnaise
½ pound fresh green asparagus, cooked, well-drained and cut in small pieces
½ teaspoon fresh lemon juice
Sea salt
White pepper, freshly ground
1½ tablespoons gelatin
¼ cup dry white wine
Watercress sprigs for garnish

White asparagus tips for garnish
Lemon and lime slices for garnish

Place cream cheese and cream in a large mixing bowl and beat until smooth. In a food processor, purée the watercress, parmesan cheese, mayonnaise, cooked asparagus, and lemon juice until smooth - season with salt and pepper. Fold asparagus mixture into cream cheese mixture and set aside.

Combine gelatin and wine in a small bowl, let stand 5-10 minutes. In a small pan, bring hot water to a simmer, set the bowl in the pan, and stir until gelatin dissolves. Cool slightly. Fold the cooled gelatin into the asparagus mixture. Spoon asparagus mixture into prepared pan, smooth top, cover and refrigerate 3-4 hours, or until filling is set.

Run the tip of a knife around the edge of pan to loosen, ease the side of pan carefully away from mousse, with mousse still on pan bottom. Place on a large serving plate and garnish with watercress sprigs, white asparagus tips, lemon and lime slices, and enjoy with crostini, crackers, bread squares or rounds.

TUSCAN-STYLE STUFFED YAKIMA TOMATOES
"Signature"

"Cooking with Erika"
Created and demonstrated this on local, weekly TV segment, aired during year 2001

Serves: 6

2 cups tightly packed basil leaves
½ cup pine nuts
½ cup extra-virgin olive oil
½ cup freshly grated Pecorino Romano cheese
Pepper, freshly ground
6 medium red beefsteak or fancy heirloom tomatoes
Sea salt
½ pound Mezzi-Tubetti pasta, (Avail. in most supermarkets)
1 teaspoon of sea salt
1 cup sun-dried tomatoes, packed in olive oil, drain and julienne
Pepper, freshly ground
¼ cup Italian parsley, chopped for garnish
Lettuce leaves, for garnish

Process basil, pine nuts, olive oil, pecorino cheese and a dash of pepper in a food processor or blender until smooth and transfer to a large bowl and set aside.

Meanwhile, cut tops off tomatoes and scoop-out seeds and flesh with a melon-baler or small spoon. Sprinkle tomatoes lightly with salt.

Dice tomato-flesh and place in bowl with the basil mixture, cover and set aside.

Bring 2 quarts of water to a boil and add 1 teaspoon of salt and pasta - cook until al-dente, about 6-8 minutes, drain - add pasta while hot to diced tomatoes and basil mixture.

Fold-in sun-dried tomatoes, season to taste with salt and pepper - toss lightly.

Line a large serving platter with lettuce leaves, arrange tomatoes on top of lettuce and fill tomatoes with pasta mixture.

Sprinkle with parsley, and enjoy with crusty Italian bread and a glass of Italian red wine.

Note: Yellow heirloom tomatoes, brandy-wine beefsteak tomatoes, grapefruit tomato and a variety of other heirloom tomato seeds are available thru mail order.

SPINACH GNOCCHI with YELLOW TOMATO SAUCE

Serves: 6

2 pounds Yukon gold potatoes
2 packages (10-ounces each) ready to use spinach leaves
1 small egg, slightly beaten
¼ teaspoon nutmeg, freshly ground
1½ cups of all-purpose flour
Sea salt
¼ cup of unsalted butter, melted, plus extra for greasing baking dish
¼ cup Parmesan cheese, freshly grated

Place potatoes in a large saucepan, cover with water and bring to a boil. Reduce heat and simmer for 30-35 minutes, or until tender when pierced with the point of a sharp knife or prongs of a fork. Drain and allow potatoes to cool before peeling. Mash potatoes in a large bowl until smooth and set aside.

Meanwhile, bring 2 inches of salted water to a boil in a large saucepan, add spinach leaves to saucepan and cook until wilted stirring occasionally, about 2 minutes. Drain spinach, reserving ¼ cup cooking liquid. Squeeze out as much liquid as possible from the spinach. Purée spinach in a food processor, or blender, add reserved cooking liquid 1 tablespoon at a time if necessary to help purée and scraping down sides of the processor bowl occasionally. Transfer puréed spinach to bowl with potatoes, mix in egg, nutmeg and enough flour until soft and slightly sticky dough forms. Season the dough to taste with salt. Dust baking sheet with remaining flour. Working in batches and using floured hands, roll ¼ cup of dough on a lightly floured work surface to form a 12-inch long rope. Cut formed dough into 1-inch pieces, and then roll each piece between palms to form an oval ball. Transfer gnocchi to floured baking sheet. Repeat rolling, cutting, shaping, and placement of remaining dough on baking sheet.

**Preheat oven to 400°F
Butter a 9 x 13 inch baking dish**

Working in batches, add gnocchi to a large saucepan of boiling, salted water and cook until gnocchi rise to surface, about 3-4 minutes. Using a slotted spoon, remove gnocchi from the water, drain, and transfer them to prepared baking dish.

Drizzle melted butter over gnocchi, and carefully toss to coat. Sprinkle gnocchi with Parmesan cheese, and bake 10 minutes, or until golden. Transfer gnocchi to a large serving dish and spoon yellow tomato sauce over gnocchi.

Note 1: For quicker preparation, add finely chopped raw spinach to the potato mixture instead of cooked spinach.

Note 2: Yellow tomato sauce can be made ahead and kept warm until ready to use, or it can be made while gnocchi are baking. *See Yellow Tomato Sauce recipe on next page.*

YELLOW TOMATO SAUCE

1 tablespoon of extra virgin olive oil
½ cup of onions, chopped
2 cloves garlic, minced
1 cup yellow sun-ripened tomatoes, chopped
Pinch of sugar
1/3 cup of dry white wine
½ cup whipping cream
Sea salt
Pepper, freshly ground
1 tablespoon fresh oregano, chopped
1 tablespoon of fresh Italian parsley

In a medium saucepan, heat oil on medium heat, add onions and sauté until onions are soft, about 5 minutes. Add garlic, tomatoes, sugar and wine – cook 10 minutes. Add cream, turn heat to medium-low, season with salt and pepper to taste – cook 5 more minutes, stir-in oregano and parsley. Enjoy served over gnocchi, or your favorite pasta.

MOZZARELLA-TOMATO-BALSAMIC VINAIGRETTE
"Signature"

"Cooking with Erika"
Created and demonstrated this on local, weekly TV Segment, aired during year 2001

Appetizer – 4-6 servings

2 pounds fresh mozzarella cheese packed in water, drained.
4 large red tomatoes
2 large yellow tomatoes
2 large orange tomatoes
3 tablespoons good quality imported balsamic vinegar
Pinch of sugar
1-2 tablespoons extra virgin olive oil
Sea salt
Pepper, freshly ground
1 tablespoon fresh oregano, chopped
1 tablespoon fresh Italian parsley, chopped
Basil leaves for garnish

Cut mozzarella cheese and tomatoes in ½ inch slices. In a small bowl, combine balsamic vinegar, oil, sugar, salt and pepper. Alternate cheese and tomato slices on a large serving platter. Drizzle balsamic vinaigrette over mozzarella and tomato slices, sprinkle with oregano and parsley, and garnish with basil leaves.

Enjoy with crusty French bread slices or crostini.

PASTA SOUFFLÉ
"Signature"

Serves: 8

1 pound of Acini Di Pepe pasta, (Avail. in supermarkets)
1 teaspoon of sea salt
2 eggs lightly beaten
1 cup whipping cream
½ cup freshly grated Parmesan cheese, plus extra for dusting
½ cup mascarpone cheese
2 tablespoons shallots, minced
Sea salt
Pepper, freshly ground
1 tablespoon of garlic, minced
2 tablespoons watercress leaves, finely chopped
Unsalted butter, for greasing

Bring 4-quarts water to a boil, add salt and pasta - stir frequently - cook 5-6 minutes, remove from heat, drain and transfer to a shallow dish - let cool.

Preheat oven to 350°F

Butter 8, 2/3-cup ramekins, dust lightly with Parmesan cheese, arrange ramekins in a large baking pan and set aside.

In a large bowl, blend cooled pasta with eggs, cream, Parmesan and mascarpone cheeses, shallots, season with salt and pepper, add garlic, watercress and mix well.

Spoon equal amounts of pasta mixture into prepared ramekins and pour enough hot water into pan to come halfway up the sides of the ramekins.

Bake 35-40 minutes or until top is golden brown.

Remove ramekins from water, let cool 10-minutes, loosen soufflés with sharp knife, invert onto warmed individual plates, and enjoy with spinach salad.

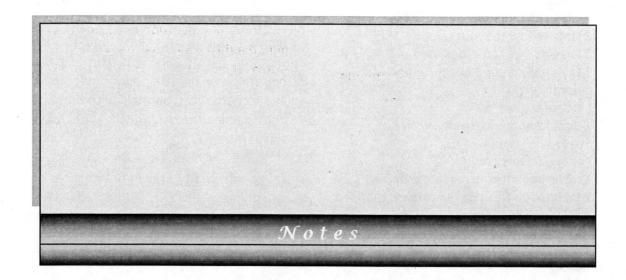

Notes

WALLA WALLA SWEET ONION TART
"Signature Heart Healthy '2001' Version"

Serves: 8

3 cups of all-purpose flour, plus extra
1 teaspoon of sea salt
1 cup of warm water (105-115°F)
1½ teaspoons of dry yeast
¼ teaspoon sugar
2 tablespoons of extra virgin olive oil, plus extra for brushing dough

2 tablespoons of extra virgin olive oil
6 medium-size Walla Walla sweet onions, thinly sliced
2 eggs, preferably omega 3 eggs
1 teaspoon of sea salt
1 teaspoon pepper, freshly ground
1 teaspoon of sweet paprika
1 teaspoon of caraway seeds
3 tablespoons of light sour cream
1 tablespoon all –purpose flour
½ cup low fat Swiss cheese

Preheat oven to 400°F
Spray a 10-inch spring-form pan with "all natural" cooking spray.

Mix 3 cups of flour and salt in a large bowl forming a well in the center - add water, yeast and sugar to the well. Stir until yeast dissolves and gradually mix in the flour, plus 2 tablespoons of oil to form soft dough.

Turn dough out onto floured surface and knead until smooth, about 3-5 minutes.

Roll out dough to a 10-inch round, about ½-inch thick.

Transfer dough to prepared spring-form pan, brush dough lightly with oil, cover with a large tea towel, and set aside.

Meanwhile, heat 2 tablespoons of oil in a large skillet over medium heat. Add onions and sauté until soft, about 3-5 minutes, let cool slightly.

In a medium bowl, beat together eggs, and add salt, pepper, paprika, caraway seeds, sour cream and flour.

Stir in cheese, spread cooled, cooked onions over dough, top with egg mixture and bake 20-30 minutes or until onion filling is set and golden brown on top.

Remove onion tart from oven, cut into wedges and enjoy warm.

Notes

183

POLENTA
With
CARAMELIZED WALLA-WALLA SWEET ONIONS
"Signature"

"Cooking with Erika"
Created and demonstrated this on local, weekly TV segment, aired during year 2001

Serves: 4

6 cups water
1 teaspoon of sea salt
2 cups of polenta
2 tablespoons extra virgin olive oil, plus extra for greasing
½ teaspoon freshly ground pepper
1-2 tablespoon(s) garlic, minced

2 teaspoons extra virgin olive oil
2 cups sweet onions, thinly sliced
1/8 teaspoon of sugar
½ teaspoon sea salt
¼ teaspoon pepper, freshly ground

Brush bottom and sides of a deep medium-size bowl lightly with olive oil and set aside.

In a large, deep non-stick saucepan over high heat, bring water and salt to a boil, and gradually stir-in polenta.

Reduce heat, simmer gently and stir often using a long handled wooden spoon (preventing polenta from sticking to sides of saucepan) until mixture is very thick, about 30 minutes. Stir-in olive oil, pepper and garlic - cook 2 more minutes.

Turn off heat, spoon polenta into prepared bowl, cover to keep warm.

In a large skillet over medium-high heat, heat oil and add onions, sugar, salt and pepper - sauté until onions are golden, about 15 minutes, stirring often.

Invert polenta onto a large, flat plate to un-mold, retaining shape of the bowl.

Cut polenta into thick slices, transfer to 4 warmed serving plates and spoon caramelized onions over polenta.

Enjoy hot with a garden salad and natural dressing. See Index.

Notes

OVEN ROASTED PORTABELLA MUSHROOMS
With
GOAT CHEESE and SHRIMP
"Signature"

Serves: 8

4 large portabella mushrooms, stems removed and wiped clean with damp paper towels
¼ cup Spanish olive oil, plus 2-tablespoons
Sea salt
Pepper, freshly ground

1½ cups goat cheese, such as Montrachet
2 cloves garlic, minced
1 large shallot, peeled and chopped
1 tablespoon of sweet paprika, Spanish paprika preferred
2 cups fresh or frozen salad shrimp, coarsely chopped
¼ cup parsley, freshly chopped, plus extra for garnish
Tomato wedges, for garnish

Preheat oven to 425°F

Brush both sides of mushroom caps with oil and arrange them on a baking sheet, sprinkle each with salt and pepper – roast for 10-15 minutes, or until almost tender.

While mushrooms are roasting, prepare goat cheese mixture.

In a medium bowl, combine goat cheese, garlic, shallots, paprika, shrimp, parsley and 2-tablespoons remaining oil and season with salt.

Remove roasted mushrooms caps from oven – turn oven to 400°F.

Spread about ¼ cup of goat cheese mixture evenly over each cap, return mushrooms to oven and bake 6-10 more minutes, or until golden brown and bubbly.

Remove mushroom from oven and cut each into 4 serving pieces.

Transfer to a pre-warmed large platter and enjoy with your favorite Sangiovese, Red Zinfandel, or Syrah and Spanish Sherry.

Chef's note: if Using frozen shrimp, defrost overnight in the refrigerator and pat shrimp dry with paper towels before using.

Notes

SPANISH STYLE
BAKED WILD MUSHROOMS

Serves: 4 - 6

3 tablespoons Spanish olive oil, plus extra
for oiling baking dish
2 pounds wild mushrooms, such as
chanterelle, morel, porcini or hedge hog,
cleaned and coarsely chopped
2 cloves garlic, minced
2 large shallots, peeled, chopped
2 teaspoons Spanish paprika
Sea salt
Pepper, freshly ground
2 tablespoons Spanish Brandy (Avail. at
Liquor stores)
¼ cup parsley, freshly chopped
2 tablespoons unsalted butter
1½ cups dried breadcrumbs

Preheat oven to 400°F

Heat olive oil in a large, deep skillet over
medium-high heat, add mushrooms and
cook until almost golden brown, about
6-8 minutes.

Add garlic, shallots and paprika – cook
1-more minute or until shallots are soft
and season with salt and pepper.
Sprinkle with brandy, stir-in parsley and

transfer to a large, lightly oiled round
baking dish.

In a small saucepan, melt butter over
medium-low heat, add breadcrumbs,
and stir until breadcrumbs are moist.

Sprinkle breadcrumbs over mushrooms,
bake for 10-15 minutes or until topping
is golden brown. Serve hot.

Note: Mushroom season is an exciting
time of year in Europe as well as it is in
the USA, especially in Spain, Italy,
Germany, England, France, Bulgaria,
Hungary, Poland and Russia to name a
few; it's a time when seasonal
excitement energizes many people to
scour wooded areas hunting for
mushrooms to add to their favorite
soups, stews, egg, meat and poultry
dishes at home.

It also is the time when excellent
mushroom entrées, partnering with wild
game dishes, dot restaurant menus
everywhere in Europe as well as in my
USA Fine Dining Establishment. Guten
Appetit!

Notes

186

POLENTA
With
RIESLING WINE and WILD MUSHROOMS
"Signature"

Serves: 6-8

POLENTA

1 tablespoon of extra virgin olive oil
1 tablespoon unsalted butter
2 large cloves garlic, minced
2 cups of dry Riesling wine
4¼-5 cups chicken stock, vegetable stock or water
1 cup whipping cream
4 cups whole grain yellow corn meal
½ cup Parmesan cheese or Grana Padana, freshly grated
¼ teaspoon of sea salt
½ teaspoon mélange pepper, freshly ground
¼ cup watercress leaves, chopped

WILD MUSHROOMS

2 tablespoons of extra virgin olive oil
2 teaspoons unsalted butter
3 cups of fresh oyster mushrooms, coarsely chopped
3 cups of fresh Shiitake mushrooms, coarsely chopped
1 cup of onions, chopped
Pinch of sugar
½ teaspoon of sea salt
¼ teaspoon pepper, freshly ground
1 teaspoon of sweet paprika
2 tablespoons Italian parsley, freshly chopped
Lemon wedges for garnish
Tomato wedges for garnish

To make polenta: Place a nonstick large saucepan over medium heat. Add olive oil and butter, when oil and butter is hot, add garlic, wine, 4 cups stock or water and cream - bring to a slow boil and gradually add corn meal to hot liquid whisking, with a wire whisk, constantly at first then stir with a large wooden spoon as the mixture begins to thicken. Reduce heat to low so that it no longer bubbles.

Cook covered, about 25-30 minutes or until thickened stirring occasionally - stir in the cheese. Polenta should be creamy, but not loose. Season with salt and pepper and add more liquid if necessary. Stir in watercress and keep warm.

To prepare mushrooms: In a large, deep skillet heat oil and butter over medium-high heat, add mushrooms and fry until they start to color. Continue to cook for 2-3 minutes, add onions and sugar and cook 2 more minutes - stir in salt, pepper, paprika and parsley. Adjust seasoning if needed.

Spoon polenta on warmed serving plates top with mushrooms, garnish with lemon and tomato wedges and enjoy.

SPINACH PESTO
With
FETTUCCINE NESTS and GORGONZOLA SAUCE
"Signature"

"Cooking with Erika"
Created and demonstrated this on local, weekly TV segment, aired during year 2001

Serves: 4-6

SPINACH PESTO

4 cups packed fresh spinach leaves, chopped
½ cup of extra virgin olive oil
½ teaspoon white pepper, freshly ground
½ teaspoon of fine sea salt
1 cup of pine nuts
¼ cup garlic, chopped
¼ cup Italian parsley, freshly chopped
½ cup Walla-Walla sweet onions, chopped
¼ cup grated Parmesan cheese of good quality
¼ cup grated Pecorino or Romano cheese of good quality
Sea salt
Pepper, freshly ground
Tomatoes for garnish

Place spinach in a blender or food processor and add olive oil, pepper and salt. Purée until smooth and transfer to a bowl. Place pine nuts, garlic, parsley, onion and cheese in a food processor, or blender, and blend on high speed until a smooth paste forms.

Fold into spinach purée, mix well, and add more salt and pepper if desired.

Transfer pesto to a small saucepan to keep it warm, on low heat, stirring occasionally until ready to serve.

GORGONZOLA SAUCE

¼ cup whipping cream
¼ cup dry white wine, such as Riesling
½ cup crumbled Gorgonzola cheese of good quality

In a medium saucepan, slowly bring cream to a boil, turn heat to medium low, add wine, cook 5 minutes, turn off heat, add Gorgonzola cheese and whisk until cheese is melted. Season with salt and pepper, keep warm on low heat, stir occasionally - avoid boiling.

FETTUCCINE

8 ounces nested egg noodle fettuccine (Preferably Real Torina, Avail. in Specialty food stores)
8 ounces nested spinach fettuccine
Water
2 teaspoons sea salt
2 tablespoons extra virgin olive oil

Egg noodle fettuccine: In a large pot, bring three quarts of water to a boil, add 1 teaspoon of salt, egg noodle fettuccine and cook 6-8 minutes. Drain. Transfer to a large platter, lightly drizzle with one-tablespoon of oil and toss.

Prepare spinach fettuccine: In a large pot, bring three quarts of water to boil, add remaining 1-teaspoon of salt, the spinach fettuccine and cook 6-8 minutes. Drain. Transfer to a large platter and drizzle with remaining 1 tablespoon of oil and lightly toss.

Arrange both fettuccine nests onto warmed plates, spoon warm spinach pesto over egg noodle fettuccine and spoon the Gorgonzola sauce over spinach fettuccine. Garnish with tomato wedges and enjoy two delicacies in a single meal – excellent to say the least.

Note: Pesto freezes well and when tightly sealed it may be kept refrigerated for up to 7 days. Stir before using.

OVENBAKED GOURMET GRITS
"Signature"

"Cooking with Erika"
Created and demonstrated this on local, weekly TV segment, aired April 4, 2001

Serves: 8

GRITS

4 cups of water
1 cup whipping cream
1 cup dry white wine, or
extra virgin olive oil
2 teaspoons sea salt
4 tablespoons unsalted butter or extra virgin olive oil
1½ cups grits
2 teaspoons pepper, freshly ground
1 cup of white cheddar cheese, of good quality, shredded
4 eggs, well beaten
Unsalted butter or extra virgin olive oil for greasing
1 tablespoon of fresh parsley, chopped

Preheat oven to 345°F

In a large saucepan, bring water, cream and wine to a boil and add salt, butter, grits and pepper. Reduce heat to medium-low and cook until thick stirring constantly. Remove from heat stir in cheese and add eggs stirring rapidly.

Pour grits mixture into a large, well buttered, casserole dish. Bake for 1-hour, or until set and golden brown. Garnish with parsley.

For a great tasting combination, serve with "Sautéed Vodka Shrimp", see recipe on page 111.

Note: Grits can be prepared 1-day ahead, kept refrigerated, for next day baking.

PISTACHIO PESTO

Serves: 4

½ cup shelled unsalted pistachios
1 bunch basil leaves, stems removed,
about ½ cup
4 garlic cloves, peeled
4 ounces prosciutto, diced small
¼ cup heavy cream
3 tablespoons extra virgin olive oil
3 tablespoons freshly grated Pecorino
Romano Cheese

In a frying pan over medium heat, lightly toast pistachios 3-5 minutes - avoid burning them - to bring out their fullest flavor and natural oil. Coarsely chop basil, pistachios and garlic together, transfer to a food processor and purée with prosciutto while slowly adding cream. Add oil, cheese and purée for 1-second. Spoon into a glass bowl and serve with your favorite pasta.

SPINACH PESTO
"Signature"

"Tempting flavor and easy to make"

"Cooking with Erika"
Created and demonstrated this on local, weekly TV segment, aired during year 2001
"Heart Healthy"

Serves: 4

4 cups spinach leaves, washed, stems removed and coarsely chopped
1 large onion, chopped
¼ cup extra virgin olive oil
1 cup of parsley, chopped
½ cup pine nuts
¼ cup garlic cloves
Fine sea salt

Pepper, freshly ground

Blend all ingredients in food processor until coarse purée forms and season with salt and pepper. (Pesto can be enjoyed with your favorite pasta or on toasted French bread slices.)

PUMPKIN-CARROT-PARSNIP SOUFFLÉ
"Signature"

"Cooking with Erika"
Created and demonstrated this on local, weekly TV segment, aired during year 2001

Serves: 8

1-2 pounds fresh pumpkin, peeled seeded and cut into 1-inch cubes, about 4-cups
1 large carrot, peeled, cut into small pieces, about 1-cup
1 large parsnip, peeled, cut into small pieces, about 1-cup
1 small onion, chopped
1 teaspoon of sea salt

4 large eggs
½ cup whipping cream
½ cup sour cream
½ teaspoon freshly grated nutmeg
½ teaspoon sea salt
½ teaspoon pepper, freshly ground
½ cup freshly grated Parmesan cheese of good quality
4 tablespoons all-purpose flour
Butter for greasing
1 cup of unsalted pistachio nuts, finely ground

Preheat oven to 350°F

Place pumpkin, carrots, parsnip, onion and salt in a large saucepan, and add enough water to cover the vegetables and bring to a boil. Reduce heat and cook for about 6-8 minutes or until vegetables are tender when pierced with the tip of a small knife or the prongs of a fork. Drain and transfer cooked vegetables to a blender and purée in batches until smooth. Transfer to a large bowl, and cool slightly.

In a medium size bowl, blend together eggs, cream, sour cream, nutmeg, salt, pepper, cheese and flour adjusting seasoning if needed. Stir egg mixture into cooled vegetable purée, and mix until well combined. Lightly butter eight 4-ounce ramekins, sprinkle each with pistachio nuts, spoon equal amounts of puréed vegetables into each ramekin, set ramekins in a shallow, large baking pan and pour enough hot water into the pan to a level halfway up the sides of the ramekins.

Bake 35-40 minutes or until soufflés are set and puffing up slightly. Let soufflés cool 5 minutes before un-molding onto plates. Enjoy garnished with watercress and crusty French bread slices.

THE ULTIMATE VEGETARIAN DISH

Serves: 4

1 small head of cauliflower, cut into small florets, preferably organic
¼ teaspoon black caraway seeds, optional – available at Middle Eastern Food Stores
2 medium sun ripened tomatoes, trimmed and halved-parallel to ends
2 tablespoons of balsamic vinegar, of good quality
½ pound carrots, trimmed on both ends, peeled, cut into strips, preferably organic
1½ pounds baby bok choy, trimmed and halved-lengthwise
4 teaspoons of fresh orange juice
½ pound of fresh shiitake mushrooms, stems removed, thinly sliced
¼ teaspoon sugar
¼ teaspoon sweet paprika
½ pound white or green asparagus, trimmed, peeled, if desired, cut into 1½ inch pieces
½ cup extra virgin olive oil
Sea salt
Mélange peppercorn, finely ground

2 cups orzo pasta, cooked, and seasoned with 2 teaspoons turmeric and
1-2 teaspoon extra virgin olive oil, kept warm

2 cups beluga lentil, cooked and seasoned with
1-2 teaspoon balsamic vinegar, kept warm

¼ cup flat leaf parsley, chopped for garnish
1 bunch of watercress leaves, for garnish

Preheat oven to 400°F

Prepare cauliflower: Toss cauliflower and 1½ tablespoons of oil in a large bowl, spread cauliflower on a medium baking sheet, spaced apart, sprinkle lightly with salt, pepper and caraway seeds - roast 15 minutes - turn florets and continue roasting them until tender, about 10-15 minutes longer. Transfer cauliflower to a large pre-warmed dish, cover with foil and keep warm.

Prepare tomatoes: Place tomato halves on a medium ovenproof baking dish, sprinkle them lightly with salt and pepper, drizzle with one tablespoon of oil and 2 tablespoons of balsamic vinegar – roast 10-15 minutes.

Note: While cauliflower and tomatoes are roasting, cook all vegetables and pre-warm serving plates.

Prepare bok choy: Heat 2 teaspoons of oil in a large saucepan over medium-high heat, add bok choy, orange juice, and sprinkle lightly with salt and pepper. Turn heat to medium, cover partly with lid and cook for 8-10 minutes, or until tender turning once or twice - keep warm.

Prepare mushrooms: Heat 2-tablespoons of oil in a large skillet over medium-high heat, add mushrooms, sugar and paprika, turn heat to medium and cook until mushrooms are crisp, about 10-minutes, stirring occasionally, lightly season with salt and pepper and keep warm.

Prepare carrots: Cook carrots in lightly salted boiling water for 2-3 minutes, until just tender, drain, and drizzle cooked carrots with 1 teaspoon of oil and keep warm.

Prepare asparagus: Cook asparagus in lightly salted boiling water for 2-3 minutes (6-8 minutes for white asparagus) until just tender, drain and drizzle cooked asparagus with 1-2 teaspoons of oil - keep warm.

Assemble dishes: Place a metal ring in the center of each pre-warmed large dinner plate. Fill each ring with ½ cup of warm orzo pasta, smooth out the top and remove rings. Set one tomato half on top of orzo pasta, garnish each tomato with mushrooms, and surround pasta with ½ cup of lentil and vegetables. Drizzle some of the vegetable pan dripping over each serving, garnish with parsley and watercress leaves.

Center:

Orzo Pasta, Tomato & Mushrooms

Top Clockwise:

Carrots, Lentil, Cauliflower & Bok Choy

Enjoy!

ARUGULA-LETTUCE-SORREL PESTO LASAGNA
"Signature"

"Cooking with Erika"
Created and demonstrated this on local, weekly TV segment, aired during year 2001
"Heart Healthy"

Serves: 6-8

PESTO

2 tablespoons extra virgin olive oil, plus extra
2 cups arugula leaves, chopped
1 cup green lettuce, coarsely chopped
1 cup of sorrel leaves, stems removed, chopped
¼ cup pine nuts
1 tablespoon of fresh lemon juice
4 cloves of garlic, peeled
1 small onion, chopped
Sea salt
Pepper, freshly ground

In a food processor, place oil, arugula, lettuce, sorrel, pine nuts, lemon juice, garlic and onion, process into a thick paste, and season with salt and pepper.

BÉCHAMEL SAUCE

2 tablespoons unsalted butter
1/3 cup of shallots, minced
¼ cup all-purpose flour, plus 2 tablespoons
3 cups skim milk
¼ teaspoon freshly ground nutmeg
Sea salt
Pepper, freshly ground

In a medium saucepan, melt butter over medium-low heat, and add shallots - sauté 1-2 minutes. Reduce heat to low, add flour, whisk until smooth and whisk-in milk.

Bring to a boil, whisking constantly and cook on low heat until slightly thickened, stirring often, about 15-20 minutes. Add nutmeg, season with salt and pepper. Let sauce cool slightly.

Note: Cook sauce at least 15-minutes – sauce should not taste pasty or flour-like.

NOODLES

16 lasagna noodles
2 teaspoons sea salt
½ cup low-fat ricotta cheese, drained refrigerated overnight in a strainer-liquid discarded
8 tablespoons freshly grated Parmesan cheese of good quality

Cook noodles in a large pot of boiling, salted water until just tender, but still firm to the bite, about 8-10 minutes. Drain, and lay out noodles to cool on untreated, clean cloth that has been dipped in warm water and well wrung out then cover with another damp warm cloth to keep noodles from drying out until ready to use. Lightly oil a 13x9x2-inch baking dish.

Preheat oven to 375°F

Spread ½ cup of béchamel sauce over the bottom of prepared dish, cover with

4 noodles overlapped, spread 1/3 of pesto over noodles and top with sauce to cover.

In a small bowl, combine ricotta with 2 tablespoons Parmesan cheese, spread over sauce. Repeat layering twice using 4 noodles, ½-cup béchamel, and 1/3 of pesto. Cover with 4 noodles and spread remaining béchamel over the top layer of noodles. Sprinkle with remaining Parmesan cheese. Cover lasagna loosely with foil. Bake 30 minutes, uncover and bake until bubbly, about 15 minutes. Let stand 5-10 minutes. Cut into squares and enjoy.

GRILLED VEGETABLES with MANGO-CURRY DIP

Serves: 6

MARINADE

½ cup extra virgin olive oil, plus extra for brushing grill
½ teaspoon pepper, freshly ground
1 teaspoon of sweet paprika
1 teaspoon of ground turmeric

VEGETABLES

2 red bell peppers, seeded, cut into 6 wedges
2 yellow bell peppers, seeded, cut into 6 wedges
2 sweet onions cut into thick wedges
6 medium button mushrooms, stems removed
6 large Roma tomatoes, halved

MANGO-CURRY DIP

2 cups ripe mango, diced, puréed
2 tablespoons fresh limejuice
2 tablespoons mild curry powder
1 cup plain yogurt, drained overnight in refrigerator, liquid discarded
1 tablespoon of extra virgin olive oil
Fine sea salt

In a large shallow glass dish, combine ½ cup of oil, salt, pepper, paprika and turmeric. Add vegetables and gently toss until well coated.

Thread vegetables on bamboo skewers, lightly brush grill rack with oil, prepare barbecue, set heat to medium-high.

Grill vegetables until slightly charred, turning occasionally, about 8-10 minutes.

MANGO DIP

In a medium bowl, combine puréed mango, add limejuice, curry powder, yogurt, oil, and season with salt. Refrigerate until ready to serve.

Arrange grilled vegetables on a large serving platter, spoon mango-curry dip into small glass serving bowls and serve with fresh, or grilled, French bread slices.

OVEN BAKED-STUFFED MUSHROOM CAPS
With
PENNE PASTA and BROCCOLI FLORETS

Serves: 4

MUSHROOMS & STUFFING

8 large brown mushroom caps, cleaned, stems removed
Sea salt
Pepper, freshly ground
¼ cup extra virgin olive oil
8 ounces goat cheese, such as Montrachet
¼ cup of Parmesan cheese, freshly grated
3 tablespoons of whipping cream
4 tablespoons watercress leaves, chopped

PASTA

1 pound of penne pasta
Sea salt
2 teaspoon of extra virgin olive oil
2 pounds broccoli florets, cooked and kept warm, for garnish

RIESLING SAUCE

1 teaspoon of unsalted butter
1 large shallot, peeled, chopped
½ cup dry Riesling wine
1 cup of whipping cream
Sea salt
Mélange peppercorn, freshly ground

4 <u>optional</u> Italian or German sausages

Preheat oven to 400°F

To prepare mushrooms: Lightly brush an ovenproof dish with oil, place mushrooms in the dish, brush each mushroom with oil, sprinkle each with salt and pepper and set aside.

To prepare filling: In a medium bowl, combine goat cheese, Parmesan cheese, cream and watercress, season lightly with salt and pepper. Fill each mushroom cap with a spoonful of goat cheese mixture, drizzle again lightly with oil and bake for 15-20 minutes or until the top of filling is golden brown and mushrooms are tender.

Prepare pasta while mushrooms are baking: Cook pasta in boiling, salted water until tender to the bite, about 10-12 minutes or according to package instructions. Drain pasta, transfer to a warm large bowl, drizzle with 2 teaspoons of oil and toss, cover and keep warm while pasta is cooking make the sauce.

To prepare sauce: In a medium saucepan, heat butter over medium heat, add shallots and sauté for about 1-minute, or until soft - add wine and cook 1-minute - turn heat to medium low, add cream and cook 6-minutes — turn heat to low, season with salt and pepper, keep warm.

To serve: Divide pasta among 4 pre-warmed serving dishes, place 2 mushroom caps alongside pasta, garnish with broccoli florets, drizzle sauce over pasta and serve as a vegetarian dish, or with meat. _See Note, below._

Note: To convert this vegetarian dish to a meat dish, cook sausage in a medium skillet heating 2 teaspoons of extra virgin olive over medium-high heat and adding 4 sausages of choice to skillet – cook until browned on all sides, about 12-15 minutes. Place cooked sausage on top of pasta and enjoy.

Convertible vegetarian dish – Oven Baked-stuffed Mushroom Caps with Penne Pasta and Broccoli Florets –

Photo shown with optional sausage

Shiitake - Round-cap mushrooms

Oyster - Irregular shape mushrooms

GOAT CHEESE-HERBS stuffed ZUCCHINI BLOSSOMS

Serves: 6

24 zucchini blossoms, a summer squash
½ cup mascarpone cheese
½ cup goat cheese, such as Montrachet
2 tablespoons extra virgin olive oil
1 small, sweet onion, chopped
3 cloves garlic, minced
¼ cup Italian parsley, freshly chopped
¼ cup watercress leaves, freshly chopped
Sea salt
Pepper, freshly ground
Flour for dusting blossoms
2 eggs, slightly beaten with 1 tablespoon of
fresh lemon juice
Light olive oil or grape seed oil, for frying

Wash blossoms and trim off stem ends. In a medium bowl, blend mascarpone, goat cheese with extra virgin olive oil and add onion, garlic, parsley and watercress - season with salt and pepper. Spoon a teaspoon of filling into each blossom, twist ends to seal in the filling, roll blossoms in flour to coat lightly and dip in beaten egg mixture.

Heat ¼ inch of light olive oil or grape seed oil in a large deep frying pan, over medium-high heat, add coated blossoms, fry turning once, about 3-minutes, until golden brown. Drain on paper towels and arrange fried blossoms on a pre-warmed large serving dish.

Serve as a side dish or as an appetizer, also known as tapas (Spanish) or hors d'oeuvre (French).

A little information about squashes: Zucchini is a soft-skin summer squash member of the gourd family, generally available April through September. The peak season for winter squashes is usually between October and March. Look for availability of blossoms before and during both harvest periods. Blossoms are very delicate and should be kept cool and dry, if possible, during transport from place of purchase to your refrigerator. The flesh (fruit) of most all squash are edible, some of which, can be eaten raw, and the flesh of some other squashes, like pumpkin, must be cooked, but the flesh of some varieties of hard shell gourd are not edible. Summer squashes usually will have soft skin whereas winter squashes, like pumpkin and non-edible gourds have hard shells. You'll usually see hollowed out shells of non-edible gourd used as hanging displays at markets as well as decoratively painted or used as flower containers.

A test kitchen or series of tests aren't necessary to determine quality and freshness of zucchini - it is fresh when it resists slightly physical bending and it easily snaps in two when more pressure is applied or its skin color appears silky and smooth and flesh is juicy light in color. Zucchini is not fresh when it is bendable and does not easily break in two, or when its skin color has lost its luster and has darkened or is shriveled, and flesh is dryer and pitted.

Stuffed Zucchini Blossoms, see Recipe on previous Page

Zucchini Soufflé, see Recipe on Page 204

ZUCCHINI au GRATIN

Serves: 4

½ cup freshly grated Parmesan cheese
1 tablespoon garlic, minced
3 tablespoons fresh mixed herbs, chopped, such as: sage, thyme, watercress and parsley
Soft unsalted butter for greasing
2-3 medium green zucchini, cut into ¼ inch slices
1 teaspoon of fine sea salt
1 teaspoon freshly ground white pepper
2 eggs, beaten
½ cup whipping cream
2 tablespoons extra virgin olive oil

Preheat oven to 350°F
Butter a 2-inch deep heatproof dish

In a small bowl, mix together cheese, garlic and herbs. Arrange one layer of zucchini slices over bottom of prepared dish, sprinkle with salt and pepper and then a sprinkling with ½ of cheese mixture.

In a small bowl, combine eggs and cream. Arrange second layer of sliced zucchini over cheese mixture and another sprinkle of salt and pepper.

Pour egg and cream mixture over zucchini, drizzle with oil and sprinkle remaining cheese mixture on top of the egg-cream mixture.

Bake 25-30 minutes, or until top is golden brown. Enjoy with fish or meat dishes.

ZUCCHINI BLOSSOM

STUFFED ZUCCHINI BOATS with YELLOW TOMATO SAUCE
"Signature"

"Cooking with Erika"
Created during year "1976" and demonstrated on local, weekly TV Segment, aired during year 2001

Serves: 4

4 medium-size green zucchini, halved with pulp removed, chopped and reserved
Sea salt
Pepper
8 ounces sweet Italian sausage, casing removed and crumbled
½ cup onion, chopped
¼ cup homemade breadcrumbs
2 tablespoons Italian parsley, chopped
2 tablespoons sour cream
1 egg
1 teaspoon of sweet paprika, Avail in supermarkets
½ cup of whole milk mozzarella, cut in strips (preferably water packed) and drained
3 tablespoons extra virgin olive oil

Preheat oven to 350°F

Place zucchini boats in a shallow, glass, baking dish. Sprinkle lightly with salt and pepper and set aside.

In a medium bowl, mix together sausage, onion, chopped zucchini pulp, breadcrumbs, parsley, sour cream, egg and paprika. Spoon sausage mixture into each zucchini boat, and sprinkle each boat with olive oil and bake for 35 minutes. Remove zucchini boats from oven, top each with mozzarella and bake them 10-15 more minutes, or until lightly browned and bubbly on top.

YELLOW TOMATO SAUCE - makes about 4 cups

3 tablespoons extra virgin olive oil
½ cup onions, finely diced
2 large garlic cloves, peeled, minced
6 large yellow tomatoes, puréed
Sea salt
Pepper, freshly ground
1 tablespoon fresh basil leaves, chopped
1 tablespoon fresh oregano leaves, chopped
1 tablespoon fresh Italian parsley, chopped

Heat olive oil in a medium saucepan over medium heat, add onions and sauté until onions are soft, but not brown, about 1-2 minutes. Add garlic and sauté 1-2 seconds.

Add puréed tomatoes to the onion-garlic mixture, season with salt and pepper, and simmer for 20-30 minutes — sauce will reduce and thicken slightly - Add basil, oregano and parsley, keep warm.

To enjoy: Spoon sauce onto a large serving platter, arrange zucchini halves on top of sauce and serve immediately with a side dish of hot basmati rice (see Page 242) and extra sauce. Substitute with red or orange tomatoes if yellow tomatoes are not available.

SAVORY ZUCCHINI TART with TOMATO SALAD

Serves: 4

DOUGH

1¾ cups unbleached all-purpose flour, plus extra
½ teaspoon sea salt
1 stick of unsalted butter, cubed, plus extra for greasing
1 egg
3 tablespoons of cold water

In a medium bowl, combine the flour and salt – work-in the butter with your fingers until the mixture resembles coarse meal. Add egg and 3-tablespoons of cold water, and knead gently until the mixture comes together - add a little more water or flour if needed. Shape into a ball, wrap in plastic and refrigerate for at least 30 minutes.

FILLING

2 tablespoons extra virgin olive oil
½ pound zucchini, sliced into ½ inch coins
Sea salt
Pepper, freshly ground
1 teaspoon fresh Italian parsley, minced
1 cup of provolone, coarsely shredded, preferably imported from Italy
5 ounces prosciutto, cut into thin strips
1 egg with 1 tablespoon of cold water, beaten together in a small bowl

Heat oil in a large skillet on medium-high heat, and add zucchini, sauté about 1-2 minutes, season with salt and pepper, and sprinkle with parsley. Transfer to a large plate lined with a paper towel and let cool.

Preheat oven to 400°F

Roll the dough out on a lightly floured surface to a thickness of 1/10 inch. Butter an 8-inch tart pan, line it with dough, cut off excess and fill with zucchini, provolone and prosciutto. Gather and roll out excess dough, cut it into narrow ribbon-like strips and space strips to cover filling. Next, press ends of strips firmly against pastry sides, brush the top with beaten egg and bake 30 minutes, or until golden on top.

TOMATO SALAD

2 tablespoons extra virgin olive oil
3 tablespoons balsamic vinegar
½ cup Walla Walla sweet onion, chopped
¼ teaspoon sugar
Sea salt
Pepper, freshly ground
1 tablespoon fresh Italian parsley, chopped
1 tablespoon fresh basil leaves, chopped
1 tablespoon watercress leaves, chopped
4 each ripe tomatoes - red, yellow and green zebra, cut into slim wedges

In a large glass bowl, combine oil, vinegar, onion and sugar and season with salt and pepper. Stir-in parsley, basil and watercress, add tomato wedges, toss lightly and set aside.

To enjoy: Arrange a slice of zucchini tart on a serving plate and spoon tomato salad into a small glass bowl and serve with crusty French bread and your favorite crisp white wine.

Left - Yellow Tomato Sauce, Page 207

Right - Zucchini Boats, Page 207

Front center - Savory Zucchini Fritters, see below

ZUCCHINI FRITTERS

Serves: 6-8

1 pound, about 3½ - 4 cups, zucchini, coarsely grated
2 eggs, beaten
½ cup sweet onion, peeled, chopped
1/3 cup all-purpose flour
½ cup Parmesan cheese, freshly grated
½ teaspoon sea salt
½ teaspoon pepper, freshly ground
Light olive oil or grape seed oil, for frying

To make fritters: Place zucchini in a clean dishtowel, squeeze out any excess liquid, discard liquid. Place zucchini in a large bowl, and combine with eggs, flour, cheese, salt and pepper.

Heat 2-3 tablespoons of oil in a large frying pan, add 2 tablespoons of zucchini mixture for each fritter and cook three fritter at a time, for about 2-3 minutes, over medium heat on each side until golden.

Drain fritters on paper towels, and keep them warm while cooking remaining fritters – add 2-3 tablespoons of oil to the pan, if necessary.

Zucchini fritters are excellent served with fruity chutney, a salsa, or as a side dish to chicken, pork or fish.

ZUCCHINI SOUFFLÈ

Serves 6

garlic, cream, cheese, parsley and mascarpone - season with salt and pepper, divide the zucchini mixture among the prepared ramekins, then place them in a roasting pan, pour hot water into the roasting pan, to come halfway up the outsides of the ramekins. Bake for 30-35 minutes.

The mixture should have risen and be firm to a light touch in the center and should not wobble excessively when given a light push.

Remove soufflé from oven and let them cool for about 5 minutes. Slide a knife blade around inside of ramekins and invert the soufflé on to warmed serving plates. Garnish with tomato wedges.

4 cups finely grated zucchini
2 eggs, beaten
4 tablespoons all-purpose flour
1/3 cup of sweet onions diced
2 garlic cloves, minced
4 tablespoons whipping cream
6 tablespoons Parmesan cheese, freshly grated
2 tablespoons parsley chopped
1/3 cup of mascarpone cheese
Sea salt
Pepper, freshly ground
Extra virgin olive oil, for greasing ramekins

Preheat oven to 350°F
Lightly oil 6 ramekins and set aside

Place grated zucchini in a clean dishtowel, squeeze out any excess liquid and discard liquid. Place zucchini in a large bowl and add eggs, flour, onion,

Fresh Zucchini Blossoms & Beans

SAUTÉED EGGPLANT and BULGUR
With
GARLIC TOMATOES

Serves: 4

2 large, fresh eggplants, peeled and sliced
2-inches thick
2 eggs
6 tablespoons dry white wine
4 tablespoons all-purpose flour
¼ teaspoon of sea salt
¼ teaspoon pepper
6-8 tablespoons light olive oil, plus extra

1½ cups bulgur grain
Water
1 teaspoon of sea salt

1 tablespoon of extra virgin olive oil
3 cloves garlic, chopped
2 large yellow tomatoes, cubed
2 large red tomatoes, cubed
2 green tomatoes, cubed
¼ cup of fresh basil leaves, coarsely
chopped
1 teaspoon lemon juice, freshly squeezed
2 tablespoons grated Parmesan cheese
Basil leaves and lemon slices for garnishes

In a shallow dish, mix eggs with wine, blend-in the flour, and season with salt and pepper. Dip eggplant in egg mixture to coat all sides. Heat oil in a large skillet, sauté eggplant, turning once, until eggplant is golden brown on both sides.

Transfer to a warm, large plate, tent with foil to keep warm.

In a medium saucepan, cook bulgur in plenty of boiling, salted water for 10-minutes and drain.

In another large skillet, heat oil, add garlic and cooked bulgur, and sauté 1-minute - stirring often.

Add tomatoes and basil, sauté 5-6 minutes, season with salt, pepper, if needed, and add lemon juice. Keep warm.

To enjoy: Mound cooked tomatoes and bulgur mixture on 4 warmed plates, sprinkle with Parmesan cheese, place slices of eggplant around bulgur-tomato mixture, and garnish with basil and lemon slices.

Note: Bulgur is a wheat berry, which has had its bran removed, it then is steamed, dried and ground into various degrees of coarseness; it has a nutlike flavor, texture and a uniform golden-brown color; it is used for salads, stews or cooked like rice.

RICOTTA-ARUGULA DUMPLINGS

Serves: 4

1 pound of whole milk ricotta cheese, drained overnight in refrigerator, discard liquid
1 cup all-purpose flour
1 large egg
½ pound arugula leaves, chopped
½ teaspoon sea salt
¼ teaspoon pepper, freshly ground
Flour for dusting
1 teaspoon of sea salt
6 tablespoons unsalted butter, melted
2 tablespoons parmesan cheese, freshly grated

In a medium bowl, mix together ricotta, flour, egg, arugula, ½ teaspoon salt and ¼ teaspoon pepper with a wooden spoon until well incorporated.

Turn ricotta-arugula mixture out onto a lightly floured surface and shape dough into small oval dumplings with well-floured hands.

Bring 4-quarts of water and 1-teaspoon of salt to a boil. Add dumplings, turn heat to medium and boil until they rise to the surface.

Using a slotted spoon, transfer dumplings to a large serving platter, spoon butter over dumplings, and sprinkle with cheese. Enjoy!

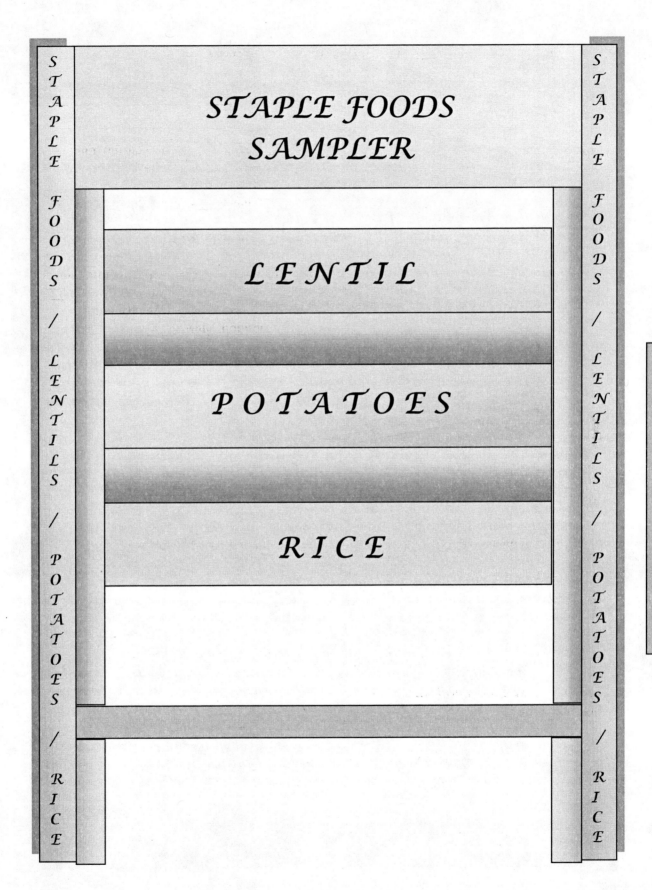

STAPLE FOODS
SAMPLER

LENTIL

POTATOES

RICE

LENTILS

Lentils are probably one of the first pulses crops (a variety of the legumes family like beans, and peas) to be domesticated. Originating in the fertile crescent of the Near East, and said that lentils date back to the beginning of agriculture itself, as the earliest carbonized remains (10,000 years old) were apparently unearthed on the banks of the Euphrates river in Northern Syria.

Cultivation of lentils since then spread to Greece to Southern Bulgaria, Crete, Hungary, Czechoslovakia, Switzerland, Germany and even France. Ancient Greece regarded lentils as a poor man's food, the Assyrians grew lentils in gardens at Babylon, and the practice of cultivating lentils crops continued its spread Eastward into India and China.

During the early 16th Century, Spanish and Portuguese introduced lentils to the new world and introduced it to America during World War I. Apart from being one among other staple foods originated in the Near East and India where it is an important source of protein, lentils is a very favorable source of protein for many adhering to vegetarian-style diets. In America and Europe lentils are generally used in soups, whereas, in the Near East lentils are more widely used in stews, salads as well as in soups and many other food concoctions. Lentil salad often forms part of the French Hors D'oeuvres table and in Germany puréed lentils may at times be an excellent substitute for potatoes served as an accompaniment to pork and other meats.

Lentils, one of the least known legumes of today, are available year round in most supermarkets or Middle Eastern markets. They are classified according to size, color of seed coat and the color of the inside. There are three common varieties; they are the large seeded types with pale green seed coats and smaller types with darker seed coats like the brown or nearly black variety, and the small frequently split, bright orange or red lentils from which the seed coat has been removed. Lentils are low in fat and rich in carbohydrates, protein, calcium, iron, phosphorus and "B" vitamins.

SWEET-SOUR LENTIL SOUP
"Signature"

Serves: 6

1 2/3 cups of dried lentils - brown, green, yellow or red, rinsed
3 quarts vegetable stock or water
1 teaspoon of extra virgin olive oil
½ cup of onion, chopped
½ cup Yukon gold potatoes, peeled and diced
½ cup of carrots, peeled and diced
1 stalk of celery, sliced
¼ cup celery root, peeled and diced
Sea salt
Pepper, freshly ground
½ teaspoon of sugar
1-2 teaspoon(s) apple cider vinegar
Parsley, chopped for garnish

Place lentils in a large stockpot, cover with 3 quarts stock or water, add 1 teaspoon of salt, bring to a boil, turn heat to medium-low, cover and simmer for 30 minutes or until almost tender.

In a large saucepan, heat oil, add onions, potatoes, carrots, celery stalk and celery root and sauté until vegetables are almost tender stirring often. Add vegetables to simmering lentils, cook for 15-20 more minutes and season to taste with salt and pepper. Stir in sugar and vinegar.

Lentil soup should have a pleasantly balanced sweet and sour flavor. Add a bit more sugar and vinegar, if needed.

Ladle soup into soup bowls, sprinkle each with parsley and enjoy with crusty French bread slices.

HEARTY LENTIL SOUP

Serves: 4

3 tablespoons extra virgin olive oil
1 cup sweet onions, finely chopped
2/3 cup of carrots, peeled and chopped
½ cup parsnip, peeled and chopped
1¼ cup dried green lentils, rinsed
5½ - 6 cups chicken stock or vegetable stock
Sea salt
Pepper, freshly ground
2 tablespoons fresh parsley, chopped

Heat oil in a large saucepan over medium heat and add onions, carrots, parsnip and sauté until slightly softened, about 5-minutes. Remove vegetables and set aside. Add lentils and stir 1-minute. Add 5½ -cups of stock and bring to boil, reduce heat to medium-low, cover and simmer until lentils are tender, stirring occasionally, about 30-40 minutes. Add reserved vegetables and simmer 10-more minutes. Season with salt and pepper, stir-in parsley and enjoy with crusty bread.

Chef's note: If thinner soup is desired, add more stock ¼ cup at a time.

BELUGA LENTILS
With
SAUTÉED SHRIMP and ORANGE-PERNOD-HERB SAUCE
"Signature"

Serves: 4

BELUGA LENTIL

1 cup black lentils, rinsed (Available in specialty food stores)
4 cups water
2 teaspoons sea salt
3 tablespoons extra virgin olive oil
¼ cup sweet onions, chopped
Pinch of sugar
½ tablespoons garlic, minced
2 medium tomatoes, peeled, seeded and chopped
¼ cup cucumbers peeled, seeded, chopped
1 teaspoon of fresh lemon juice
1 tablespoon of balsamic vinegar
Sea salt
Pepper, freshly ground
Lemon wedges, for garnish

Place rinsed lentils in a medium saucepan, cover with 4-cups of cold water, add salt, bring to a boil, turn heat to medium-low, cover with lid and cook for 35-minutes, stirring occasionally. Drain lentils and shake off excess water. In a large skillet, heat 2-tablespoons of oil over medium-high heat, add onions and sugar, sauté 12-minute, add garlic, tomatoes, cucumbers and sauté for 6-minutes stirring often.

Turn heat to low. Stir-in lentils, lemon juice, balsamic vinegar, and remaining 1-tablespoon oil, and season with salt and pepper. Keep warm.

SHRIMP

1 bottle (8-ounces) clam juice
¼ cup fresh orange juice
3 tablespoons unsalted butter
2 tablespoons garlic, minced
1½ pounds of cooked, shelled medium-size shrimp
2 tablespoons Pernod (Avail. in Liquor Stores)
¼ cup watercress leaves, chopped, plus extra for garnish
Sea salt
Pepper, freshly ground

Bring clam juice and orange juice to a boil over medium-high heat in a large skillet. Boil until the liquid has reduced by half, about 5-6 minutes. Transfer reduced liquid to a small bowl and set aside. Without rinsing the skillet, return it to medium-high heat, add butter and garlic. Cook until garlic starts to sizzle, but not browned. Turn heat to medium-low, add shrimp and the reserved liquid, stir-in Pernod and watercress and season with salt and pepper, if needed. Keep warm.

Spoon equal amounts of lentil mixture onto 4-large warmed serving plates, arrange portions of shrimp on top of lentils, drizzle any remaining sauce over shrimp. Garnish with lemon wedges, sprinkle with watercress and enjoy.

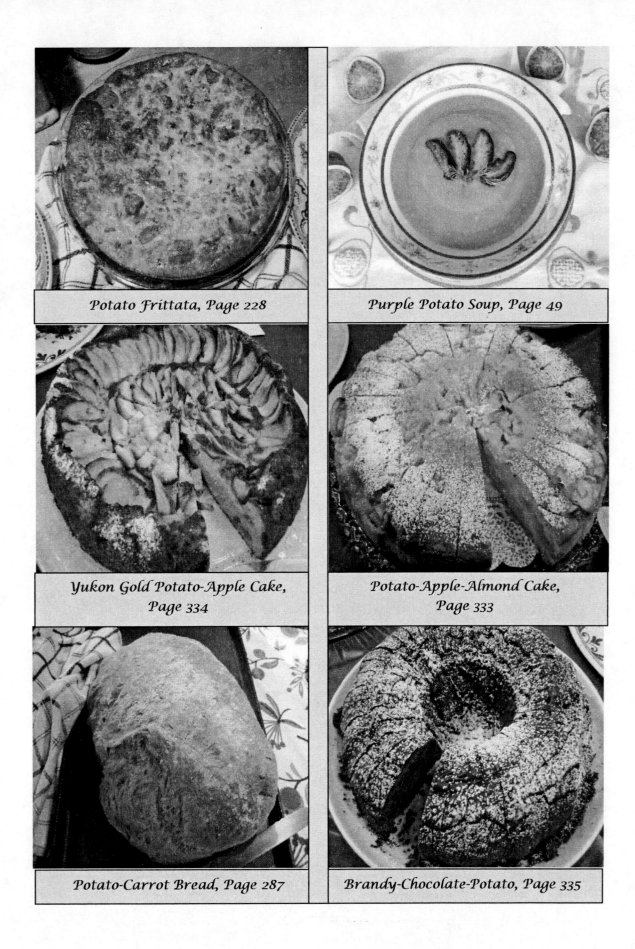

Potato Frittata, Page 228

Purple Potato Soup, Page 49

Yukon Gold Potato-Apple Cake,
Page 334

Potato-Apple-Almond Cake,
Page 333

Potato-Carrot Bread, Page 287

Brandy-Chocolate-Potato, Page 335

POTATO HIGHLIGHTS

PURPLE

BLUE

CRANBERRY

FINGERLINGS

YELLOW FINN

YUKON GOLD

SWEET POTATO

YUCCA ROOT

POTATOES

Varieties of potatoes from distant countries have found their way into American farms and markets - enjoyed in households and restaurants in a variety of preparations. Myself, having created several original recipes introducing purple and blue Peruvian potatoes, as vegetarian-main entrées, soups, salads, and as accompaniments to other dishes to patrons today as I did years ago, in my Western Washington Restaurant, I've decided to share some of those and some more recent creations with you in this cookbook.

In my previous cookbook, "A Touch of Europe® Cookbook - Bringing Fresh to the Table Naturally", published April 2005, I touched on ancient history of potatoes, and for purpose of this cookbook, I'm elaborating a little more on that theme but nudging a bit closer to modern times - remembering that practically everything new began with a ancient, historical action, event or discovery.

To begin with, I believe potatoes are healthier than given credit for.... For example, the high nutrient level in a single potato is a worthy health benefit, but there will be more reasons covered as to why that is in subsequent paragraphs. Remember purple and blue!

Even though it may seem that potato consumption has dropped a bit, they still are widely consumed these days, especially the so-called French-fried potatoes. But it is quite possible the cause may be the notion that this vegetable family possesses exceedingly high bad carbohydrates - categorically placing potatoes as an undesirable part of diets - when actually, it is what potatoes are topped with, stuffed with, cooked in or fried in, or when overly salted, that should warrant any concern over fat content, calorie count or health concern - not the potato. For example, a baked potato, by itself, only has about 20 grams of carbohydrates, starch, and if stored properly, its sugar level remains quite low - but more on that later.

Recalling when the European public's awareness of the success of Queen Julia of Holland's potato diet during early 1980's became known, it grew into a nationally favored diet highly promoted in Germany, Austria and other European countries. And, from my personal experience while on a potato diet, results for me and other participants in a "stay-in" European Spa environment over a two-week period (in Germany) was weight loss, my energy levels increased and I felt much healthier because of the high nutrient levels of potatoes in well regulated, appropriately apportioned dietary meals that contained lots of fiber, and filling up on fiber meant consuming fewer calories. <u>*Continued on next page.*</u>

POTATO HIGHLIGHTS

213

For illustrative purposes only, a partial example could be: One baked potato, about 20 grams of carbohydrates-starch for energy with its vitamins B and C combined with fiber, like whole wheat grain or rye bread, rather than refined and whole wheat grain or rye bread rather than refined and whole fruits rather than processed. Why "whole", because I believe refining removes fiber, and obviously, the natural nutritional benefits of "whole" foods are reduced.

If there aren't any medical or allergenic reasons against doing so, enjoy an occasional potato in your diet while being discretionary on what its toppings are or whatever else might accompany the potato.

Furthermore, potatoes are very low in kilojoules (kilocalories), as referenced in the European metric measures system – an equivalent of 4,185.5 joules equals 1-calorie. Potatoes contain only 1 gram of fat per 150 grams of potato, and there is as much potassium in one large potato as there is in one-half of a banana.

As best as I can determine, the purple, blue and cranberry red potato varieties yield the most favorable nutritional values of any other variety, plus their use in preparations are practically unlimited and they make for showy presentations. But I tend to consider these varieties most versatile and aptly adaptable in the gourmet category, as you will see in the following recipes – without going too extreme for the purpose of this book.

COOKING DURATION

Purple and blue potatoes are delicious fried, boiled, baked or steamed. Color is well retained when not overcooked. Both varieties are late easy growing-high yielding and cook faster than yellow or white varieties. Over-cooking causes mushiness and crumbliness. Cook small potatoes (golf ball size) 10-15 minutes. Medium (between golf ball-baseball size): 15-20 minutes. Large (baseball-softball size): 25-30 minutes.

Cranberry red potatoes cook quickly – small size: 10-15 minutes, medium: 15-20 minutes and large 25-30 minutes. This potato variety has an earthy flavor and creamy texture, thin skin and peels easily.

Butterball potatoes are rounder, with similar texture, but have more intense color and flavor than the small-medium size, thin skin, Yellow Finnish potatoes or the larger, better known Yukon Gold potato.

Purple and blue potatoes, which shoppers may have noticed displayed in supermarkets and passed them by without taking a second look, possess excellent potato flavor. The only visible difference is their solid color, except for the purple variety, shown in color on page 219 with the fingerling potato has a white outer ring between skin and purple flesh - not visible until peeled or halved.

(Opposite photo - Left to Right - Royal Blue, Butterball and Cranberry Red) See color page 236.

Apart from excellent flavor, their antioxidant level is equal to that of blueberries, a health benefit that deserves a second look - antioxidant accounts for their brilliant color too. These true, genetically unaltered, naturally purple and blue vegetables originated in the Peruvian Andes and regarded there as the king of all potatoes, which are presumed to have been the first to be harvested and prepared for serving only to Inca kings. This is because purple and blue, are usually regarded as symbolic colors associated with royalty, and thus only kings were worthy of the health benefits of these delicious earthy-flavored, low starch, nutritional tubers. Through the years, these potatoes became available to us peasants so we also can take advantage of the benefits these flavorful morsels provided to them.

Basically, these potatoes are at least as versatile as the well-known all-purpose potatoes because they taste great in both simple and complex concoctions.

(Opposite photo - Purple Potato Salad- See Recipe on Page: 222)

The recipes I've created for publishing in this cookbook combine the exact amounts of ingredients, seasonings and herbs that are best used with these potatoes to yield balanced flavor that I believe everyone will enjoy. They make excellent potato salad, great potato soups and they taste delicious whether roasted, fried, baked, steamed, or prepared for use as an accompaniment or as a main dish.

<u>And yes, they taste exactly like potato because they are potato - only their natural colors are different.</u>

<u>Note:</u> Embedded black & white photos in text for illustrative and referencing purposes only. Subsequent pages may show specimens in color.

Returning briefly to history, there are in excess of 200 potato varieties in the world and most of them originated in Peru and because of that, I personally refer to Peru as the world's potato capital. But, in my teen years in Germany, my original homeland of birth, I thought Germany was the potato capital of the world because potatoes were so often served back home.

(Opposite photo - Left to Right
Fingerling potatoes, a favorite in Germany and other parts of Europe, and Purple potatoes, notice the white outer ring.) See color page 236.

Later in life I found that potatoes were abundantly available - a staple food, but one that has many possibilities. I find intrigue behind the origins of foods so intensely I feel compelled to share some of its details - such an abundance of history that it's difficult to comprehend all of it in a short period of time, but one thing in common with some foods - there always seems to be an initial link with Royalty from various lands at one time or another, or from an adventurer or from the likes of the blowing wind spreading pollen from one area's crops to another so to speak.

I found that Peru is home to the International potato center with a research facility that has catalogued hundreds of native tubers including some near extinction in a rainbow of colors - golden yellow to deep purple. One of the deep purple varieties, because of its color intensity, is oftentimes referred to as black potato. Then, in 1984 the cranberry red potato (also known as the all-red potato) was developed from a potato exchange.

(Opposite photo – Hand formed Cranberry Red Potato Dumplings – See Recipe on Page: 223 and color page 236.

Also developed was a potato named "Bison" to grow well in draught conditions; it has earthy flavor; cooks quickly; peels easily, and makes excellent potato salad, French fries - baked or fried - potato soups and stews are few of many preparative ways to enjoy these and other varieties of potatoes.

In the Andes, potatoes are also set out to freeze in the cold mountain nights, then dehydrated in the highlands sun each day until they become freeze-dried pebbles, a preserving process designed for storing them over long periods of time - a very interesting and natural way to preserve potatoes, ensuring availability

216

over the winter months. These freeze-dried potatoes often make-up a delicious, rich pork- potato-rice and peppers stew.

The potato seed is very hardy and adaptable to growing conditions below sea level, even behind the Dutch dykes to almost 14,000 feet up the chilly Peruvian Andes and Himalayas. In some parts of Europe, it is said that the potato was cursed as being a food of evil when first introduced to Europe because it was unmentioned in the bible, and thus the Scots refused to eat them. But

apparently Catherine the Great, among other Royal Europeans, were convincing enough to bring about public acceptance of this humble, delicious (staple) vegetable.

(Opposite Photo - Potato Frittata, use Yellow Finn or Butterball Potatoes, see Recipe on Page 228.)

It's interesting to know that a field of potatoes yields more nutrition in less growing time and space and survives harsher climates than many other major staple foods like, corn or wheat; that one potato provides 600 – 800 mg. of potassium, essential in maintaining a healthy body, and that six-ounces of potato contains three grams of highly digestible protein and carbohydrates, which provide our body with necessary sources of energy – containing nearly as much as is contained in a half glass of milk. Factoring protein benefits of potatoes in with its nutrient values, vitamins B and C, and the good carbohydrates, in my estimation, potentially could be considered a wholesome meal all by itself.

I have always stood by the assumption that potatoes consumed in reasonable portions, are not weight gaining culprits.

(Opposite photo - color intensity of red cranberry, purple and butterball potatoes heightens during cooking.) See color page 236.

It's my emphatic belief, the toppings, accompaniments, and the substance (liquid) in which the potato is cooked, are the calorie and fat boosters rather than the potato. All-in-all the golden rule "portion control" and making "healthy choices" still rules, in my opinion. Now you can tease your palate with the following recipes, enjoy.

POTATO GRATIN
With
GOAT CHEESE and TOMATO SALAD

"Cooking with Erika"
Signature recipe created to demonstrate it on local, weekly TV segment, aired during year 2001

Serves: 4-6

1 cup of whole milk
1 cup whipping cream
1 cup crumbled soft, fresh goat cheese, such as Montrachet
1 garlic clove, minced
¼ cup Swiss cheese, of good quality
1½ teaspoons sea salt
½ teaspoon pepper, freshly ground
¼ teaspoon freshly ground nutmeg
2 pounds Yukon gold potatoes, peeled, thinly sliced
2 teaspoons fresh Italian parsley, chopped
1 teaspoon fresh chives, chopped

Preheat oven to 350°F
Generously butter 11x7x2 inch glass-baking dish.

Whisk first 8 ingredients in a medium bowl to blend.

Arrange 1/3 of potatoes in bottom of prepared dish. Pour 1/3 of cream mixture over.

Repeat layering potatoes and cream mixture 2 more times.

Bake uncovered until potatoes are tender and top is golden brown, about 1 hour. Sprinkle with parsley and chives before serving.

TOMATO SALAD

¼ cup red onions, chopped
2 tablespoons balsamic vinegar, of good quality
1 teaspoon of extra virgin olive oil
½ teaspoon sea salt
½ teaspoon pepper, freshly ground
¼ teaspoon sugar
4 large vine ripened tomatoes, cut into slim wedges
1 tablespoon fresh Italian parsley, chopped
1 tablespoon fresh chives, chopped
1 tablespoon fresh dill, chopped

Mix the first 3 ingredients in a medium glass bowl and blend - season with salt, pepper and sugar. Add tomatoes, parsley, chives, dill, and toss lightly. Enjoy with potato gratin.

PURPLE POTATO-PROSCIUTTO BAKE
"Signature"

Serves: 6

6 large purple potatoes, scrubbed
Extra virgin olive oil, for brushing potatoes
½ cup Parmesan cheese, freshly grated
1 cup prosciutto or Westphalian ham, chopped
½ cup sweet onions, finely minced
2 tablespoons Italian parsley, chopped
¾ cup unsalted butter, melted
Sea salt
Pepper, freshly ground
1 cup of fresh-white breadcrumbs

Preheat oven to 425°F

Brush potatoes lightly with olive oil, arrange them on a large baking sheet and bake 45-50 minutes. Let potatoes cool slightly, cut in half lengthwise and scoop out almost all of their pulp leaving enough so that halves are still firm.

Put pulp through a ricer into a medium bowl and add cheese, prosciutto or Westpahlien ham, onion parsley, ½ cup melted butter, salt and pepper to taste, mix thoroughly - stuff each potato half with mixture, sprinkle with breadcrumbs to cover and drizzle each with remaining butter.

Preheat oven to 400°F

Arrange potatoes in a roasting pan and bake 10-15 minutes or until golden on top. Arrange baked potatoes on a warmed, large platter and serve hot.

Chef's Note: If possible, avoid purchasing potatoes that have green tinted skins or green spots because they may have been improperly stored or were exposed to direct sunlight. Spots and sprouts may contain solanine, a bitter, toxic crystalline compound, affecting nightshade plants, such as potatoes and tomatoes. If purchased, scrape away green spots and remove sprouts from potatoes before cooking. I suggest peeling and cooking blemished potatoes using a recipe that does not suggest cooking or baking them with skins on. Proper storage for potatoes is in a cool, dark, dry, well-ventilated area. Storing potatoes in a refrigerator or other confined space turns natural potato starch into sugar. Emphasis on proper handling, storing and preparation means everything to yield best results.

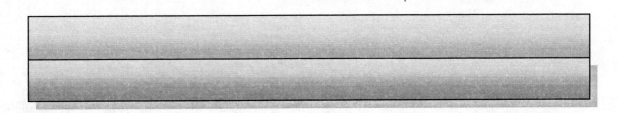

PURPLE POTATO-OYSTER MUSHROOM LASANGA

"Signature" – My original, among other identified recipes in this cookbook created for, and personally demonstrated recipe, showcased & served this dish for and to the Washington State Potato Seed Commission at the Washington State University Exploratory Laboratory, November 17, 2006)

Serves: 8

8 large purple potatoes
Sea salt
Mélange peppercorn, freshly ground

Cook potatoes in a large pot of boiling water until just tender, about 20-25 minutes, (do not overcook). Drain well and cool. Peel potatoes and cut into ½-inch slices and set aside.

BÉCHAMEL SAUCE

5 tablespoons unsalted butter
¼ cup all-purpose flour
2½ cups whole milk, hot
½ cup dry white wine
1½ teaspoons sea salt
½ teaspoon white pepper, freshly ground
½ teaspoon nutmeg, freshly grated
4 cloves garlic, minced

Melt butter in a 2-3 quart saucepan over moderate heat, whisk in flour until smooth – cook whisking frequently, until pale golden, about 1-2 minutes. Add hot milk, 1- cup at a time to butter mixture, whisking constantly until very smooth. Add wine, bring sauce to a boil whisking - cook on low-medium heat still whisking, about 5-minutes. Turn off heat and whisk-in 1½ teaspoons salt, ½ teaspoon white pepper, ½ teaspoon nutmeg and ¼ cup of minced garlic. Let sauce cool to room temperature – stir occasionally.

CHEESE FILLING

2 cups whole milk ricotta cheese, drained overnight, refrigerated discard liquid
1½ cups parmigiano reggiano or parmesan cheese, freshly grated
6 cloves garlic, minced
16 ounces arugula, coarsely chopped
Sea salt
Mélange peppercorn, freshly ground

In a large bowl, mix together Ricotta cheese, 1 cup of parmigiano or parmesan cheese and ¼ cup of minced garlic, stir-in the chopped arugula, season lightly with salt, mélange pepper, and set aside.

MUSHROOM FILLING

6 tablespoons extra virgin olive oil, plus extra for oiling pan
1 pound of oyster mushrooms, cleaned and coarsely chopped
1 cup of shallots, peeled and coarsely chopped
Sea salt
Mélange peppercorn, freshly ground

Heat 6-tablespoons of oil in a large, deep skillet over medium-high heat, add mushroom and cook until golden brown, stirring often. Add shallots and cook 1-2 minutes, season with salt and mélange pepper. Using a slotted spoon, transfer mushrooms mixture to a bowl and let cool.

ASSEMBLE and BAKE LASANGA

Middle position an oven rack and preheat oven to 375°F

Lightly oil a 13 x 9 inch lasagna pan and cover the bottom with a layer of potatoes, sprinkle potatoes lightly with salt and mélange pepper, spread enough ricotta cheese mixture on top of the potatoes to cover, about ½ cup. Completely cover ricotta with about ½ cup of béchamel sauce. Place another layer of potatoes over the sauced ricotta and sprinkle potatoes lightly with salt and mélange pepper. Top with mushroom mixture to cover potatoes, spoon some of the sauce to cover mushrooms, about ½ cup, top with another layer of potatoes, sprinkle potatoes lightly with salt and pepper, top potatoes with remaining ricotta mixture and a final layer of potatoes lightly sprinkled with salt and mélange pepper. Spoon the remaining sauce over potatoes and sprinkle remaining ½ cup parmigiano-reggiano, or parmesan, cheese over the sauce. Bake lasagna uncovered until edges are bubbling and pale golden on top, about 35-45 minutes. Let lasagna stand 10-15 minutes before serving.

PURPLE MASHED POTATOES with GOAT CHEESE and CHIVES
"Signature - 1989"

Serves: 6

4 pounds medium purple potatoes, peeled and cut into 2-inch pieces
2 teaspoons sea salt
½ cup whole milk (warm)
¼ cup unsalted butter, softened
2 garlic cloves, minced
¼ cup sour cream
Sea salt
White pepper, freshly ground
1½ cups soft goat cheese, such as Montrachet
¼ cup chives, chopped

3 yellow tomatoes cut into wedges, for garnish
3 orange tomatoes cut into wedges, for garnish

Cook potatoes in a large pot of boiling, salted water until tender when pierced with a fork, about 14-minutes. Drain well, transfer to a large warm bowl, add milk, butter and garlic and sour cream, mash until mixture is light and fluffy - season to taste with salt and pepper.

In a small, nonstick saucepan, heat goat cheese over medium-low heat, stir until cheese melts, turn off heat, divide mashed potatoes among 6 warmed plates, spoon a dollop of warm goat cheese on top of each serving. Sprinkle chives over each serving and enjoy with yellow and orange tomato wedges, or serve with chicken, pork and salmon.

PURPLE POTATO SALAD
"Signature-1990"

Serves: 4

6 medium purple potatoes, cooked, peeled, thinly sliced
3 tablespoons safflower oil
2 teaspoons white balsamic vinegar
¼ teaspoon sea salt
¼ teaspoon pepper, freshly ground
Pinch of sugar
¼ cup homemade mayonnaise (See Page 272)
1 tablespoon chives, freshly chopped
1 tablespoon parsley, freshly chopped

Place potato slices in a large bowl and set aside. In a small bowl, combine oil, vinegar, salt, pepper and sugar. Pour mixture over potatoes and toss gently. Mix in mayonnaise, chives and parsley. Adjust seasoning to taste. Best when served at room temperature. _Note:_ One-fourth cup of finely chopped sweet onions can be added, if desired.

> *Note: For convenience and illustrative purposes, Purple Potato Salad recipe also appears in the salad section.*

OVEN ROASTED SWEET PAPRIKA POTATOES

Serves: 4-6

1 large purple potato, cut into 6 lengthwise wedges
1 large red cranberry potato, cut into 6 lengthwise wedges
6 small butterball potatoes, halved
¼ cup extra virgin olive oil
Sea salt
1½ tablespoons sweet paprika

Preheat oven to 400°F

Place potatoes on a large baking sheet, drizzle oil evenly over potatoes, sprinkle lightly with salt and paprika and bake 35-40 minutes or until tender when pierced with a fork – turn once during baking.

CRANBERRY RED POTATO DUMPLINGS

"Signature" – My original, among other identified recipes in this cookbook created for, and personally demonstrated this and other recipes, for the Washington State Potato Seed Commission at the Washington State University Exploratory Laboratory, Prosser, WA., November 17, 2006)

Serves: 6

2 pounds red cranberry potatoes, scrubbed clean
1¼ cups all-purpose flour or potato starch
1½ teaspoons horseradish
1 large egg, slightly beaten
¼ teaspoon white pepper, finely ground
1½ tablespoons sea salt

Cook potatoes in boiling water until tender, about 25-30 minutes, drain, slightly cool and peel. Transfer potatoes to a large shallow dish, loosely cover with plastic wrap and refrigerate overnight.

Next day, finely grate potatoes into a large bowl, add flour or cornstarch, horseradish, egg and pepper – mix until smooth. Dust hands lightly with flour and form 6-round dumplings.

Fill a large saucepan with water, add salt and bring to a boil – turn heat to medium-low and carefully drop dumplings, one at a time, into gently boiling water – cook 10-15 minutes or until they turn and float to the surface. Remove dumplings with a slotted spoon, arrange dumplings on a pre-warmed, shallow dish and serve with roast pork or as a vegetarian dish with pink peppercorn sauce – *see recipe below.*

PINK PEPPERCORN SAUCE

Makes: 6 servings

1½ cups whipping cream
½ cup Late Harvest Riesling wine
½ teaspoon sea salt
¼ teaspoon white pepper, freshly ground
½ teaspoon pink peppercorn
½ cup watercress leaves, chopped

In a medium saucepan, bring cream to a gentle boil, add wine and simmer on medium-low heat for 10-15 minutes. Turn heat to low.

Season with salt and white pepper, stir-in pink peppercorns and watercress and transfer to a pre-warmed sauce boat and serve with dumplings.

FRENCH FRIED POTATOES

Remembering the great tasting French fries in Germany offered at nearly every kiosk and kiosks were everywhere, including Holland and even in Belgium. The delicious mayonnaise was a typical accompaniment to Belgian French fries that seemed to combine flavors, letting the palate detect the potato and mayonnaise, rather than one flavor overpowering the other - balanced. Especially in Europe, balanced flavor is a consumer's typical expectation. Paprika and other types of sauces were optional choices, but their flavor strengths are intentionally concocted to enhance their own as well as the flavor of food served with it, rather than cover it up. Delicious!

Venturing a little deeper into the world of French fries raises the question, "where did they originate"? Today, the answer is still under debate, speculation and riddled with guesswork! But some people in Belgium claim that French fries originated there, while I can't say for sure, they surely tasted like an original - flavor was paramount over others I've tasted, but when in Germany, I enjoy Pomes Fritz mit majonäse as well as those in Holland and elsewhere. While I am quite particular about sauces, I just enjoy eating quality potatoes. I don't know of many people who dislike a nutritious potato.

I might add though, flavor of French fried potatoes will always vary depending on the type of fat or oil used in the deep fat frying process. Deviant flavor also results when battered potatoes are deep-fried. Writing this revives thoughts, that maybe Italy's Fritto Misto (FREE-toh MEES-toh) deep fried mix of battered vegetables included battered strips of potatoes. Unfortunately, we didn't try dishes with potatoes in Italy because we couldn't pass up on all of the excellent fish, seafood and pasta dishes while we were vacationing there, but as I write this, I think we might have missed out on something we should have tried. One thing for certain, an identical variety of potato deep fried in goose fat, pig lard, olive oil, vegetable oil or in other varieties of oil, as you may know, will invariably yield different flavor and texture whether or not battered. It's all a matter of preference and concerns.

In Germany, Pomes Fritz are traditionally thickly sliced and deep fried in goose fat, like in Belgium, and in some other European countries. Goose fat is regarded as one of the healthiest of fats and it's also one that has excellent flavor. But, today's emphasis in some parts of the world toward reducing consumption of fats seems to loosely imply that all fats fit into one negative category, which could cause diminishing use of some of those natural, traditional fats that I believe are healthier. I for one am not in agreement with replacing anything we ingest with chemically modified solutions that, in my opinion, present more of a health concern than as nature intended.

Returning to natural though, great alternatives I like for deep-frying are light olive oil, grape seed oil and peanut oil. I especially like deep frying potatoes in olive oil because of its refreshing, lingering light flavor that leaves potatoes a bit crispy on the outside, (depending on thickness of cut), soft inside but not mushy, and it doesn't leave an oily after taste. Potatoes deep-fried in any one of those three oils will, of course, have slightly different flavor, but whichever oil used, the potatoes taste great, like potato - not oil; there are fewer calories, and it may be found that heavy use of salt or commercial sauces most likely would be unnecessary because flavor needs little adjusting.

Potatoes destined for the deep fryer should be freshly peeled, sliced and not held soaking in ice water, unless you want to remove starch from the potatoes along with some of the flavor. When dry potatoes are introduced to the deep fryer, there is less chance of splattering; less dilution of oil, which simply means there will be less grease splatter to clean up afterward. Enjoy potato flavor!

L. - Purple / C. - Butterball / R. - Cranberry Potatoes

TRI-COLOR FRIES

"Signature" - My original, among other identified recipes in this cookbook created for, and personally demonstrated this recipe for the Washington State Potato Seed Commission at the Washington State University Exploratory Field, Patterson, WA., September 2, 2005)

Serves 6-8

2 large purple potatoes, peeled
2 large red cranberry potatoes, peeled
6 medium butterball potatoes, peeled
Light olive oil for deep-frying

Cut potatoes in even strips (or use a potato cutter tool), deep fry potato strips in batches for 5-minutes at 325°F, drain on paper towels and let cool 10-minutes. Increase heat to 375°F – fry until potatoes are nicely browned and crisp. Drain again on paper towels and serve hot with a sprinkling of sea salt. Twice fried, Belgian-style!

Enjoy with Red Bell Pepper-Goat Cheese Dip Sauce, Recipe on Page 227

225

SAUTEED (RED) CRANBERRY POTATOES
With
FRESH HERBS and PECORINO ROMANO CHEESE
"Signature"

Serves: 6-8

8 medium cranberry potatoes
2 tablespoons extra virgin olive oil
2 tablespoons unsalted butter
Fine sea salt
Mélange peppercorns, freshly ground
2 tablespoons fresh rosemary, chopped
2 garlic cloves, minced
½ cup Pecorino Romano cheese, freshly grated
2 tablespoons chives, freshly chopped
2 tablespoons Italian parsley, freshly chopped
Yellow tomato wedges, for garnish

Cook potatoes in a large saucepan of boiling water until tender when pierced with a fork, about 15-20 minutes.

Drain well and transfer to a large shallow dish – let cool, peel and cut potatoes into halves.

Divide oil and butter between 2 nonstick large skillets.

Turn heat to medium-high and divide potatoes, cut-side down among skillets, sprinkle potatoes lightly with salt and pepper.

Brown potatoes turning once until a light crust forms, about 1-minute per side.

Turn heat to medium-low, add rosemary and garlic - sauté 2-more seconds. Sprinkle each potato with cheese, cover skillets with lids and cook one more minute.

Turn off heat, transfer potatoes to a large warmed serving platter, sprinkle potatoes with chives and parsley, garnish with tomato wedges and serve hot.

Excellent served with chicken, pork, fish or sour cream-cucumber salad.

Notes

RED BELL PEPPERS-GOAT CHEESE DIP SAUCE

"Signature" – My original, among other identified recipes in this cookbook created for, and personally demonstrated this recipe for the Washington State Potato Seed Commission at the Washington State University Exploratory Field, Patterson, WA., September 2, 2005)

Serves: 6-8

2 cups red bell pepper, seeded and chopped
½ cup extra virgin olive oil
1 tablespoon of sweet paprika
½ teaspoon sea salt
¼ teaspoon pepper, freshly ground
½ cup onion, chopped
2 cloves garlic, chopped
1 cup of goat cheese, such as Montrachet

Place red peppers in a food processor, and add oil, paprika, salt, pepper, onion and garlic - purée until smooth, about 2-3 seconds. Add goat cheese and purée 1-more second. Transfer pepper mixture to a glass bowl - refrigerate until ready to serve.

POTATO FRITTATA

Serves: 6

4 medium yellow Finn or butterball
potatoes, cooked, peeled and thinly sliced
¼ cup extra virgin olive oil, plus extra for
greasing dish
1 teaspoon of sea salt
½ teaspoon pepper, freshly ground

Lightly oil a heatproof 10-inch round
baking dish and set aside

6 large eggs, organic preferred
1 tablespoon of sweet paprika
¼ cup whipping cream
¼ cup watercress leaves, chopped
1 cup Emmenthaler cheese, grated
¼ teaspoon sea salt

Preheat oven to 400°F

In a large skillet, heat oil over medium-high heat, add sliced potatoes, sprinkle with salt and pepper and cook stirring occasionally until light brown, about 10-15 minutes. Transfer to prepared dish.

In a large bowl, combine eggs, paprika, cream, watercress, cheese and salt – pour mixture over potatoes and bake until puffed and golden brown, about 20-30 minutes. Remove from oven and cut into 6 wedges and serve hot.

SPANISH STYLE POTATO SALAD
"Signature"

Serves: 6

2 pounds small butterball potatoes or
Red cranberry potatoes, boiled, peeled and
sliced about 1/8 inch thick
Sea salt
½ cup Spanish olive oil
2 tablespoons fresh lemon juice
2 tablespoons fresh orange juice
¼ cup sweet Spanish onions
¼ cup fresh chives, finely chopped
2 tablespoons fresh dill, finely chopped
2 tablespoons small Spanish capers,
drained (see list of supply sources)
Sea salt

Pepper, freshly ground

Arrange and layer potato slices in a large, shallow serving dish. Lightly sprinkle each layer with salt and pepper. In a small bowl, combine olive oil, lemon juice, orange juice, onions, chives, dill and capers - season to taste with salt and pepper. Pour marinade over layered potatoes and let stand at room temperature for at least 2-3 hours before serving.

BUTTERBALL POTATOES with SAFFRON-SHERRY SAUCE
"Signature"

Serves: 8

3 teaspoons unsalted butter
16 small potatoes, cooked and peeled
(butterball potatoes preferred)
2 cloves garlic, minced
2 large shallots, peeled, chopped
1½ teaspoons sea salt
½ teaspoon pepper, freshly ground

1 cup whipping cream
¼ cup cream sherry
½ teaspoon saffron, steeped in 1-2
tablespoon hot sherry or water for about
2-minutes
¼ cup watercress leaves, coarsely chopped

In a large deep skillet, heat butter over medium-high heat, add potatoes and sauté until potatoes are golden brown, stirring occasionally. Turn heat to medium, add the garlic and shallots - cook until shallots are soft, about 1-minute. Sprinkle with salt and pepper, stir-in whipping cream, the sherry, saffron, or water-saffron mixture, and cook gently for 1-2 more minutes. Stir-in watercress and divide evenly among 8 shallow serving dishes and *enjoy!*

PARSNIP-POTATO PURÉE

Serves: 4-6

2 medium parsnips, peeled and cut into small cubes
6 medium Yukon gold potatoes, peeled and cut into small cubes
2 teaspoons of sea salt
2 tablespoons unsalted butter
¼ teaspoon pepper, freshly ground
2 tablespoons sour cream
Fresh parsley, minced, for garnish

Cook parsnip and potatoes in boiling, salted water until tender, about 15-20 minutes. Remove from heat and drain well and add butter, pepper and sour cream. Whip until light and fluffy, season with salt and pepper, if needed, transfer to a warmed serving bowl and sprinkle with parsley. *Enjoy.*

BAKED POTATO
With
ZAPPY AVOCADO DIP
"Signature"

Serves: 6

6 large baking potatoes
Extra virgin olive oil

2 large, ripe avocados, pits removed, peeled and chopped
2 tablespoons of fresh lemon juice
¼ teaspoon of sea salt
1 pound of cream cheese, softened
½ cup of sour cream
2 small green zucchini, coarsely chopped
2 large red bell peppers, seeded and chopped
2 red chili peppers, seeded and chopped
1 cup of sweet onions, chopped
1 teaspoon green Tabasco sauce
½ teaspoon paprika
¼ cup of fresh chives, chopped
Sea salt
Pepper, freshly ground

Preheat oven to 400°F

Scrub potatoes, pat dry and prick with fork.

Brush potatoes with oil, place on a cookie sheet and bake for 45-50 minutes or until potatoes are tender.

Let potatoes cool 5-minutes.

Purée avocados with lemon juice, ¼ teaspoon of sea salt and set aside.

Using electric mixer, beat cream cheese, sour cream and avocado purée in a large bowl until smooth - fold in zucchini, bell peppers, chili peppers, onions, Tabasco sauce, paprika and half of the chives - season to taste with salt and pepper.

Make two crosscuts in the top of the baked potatoes, spread open with your fingers.

Arrange potatoes on a large platter or on individual plates, and spoon avocado mixture over the top of each potato, sprinkle with remaining chives and serve with tomato wedges.

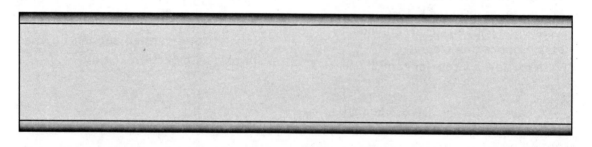

POTATO ROLL
With
PROSCIUTTO and BELL PEPPERS

Serves: 6

1 pound of Yukon gold potatoes
7 tablespoons of unsalted butter
2 egg yolks
¼ cup Parmesan cheese, freshly grated
½ teaspoon sea salt
½ teaspoon pepper, freshly ground
½ teaspoon nutmeg, freshly grated
½ pound of prosciutto, very thinly sliced, if not procured sliced
¼ cup of all-purpose flour
1 red bell pepper, seeded, diced
1 yellow bell pepper, seeded, diced
½ cup of black olives, pitted and chopped
Sea salt
Pepper, freshly ground
2 tablespoons of balsamic vinegar of good quality
½ pound arugula leaves, chopped

Boil potatoes until tender when pierced with a knife. Drain, cool, peel and pass them through a ricer into a large bowl. Let cool to room temperature. Add to the potatoes - 2 tablespoons of butter, the egg yolks, Parmesan, ½ teaspoon salt, ½ teaspoon pepper and nutmeg.

On parchment paper, arrange 6 slices of prosciutto, side by side, so as to form a rectangle. Spread a single layer of potato mixture over prosciutto, about ½ inch thick, and lifting parchment paper as you go, roll ingredients neatly,

making sure that the potato mixture is completely covered by prosciutto.

Refrigerate the roll for 1-hour or until the mixture solidifies. Remove parchment paper, cut the roll into 12-14 equal slices and arrange them on a lightly floured baking sheet.

Heat 1-tablespoon of butter in a large skillet, and over medium heat, brown the potato slices until golden in color on both sides, about 2 minutes per side, in 4 separate batches using 1 tablespoon of butter for each batch. Transfer cooked potatoes to a large pre-warmed platter.

Meanwhile, in another skillet, cook bell peppers and olives in remaining tablespoon of butter for 5 minutes, season with salt and pepper, add balsamic vinegar and cook 1 minute, spoon over warm potato slices, sprinkle with arugula.

<u>Note:</u> if prosciutto is unobtainable, very thinly sliced Black Forest Ham is an excellent alternative. Arrange slices on a large, warmed serving platter. Dice and cook any remaining prosciutto in the same skillet until slightly golden, transfer and mound it in the center of the platter, enjoy!

SWEET POTATO-CELERY-APPLE BISQUE (beesk)
"Signature"

Serves: 6

3 tablespoons extra virgin olive oil
2 pounds sweet potatoes, peeled, cut into small pieces
1 cup sweet Walla-Walla onions, coarsely chopped
2 cloves garlic, chopped
1 cup of celery root, peeled, cut into small pieces
2 large wine-sap apples or golden delicious, peeled, cored and cut into small pieces
2 teaspoons sea salt
½ teaspoon white pepper, freshly ground
¼ cup dry white wine
6 cups water
¼ cup whipping cream
¼ cup crème fraîche for garnish (See Index)
¼ cup chives, freshly chopped, for garnish
Apple slices, for garnish

On medium-high heat, heat oil in a large saucepan and add potatoes, onions, garlic, celery root, apple and cook — stirring for about 2-3 minutes. Add salt and pepper, wine and 6-cups water — bring to a boil, turn heat to medium-low and cook until vegetables are tender, about 15-20 minutes.

Cool slightly, transfer bisque (soup) to a blender or food processor and purée in batches until smooth - return purée to a clean saucepan, add cream and cook gently on medium-low heat for 5-10 minutes and season with salt and pepper, if needed.

Ladle bisque into warm soup bowls and garnish servings with a small dollop of crème fraîche, a sprinkle of chives and apple slices. Enjoy!

<u>*Note:*</u> Traditional bisque (beesk) is a French cream soup made of puréed fish, shellfish, poultry, meat or vegetables and traditionally thickened with rice.

Try the traditional addition of a tablespoon of precooked hot rice to add thickness, flavor and substance.

Notes

POTATO-ONION PURÉE

Serves: 4

4 large Yukon gold potatoes, peeled and quartered
1 teaspoon of sea salt
1 medium onion, peeled and quartered
2 teaspoons unsalted butter
¼ teaspoon white pepper, freshly ground
2 tablespoons sour cream
1 tablespoon fresh parsley, chopped for garnish

Cook potatoes and onions in a large pot of salted, boiling water until tender, about 25-30 minutes. Drain and transfer potatoes to a warmed bowl, add butter, pepper, sour cream, and whip until light and fluffy. Garnish with parsley. Excellent served with poached salmon, see Index.

MASHED SWEET POTATOES

Serves: 6

1½ pounds sweet potatoes, peeled and cubed
1 medium parsnip, peeled and cubed
Water
1 teaspoon of sea salt
¼ cup whipping cream (hot)
2 tablespoons unsalted butter
Pinch of cinnamon
Pinch of nutmeg, freshly ground
¼ teaspoon ground cardamom
Sea salt
Pepper, freshly ground
Rosemary Sprigs, for garnish

Place potatoes, parsnip and 1-teaspoon of salt in a large saucepan, cover with water and bring to a boil. Turn heat to medium and cook 15-minutes or until tender when pierced with a fork. Drain and transfer to a large warm bowl, add cream, butter, cinnamon, nutmeg and cardamom. Whip until smooth and fluffy and season with salt and pepper, if needed. Garnish with Rosemary sprigs and serve with braised short ribs and your favorite Merlot.

SWEET POTATO GRATIN
With
PARMESAN BREADCRUMBS
"Signature"

"Cooking with Erika"
Created and demonstrated this on local, weekly TV segment, aired during year 2002.

Serves: 8 – 10

3 tablespoons of unsalted butter
2 cups thinly sliced onions
Sugar
4 cups redskin sweet potatoes, peeled,
cooked, mashed and cooled
½ teaspoon sea salt
½ teaspoon freshly ground pepper
¾ cup whipping cream
2 large eggs, slightly beaten
1 teaspoon freshly grated nutmeg
1 cup Jarlsberg cheese, grated
2 tablespoons unsalted butter, plus extra
for greasing baking dish
2 cups dry, plain breadcrumbs
½ cup Parmesan cheese, freshly grated
2 tablespoons fresh parsley, chopped

Preheat oven to 350°F
Butter a 13x9x2-inch glass-baking dish

In a large skillet, melt 3 tablespoons of butter, over medium-high heat, and add onions, a pinch of sugar and sauté until golden, about 8-minutes stirring often.

Place sweet potatoes in a large bowl, stir-in salt, pepper, cream, eggs, nutmeg and grated Jarlsberg cheese and mix until well combined.

Spread sweet potato mixture into prepared baking dish, and spread onions on top of potato mixture.

Melt 2-tablespoons of butter in a small saucepan, add breadcrumbs and Parmesan cheese stirring constantly over low heat, about 1-2 minutes.

Sprinkle breadcrumb mixture over onions and bake uncovered until top is golden brown, about 35-40 minutes.

Enjoy with spinach salad and crusty French bread.

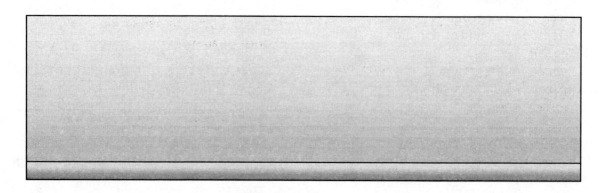

Opposite photo L – R
Royal Blue, Butterball &
Cranberry potatoes

Below photo L – R
Fingerling & Purple potatoes

Below-Center – Colors of
Cranberry Red, Butterball
and Purple potatoes
intensify when cooking

Below – Right – Cranberry
Red Potato Dumplings

Background photo is the actual surface of Purple Potato-Oyster Mushroom Lasagna fresh
out of the oven and shown centered is an embedded photo of serving, see Page 220.

1 - Peel yucca with peeler

2 - Crosscut & split pieces

3 - Boil halved yucca

4 - Cooked - remove vein

Yucca-Shallots-Garlic & Broccoli , see page 238

Ready to enjoy with broccoli and squeeze of lemon

CASSAVA

Cassava, pronounced (cah-SAH-vah) also known as yucca, the Spanish translation for cassava and manioc - cassava is a white starchy tropical vegetable, a staple food, originally grown by indigenous people inhabiting Columbia, Venezuela, Brazil and Peru. Because of its abundance, versatility and availability, its use has spread, to many non-Latin populations, including the U.S., but is most commonly known as "yucca". For that reason, all subsequent references to this tuber will be "yucca".

Yucca can be boiled, baked or fried; it can be served hot or cold; it is delicious in soups, stews and salads; it can be prepared as an accompaniment; it can be stuffed; it can be prepared as an vegetarian dish, or it can be milled into flour. (Continued on next page)

236

Fresh yucca potatoes contain high levels of vitamin C, carbohydrates and only 120 calories per 3.5 ounces serving. Typical market size is between 9-15 inches in length, they have a thick, dark brown skin resembling tree bark and white flesh when peeled.

Once cooked and center-cut lengthwise, the tough string like fiber in center can easily be removed for discarding. Or, you can cut yucca crosswise into 3-inch sections with a sharp knife, stand a section upright (cut-end down) on a cutting board – starting at the top of the tuber, slice a strip of peel and fibrous layer off with downward slicing motion, repeating motion until only flesh of yucca remains. Immerse yucca in cold water, adding 1-teaspoon of fresh lemon juice to prevent discoloration. Select firm roots that are odorless, hard and free of cracks. To prevent mushy results, do not overcook.

Whole, fresh yucca is available, nowadays, in many supermarkets and ethnic food stores. Peeled, pre-cut, packaged frozen yucca is also available. To use yucca, follow the package cooking instructions. Frozen yucca requires about 20-30 minutes cooking time, but add 1 clove garlic and 1-2 teaspoons of fresh lemon juice when doing so.

OVEN ROASTED YUCCA

Serves: 4-6

1 pound fresh yucca, cut into 3-inch pieces and peeled, or
1 pound peeled, cut frozen yucca (Avail. in Ethnic Food Stores)
2 tablespoons fresh lemon juice
1 tablespoon of sea salt
½ tablespoon pepper, freshly ground
4 tablespoons extra virgin olive oil
¼ cup watercress leaves, chopped

In a medium size saucepan, cover yucca with cold water, add lemon juice and salt – bring to a boil, turn heat to medium-low and simmer covered for 20-30 minutes or until tender.

Preheat oven to 350°F

Transfer yucca with a slotted spoon to a cutting board, let cool and cut lengthwise into ¾-inch wide wedges, remove and discard the thin woody center core. Arrange yucca on a baking sheet, drizzle oil over each piece, sprinkle with pepper and bake for about 10-15 minutes or until golden brown and crisp on top. Serve with fresh spinach salad or green beans.

YUCCA with SAUTEED SHALLOTS, GARLIC
And
BROCCOLI FLORETS
"Signature"

Serves: 4

1 pound of fresh yucca root, peeled, cut into 3-inch sections.
2 teaspoons fresh lemon juice
1 teaspoon of sea salt
1 tablespoon unsalted butter
2 tablespoons of extra virgin olive oil
1 cup of shallots, peeled, chopped
4 cloves of garlic, peeled, chopped
¼ teaspoon sea salt
¼ teaspoon mélange peppercorn, freshly ground
½ cup fresh Italian parsley, for garnish
1½ pounds of cooked broccoli florets, kept warm

Place yucca in a medium saucepan, cover with cold water - add 2 teaspoons of lemon juice and salt.

Bring to a boil, turn heat to medium-low, cover and cook for about 25-30 minutes or until tender.

Using a slotted spoon, transfer yucca to a cutting board, to cool. Cut yucca lengthwise into ¾ inch wide pieces, discarding the thin woody core. See steps 1-4 on page 236.

In a medium skillet, heat butter and oil over medium heat, add shallots and garlic -cook until soft, about 2 minutes - season with salt and pepper, add yucca pieces to the skillet and sauté until they are heated through.

Transfer yucca to a pre-warmed serving platter, spoon shallots and garlic drippings from skillet over yucca, garnish with broccoli florets and parsley.

Note: Frozen, peeled yucca and fresh yucca are available in Ethnic food shops, and some supermarkets.

238

CREAM of YUCCA-CAULIFLOWER, SAFFRON SOUP
With
PRAWNS
"Signature"

Serves: 4-6

1½ tablespoons of unsalted butter
½ cup sweet onions, chopped
1 medium head of cauliflower, trimmed, cut into small florets
4-5 cups hot chicken stock or water
1½ cups yucca potatoes, cooked and cubed
¼ cup whipping cream
½ teaspoon saffron threads or 2 teaspoons ground turmeric
1 tablespoon cream sherry
Sea salt
White pepper, freshly ground
1 bunch of watercress leaves, chopped for garnish
4-6 cooked, peeled prawns, for garnish

For Yucca Potatoes, please see preparation instructions on Page 236.

Melt butter in a large saucepan over medium-low heat, add onions and sweat them for 1-2 minutes, stirring often.

Add cauliflower, 4-cups chicken stock or water, bring to a boil, turn heat to medium and cook until cauliflower is tender, about 10-15 minutes -add cooked, cubed yucca and cook 1-2 minutes. Let soup cool slightly.

Transfer soup to a blender or food processor and purée in batches until smooth, then transfer soup to a clean saucepan, stir-in cream, saffron or turmeric, cook soup on medium-low heat until heated through.

Turn heat to low, stir-in sherry and season with salt and pepper.

Ladle soup into soup bowls, garnish each with a few leaves of watercress and place one prawn on top of watercress.

Note: In a small skillet, heat 1 teaspoon of extra virgin olive oil on medium-high heat, add ¼ teaspoon of sea salt and prawns - cook quickly for 1-2 seconds — to warm prawns through being careful not to overcook them.

Notes

RICE

<u>Introduction:</u> In Asian territories, rice is regarded as a gift of the gods. China references it as a gift of animals after China recovered from severe periods of floods. Henceforth, after its lands drained and dried, came the sowing of the long yellow seeds discovered hanging from a dog's tail. So it's said, cultivation of rice took place - and as with anything of nutritional value - the process of diffusion took hold and rice eventually was introduced all over the continent. Apart from its staggered long distance pathway to California in the 20th century the origin of rice, however, is likely to still be on the debating block and because the plant is of such antiquity it is said that the precise time and place of its first development will probably never be known. It is however, certain that the domestication of rice ranks as one of the most important developments in history for this grain has fed more people over a longer period of time than any other known crop.

I don't profess to be an authority on every underlying nutritional benefit of rice, a main course and staple food in Asian households, (except from my own observation and interest in research), but over there, there aren't many choices available to the populace other than plentiful vegetables and legumes which provide favored high-fiber and protein, for example. After having said that, and from what I've read in Journals, on the surface, it appears that unfavorable health conditions like obesity, and risk factors like heart disease, diabetes, strokes, kidney and cancer is categorically much lower compared to some non-Asian countries, lower cholesterol included. That's not to say that they don't have other types of health problems, but that's another story. In contrast though, I often wonder if results therefore would be different if animal-based and other like food choices were more readily available and more affordable to everyone, or if lifestyles there were less labor intensive. I think it would make an interesting study. To me, a balanced diet is one that is all-natural and encompasses all that one enjoys in moderation and taking advantage of all nutritional benefits natural and fresh foods have to offer.

Asians subsist on grains and vegetables daily, while elsewhere in the world, it's obvious the frequency and quantity of rice consumption varies in as much as it does with its presence in soups, in other preparations or covered with toppings of sorts, or as an accompaniment to other foodstuffs but usually not consumed on its own – as a meal. Considering the benefits of rice, and from my point of view, consuming some of it is better than none, but how much of it is best? Is it the amount and regularity of consumption that promotes such health benefits? One thing for certain is that the nutritional benefits of unpolished rice like, basmati, jasmine or brown rice with their fragrance combined with loads of fiber, happen to be some of my foremost favorites.

Unscientifically, I believe the more natural rice is, the more beneficial it is to health. I also believe that modern day methods over-processes rice (there are *some exceptions), affecting true values of nutritional potency levels - the full nutritional benefits inherent in its unaltered state. Further, and descriptively, unpolished (natural-unprocessed) rice is brown, containing natural fiber, nutrients and thiamine that processing removes, but it is good to know that at least some of the nutrients removed by commercial processing methods are artificially replaced, however. Comparatively though, I believe the equivalence of potency levels in artificial additives is weaker, and if so, food labels should reveal the difference, especially if potency values are significantly different from that of unprocessed rice. Here are a few of my favorite, flavorful creations, to add to your collection. Enjoy the nutritional benefits of rice as often as you can!*

BASMATI RICE SOUFFLÉ
"Signature"

Serves: 4

2 cups white or brown basmati rice, water rinse until water is clear, cooked and cooled
2 eggs, slightly beaten
½ cup of sweet onions, chopped
½ cup of sour cream, organic preferred
¼ cup of watercress leaves, chopped
Sea salt
Pepper, freshly ground
Unsalted butter for greasing

Preheat oven to 350°F
Butter four 2/3-cup soufflé dishes

In a medium bowl, mix together rice, eggs, onions sour cream, watercress and season with salt and pepper. Divide mixture among 4-soufflé dishes – place dishes in a medium roasting pan or a deep medium-size baking dish and surround the soufflé dishes with hot water up to within ¼ inch of rims. Bake for 25-30 minutes or until soufflés have slightly risen and are firm to the touch. Remove pan from oven, carefully remove soufflés from the water bath and let cool slightly. Run a small sharp knife around soufflés to loosen from dish and gently un-mold soufflés onto warm serving plates.

SAFFRON RICE

Serves: 4

1 cup of white basmati rice
1¾ cups of water
1 teaspoon of sea salt
Pinch of saffron, soaked in 1-tablespoon of hot water

Rinse rice under running cold water until water is clear and drain thoroughly. Combine rice, water and salt in a 3-quart saucepan. Bring to a boil, stirring once. Cover, reduce heat and simmer 15 minutes. Remove from heat and let stand covered 5-minutes. Add saffron, fluff with fork and enjoy with chicken, lamb, pork or fish.

PLAIN BASMATI RICE

Serves: 6

2 cups white basmati rice, or good quality long grain rice
2 tablespoons clarified butter, or 2 tablespoons extra virgin olive oil
3 cups hot water
2 teaspoons sea salt

Place rice in a bowl and cover with cold water. Stir with fingers to loosen starch, and pour through a sieve to drain. Rinse under running cold water until water is clear and drain thoroughly. Heat butter or oil in a heavy pan, add rice and stir over medium heat for 2 minutes until grains are well coated with fat. Pour-in hot water, and add salt. Stir occasionally until boiling, reduce heat, cover pan with lid and leave over low heat for 20 minutes. Turn off heat and leave for 5-10 minutes before serving. Fluff with fork.

HIMALAYAN-STYLE RICE SALAD
With
FRESH PEARS
"Signature"

Serves 6-8

3½ cups of water
½ cup orange juice, freshly squeezed
1 teaspoon of sea salt
2½ cups Himalayan rice, rinsed thoroughly under cold running water until water is clear, drained

2 cups ripe comice or bosc pears, peeled, cored and chopped
½ teaspoon sea salt
¼ teaspoon white pepper, freshly ground
¼ cup walnut oil
1/3 cup raspberry vinegar
½ cup sweet onions, finely chopped

Bring water and orange juice to a boil in a large saucepan, add salt and rice, cover and cook on medium-low heat for 25-30 minutes stirring occasionally. Transfer rice to a heat proof, large glass bowl, cover with plastic wrap and chill for 2 hours.

Prepare rice salad: In a large glass bowl, combine pears, salt, pepper, oil, vinegar and onions — add chilled rice and gently mix together and adjust seasoning if needed. Enjoy with grilled chicken, lamb or pork.

BLACK (SWEET) THAI RICE

Serves: 4

1 cup of black Thai rise, rinsed thoroughly under cold running water until water is clear, drained
1½ cups of water
¼ teaspoon of sea salt

In a medium saucepan, combine rice and water. Bring to a boil, cover and simmer over low heat until the water has been absorbed and the rice is tender, about 15-20 minutes. Stir occasionally. Stir in salt and fluff with fork. *Note: The texture of this excellent tasting rice, native to Thailand, is semi-firm, but not mushy or hard to the bite. In its cooked, un-sauced state, it closely favors a nutty, raisin-like flavor. Serve with your favorite meat or vegetable dish.* For the Gourmand wanting extra flavor, add truffle oil, extra virgin olive oil or butter. *Enjoy!*

BAMBOO RICE, what is it?

Chlorophyll is extracted from young green bamboo plants and infused with short grain white rice to give it its light green color and clean, refreshing flavor. The light, almost green tea leaf flavor makes this rice a wonderful complement to chicken, fish, vegetables and salads. Cooked bamboo rice, with its very aromatic, slightly grainy and slightly sticky texture, most likely will be a welcomed addition to any dish.

PLAIN BAMBOO RICE

Serves: 4-5

2 cups of water
1¼ cups of bamboo rice, rinsed under cold running water until water is clear, drained thoroughly
¼ teaspoon sea salt
¼ teaspoon white pepper, freshly ground
¼ cup watercress leaves, chopped
2 tablespoons almond oil (Avail in supermarkets)

Bring water to a boil in a medium saucepan — add rice and salt, cover and cook on medium-low heat 12-15 minutes stirring occasionally. Turn off heat and season with more salt if needed. Stir-in pepper, watercress and oil, let stand 2-3 minutes covered. Serve with chicken, lamb, fish, sautéed mushrooms or braised bokchoy.

BAMBOO RICE PUDDING
With
ORANGE SAUCE and TOASTED MACADEMIA NUTS
"Signature"

Serves 4-6

RICE

2 cups whole milk
½ cup of sugar
½ teaspoon sea salt
1 tablespoon of unsalted butter
1 tablespoon Orange Liqueur or freshly squeezed orange juice
1¼ cups of bamboo rice, rinsed thoroughly under cold running water until water is clear, drained

SAUCE

1¼ cups orange juice, freshly squeezed
3 tablespoons super fine sugar
2 teaspoons orange zest, finely grated
¼ cup of unsalted butter, chilled and cut into small cubes
¼ cup Orange Liqueur or Cognac
½ cup toasted macadamia nuts, chopped
4-6 fresh strawberries, for garnish

<u>To make rice pudding:</u> Bring milk to a boil in a medium saucepan, turn heat to low and add sugar, salt, 1 tablespoon butter, orange liqueur or orange juice and rice – again bring mixture to a boil, turn heat to medium-low stirring often - cook 15-20 minutes, turn off heat, cover and let stand 5-minutes.

<u>To make sauce:</u> Bring orange juice, sugar and orange zest slowly to a boil in a medium saucepan.

Continue boiling mixture on medium-low heat, stirring occasionally until liquid becomes syrupy, about 10-minutes.

Whisk ¼ cup butter into hot liquid, piece by piece, until its consistency is smooth.

Remove saucepan from heat and add orange liqueur or cognac. Serve sauce immediately or kept warm for 10-15 minutes.

Spoon warm rice pudding into 4-6 glass bowls, and spoon orange sauce over each serving, garnish each with nuts and strawberries.

<u>Note:</u> Rice pudding may also be served chilled. If served chilled, refrigerate it for 3-4 hours, stir occasionally and enjoy with warmed orange sauce or topped with orange-sweetened fresh whipped cream.

SALADS

ASPARAGUS-SPINACH SALAD
With
HONEY-LEMON-LIME-HERB DRESSING
"Signature" House Dressing-since 1978

This dressing was served over the salad as the second of five course "sit-down" dinner prepared for 140 guests at the combined "1999" Asparagus Festival and Spring Barrel Tasting, Sunnyside, Washington State. (April 24, 1999)

This "natural salad", with its beautiful presentation, was also featured on the front cover of the "Northwest Palate Magazine" with event details inside its April-May 2000 edition, a preamble to the upcoming "2000" celebration, and the recipe was also selected for inclusion in NW Palate magazine's 20th Anniversary (March-April-2007) issue featuring the "Best of the Northwest" Recipes & Wines, People & Places

Serves: 4

10 ounces of young, tender spinach leaves, washed and trimmed
1½ pounds fresh asparagus tips, cooked
4 yellow tomatoes cut into wedges
4 red tomatoes cut into wedges
1 tablespoon safflower oil
1 tablespoon fresh lemon juice
1 tablespoon fresh limejuice
1 tablespoon honey, good quality
1 tablespoon chives, chopped
1 tablespoon parsley, chopped
1 tablespoon arugula or watercress leaves, chopped
Sea salt
Pepper, freshly ground

Arrange spinach leaves on 4 salad plates. Arrange asparagus tips on top of spinach, garnish with yellow and red tomato wedges.

DRESSING

In a small bowl, combine oil, lemon and limejuices, honey, herbs, and season with salt and pepper. Spoon dressing over salad and enjoy with toasted French bread slices.

Delightfully refreshing, Natural and Heart Healthy
(Simply one favorite of several of my signature dressings)

ANTIPASTO SALAD
With
WATERCRESS-ARUGULA DRESSING

Serves: 6

½ cup watercress leaves, coarsely chopped
½ cup of arugula leaves, coarsely chopped
¼ cup fresh basil leaves, coarsely chopped
1 clove of garlic
½ teaspoon sea salt
½ teaspoon pepper, freshly ground
¼ cup extra virgin olive oil

½ pound thinly sliced prosciutto
2 each 8-ounce balls of fresh water packed mozzarella cheese, drained, thinly sliced
2 medium-ripe, full-flavored red beefsteak tomatoes, thinly sliced
2 medium-ripe full-flavored yellow beefsteak tomatoes, thinly sliced
1 large red bell pepper, seeded, thinly sliced
1 large yellow bell pepper, seeded, thinly sliced
6 hard-boiled eggs, shelled, sliced into ¼-inch thick rounds
¼ cup Kalamata olives, pitted, and coarsely chopped

Combine watercress, arugula, basil, garlic, salt and pepper in food processor and blend to coarse purée. With machine running, gradually blend-in oil and transfer mixture to a small glass bowl.

Arrange prosciutto around the outer edge of a large serving platter, arrange cheese slices inside the circle of prosciutto, and arrange tomato slices within the center-circle of cheese. Tuck-in egg slices, top with pepper slices, sprinkle salad with chopped olives, and drizzle with some of the dressing. Enjoy with remaining dressing and plenty of crusty Italian bread.

Note: Remove mozzarella from refrigeration and discard drained water. Place cheese in a small bowl of warm water to bring it to room temperature. Drain and proceed with recipe. Supply sources for Di Bufala Mozzarella, an excellent whole milk mozzarella, is available via Internet.

Notes

247

BEET-ARUGULA-BABY SPINACH SALAD
With
VODKA-ORANGE DRESSING
"Signature"

"Cooking with Erika"
Created and demonstrated this on local, weekly TV segment, aired during year 2001

Serves: 4-6

2 pounds fresh beets, julienne (cut into strips)
2 tablespoons fresh orange juice
1 teaspoon of sea salt
¼ teaspoon of freshly ground white pepper
½ teaspoon sugar
1 tablespoon white wine vinegar
1 cup water

1 pound of arugula leaves, stems removed
1 pound baby spinach leaves
2 large oranges, cut away peel and pith, slice and cut slices in half

VODKA-ORANGE DRESSING

2 tablespoons safflower oil
1 tablespoon white wine vinegar
1 teaspoon of vodka
4 tablespoons fresh orange juice
Pinch sugar
½ cup onion, finely diced
Sea salt
White pepper
1 tablespoon fresh parsley, chopped
1 tablespoon fresh dill, chopped

Preparing Beets: Place beets in a medium saucepan and add orange juice, salt, pepper, sugar, vinegar and water. Bring to a boil, turn heat to medium-low and cook for 6-10 minutes, stirring occasionally. Transfer to a heatproof glass bowl, refrigerate for at least 2-4 hours.

To make Dressing: In a small bowl, combine the oil, vinegar, vodka, orange juice, sugar and the onion - season with salt and pepper - stir-in parsley and the dill.

Assembling Salad: Drain beets, and equally divide the arugula and spinach among 4-6 large plates, mount beets in center of arugula and spinach leaves. Arrange orange halves over beets, spoon dressing over beet salad and enjoy with crusty French bread.

CARROT-APPLE SALAD
"Signature"

"Cooking with Erika"
Created and demonstrated this on local, weekly TV segment, during year 2001
"Heart Healthy"

Serves: 4

4 medium carrots, peeled, coarsely shredded
2 apples, peeled, cored, coarsely shredded
2 teaspoons fresh limejuice
2 ounces shelled walnut halves, coarsely chopped plus 4-walnut halves for garnish
2 teaspoons orange honey (Avail. at Health Food stores)
½ cup low-fat plain yogurt, drained overnight in refrigerator
1 tablespoon watercress leaves, chopped

In a medium bowl, combine carrots, apples and limejuice.

In a small bowl, mix together chopped walnuts, honey, yogurt and watercress. Pour half the yogurt dressing over carrot mixture. Let stand 15 minutes. Spoon the remaining dressing over carrot mixture just before serving. Top with reserved walnut halves and enjoy.

SUN RIPENED HEIRLOOM TOMATO SALAD
"Signature"

Serves: 4

2 pounds of sun ripened heirloom tomatoes, cut into bite-size pieces (tomatoes, such as,
Brandy-wine, great white beefsteak, yellow pear, yellow giant Belgium beefsteak, green zebra or red beefsteak - available at farmer's markets, market stands and food stores.)

¼ teaspoon sea salt
1 small onion, peeled, chopped

2-3 tablespoons of white balsamic vinegar, available in supermarkets and supply sources via Internet
2-3 tablespoons grape seed oil, available in supermarkets and nutrition stores
1-2 teaspoon of sugar
¼ teaspoon sea salt

¼ teaspoon white pepper, freshly ground
1 cup mixed fresh herbs, chopped (such as dill, chives, parsley, watercress and sorrel)

Place tomatoes and onions in a large glass bowl, add ¼ teaspoon of salt and toss gently, set aside.

In a small bowl, combine vinegar, oil, sugar, salt and pepper – stir-in the herbs and pour over tomato salad - toss very gently - adjust seasoning, if needed. Serve at room temperature. Excellent by itself, with homemade bread, grilled meats or fish. _Note:_ Never refrigerate fresh tomatoes – refrigeration will cause loss of texture and flavor.

CRAB SALAD with CITRUS DRESSING
"Signature-1978"

Serves: 4 - 6

CITRUS DRESSING

1 clove garlic, chopped
3 tablespoons anchovy paste
4 tablespoons flat leaf parsley, finely chopped
1 tablespoon of fresh limejuice
1 tablespoon of fresh lemon juice
1 tablespoon of fresh orange juice
2 tablespoons white Balsamic vinegar
¼ cup crème fraîche, or organic sour cream
½ cup of homemade mayonnaise (preferred)
Sea salt
Pepper, freshly ground
1/3 cup fresh chives, chopped for garnish
Lemon, lime and orange wedges for garnish

Place garlic, anchovy paste, parsley, lime, lemon, orange juice and vinegar in a blender, or food processor, and purée until mixture is smooth. Transfer to a medium bowl, whisk in crème fraîche or sour cream and mayonnaise. Whisk until dressing has a smooth consistency, season with salt and pepper if needed, and refrigerate until ready to use.

Preheat broiler

1 cup of toasted pecans or walnuts

To prepare pecans or walnuts:
Spread pecans or walnuts on a baking sheet and toast for 1-2 minutes, or until brown taking care to avoid burning. Let cool and chop coarsely.

CRAB SALAD

2 pounds fresh cooked crabmeat, such as Dungeness crab, (If unavailable, frozen or canned crab may be used)
1½ cups dessert apples, such as Red or Golden Delicious, peeled, cored, diced
1½ cups ripe Bosc pears, peeled, cored, diced
1 cup of ripe mango, peeled, diced
1 cup of firm blue cheese, such as Stilton, crumbled
6 cups young salad leaves, such as bib lettuce

To assemble salad:
Place crabmeat, apples, pears, mango, cheese and nuts in a large bowl and toss gently with half of the dressing. Place salad leaves on 4-6 large serving plates, and arrange crab mixture on top. Drizzle each with more dressing, sprinkle with chives, and garnish with lemon, lime and orange wedges. Serve chilled. Enjoy as a first slices and a glass of your favorite dry Riesling wine.

SUMMER SALAD and GORGONZOLA-HERB DRESSING
"Signature"

Serves: 6

DRESSING

1/3 cup fresh Italian parsley, chopped
1/3 cup Gorgonzola cheese, of good quality
1/3 cup of sour cream, preferably organic
3 tablespoons mayonnaise (Homemade preferred)
1/3 cup of well-shaken buttermilk
1 tablespoon white vinegar
¾ teaspoon sea salt
½ teaspoon Pepper, freshly ground
¼ cup fresh chives, finely chopped
¼ cup arugula leaves, chopped

Blend parsley, cheese, sour cream and mayonnaise in a food processor until smooth. Blend in buttermilk, vinegar, salt and pepper. Transfer to a bowl and stir-in chives and arugula.

SALAD

2 large heads red-leaf lettuce, thinly sliced, cross-wise
4 yellow or orange vine-ripened tomatoes, sliced
4 red vine-ripened tomatoes, sliced
3 cucumbers, peeled and thinly sliced

Arrange lettuce on 6 serving plates. Arrange tomatoes and cucumbers on top of lettuce, spoon dressing over salad and enjoy with crostini slices.

PURPLE POTATO SALAD
"Signature"

Serves: 4

6 medium purple potatoes, cooked, peeled, thinly sliced
3 tablespoons safflower oil
2 teaspoons white balsamic vinegar
¼ teaspoon sea salt
¼ teaspoon pepper, freshly ground
Pinch of sugar
¼ cup homemade mayonnaise (See Page 272)
1 tablespoon fresh chives, chopped
1 tablespoon fresh parsley, chopped

Place potato slices in a large bowl and set aside. In a small bowl, combine oil, vinegar, salt, pepper and sugar. Pour mixture over potatoes and toss gently. Mix in mayonnaise, chives and parsley. Adjust seasoning to taste.

Best when served at room temperature.

Note: One-fourth cup of finely chopped sweet onions can be added, if desired. Purple potatoes taste like potato and nutritional values are higher than most familiar potato varieties.

CUCUMBER - RED ONION SALAD
"Signature"

Serves: 4

2 large cucumbers, trimmed on both ends, peeled and thinly sliced
1 small sweet red onion, peeled, chopped
¼ teaspoon sea salt

3-4 tablespoons of white balsamic vinegar, available in most supermarkets
½ tablespoon of sugar
¼ teaspoon sea salt
¼ teaspoon white pepper, freshly ground
2-3 tablespoons grape seed oil, preferably imported from France, available in supermarkets and nutrition stores
½ cup of fresh mixed herbs, chopped (herbs, such as, dill, chives and parsley)

Place cucumbers and onions in a large glass bowl, sprinkle with ¼ teaspoon of salt, and toss gently and set aside.

In a small bowl, combine 3 tablespoons of vinegar, the sugar, ¼ teaspoon of salt, pepper and 2-tablespoons of oil – stir-in fresh herbs – pour dressing over cucumber salad, toss gently and adjust season, if needed. Serve chilled. Excellent served with parsley potatoes, grilled meats and fish dishes.

SUMMER FRUIT SALAD
With
COINTREAU FLAVORED WHIPPED CREAM
"Signature"

Serves: 4 - 6

1 small honeydew melon
1 papaya
8 ounces fresh raspberries
8 ounces fresh blueberries
4 ripe apricots, halved, pits removed, diced
8 ounces fresh strawberries, halved
3 tablespoons of sugar
½ cup Late Harvest Riesling wine

Slice melon into 8-wedges, remove rind, discard seeds and cut flesh into cubes. Cut the papaya in half, scoop out and discard seeds, peel and cut flesh into cubes. Combine fruits in a medium-glass bowl, sprinkle with sugar, pour wine over fruit, gently toss, cover with plastic wrap, and refrigerate until ready to use.

COINTREAU FLAVORED WHIPPED CREAM

1 cup whipping cream
1 tablespoon of confectioner sugar
2 tablespoons Cointreau Liqueur
1 tablespoon unsalted pistachio nuts, chopped for garnish

In a medium bowl, beat cream and confectioner sugar until soft peaks form, add Cointreau and beat until stiff peaks form. Spoon whipped cream over fruit, sprinkle with pistachio nuts, and enjoy!

GARDEN SALAD with HERB DRESSING

Serves 4-6

1 small head of bib lettuce, torn in bite-size pieces
1 small head of red-leaf lettuce, torn in bite-size pieces
1 red bell pepper, pith and seeds removed, thinly sliced
3 medium vine ripened tomatoes, cut into wedges
10 pimiento stuffed olives, cut in half
1 cucumber, peeled and thinly sliced

HERB DRESSING

3 tablespoons white wine vinegar or white balsamic vinegar
2 tablespoons extra virgin olive oil
Sea salt
Pepper, freshly ground
Pinch of sugar
1 tablespoon fresh Italian parsley, chopped
1 tablespoon fresh basil, chopped
1 tablespoon fresh watercress, chopped

To make Garden Salad: In a small bowl, whisk together vinegar, oil, season with salt, pepper and add sugar. Stir-in the parsley, basil and watercress.

Assemble Salad: Place lettuce, bell pepper, tomatoes, olives and cucumbers in a large bowl, pour herb dressing over salad, and toss lightly - enjoy with polenta – see Recipe Index.

SPINACH SALAD

12 cups baby spinach leaves, washed, dried thoroughly and transferred to a large glass bowl

In a small bowl, mix together 6-8 tablespoons extra virgin olive oil, 8-tablespoons white balsamic vinegar, 1-teaspoon salt, 1-teaspoon pepper, a pinch of sugar, 6-8 tablespoons of chopped, sweet onions and 6-tablespoons of chopped fresh parsley. Spoon herb dressing over spinach and toss lightly and adjust seasoning, if needed.

Heirloom Tomato Salad, Page 249 / Cucumber-Red Onion Salad, Page 252

253

Notes

Dandelion Crepes with Black Currant Jam, Page 260

Dandelion Purée with Boiled Egg Halves, Page 260

Oven ready Pizza /// Dandelion Onion-Buffalo Cheese Pizza, Page 263

Dandelion-Riesling-Feta Cheese Bread, Page 282

Dandelion-Pesto over Creamy Polenta, Page 259

DICOTYLEDON

Did you know that dandelion is a yellow-flowered composite plant of the dicotyledonous herb family, which has two seed leaves? I'm sure you do! But, for all who may not have known this, consider that if untreated dandelions seasonally appear in your lawn, you may always have something to eat, or you may not need to make regular coffee, or you may want to add another variety of honey to your pantry, or you may want to add  another variety of wine to your wine cellar. What is this you say?

Here is how the parts of whole cultivated or wild dandelions can be used to yield all of that except use of stems, which are discarded: Its jagged-edged, tangy leaves (similar tanginess to endive leaves) are delicious in salads, its roots can be roasted and ground to make dandelion coffee, its blossoms can be made into a honey, and its fresh yellow flowers can be made into dandelion wine.

In this "Dandelion" section I've created deviant recipes you can add to the above mentioned, but first, here is more information about dandelion that may be of interest - in Europe dandelion blossoms are commonly used in jellies and jams, blossoms that are dipped in batter and deep fried (as are zucchini blossoms in Italy) make quite a tasty snack or as a side dish with a main meal.

If you want dandelions readily available as an excellent source of Vitamin A, Iron and Calcium and the presence of dandelions in your green lawn is undesirable, then you may want to consider cultivating them in a raised, screened bed and deadheading unused flowers to prevent contaminating your lawn by seeds straying outside preferred confined space. On the other hand, this paragraph can be disregarded if you prefer dandelions accenting your green lawn then, there is a possibility that, with a subtle breeze, you will be sharing your source of Vitamin A. Iron and Calcium with your neighbors whether or not they need it or even want it.

 Another inherent character of the dandelion is that flavor in their leaves are slightly bitter and tangy, but if you prefer to alter flavor intensity, change water once or twice during cooking. Additionally, when blanching dandelion leaves, cover them with water, add a pinch of salt and sugar, drain and place them in ice water, drain again, chop, and refrigerate them covered. In salads, dandelions are best when served chilled.

DANDELION in PUFF PASTRY
"Signature"

Serves: 4

PUFF PASTRY

½ package of frozen puff pastry sheets, (1 sheet)
Flour for rolling out pastry
2 egg yolks, slightly beaten with 1 teaspoon of brandy

DANDELION

4 cups of untreated dandelion leaves, washed thoroughly, drained well and coarsely chopped
1/3 cup of sour cream, organic preferred
¼ cup of sweet onions, chopped
1/3 cup of fresh parsley, chopped
½ cup of Emmenthaler cheese, freshly shredded
¼ cup of mascarpone cheese
Sea salt
Pepper, freshly ground

Prepare dandelion: In a medium bowl, combine, dandelion, sour cream, onion, parsley, Emmenthaller and mascarpone cheese, season with salt and pepper – set aside.

Thaw pastry sheet at room temperature for 30-minutes

Preheat oven to 400°F

Unfold pastry onto a lightly floured surface, roll into 14-inch squares and cut into four 7-inch squares

Spread ¼ cup of filling in center of each square, brush edges with egg mixture. Fold each corner to center to cover filling and seal edges of squares. Place the seam side down on baking sheet. Brush with remaining egg mixture and bake 25-minutes or until golden brown. Serve warm.

Baked Zita-Dandelion Casserole

Recipe on Page 264

Serves: 4-6

PESTO

3 garlic cloves
4 cups dandelion leaves, thoroughly washed, paper towel dried and coarsely chopped
2 cups fresh Italian parsley, coarsely chopped
½ teaspoon sea salt
¼ teaspoon white pepper, freshly ground
¼ teaspoon sugar
6-8 tablespoons extra virgin olive oil
¼ cup pine nuts
½ cup parmesan cheese, freshly grated, plus extra for garnish

4-6 cups hot polenta, see Index

In a food processor, finely chop garlic and add dandelion, parsley, salt, pepper, sugar, 6 tablespoons oil and pine nuts. Process to combine and add remaining 2 tablespoons of oil and cheese, process 2-3 seconds and transfer to a bowl. Pesto can be made 2- days ahead. Cover with plastic wrap and refrigerate.

Spoon 1 cup polenta onto each dinner plate, spoon pesto on top of each serving, sprinkle each with remaining cheese. Serve immediately with crusty Italian bread slices.

DANDELION (aka, Lion's Tooth) PURÉE & EGG HALVES
"Signature"

Serves: 4

2 pounds of untreated young dandelion leaves, washed, thoroughly
½ teaspoon of sea salt
¼ teaspoon white pepper, freshly ground
1 tablespoon unsalted butter
Pinch of sugar
1/3 cup of whipping cream
4 large organic eggs, hardboiled (8-9 minutes), shelled and halved

In a large saucepan boil dandelion leaves in salted water for 10-minutes. Drain. Place in a blender or food processor and purée until smooth. Transfer purée to a clean saucepan, add pepper, butter, sugar and cream – cook on low heat for 5-10 minutes. Adjust seasoning if needed. Spoon dandelion purée onto 4 warmed serving plates, place 2 egg halves on top of purée and serve with crusty French bread slices.

Time and money saver note: Cook eggs while dandelions are cooking. Reserve the dandelion water for use as a base for soups or sauces. Dandelion water may be kept frozen up to 4-months.

DANDELION CREPES
"Signature"

Serves: 4

1 cup of all-purpose flour
¼ teaspoon of sea salt
2 tablespoons super fine sugar
2 large organic eggs
1 cup of whole milk, organic preferred
2 tablespoons melted unsalted butter
1½ cups untreated dandelion blossoms, rinsed in cold water, patted dry with paper towels and coarsely chopped
4-6 teaspoons of unsalted butter
Confectioner sugar for dusting crepes
Black currant jam for garnish

In a medium bowl, combine flour, salt, sugar, eggs and milk, stir-in melted butter and dandelion blossoms and mix well.

Melt 1 teaspoon of butter in an 8-inch nonstick skillet over medium heat. Pour ¼ cup of batter into skillet, cook until lightly browned on one side, then flip to other side and repeat with remaining butter and batter.

Transfer pancakes to 4 pre-warmed serving plates, dust each serving with confectioner sugar and spoon a dollop of jam on each pancake. Serve immediately.

DANDELION SALAD
"Signature"

Serves: 4

1½ pound of tender young (untreated) dandelion leaves, washed thoroughly, drained well and cut into bite size pieces
4 sun ripened tomatoes, cut into wedges
½ cup of organic red onions, chopped
1/3 cup of extra virgin olive oil
3-4 tablespoons of white balsamic vinegar
2 garlic cloves, minced
¼ teaspoon of sugar
¼ teaspoon sea salt
Pepper, freshly ground
¼ cup of Italian parsley, chopped
1/3 cup of Parmesan cheese, freshly grated

Place dandelion leaves and tomatoes in a large glass bowl, sprinkle lightly with salt and pepper and toss gently. In a small bowl, combine onions, oil, vinegar and garlic and sugar and season to taste with salt and pepper, add parsley and pour dressing over salad and toss gently. Divide tossed salad among 4 salad plates, sprinkle each serving with Parmesan cheese and serve with crusty Italian bread. Bono Appetito!

DANDELION-SORREL SOUP
"Signature"

Serves: 4-6

3 cups of young, untreated dandelion leaves, washed thoroughly, chopped
2 cups loosely packed sorrel leaves, chopped
1 medium Yukon gold potato, peeled and diced
½ cup Walla Walla sweet onions, chopped
2 cloves of garlic, minced
6 cups of chicken stock or water
2 tablespoons unsalted butter
¼ cup all-purpose flour
3 tablespoons of whipping cream
Sea salt
Pepper, freshly ground
Crème fraîche for garnish

Place dandelion, sorrel, potato, onion, garlic, stock or water in a large saucepan and bring to a boil. Reduce heat and simmer for 10-15 minutes and purée in batches in a blender or food processor. Melt butter in a large saucepan over medium-low heat, stir-in flour and cook 1-minute without browning. Remove from heat, whisk-in puréed soup. Return to heat and bring slowly to a boil stirring constantly. Turn heat to medium-low, and add cream - cook 5-minutes - season with salt and pepper, if needed. Ladle into soup bowls and garnish each serving with a dollop of crème fraîche.

DANDELION-SPINACH SALAD
"Signature"

Serves: 4

4 cups untreated young dandelion leaves, washed thoroughly and chopped
1 cup firmly packed baby spinach leaves
2 tablespoons extra virgin olive oil
½ teaspoon sea salt, or to taste
¼ teaspoon pepper, freshly ground, or to taste
Juice of 1 orange, freshly squeezed
Juice of 1 lemon, freshly squeezed

1/3 cup of Parmesan cheese, freshly grated

Place dandelion and spinach in a large glass bowl. In a small bowl, combine oil salt, pepper, orange and lemon juices – mix well – pour dressing over salad and toss. Add cheese and toss again. Adjust seasoning if needed and serve.

DANDELION VINEGAR
"Signature"

Makes about 4 cups

Fill a 1-quart jar with 4-cups of washed, loosely packed untreated dandelion leaves
Top-off the jar with pear vinegar (Avail. in Supermarkets)
Cap jar and let set for 4-weeks

Strain the mixture through a piece of cheesecloth into a large glass bowl. Discard dandelion leaves, transfer mixture to a clean large jar or bottle and store in the refrigerator for up to 2-months. Add dandelion vinegar to salad dressings, meats and vegetables. _Note:_ For refreshing skin, steep 1-cup of untreated (chemical-free-untainted) dandelion blossoms in 1-pint boiled spring water for 1-hour. Let mixture cool slightly, strain mixture through a piece of cheesecloth into a bowl and discard blossoms. Wash face with cooled dandelion water.

DANDELION-CARAMELIZED ONION-BUFFALO CHEESE PIZZA
"Signature"

Makes: one 10" pizza

PIZZA DOUGH

2/3 cup warm spring water (115°F)
¼ teaspoon sugar
2 teaspoons active dry yeast
2 cups all-purpose flour, plus extra for dusting baking sheet
1 teaspoon sea salt
2 tablespoons extra virgin olive oil, plus extra for oiling bowl and brushing dough
Mélange peppercorns, freshly ground
3 cloves garlic, finely chopped

TOMATO SAUCE

1 pound ripe Roma tomatoes
2 tablespoons extra virgin olive oil
2 cloves garlic, finely chopped
½ teaspoon sea salt
¼ teaspoon pepper, freshly ground
1/3 cup dandelion leaves, coarsely chopped

TOPPING

1 tablespoon extra virgin olive oil
1 medium sweet onion, thinly sliced
¼ teaspoon sugar
¼ teaspoon sea salt
¼ teaspoon mélange peppercorns, freshly ground
2 cups dandelion leaves, coarsely chopped
½ cup Grana Padana cheese, freshly grated
8 ounces buffalo cheese, thinly sliced

To make Pizza dough: Combine warm water, sugar and yeast in a large bowl, proof until foamy, about 5-10 minutes. Sift together flour and salt, add to proofed yeast, add oil and beat until smooth. Turn out onto a lightly floured surface, and knead dough 3-5 minutes. Lightly grease a large bowl with oil and place the dough in the bowl – turn to coat overall, cover with plastic wrap and let dough rise in a warm place until size doubled, about 2-hours. Punch dough down, cover with plastic wrap and let it rise in a warm place, about 30 minutes. While dough is rising, make sauce and prepare toppings.

To make tomato sauce: Scold, skin and chop tomatoes, place tomatoes in a medium saucepan, add oil, garlic, salt and pepper, bring to a boil, turn heat to medium-low stirring often – cook until tomatoes mixture becomes a thick purée, about 35-45 minutes. Turn off heat, stir-in 1/3 cup dandelion leaves and let sauce cool. In a large skillet, heat 1-tablespoon of oil over medium-high heat, add onions, sugar, salt and pepper – sauté until golden brown, about 6-8 minutes, stirring often – let cool. **Preheat oven to 425°F**

To prepare and assemble pizza: On a dry work surface dusted lightly with flour, roll dough into a large round, about 11-inches in diameter, then fold over ½ inch all the way round. Place dough on a lightly floured, large round baking sheet, or pizza pan, lightly brush dough with olive oil, and lightly sprinkle with mélange peppercorns and garlic. Spread tomato sauce over the top, arrange onions on top, sprinkle dandelion over onions, sprinkle Grana Padana cheese over dandelion and arrange sliced mozzarella cheese on top of dandelion. Bake 20-25 minutes, or until dough is golden brown and cheese has melted – serve hot.

BAKED ZITA-DANDELION CASSEROLE

Serves: 4-6

1 pound zita pasta
2 teaspoons sea salt

3 cups sun-ripened tomatoes, chopped and puréed
½ teaspoon sea salt
1 teaspoon mélange peppercorn, finely ground
2 tablespoons extra virgin olive oil
3 cloves garlic, minced
2 tablespoons tomato paste, preferably organic
¼ cup whipping cream
¼ cup Riesling wine
1 cup dandelion leaves, thoroughly washed, patted dry with paper towel and coarsely chopped
Pinch of sugar
¼ cup parsley, finely chopped
Sea salt
½ cup goat cheese, preferably imported
½ cup parmesan cheese, freshly grated, preferably imported
½ cup fontina cheese, freshly grated, preferably imported

Place puréed tomatoes, salt, pepper, oil, garlic, tomato paste, cream and wine in a medium saucepan, bring to a boil, turn heat to low and simmer 25-30 minutes, or until tomato sauce is slightly thickened.

Add dandelion and sugar, cook 5-minutes, turn off heat, stir-in the parsley, season with salt if needed, and set aside.

Preheat oven to 400°F

In a large saucepan, bring water to a boil, add 2-teaspoons salt and pasta, cook for 10-14 minutes, or until al dente. Drain.

Transfer pasta to a large heatproof baking dish, sprinkle with half of cheeses, spoon sauce over and gently mix pasta to coat with cheese and sauce.

Sprinkle remaining cheeses on top of pasta and bake for 15-minutes, or until cheese is golden brown and bubbly on top.

Remove casserole, let rest 5-minutes.

Spoon equal portion onto 4-6 preheated dinner plates.

Enjoy with crusty Italian bread, garden salad and Chianti or Sangiovese.

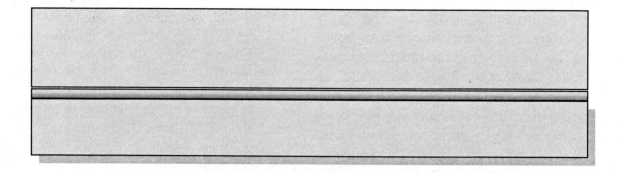

264

SAUCES

SALSA

STUFFING

Etc.

BÉCHAMEL SAUCE- on the light side

Makes about 2¾ cups

2 tablespoons unsalted butter
1/3 cup of shallots, minced
½ cup all-purpose flour
3 cups skim milk, organic preferred
¼ teaspoon freshly ground nutmeg
Sea salt
Pepper, freshly ground

Melt butter in a medium saucepan over medium-low heat, add shallots, and sauté 1-2 minutes. Reduce heat to low, add flour, whisk until smooth, whisk-in milk, and bring to a boil whisking constantly - cook on low heat until slightly thickened, stirring often, about 8-10 minutes. Add nutmeg, season with salt and pepper. Excellent served with potatoes, vegetables, lasagna and casseroles.

GARLIC SAUCE

Makes about ½ cup

3 garlic cloves, peeled
½ teaspoon sea salt
½ cup of extra virgin olive oil, of good quality
1 slice white bread, crust removed
1 tablespoon white wine vinegar, preferably Italian

Crush garlic and salt in a mortar until creamy paste forms. Begin adding olive oil while beating paste with a pestle and add oil as much as paste will absorb. Soak bread in warm water for 5 minutes, squeeze bread dry and add to the garlic emulsion along with the vinegar. Work bread in until it is perfectly incorporated. Refrigerate sauce until serving time. Enjoy with vegetables or meat. _Note:_ Recipe can be doubled and sauce can be kept up to 1 week, refrigerated.

PEPPERCORN WINE SAUCE

Makes about 1¾ cups

1½ cups whipping cream
½ cup Late Harvest Riesling Wine
½ teaspoon sea salt
¼ teaspoon white pepper, freshly ground
1 teaspoon pink peppercorns
1 bunch watercress leaves, coarsely chopped

In a medium saucepan over medium heat, bring cream to a slow boil, turn heat to medium-low and cook gently for 3-minutes. Add wine, salt and pepper and cook 10-minutes or until slightly thickened. Add pink peppercorn, turn heat to low and stir-in watercress. Excellent with chicken, pork, turkey, veal, halibut, salmon, lobster and shrimp.

PEAR-BRANDY SAUCE

Serves: 6

1 tablespoon unsalted butter
¼ cup shallots, peeled, chopped
¼ teaspoon sugar
3 large pears, peeled, cored, chopped
¼ cup brandy
1/3 cup Late Harvest Riesling wine
1 cup whipping cream
Sea salt
Pepper, freshly ground
½ teaspoon Mrs. Dash original seasoning
1 tablespoon watercress leaves, chopped
Lemon and Lime wedges, for garnish

Melt butter in a medium saucepan over medium heat, add shallots and sugar, and sauté until shallots are soft, about 2-minutes and add pears. Cook 3-minutes, stir-in the brandy, wine, and cream. Simmer until flavors blend and sauce thickens slightly, stirring frequently, about 10-minutes. Season with salt and pepper, and add Mrs. Dash seasoning. Stir in the watercress, and keep warm until ready to serve.

Excellent with pork chops, chicken, and wild game, such as, venison, quail and pheasant.

YOGURT-CARDAMOM SAUCE

Serves: 6

2 tablespoons grape seed or pumpkin oil
3 medium onions, finely chopped
2 small cinnamon sticks
2 large black or green cardamom, finely ground, (Avail. Middle Eastern food markets)
1 teaspoon fresh ginger root, peeled and finely chopped
1 teaspoon of garlic, minced
1 teaspoon of sea salt
½ cup of unsweetened whole milk yogurt, drained (Drain overnight in a fine strainer, refrigerated – discard liquid)
2/3 cup of water
Fresh cilantro leaves, finely chopped for garnish
1 fresh green chili, seeded, finely chopped

In a medium saucepan, heat oil over medium-high heat and sauté onions until golden brown.

Add cinnamon sticks and cardamom to the pan, lower heat and stir-fry 5 more minutes. Add ginger, garlic, salt, yogurt and water, and stir to mix well.

Remove cinnamon stick and discard. Transfer sauce to a serving bowl and garnish with chopped cilantro and chilies. Enjoy sauce over meatballs with basmati rice and tomato wedges, or lamb kabobs.

ORANGE-TOASTED MACADAMIA NUT SAUCE

Makes about 1½ cups

1¼ cups orange juice, freshly squeezed
3 tablespoons super fine sugar
2 teaspoons orange zest, finely grated
¼ cup of unsalted butter, chilled and cut into small cubes
¼ cup Orange Liqueur or Cognac
½ cup toasted macadamia nuts, chopped
4-6 fresh strawberries, for garnish

Bring orange juice, sugar and orange zest slowly to a boil in a medium saucepan. Continue boiling mixture on medium-low heat, stirring occasionally until liquid becomes syrupy, about 10-minutes. Turn heat to low and whisk butter into the hot liquid piece by piece until its consistency is smooth. Remove saucepan from heat and add orange liqueur or cognac. Serve with a sprinkling of nuts and garnish with strawberries. Excellent over vanilla or rice puddings, pancakes or pound cake.

APPLE CHUTNEY
"Signature"

Makes about 6 cups

3 pounds apples, such as Golden Delicious, Pink Lady, or Granny Smith, peeled, cored and chopped
1 pound of onions, chopped
1½ cups of sugar
½ cup of water
1 ¼ – 1½ cups apple cider vinegar
½ cup golden raisins
2 tablespoons ginger root, peeled, chopped
1 teaspoon of ground cinnamon
½ teaspoon cardamom, ground
3 red Chile peppers, seeded, coarsely chopped
½ teaspoon of sea salt
¼ teaspoon pepper, freshly ground

In a large saucepan, combine all ingredients and bring to a boil. Simmer until mixture thickens, and while hot, ladle into 6 – ½-pint sterilized canning jars. Seal the jar, label contents, and date. Sealed chutney can be stored up to 3-months. Refrigerate after opening.

Serve apple chutney as a side dish with Chicken, Lamb, Pork or Turkey.

<u>Note:</u> The mixture can be thinned with ¼ cup of vinegar or water if it becomes too thick. Adjust seasoning if needed.

TRI-COLOR BELL PEPPER SAUCE
"Signature"

Serves: 4-6

6 roasted red pepper, chopped
6 roasted yellow peppers, chopped
6 roasted green peppers, chopped
¾ cup of extra virgin olive oil
1½ cups sweet onions, chopped
3 tablespoons of garlic, minced
¾ cup of white wine
3 tablespoons of whipping cream
Sea salt
Pepper, freshly ground

Place red peppers in a blender, and add ¼ cup oil, ½ cup onion, 1 tablespoon of garlic and purée until smooth.

Place red pepper purée into a small saucepan, add ¼ cup of wine. Stir in 1-tablespoon cream, cook for 5 minutes on medium-low heat, and season with salt and pepper. Without combining, repeat process for each the yellow and green peppers. Serve with your favorite pasta.

To enjoy: Place pasta, such as linguine, in a large shallow serving dish and alternately spoon over with the red, yellow and the green pepper sauces for excellent flavor and striking presentation.

BASIC TOMATO SAUCE

Makes about: 5-6 cups

½ cup sweet onions, finely diced
¼ cup extra-virgin olive oil
2 tablespoons garlic cloves, minced
4 pounds very ripe plum tomatoes
Sea salt
Pepper, freshly ground
Pinch of sugar
2 tablespoons dry red wine
1½ tablespoons fresh basil leaves, chopped
2 tablespoons of fresh Italian parsley, chopped

Sauté onion in olive oil in a large saucepan over medium heat until soft, about 3-5 minutes, add parsley and garlic, and sauté until the garlic is soft but not brown, about 2 seconds – turn off heat. Quarter the tomatoes and pass them through a food mill using the disc with the largest holes. Add the puréed tomatoes to the onion and garlic mixture. Season with salt, pepper and sugar, add wine and simmer 25-30 minutes or until sauce has reduced slightly. Stir-in basil, parsley and enjoy with your favorite pasta. Easy! Quick! Flavorful!

AVOCADO SALSA
"Signature"

Serves: 4

2 cups avocado, peeled, pit removed, chopped
1 cup vine-ripened tomatoes, chopped
½ cup onion, chopped
2 tablespoons fresh limejuice
½ cup green peppers, seeds removed, chopped
1 tablespoon of extra virgin olive oil
¼ cup fresh cilantro, chopped
Sea salt

Pepper, freshly ground
Pinch of sugar
1 teaspoon of sweet paprika

Combine all ingredients in a glass bowl, season with salt, pepper, sugar and paprika, toss, and refrigerate up to 2-hours before serving. Excellent served with chicken and pork.

GARLIC CUSTARD

Excellent as a first course, served with baby spinach leaves lightly drizzled with olive oil and a sprinkling of Parmesan cheese, sea salt and cracked black pepper.

Serves: 4-6

14 large cloves garlic, peeled, preferably organic
¼ cup extra virgin olive oil
1 cup of chicken stock
2 cups whipping cream
4 eggs
1/8 teaspoon of sugar
½ teaspoon of freshly ground white pepper
Sea salt
Natural cooking spray, preferably Pam

Preheat oven to 350°F

Place garlic cloves and oil in a medium ovenproof dish, toss until well coated and bake for 25-30 minutes. Strain garlic and discard oil.

In a medium saucepan, add stock, garlic and 1-cup of cream. Bring to a boil, and reduce heat to simmer to reduce mixture to 1-cup and purée mixture until smooth and thick.

In a bowl, whisk together eggs, remaining 1-cup of cream and garlic purée and season to taste with sugar, pepper and salt.

Coat 4-6 custard cups (6-ounce size ramekins) with cooking spray and fill each with garlic mixture. Place ramekins in a large ovenproof dish, pour hot water a third of the way up the ramekins and bake for 35-40 minutes.

Remove from oven, let cool slightly. Run a thin knife blade around the edge to loosen custard from ramekins. Center a warm plate over each ramekin, flip over and un-mold custards onto plates. Enjoy warm with crusty French bread or Italian crostini.

BASIC MAYONNAISE

Makes: about 2 cups

3 egg yolks
2 teaspoons Dijon-style mustard
¼ teaspoon sea salt
1 tablespoon of fresh lemon juice
White pepper, freshly ground
1¼ - 1½ cups extra virgin olive oil or grape seed oil

Place egg yolks and mustard in a food processor bowl fitted with a metal blade. Pulse-process for about 30 seconds, or until blended. Add salt, lemon juice and pepper, process for about 15-seconds longer. With the machine running, add just a few drops of oil to begin with and continue adding oil until all oil has been incorporated, and the mixture has emulsified. Adjust flavor of the mayonnaise as needed, if mayonnaise appears too stiff, add a few drops of water - stir to combine. Transfer to an airtight container and store in the refrigerator for up to 1-week.

Chef's tip: If oil is added too fast, or the mayonnaise separates, place an egg yolk in a small bowl, and whisk-in the separated mayonnaise just a little at a time. Continue to whisk vigorously, adding small amounts of mayonnaise each time until mixture reaches desired thickness.

CURRY-APRICOT MAYONNAISE

Makes about 1¾ cups

1½ cups mayonnaise
¼ cup apricot jam

½ tablespoon mild curry powder

Combine mayonnaise, apricot jam and curry powder in a small bowl. Can be prepared 2-days ahead, covered and refrigerated. Excellent served with grilled turkey, chicken or lamb kabobs.

HERBED MAYONNAISE

Variation: Prepare Basic Mayonnaise, extract 8 tablespoons from total yield and place in a small bowl, stirring-in 2-teaspoons of minced garlic, 2-tablespoons chopped-fresh parsley, chopped dill or chopped chives. Stir to combine, cover and store in refrigerator until ready to use.

BRANDIED APPLE-SAGE STUFFING
"Signature"

"Cooking with Erika"
Created and demonstrated this on local, weekly TV Segment, aired during year 2002

Serves: 8-10

3-4 loaves of French bread, crust removed and discarded, cut bread into ½-inch cubes, about 10-12 cups
½ cup unsalted butter, plus extra for greasing dish
1 large onion, chopped
2 large shallots, chopped
3 large apples, such as Gala, Pink Lady or Golden Delicious
1 cup dried currants
¼ cup Brandy
¼ cup apple cider
1/3 cup fresh sage, finely chopped
2 tablespoons fresh thyme, chopped
2/3 cup fresh Italian parsley, finely chopped
1 teaspoon of sea salt
½ teaspoon freshly ground pepper
2 large eggs, slightly beaten
2 cups homemade chicken stock or vegetable stock
¼ cup watercress leaves, chopped for garnish
2 tablespoons olive oil
½ pound pancetta, diced

Preheat oven to 325°F

Spread bread cubes in 2 shallow baking pans and bake in upper and lower third oven, switching position of pans halfway through the baking process, and continue baking until golden, about 20-25 minutes total. Cool bread in pans on racks, then transfer cubes to a large bowl and set aside. In a 12-inch heavy skillet, melt butter over moderate heat. Add onions and shallots, cook, stirring frequently until onions and shallots are golden brown, about 10-15 minutes. While onions and shallots are cooking, peel, core and coarsely chop apples. Boil currants, brandy and cider in a 1-quart heavy saucepan, stirring occasionally until brandy and cider are absorbed, about 6-8 minutes.

Preheat oven to 350°F

Add apples to browned onions and shallots. Add sage, thyme and parsley. Cook stirring occasionally until apples begin to soften, about 6-minutes. Add currant and apple mixtures to the bowl containing bread cubes, add salt, pepper, eggs, stock, and toss well. Transfer stuffing to a buttered 3 to 3 ½ quart shallow baking dish. Bake covered in middle of oven for 30-minutes. Uncover and bake until browned, about 30-minutes more.

In a medium skillet, heat oil over medium-high heat, and add pancetta and sauté until golden brown, about 6-8 minutes stirring often. Sprinkle watercress on top of baked stuffing and sprinkle pancetta on top of watercress. Enjoy as a side dish with turkey, chicken or pork roast.

<u>*Chef's note:*</u> Stuffing can be assembled, but not baked, 1-day ahead, covered and refrigerated. Bring to room temperature before baking.

LEMON VINEGAR
"Signature"

"Cooking with Erika"
Created and demonstrated this on local TV Segment, aired during 2001
"Heart Healthy"

Makes about 1 cup

1-2 large lemons
2 tablespoons of fresh lemon peel
1 cup white wine vinegar
A few lemon-balm leaves

Thinly pare lemon, taking care to remove none of the pith with the peel, and squeeze juice out of the lemon into a container. Measure 6-tablespoons juice and pour into a bottle. Add the peel and vinegar, add lemon-balm leaves, cork and shake the bottle well. Refrigerate at least 3 weeks, strain vinegar through cheesecloth, and return vinegar to the bottle. Store refrigerated. Use as a dressing over your favorite salad composition.

ONION-ORANGE CONFIT

Serves: 4

3 tablespoons of unsalted butter
3 pounds large, sweet onions (such as Walla Walla sweets), peeled and thinly sliced
1 tablespoon of sugar
2 tablespoons of fresh orange juice
1 teaspoon of sea salt
½ teaspoon pepper, freshly ground

In a large skillet, heat butter, add onions, sugar and sauté onions, stirring often, over medium-high heat for 30 minutes or until golden in color. Add Orange juice, simmer 2 more minutes, remove from heat, and season with salt and pepper. Enjoy as a side dish with your favorite meat, spoon over green beans or over asparagus.

<u>*Chef's note:*</u> Adjust the recipe by adding 1-2 teaspoon(s) of curry powder to the onion mixture when serving with meat, such as lamb, pork or chicken.

NOTES

Second Cookbook
Released, April 2005

The Original
A Touch of Europe®
Cookbook

"Bringing 'Fresh' to the Table –
Naturally"

www.trafford.com/04-2768

***Current – and available
in/through bookstores,
and on-line***

<<<<<< Opposite photo

First Cookbook
Released, April 1992

The Original
A Touch of Europe®
Cookbook

*"Creative Cooking
in a
Tiny Kitchen"*

To be revised

Opposite photo >>>>>>>

1. Wash Dandelion

2. Rinse Dandelion

3. Pre-measure

4. Prepare flour

5. Add Yeast Mixture

6. Yeast-flour mixtures

7. Add Wine

8. Add Oil

9. Crumble Feta Cheese

10. Add Dandelion

11. Add Onions

12. Stir - side to center

13. *Knead dough*   14. *Shape dough*   15. *Enjoy!*

Potato-Carrot Bread, Page 286

Prosciutto-Emmenthaler, Page 293

BREADS
BUTTERS   &   SPREADS

Dandelion-Riesling-Feta, Page 282

Hutzelbrot (Bread), Page 290

Bread Rolls, Page 283

Spinach-Potato Bread, Page 287

Feather-light Popovers, Page 298

Chocolate Scones, Page 294

MY VIEWPOINTS ABOUT BREAD MAKING

Make your own bread, it's easy, it isn't as time consuming as imagined, its healthier, and you personally know for sure what all ingredients you are consuming. After you've prepared and baked a couple of loaves, you just might begin enjoying your own (clean) bread every day. The only ingredients that you really need to make the best loaf of bread or rolls are simple, those are: _Organic flour, yeast, sea salt and spring water,_ which produces incomparable tasting bread. Free yourself and family of chemicals as often as you can. I therefore, do not recommend tap water, because the reactive chemicals in tap water in some way prevents full development of texture and flavor in bread making. Omit non-essential ingredients, such as, baking soda, unless you actually intend to make Irish Soda Bread, to make up for any leavening thought to be necessary or needed. I've been baking breads for many years and never have I experienced a problem rising dough, or a problem achieving light and fluffy cake batters - without using baking soda - artificial leavening action from this ingredient was never needed. Less sodium in products and time tested use of ingredients in those products results in "clean food flavor that really is trump."

Yeast, a leavening agent, ferments in breads when sugar available from the flour used interacts with added sugar, entraps carbon dioxide gas within the dough's elasticity and stretchable bulk. The expanding affects of the gas causes the kneaded dough to inflate, increasing its original bulk size. In general terms, this bread type is commonly referred to as, yeast dough bread.

Another fermentation process evolves naturally when berries, for example, break open in late fall when overripe and full of sugar and thus becomes alcoholic. This form of fermentation is caused by natural microscopic yeast organisms. The fermentation of yeast in the making of wine allows the carbon dioxide gas in grape juice to escape from the solution, that which is noticeable in the heavy surface foam that forms in fermenting wine tanks. _The way I visualized it years ago, if wine, red or white, can be great in a glass, it can and is great in bread, a natural match. That is why I, as the declared originator, created and refined breads that I term as "Wine Breads" and "Vino Breads"._ In this cookbook, I have dedicated special emphasis on such "Wine Breads" aka "Vino Breads", by exposing and sharing recipes to confirm two of many of my secret varieties that will prompt and garner ecstatic remarks from anyone who tastes them. Just as evidenced by everyone served my "Vino Breads" in my Fine Dining Establishment hold true to such remarks. _Enjoy the "Good Life" of two worlds, the "Worlds of fine Breads and fine Wines"._

I prefer using active dry yeast, which is dehydrated - this is due to yeast cells becoming dormant because of lack of moisture, a condition which promotes longer shelf life of this product. Other types are: brewer's and compressed yeasts. Brewer's is cultured yeast, essential for brewing beer and also used for some industrial nutritional purposes. Compressed-fresh yeast is a combination of yeast and starch that has a moisture content of about 70%.

To yield better tasting bread varieties, consider adding ingredients in varying, but appropriate amounts, like organic sugar, eggs and fats such as unsalted butter, extra virgin olive oil, grape seed oil or avocado oil. Also using other healthier alternative liquids such as organic milk, beer or buttermilk will subtly influence flavors you certainly will enjoy. I do not recommend using lard, or shortening, of any kind in bread or baked goods when there are healthier choices that yield much better flavor. I believe you will notice and appreciate the flavors in my dessert and bread recipes that will justify the accuracy of my comments. Organic flour, incidentally, is produced from wheat that has been grown without chemicals, fertilizers or pesticides. Both organic white and whole-wheat flour are available in most supermarket baking sections, and other suppliers of organic products can be discovered via the Internet.

ROSEMARY-RIESLING-PEAR BREAD
"Signature"

Makes 1 large loaf

4½ cups all-purpose flour, preferably organic, plus extra for kneading dough
1¼ teaspoons of sea salt
1½ tablespoons of active dry yeast
1 cup of bottled spring water, warm (115°F)
1 cup of warm dry Riesling wine (115°F
4 tablespoons extra virgin olive oil, plus extra for greasing baking sheet
1 cup dried pears, preferably organic, coarsely chopped
2 rosemary sprigs, chopped

Put flour in a large pre-warmed mixing bowl with salt, mix lightly and make a well in the center – add yeast, pour in the water and wine – add oil and gradually incorporate flour mixing to a soft dough - knead-in the pears and rosemary, with dough still in the bowl. Cover dough with a clean tea towel, place it in a warm area for 1½ hours or until its size has doubled.

Preheat oven to 380°F
Lightly grease a baking sheet

Knead dough on a lightly floured work surface, form dough into a ball and transfer it to a baking sheet.

Cover and let it rise again for 20-30 minutes in a warm place.

Bake for 45-55 minutes or until the bread sounds hollow when tapped. Remove bread from oven and let it cool on a wire rack. When tightly wrapped, bread will keep fresh up to four days, without preservatives.

Excellent served with cheese, wine tasting, with butter and jams, such as peach, apple or apricot.

MERLOT BREAD
"Signature"

Makes 1 large loaf

4½ cups of all-purpose flour, plus extra for kneading dough
1¼ teaspoon of sea salt
¼ cup of sunflower seeds, coarsely ground
1 tablespoon of anise seeds, crushed
3 teaspoons active dry yeast
¼ cup warm spring water 115°F
1¾ cups warm merlot wine 115°F
4 tablespoons extra virgin olive oil, plus extra, for greasing baking sheet and bowl

Lightly grease baking sheet, set aside

Mix flour, salt, sunflower seeds and anise seeds in a large warm bowl and make a well in the center.

In a small bowl, mix the yeast with water, add to the center of the flour mixture, pour in warm wine, add oil and mix to a fairly soft dough.

Turn out dough onto a lightly floured surface and knead for about 6-8 minutes, or until smooth and elastic.

Place dough in a warm lightly oiled bowl, cover with a clean dish towel and let it rise in a warm place for about 1-hour or until doubled in bulk.

Turn out dough onto a lightly floured surface and punch down. Gently knead 5 minutes.

Shape dough into a round ball, and place it on prepared baking sheet – cover with a dish towel and let it rise in

a warm place for 35-45 minutes or until dough doubles in size.

Preheat oven to 400°F

Bake 35-45 minutes or until the loaf has browned and sounds hollow when tapped. Let bread cool, on a wire rack, before slicing.

Note: The fine flavor and texture of this superiorly balanced Merlot bread is excellent anytime, with any food at any type of occasion or function, including wine tastings. Also, enjoy it with French brie, smoked duck breast, cream cheese, butter and black cherry jam.

DANDELION-RIESLING-FETA CHEESE BREAD
"Signature"

Makes: 1 loaf

2 teaspoons active dry yeast
¼ cup warm spring water (115°F)
¼ teaspoon sugar
3½ cups all-purpose flour, plus extra for kneading dough
1 teaspoon sea salt
1¼ cups warm, dry Riesling wine (115°F)
4 tablespoons extra virgin olive oil, plus extra for oiling bowl and baking sheet
¾ cup feta cheese, crumbled
¾ cup dandelion leaves, thoroughly washed, patted dry with paper towels, coarsely chopped
½ cup sweet onions, chopped

Combine yeast with ¼ cup of warm water and sugar in a small bowl, and let it set to dissolve, about 15 minutes. Mix flour and salt together in a large bowl.

Make a well in the center and pour-in yeast mixture, add wine, oil, goat cheese, dandelion and onions.
Using a wooden spoon, stir from the center incorporating flour with each turn, to obtain rough dough. Turn out onto a lightly floured surface and knead for about 8-10 minutes.

Place dough in a lightly oiled large, warm bowl, cover with a clean dish towel and let dough rise in a warm place for 1-hour, or until doubled in bulk.

Lightly oil a baking sheet and set it aside

Turn dough onto a lightly floured surface and punch down. Knead for 2-3 minutes, and shape dough into a round ball. Place dough on prepared baking sheet, cover with a dish towel and set aside to rise until doubled in volume, about 30-45 minutes. Meanwhile, preheat oven to 380°F and bake 45 minutes, or until bread is golden and sounds hollow when tapped.

Feta (FEH-tah) can either be a soft Greek cheese made from ewe's milk (or occasionally goat's milk) and pickled in brine: it has a white color, a crumbly texture and a salty, sour tangy flavor, or it can be a soft, white, flaky American feta-style cheese made from cow's milk and stored in brine.

ROUND BREAD ROLLS
"Signature"

"These rolls taste too good to be true, they are so easy to make, and they don't contain or need unnecessary preservatives."

Makes about 10-12 rolls

4½ cups all-purpose flour, preferably organic, plus extra for kneading
1¼ teaspoons sea salt
2 teaspoons sugar
1½ tablespoons of active dry yeast, preferably Bob's red mill yeast -
(Available at Nutrition Shop's refrigeration section)
2 cups warm bottled spring water, 115°F
Extra virgin olive oil for greasing baking sheet

Put flour in a large pre-warmed mixing bowl with salt and sugar, mix lightly and make a well in the center, add the yeast, pour-in warm water, and gradually incorporate the mix into soft dough.

Turn dough out onto a floured surface and knead for 5-minutes.

Return dough to the same bowl, cover with a warm, damp, clean tea towel and set aside, allowing it to rise in a warm place, about 1½ hours or until size doubled.

Preheat oven to 400°F
Lightly grease a baking sheet and set aside.

Knead dough again and using a sharp knife, cut dough into 8-10 even-sized pieces, lightly knead each piece, roll dough around between floured palms of hands to form ball shape.

Next, place dough balls on a floured surface and turning them around several times with your palms to produce an evenly rounded shape. Lay dough balls on prepared baking sheet without flattening them.

Cover with a tea towel and set aside – let rest for 10-15 minutes.

Bake 15-20 minutes or until lightly browned. Briefly cool rolls on a wire rack, but serve them while still warm.

<u>*Note:*</u> Rolls can be kept fresh in a tightly sealed plastic bag for up to 2-3 days, without containing preservatives. Rolls kept longer can be sliced in half and toasted in buttered frying pan, or use extra virgin olive oil, until lightly browned – to make excellent flavored crostini that can be topped with cheese, meats or smoked salmon (lox).

FOCACCIA BREAD
With
OLIVES, ONIONS and ROSEMARY

Serves: 6-8

2 cups of warm water (105-115°F)
2 teaspoons dry yeast
½ teaspoon sugar
4½ cups all-purpose flour, plus extra for dusting
2 teaspoons sea salt
4 tablespoons extra virgin olive oil
24 black or green olives, pitted and halved
2 cloves garlic, chopped
½ cup onion, thinly sliced
1 tablespoon fresh rosemary, chopped, or 1½ teaspoons dried

Place 2-cups of warm water in a large bowl. Stir-in yeast, sprinkle with sugar and stir with fork. Let stand until yeast dissolves, about 10-15 minutes. Add flour and salt to yeast mixture, stir to blend well (dough will be sticky). Knead dough on floured surface until smooth and elastic, about 10-minutes – keep adding small amounts of flour until dough no longer feels sticky. Form dough into a ball.

Oil a large bowl, add dough turning to coat, cover with plastic wrap or a clean dishtowel and let dough rise in a warm area until size doubles, about 1½ hours.

Punch down dough, knead into a ball and return to the same bowl, cover and let it rise in a warm area until doubled, about 45-minutes. Brush a 15 x 10 inch baking sheet with 1-tablespoon of oil, again punch down dough, and transfer to prepared sheet. Using fingertips, press out dough to a 13 x 10 inch rectangle, let dough rest 10-minutes. Press fingertips over dough surface, forming indentations. Drizzle remaining 3-tablespoons of oil over dough, sprinkle olives, onions, garlic and rosemary evenly over surface and let dough rise uncovered in a warm area until puffy, about 25-minutes. Bake until brown and crusty, about 20-30 minutes. Best when served warm.

A bit of history: Deriving its name from the Latin word focus, meaning "hearth" - focaccia evolved from the unleavened hearth cake consumed during mid-ages. Focaccia bread dough was patted into a flat round, and cooked directly on a hot stone or under a mound of ashes. Since then, every Italian town has created its own special version of facaccia bread. Whether soft or crisp, thick or thin, the dough is typically flavored with local herbs and olive oil. Enjoy focaccia by itself, or along with a bowl of soup – it is nothing short of excellent.

BUTTERMILK-POTATO BREAD
"Signature-1996"

Makes 1 loaf

1 large Yukon gold potato, peeled and cubed
1½ cups of mountain-spring water (Avoid using chlorinated tap water)
¼ teaspoon of sugar
1½ tablespoons active dry yeast
½ cup buttermilk
1 teaspoon snipped, fresh thyme
1½ teaspoons of sea salt
4-4½ cups of all-purpose flour, plus extra for kneading dough
1 egg yolk
2 tablespoons of water
Extra virgin olive oil, for greasing baking sheet and bowl

Place potato in a small saucepan, cover with 1½ cups of water, bring to boil, and cook over medium-low heat for 15-20 minutes, or until potato is tender.

Drain reserving ¾ cup potato liquid. Mash the cooked potato, and set aside.

Cool reserved potato liquid until lukewarm (110-115°F). Stir-in sugar and yeast, let stand 10 minutes.

Meanwhile, heat buttermilk, salt and thyme until warm (110-115°F). Stir into the mashed potato until smooth.

Transfer potato mixture to a large, warm bowl, and stir-in yeast mixture and 2 cups of flour until mixture forms soft dough.

Turn dough out onto a lightly floured surface. Gradually knead-in enough of remaining flour to make moderately stiff dough, about 6-8 minutes.

Place dough in a lightly oiled large bowl, turn once to grease surface.

Cover and let rise in a warm place until doubled (45-60 minutes).

Punch dough down. Shape into a 20-inch oval. Place dough on a lightly greased baking sheet, cover and let rise until almost double, about 30 minutes.

Preheat oven to 375°F

In a small bowl, combine egg yolk and 2-tablespoons water. Brush egg mixture over the top of loaf.

Bake for 35-40 minutes or until golden and loaf sounds hollow when tapped. Remove from baking sheet and cool on wire rack.

Note: Bread will keep fresh tightly wrapped up to 3 days unless uncontrolled consumption voids its fresh holding duration.

Delicious topped with unsalted butter, homemade jams or European cheeses.

POTATO-CARROT BREAD

(Signature – Created and demonstrated this recipe for the Washington State Potato Commission and the Washington State University Exploratory Laboratory, November 17, 2006)

Makes: 1 large loaf

4½ cups all-purpose flour, plus extra
3 teaspoons active dry yeast
½ teaspoon organic sugar
1¼ teaspoons sea salt
1½ cups of warm spring water 110 - 115°F
2 eggs, slightly beaten, room temperature
¼ cup extra virgin olive oil, plus extra

1 cup carrots, peeled and finely shredded
2 teaspoons dill, freshly chopped
2 teaspoon watercress leaves, chopped
1 cup Emmenthaler cheese, grated
¼ cup sunflower seeds, finely ground
1 cup Yukon gold potatoes, cooked, peeled and finely grated

Preparing bread dough: Mix flour, yeast, sugar and salt in a pre-warmed large bowl, add warm water, eggs and oil - stir with wooden spoon until mixture clumps together.

Turn dough out onto a lightly floured work surface and knead until smooth and elastic, about 5 minutes.

Assembling bread dough: Lightly oil a large bowl, place dough in oiled bowl and turn to coat. Cover dough first with plastic wrap and then a kitchen towel and let it rise in a warm, draft-free area until volume doubles, about 1½ hours.

Turn dough out onto a floured work surface, punch down the dough, and work-in the carrots, dill, cheese, sunflower seeds and potatoes. Knead dough into a ball and return it to the same bowl, cover and let it rise in a warm area until doubled, about 45 minutes.

Preheat oven to 380°F
Coat a 15 x 10 inch baking sheet lightly with oil.

Punch dough down again and shape into a large round, place on prepared baking sheet, very lightly sprinkle dough with flour and let it rest covered 10-15 minutes.

Bake bread uncovered until top is golden brown, about 45-55 minutes. Let it rest 30 minutes before slicing for immediate serving or refrigerate bread until ready to use.

Plastic wrapped leftover bread can be stored refrigerated up to 2 days or it can be sautéed in olive oil or butter and serve like crostini with soups or stews.

SPINACH-POTATO BREAD
"Signature"

Makes 1 large loaf or 2 small loaves

8 ounces yellow Finn potatoes, peeled and diced
2½ teaspoons active dry yeast
3¼ cups all-purpose flour, plus extra for kneading
1 cup spelt flour, plus extra for sprinkling (Avail. at Nutrition Shops)
1¼ teaspoons of sea salt
4 tablespoons extra virgin olive oil, plus extra for oiling bowl
1 ½ cups fresh baby spinach leaves, chopped
¼ cup sweet onions, chopped

Lightly grease a large baking sheet, set aside

Place potatoes in a medium saucepan, cover with water and cook until tender, about 10-15 minutes.

Drain and reserve 1½ cups of the cooking water 115°F. Mash potatoes and set aside to cool slightly.

Combine yeast, 3 cups of all-purpose flour, spelt flour and salt in a large bowl, add the reserved warm water, the potatoes, olive oil and spinach and gradually work this mixture into the flour mixture to form soft dough.

Turn out dough onto a lightly floured surface and knead for 5-6 minutes, until smooth and elastic, and place in a pre-

warmed, lightly oiled large bowl, sprinkle dough lightly with spelt flour, cover with a clean dish towel and let it rise in a warm place for 1-hour or until doubled in bulk.

Turn dough out onto a lightly floured surface, punch down and knead again for 3-4 minutes.

Shape into a plump oval loaf, place on prepared baking sheet and sprinkle again lightly with spelt flour, cover dough and let it rise in a warm place for 30-minutes or until doubled in size.

Meanwhile, preheat the oven to 400°F.

Bake for 35-45 minutes or until golden and sounding hollow when tapped. Transfer to a wire rack to cool before slicing.

OATMEAL-PEAR BREAD
"Signature"

Makes 1 large loaf

2 cups organic all-purpose flour, plus extra for kneading
3 cups organic wheat flour
¼ cup organic oatmeal (spelt flakes)
1/3 cup organic sunflower seeds, coarsely chopped
2 teaspoons sea salt
3½ teaspoons active dry yeast
1½ cups of warm water 115°F
1 cup of organic pear juice, warm (115°F)
¼ cup almond oil, plus extra for greasing and brushing

Lightly grease a baking sheet and set aside

Mix flours, oatmeal, sunflower seeds, salt and yeast in a large warmed bowl and make a well in the center – add water, pear juice and oil to the center of the flour mixture and mix to soft dough.

Knead dough on a lightly floured surface for 8-10 minutes, until smooth and elastic.

Place dough in a lightly oiled, large warmed bowl, cover with oiled plastic wrap and draped with a dishtowel - let dough rise in a warm place for 1½ hours or until doubled in bulk.

Turn out dough onto a lightly floured surface, punch down and knead for 5-minutes, shape dough into a round and place on the prepared baking sheet, cover with a clean dish towel and let rise in a warm place for 45 minutes or until doubled in size.

Preheat oven to 400°F

Bake for 1-hour or until the bread sounds hollow when tapped. If the bread begins over-browning, loosely cover it with foil for the last 10-minutes of baking.

Transfer bread to a wire rack to cool.

Excellent with orange butter, jams, cream cheese or as an open face sandwich topped with a slice of your favorite cheese or luncheon meats.

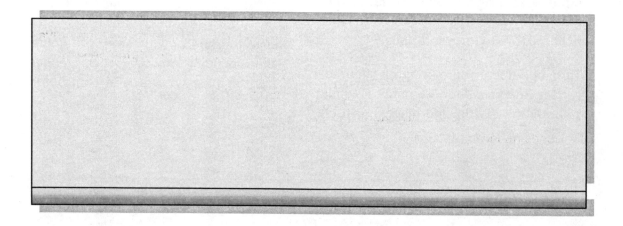

CRANBERRY BREAD
"Signature"

Excellent bread for "no sugar" and "diet conscious consumers"

Makes 1 large loaf

4½ cups all-purpose flour, plus extra for dusting, preferably organic
1½ teaspoons of sea salt
1 tablespoon of active dry yeast
1 cup of warm bottled spring water, 115°F
1 cup of warm, organic unsweetened cranberry juice, 115°F
¼ cup grape seed oil, preferably organic, plus extra for greasing baking sheet
½ cup pumpkin seeds, finely ground

Place flour in a large pre-warmed mixing bowl with salt, mix lightly and make a well in the center – add yeast and pour-in the warm water and cranberry juice.

Add oil and pumpkin seeds and gradually incorporate flour mix into soft dough.

Turn dough out onto a floured surface and knead for 5-minutes. Return dough to the same bowl, cover with a warm, clean damp tea towel and set aside to let dough rise in a warm place, about 1½ hours or until size has doubled.

Preheat oven to 380°F
Grease baking sheet and set aside.

Knead dough on a lightly floured work surface, about 5 minutes to form dough into a large ball – place it on prepared baking sheet, cover and let rise again for about 20-30 minutes in a warm place.

Bake for 1-hour or until the bread loaf sounds hollow when tapped. Cool on wire rack.

Bread will keep, when tightly wrapped, up to 4 days, and this is without the unnecessary preservative additives in the dough.

This flavorful bread is excellent without anything on it and particularly excellent with cheese, such as montrachet goat cheese, emmenthaler, stilton, and orange, whipped butter and cream cheese.

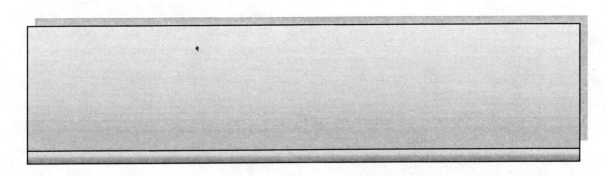

HUTZELBROT
"German Winter Fruit Bread"

Makes 2 large loaves

1 pound dried pears, coarsely chopped
1 pound dried plums coarsely chopped
1 pound dried figs, trimmed, coarsely chopped
1 pound of raisins
2 tablespoons active dry yeast
¼ cup of warm water 115°F
2 cups rye flour
3 cups all-purpose flour, plus ¼ cup, plus extra for kneading dough
1½ teaspoons sea salt
½ cup sugar, preferably organic, plus 1 teaspoon
2 tablespoons ground cinnamon
1 tablespoon of ground anise seeds
½ pound hazelnuts, coarsely chopped
½ pound almonds, coarsely chopped
About ¼ cup of grape- seed oil or melted unsalted butter, for oiling bowl and baking sheet
¼ cup kirsch wasser liqueur (clear cherry brandy), for brushing loaves (Avail. in Liquor stores)

Place pears, plums and figs in a large saucepan, cover with water and bring to a full boil – turn heat to low and cook gently for 5-10 minutes to soften fruits.

Turn off heat, transfer cooked fruits to a large bowl, stir-in raisins and let sit for 20-30 minutes.

Drain fruits and let cool - reserving 2 cups of fruit liquid. Sprinkle ¼ cup all-purpose flour over drained fruits and toss gently. Set aside.

In a small bowl, combine yeast, 1 teaspoon sugar and ¼ cup of warm water and let stand for 10-15 minutes, or until the yeast is dissolved and the mixture is frothy.

In a large bowl, stir together the flours, salt, ½ cup sugar, cinnamon, anis, hazelnuts and almonds to make a well in the center.

Add drained, warm fruits and warm (115°F) reserved fruit liquid – pour-in the yeast mixture with a wooden spoon, stir from center incorporating more flour mixture with each turn to obtain rough dough.

Transfer to a floured surface and knead until smooth and elastic, adding a little more flour as necessary, but keep dough soft.

Place dough into a lightly oiled or buttered pre-warmed large bowl, turn to coat all sides, cover with a dish towel and let rise until doubled in bulk.

Grease a large baking sheet and set aside

Punch down dough, turn dough out on a lightly floured surface, knead again a few times, cut dough in half with a sharp knife, cover dough with a dish towel and let rest 15 minutes. With hands, shape each half of dough into round loaves.

Place loaves on prepared baking sheet, cover with dishtowel and let rise until not quite doubled, about 15-20 minutes.

Preheat oven to 350°F

Bake loaves 50-60 minutes, or until loaf sounds hollow when tapped - cool bread on wire racks and brush each loaf with kirsch wasser (wasser = cherry water, a liqueur). Bread keeps well and improves with age when tightly wrapped.

Hutzlebrot is excellent low calorie breakfast bread, tastes great any time of the day and makes a delicious afternoon snack especially with orange butter, jams or cream cheese.

Enjoy it also with roast pork, goose and duck - a nutritious winter fruit, low calorie bread, great any time.

Historical background of Hutzelbrot:

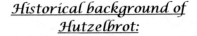

Hutzelbrot, originated in Stuttgart, Germany, legendary "Hutzelbrot." It is absolutely delicious!a natural, healthy combination of dried fruits, nuts and spices. "Hutzel" is an old world word referencing dried, winter fruits, such as apples, pears, plums and figs, "brot" means "bread". See opposite photos. It began when a storybook figurine was crafted with dried fruits and dubbed "Hutzelman", in a poem, by storyteller

Eduart Morike, during 1853, in which, he portrayed Hutzelman as a Kobold (a Goblin/Imp), that became known to everyone in Stuttgart and throughout the Land, as well as public knowledge of the many jokes surrounding the Kobold- that distinctly connected Morike with the legendary "Hutzlebrot". It is absolutely delicious!

PEAR-CARDOMOM BREAD
"Signature"

Makes 1 large loaf

4 cups all-purpose flour, plus extra for kneading
2½ teaspoons active dry yeast
1 teaspoon of sea salt
1 tablespoon ground cardamom
1¾ cups warm spring water 115°F
1/3 cup walnut oil, plus extra for greasing and brushing (see page 27)
1½ cups dried pears, coarsely chopped

Lightly grease a baking sheet, set aside

Mix flour, yeast, salt and cardamom in a large warm bowl and make a well in the center - add warm water and oil to the center of the flour and mix to soft dough.

Knead dough on a lightly floured surface for 6-8 minutes until smooth and elastic.

Place in a lightly oiled large bowl, cover with oiled plastic wrap and let it rise in a warm place for 1-hour or until doubled in bulk.

Turn out onto a lightly floured surface, punch it down, flatten it and sprinkle on the chopped pears.
Fold up and knead dough to distribute pears and let it rest for 5-10 minutes.

Shape dough into an oval loaf and place it on the prepared baking sheet, cover with lightly oiled plastic wrap, drape plastic wrap with clean, dry dish towel and let dough rise in a warm place for 30-45 minutes, or until doubled in size.

Preheat oven to 400°F

Shape dough into an oval loaf, brush dough lightly with oil and place dough on the prepared baking sheet.

Bake 40-45 minutes or until loaf is golden in color and sounds hollow when tapped.

Transfer to a wire rack to cool. Enjoy anytime, excellent with unsalted butter, orange jam, with cream cheese, or even plain.

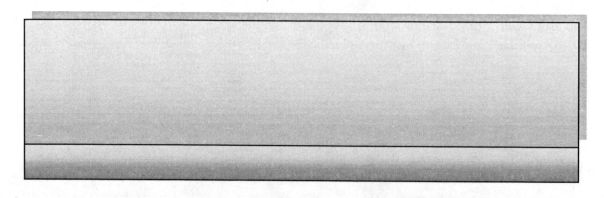

PROSCIUTTO-EMMENTHALER CHEESE BREAD
"Signature"

Makes 1 large loaf

1½ cups warm water 115°F
3 teaspoons active dry yeast
4½ cups all-purpose flour
1½ teaspoons sea salt
3 ounces prosciutto, chopped
½ cup sweet onion, chopped
½ cup emmenthaler cheese, freshly grated
¼ cup of extra virgin olive oil, plus extra for greasing bowl and brushing bread

In a small bowl, combine yeast with ¼ cup warm water, stir and let set for 15-minutes to dissolve yeast.

In a large pre-warmed bowl, combine 4¼ cups flour and salt.

Make a well in the center and pour in the yeast mixture, add prosciutto, onions, cheese, ¼ cup of oil and the remaining warm water.

Gradually incorporate flour and mix to a soft dough, adding a little extra flour if necessary.

Transfer the dough to a lightly floured surface and knead for 5-minutes or until smooth and elastic.

Lightly oil a clean large bowl, cover with a clean dish towel and set aside in a warm place to rise for about 2-hours or until doubled in bulk. Lightly grease a large baking sheet, set aside.

Transfer dough to a lightly floured surface and knead for 4-5 minutes.

Shape dough into an oval loaf, brush lightly with oil and place dough on the prepared baking sheet - cover and let it rise in a warm place until doubled in volume, about 25-30 minutes.

Preheat oven to 400°F

Bake for 40-45 minutes or until the loaf is a golden color, remove bread from oven, cool on a wire rack before slicing.

CHOCOLATE-COCONUT-ALMOND SCONES
"Signature"

Makes about 8-10 large scones

2 cups all-purpose flour, plus extra for rolling out dough
¼ cup unsweetened coco powder
1½ teaspoons of baking powder
5 tablespoons sugar, preferably organic
2 ounces almonds, finely ground
¼ cup shredded, unsweetened coconut
5 tablespoons unsalted butter, chilled and cut into small pieces
2/3 cup half and half, plus extra for brushing scones
Confectioner sugar, for dusting scones

Preheat oven to 400ºF

Into a large bowl, sift flour, coco and baking powders, stir-in sugar, almonds and coconut. With a pastry blender, cut the butter into the dry ingredients until mixture resembles fine crumbs, or rub in the butter with your fingertips. Add the half and half - stir with a fork until the dry ingredients are thoroughly moistened and will come together in a ball of fairly soft dough in the center of the bowl. Turn the dough onto a lightly floured surface, knead it very lightly, folding and pressing to mix evenly, about 30 seconds. Roll or pat dough to produce a flat round about ½ inch thick. With a floured sharp knife, cut 8-10 equal wedges. Arrange scones on an un-greased baking sheet. Brush the tops lightly with half and half and bake for 12-15 minutes or until well risen. Serve with butter, jam, or orange whipped sweetened cream.

CREAMY BISCUITS
With
ORANGE BUTTER and APPLE JAM

"Signature-1995 – one of our "High Tea" favorites"

Makes 12 biscuits

BISCUITS

2½ cups of all-purpose flour
1 tablespoon of baking powder
¼ teaspoon of sea salt
2 tablespoons of sugar
2 cups whipping cream

Preheat oven to 400°F

In a large bowl combine flour, baking powder, salt, sugar and cream to form soft dough.

Drop heaping ¼-cups of batter, about 1-inch apart, on an un-greased, large baking sheet.

Bake 18-20 minutes in the middle of oven until tops and bottoms are golden brown.

Remove biscuits from oven, cover with foil to keep warm until ready to serve.

APPLE JAM

8 large apples, such as Granny Smith, Pink Lady or Golden Delicious
2¾ cups of sugar
¼ teaspoon of ground cinnamon
1 tablespoon of fresh lemon juice
1 tablespoon of fresh limejuice

Peel, core and cut apples into small cubes and place them in a large saucepan. Add sugar, cinnamon, lemon and limejuice. Bring to a slow boil, turn heat to medium-low and cook 30 minutes, or until mixture is thick.

Transfer to a heatproof glass bowl, let cool completely, cover and refrigerate until ready to use.

To enjoy: Slice biscuits in half, spread orange butter on each half and spoon a small dollop of apple jam on top of orange butter. Enjoy for breakfast or as afternoon snack with a cup of tea.

Note: See Orange Butter on page 301. Apple jam can be made 2 days ahead, serve at room temperature.

BASIC PUFF PASTRY

Makes about 1 pound

2/3 cup unsalted butter, chilled
1-1/3 cups all-purpose flour, plus extra
2/3 cup of white cake flour
1 teaspoon of sea salt
1 teaspoon lemon juice, freshly squeezed and chilled
½ to 2/3 cup of ice water

Dough base: Melt 1-tablespoon of butter and refrigerate remaining butter. Sift flours onto a cool marble slap or board. Make a large well in center. Place salt, lemon juice, ½ cup of water and 1-tablespoon of melted butter in the center of well and, using fingertips, blend the ingredients. Then, using fingertips of both hands, gradually work in the flour to form coarse crumbs. If crumbs are dry, add more ice water, a few drops at a time. Cut dough several times with a metal spatula to be sure ingredients are blended. Do not knead the dough. Press dough into a ball - dough should be soft. Score an "x" on top of the dough with a sharp knife to prevent shrinkage. Wrap in lightly floured parchment paper or plastic wrap. Chill for ½ hour in the refrigerator.

To continue: Lightly flour remaining chilled butter, place floured butter between 2- sheets of parchment paper or plastic wrap and flatten with rolling pin. Remove top sheet of parchment or plastic wrap – fold butter in half and place it between sheets of parchment paper, or plastic wrap. Continue flattening and folding until butter is pliable, but not sticky. Butter should have same consistency as dough. Shape butter into a 6-inch square and lightly sprinkle with flour.

To complete: On a cool surface roll out dough to a 12-inch square, slightly thicker in center than at sides. Set butter in center of dough, then fold corners of dough toward center of butter, then fold sides of dough so as to envelope the butter. Place dough, seam side down, on a floured surface. Press down on top with a rolling pin to flatten dough slightly. Roll out dough to a rectangle 7 to 8 inches wide by 18 to 20 inches long and fold in thirds. Gently press seams with rolling pin to seal. Turn dough to bring seam-side to your left so dough opens like a book. This is called a turn. Again roll dough to a large rectangle and fold again in thirds. This is the second turn. Wrap dough in parchment paper or plastic wrap and refrigerate 15-30 minutes. Repeat rolling process, giving dough a total of 6 turns. Refrigerate at least 1-hour before the next turn.

Tips for using puff pastry: Let frozen puff pastry dough thaw at room temperature, roll out puff pastry dough on a lightly floured surface, roll the dough in two directions from top to bottom and from left to right. If rolled in only one direction, it will not rise evenly during baking. Cut puff pastry dough with a very sharp knife to prevent edges from sticking together, if using a pastry cutter, dip it in cold water before cutting out dough. Brush edges of pastry dough with cold water for best results.

Trimming stacked dough: Press firmly together and again roll out dough. Use small pieces and strips for decoration. Always place puff pastry dough on a baking sheet or in a pan that has been sprinkled lightly with cold water – the steam developing from the water during baking helps pastry rise. Refrigerate puff pastry dough 15-minutes before baking.

Note: Whole or cut homemade puff pastry can be packaged and frozen in small portions according to planned usage. This pastry requires more effort and time to make than do other pastries, but the effort is worth it to yield the buttery and flakiest base for any tart or pastry. However, if you are short of time, purchased sheets of frozen puff pastry can be used, but wise shoppers will research and read labels to seek out bakeries that specialize in puff pastry, producing nearest to that of homemade, which most likely will contain less to almost none of the undesirable ingredients that may be found in other commercially processed puff pastry.

RED CURRANT JAM

Created and demonstrated this on local, weekly TV Segment, aired during year 2001.

Yields about 2 pints (Recipe can be doubled)

4 cups currant pulp
3 cups sugar
2 teaspoons gin

Cook currants until soft, press through a sieve or food mill. Measure currant pulp and place pulp in a large saucepan and add sugar. Bring slowly to a boil, stirring occasionally until sugar dissolves. Cook rapidly, almost to a jelling point, about 30 minutes. As mixture thickens, stir frequently to prevent sticking. Add gin. Pour boiling hot mixture into hot jars leaving ¼ inch between liquid and jar rim. Position caps, tighten lids on jars and process 15 minutes in a boiling water bath to seal.

Note 1: Red, black and white currants, a berry typically found in Europe, may be frozen for future use. Select berries that are fully ripe. Sort, stem, wash and rinse berries carefully and drain, pat them dry with paper towels, apportion in freezer containers, seal, label and freeze.

Note 2: Mix ½ cup of stemmed currants into your favorite pound cake or muffin batter to add a fresh and fruity taste. You may also purée 1-2 cups of red currants in your blender with sugar to taste for use over ice cream or with your favorite dessert. Puréed currants may be kept refrigerated up to 1 week, or longer if frozen.

CLASSIC POPOVERS

Each Recipe on this page makes 6 large or 9 medium popovers

3 large eggs, plus 1-egg white
1 cup of whole milk
1 tablespoon unsalted butter, melted, or
1 tablespoon of walnut oil (Avail. in supermarkets)
1 cup of all-purpose flour
¼ teaspoon sea salt
Unsalted butter, for greasing

Preheat oven to 400°F

Generously grease six 2/3-cup non-stick popover tins, or nine ½ -cup non-stick muffin tins.

In a medium bowl, whisk together eggs and milk. Add butter or oil in a stream whisking. Add flour and salt, and whisk mixture until combined well but still slightly lumpy. Divide batter among tins and bake in lower third section of oven for 35 minutes. Turn heat to 375°F and bake 10 minutes more.

GRUYÉRE POPOVERS

Follow "Classic Popovers" recipe - coarsely grate ½ cup gruyére cheese

Divide half of batter among tins and sprinkle ¼ cup gruyére over batter in tins.

Divide remaining batter among tins and sprinkle remaining ¼ cup gruyére over batter, and bake popovers according to recipe above.

CURRY-CUMIN-WATERCRESS POPOVERS

Follow "Classic Popovers" recipe and add the following ingredients:

¼ teaspoon ground cumin
¼ teaspoon curry powder
2 tablespoons of watercress leaves, chopped

Whisk ground cumin and curry powder into batter, fold-in watercress, and bake popovers according to recipe for Classic Popovers. *Note:* Popovers are best served hot either plain or saturated with butter. Enjoy!

BUTTER

WHAT TO LOOK FOR, WHAT CHOICES ARE THERE & OTHER OPTIONS

Don't over-salt! Throughout this cookbook you'll notice that all recipes call for unsalted butter rather than salted butter. My rule is avoiding purchase of butter containing salt, chemical additives or purchasing any artificial substitution. Applicable also to all other consumable products in keeping preparations as organically natural as possible, putting you and me in regulative control over the amount of salt wanted, or not wanted in your diet. So then you may ask why is salt in butter? To clarify, salt in butter is meant to extend shelf life of butter and act as a flavor enhancer but I believe any dietary benefit to consumers or to a recipe deriving from this additive is nil. In retrospect, when cooking from memory or following recipes calling for butter (other cookbooks on the market usually make no distinction between preferred use of salted or unsalted butter) and now because of your awareness of this, salt shouldn't be an unintentional tag along ingredient when using unsalted butter in and among specified ingredients of a recipe considered essential to produce the flavor intended by its author. That is why all recipes in my cookbooks calling for butter specifically list unsalted butter, and substitutions will not serve any useful purpose or benefit the outcome of recipes, unless otherwise stated in this book.

In the USA, there are, however, European style unsalted butters available in supermarkets, such as Plugra, Horizon, Classique, and Tillamook to name a few that produce favorable results. Also, there are imported unsalted butters available in the USA from European countries such as from Denmark, France, Germany, Ireland, and the Netherlands. Although the latter choices are a bit more expensive, chances are they are products from farm animals that graze freely, their diet is as nature intended, and they (generally) are not over-milked. Organic farming and ranching, and consumer demand for it are on the rise, however. Fortunate are we to have one of those exceptions in the Yakima Valley, "Pride and Joy Dairy, a certified organic dairy, located close by in Granger, Washington that I'm personally most familiar with.

I highly recommend reading labels to determine the amount of butterfat products contain. Butter with a low percentage of butterfat, less than 85%, generally will produce excessive residual water causing splattering when heated, water that dilutes flavor and adds undesirable moisture in baked goods and other concoctions. Such results are not experienced with butter containing higher percentage of butterfat.

If you would like to churn your own butter - it's easy to do if you have time and here's how: Simply use organic, pasteurized whipping cream (ultra-pasteurized whipping cream will not work). Beat it as though you would whip cream - but *don't stop beating when stiff peaks form - continue beating until the milky liquid begins to separate from the butterfat. Pour the milky liquid (known as buttermilk or whey) into a separate container and store refrigerated for subsequent use in baked goods or spoon it over vegetables. What remains is sweet, creamy butter to use in place of commercial butter.*

We used to make Europeanized butter by adding a teaspoon of organic sour cream or organic plain yogurt. Yogurt was drained overnight in the refrigerator and the liquid discarded. We used 1-pint of organic, pasteurized whipping cream, 1-teaspoon of yogurt or sour cream and let it stand overnight at room temperature covered with cheesecloth before implementing the previously described churning process. This butter is freezable up to two months tightly wrapped and appropriately packaged (vacuum packed) for freezing.

For larger yield and family fun, look for an old-fashioned butter churner, or ask grandma if you can borrow hers, and involve the entire family in the churning process. Besides a healthy yield, there's a bit of exercising in it too.

<u>Chef's note</u>: To boost flavor of ordinary breads, meats, fowl and fish, use herb butter to add notable finishes to your dish, such as, spreading herb butters over bread or melting it over baked potatoes or over your favorite vegetables - to mention a few of many typical, natural applications. The following

butters may help toward that end. Enjoy!

ORANGE BUTTER

Makes about ¾ cup

1 stick of unsalted butter, softened
3 tablespoons of confectioner sugar
1 tablespoon finely grated orange zest
¼ cup of fresh orange juice

In a small mixing bowl with a hand-mixer, beat butter, confectioner sugar and orange zest until light and fluffy. Add orange juice and beat until well incorporated.

Transfer to a small glass bowl, cover with plastic wrap, and refrigerate until ready to use. Tastes excellent on warm muffins, toasted breads, crepés, sweet rolls and scones

PISTACHIO BUTTER

Makes: ½ cup

½ cup unsalted butter, softened
½ teaspoon sea salt
2 tablespoons unsalted pistachios, finely chopped
¼ teaspoon white pepper

In a medium bowl, cream butter with salt and pistachios. Place mixture on wax paper, parchment paper or plastic wrap, and roll into a cylindrical shape. Refrigerate for 2-hours.

<u>Chef's note:</u> Use as an accompaniment to roasted or grilled meats, as a spread on crostini, or on French bread.

HERB BUTTERS
"Signature"

"Cooking with Erika"
Created and demonstrated this on local, weekly TV Segment, aired during year 2002.

TO MAKE HERB BUTTERS

1-cup unsalted butter, softened along with any of the following combinations:

THYME BUTTER

2 teaspoons each fresh-snipped thyme and marjoram

PARSLEY-WATERCRESS-CITRUS BUTTER

4 tablespoons fresh-snipped parsley
2 tablespoons fresh-snipped watercress
1 teaspoon finely grated lemon zest
2 teaspoons finely grated orange zest

SUNDRIED TOMATO BUTTER

2 tablespoons oil packed dried tomatoes, drained, chopped
2 tablespoons finely chopped shallots
2 cloves of garlic, minced

CHIVES BUTTER

2 tablespoons fresh-snipped chives
2 tablespoons fresh-snipped dill
1 teaspoon finely ground mélange peppercorns

BASIL BUTTER

Makes 1 log each about 1 x 5 inches

2 tablespoons fresh-snipped basil
2 tablespoons lime zest, finely grated
1 tablespoon Italian parsley, finely chopped

Place choice of butter and other ingredients in a small bowl and stir until combined. Cover and refrigerate for 30 minutes. Shape butter into a log about 1-inch in diameter, wrap in waxed paper or plastic wrap, chill for several hours before serving.

CLARIFIED BUTTER

Melt any given quantity of sweet, unsalted butter in a heavy saucepan. Over very low heat, heat until white foam rises to the top. Skim-off the foam and continue cooking until no more foam rises and all particles in the butter sink to the bottom of the pan. Be very careful not to allow the butter to color too much. Pour off the clear purified butter from the top into a container, or remove it with a bulb baster.

The residue may be used as a final enrichment for sauces and soups. Both the clarified butter and the residue are storable up to two weeks refrigerated, or they can be kept frozen 3-months.

Chef's note: Clarified butter may be used as is or add lemon juice, salt and pepper for a simple, but excellent, sauce over a wide variety of vegetables, a combination often used in Indian cooking.

OLIVE-ONION-SUNDRIED TOMATO BUTTER

Makes about 1 cup

½ cup unsalted butter, softened
1/3 cup black olives, minced
1/3 cup sun-dried tomatoes, chopped
1 tablespoon of garlic, minced
1 tablespoon sweet onions, minced

In a medium bowl, mash together butter, olives, tomatoes, garlic and onion. Form into 2 cylinders, each about 3-inches long, wrap in plastic wrap and refrigerate. This butter can be kept frozen for up to 3-months. Enjoy with grilled meats, such as lamb, pork or chicken.

GOAT CHEESE SPREAD

"Signature" – My original, among other identified recipes in this cookbook created for, and personally demonstrated this recipe for the Washington State Potato Seed Commission at the Washington State University Exploratory Laboratory, Prosser, WA., November 17, 2006)

Make about 2 cups

8 ounces mild soft goat cheese, room temperature
8 ounces of cream cheese, room temperature
¼ cup sweet Walla Walla onions, finely chopped
1 medium apple, gala or golden delicious, peeled, cored, finely chopped
¼ cup dry white wine
Sea salt
White pepper, freshly ground
¼ cup of watercress leaves, chopped
¼ cup of fresh dill, chopped

1 teaspoon if sweet paprika, for garnish
Apple slices, for garnish

In a medium bowl, beat together goat cheese, cream cheese, onions, apple and wine until completely smooth. Season with salt and pepper, stir in watercress and dill, transfer to a glass bowl, sprinkle with paprika and garnish with apple slices. Serve with toasted bread slices, cucumber rounds, apple slices or with warm potato wedges.

Best when served at room temperature.

Also, tastes great over baked potatoes.

Goat Cheese Spread

FIGS in PORT WINE
"Signature"

Serves: 4-6

1-1/3 cup of sugar
1 cup of water
1 cup of Port wine
1 pound fresh figs, washed under running warm water, pat dry with paper towels

In a medium saucepan combine sugar and water, turn heat to medium low, and cook until sugar is dissolved, stirring constantly. Add port wine and figs turn heat to medium and cook 10-minutes. Transfer figs to a heatproof glass bowl and let cool. Cover with plastic wrap and refrigerate until ready to serve. Enjoy over vanilla ice cream, pound cakes, pancakes, or as an after dinner compote.

A bit of history

Figs are grown in the Southern part of Europe and in Africa. As of today, Germany developed fig farms on the famous Weinstrasse am Kaiserstuhl, the Odenwald and the Bodensee regions. The harvest cycle for this naturally sweet, flavorful fruit begins during July ending approximately mid November. In Turkey and South Africa, figs are green to light yellow or red to violet color. Darker figs, however, are the tastiest. Figs are storable up to 3 weeks in a cool environment, ideally, in the basement or a similar alternative other than a refrigerator. To varying degrees, refrigerating figs cause loss of aroma, also a slight loss of flavor is quite possible.

DESSERTS

CAKES

TORTES

SIGNATURE

Top Left & Right – Mixed Fruit Flans, see Page 319

Opposite Photo – Miniature Cheesecakes, foreground, see Page 322

Bottom Left – Chocolate-Eggnog-Apple Torte, see Page 336

Bottom Right – Cinnamon-Brandy-Chocolate-Potato Cake, see Page, 334

Napoleon, Page 342 / Yukon Gold Potato-Apple Cake, Page 333

L. Red Gooseberry Cake, Page 316 / R. Bing Cherry Cake, Page 315

Figs in Port Wine, Page 304 / Potato-Apple-Almond Cake, Page 332

Above Right - Lighter appearance - less flavor - contains salt and baking soda

Salt (not shown) and above active baking soda - are not needed to get most flavor, and leavening results - salt reduced the flavor of chocolate and produced a lighter appearance; harder texture; there was no appreciable difference in height; there was a salty-chalky aftertaste, and a bloated feeling presumed from baking soda, was detected compared to cookies without these two sodium compound ingredients. Results of a taste test conducted between these two versions using identical processing method and both were independently baked in the same oven set at the same temperature.

THE BEST EVER CHOCOLATE COOKIES

(No salt – No baking soda)

Makes about 30 cookies

½ cup plus 2 tablespoons unsalted butter
1 cup of light brown sugar
1 tablespoon of hazelnut liqueur

1 2/3 cups all-purpose flour
1/3 cup plus 1 tablespoon unsweetened coco powder
¼ teaspoon baking powder
½ teaspoon ground cinnamon
1 tablespoon finely ground coffee
8 ounces bittersweet chocolate, coarsely chopped

Using a mixer with paddle attachment, place butter in a large bowl, beat at medium speed until soft and creamy. Add sugar and hazelnut liqueur and beat 1-2 more minutes.

Sift together flour, coco, baking powder, cinnamon and coffee - reduce mixer speed to low, add dry ingredients –

incorporate, toss-in chopped chocolate and again mix to incorporate.

Turn dough out onto work surface, divide in half and shape each into a 1½ inches diameter log. Plastic wrap logs and chill at least 1-2 hours.

Middle position a rack in oven and preheat oven to 325°F
Line two baking sheets with parchment paper

Using a sharp knife, slice logs into ½ inch thick discs and place cookies on prepared baking sheets, spacing each about 1-inch apart.

Bake one sheet of cookies at a time for about 12 – 15 minutes - cookies will be soft. Transfer from oven to a cooling rack - let cookies cool before removing them from the baking sheet. Enjoy!

Notes

ALMOND SHORT CAKES -
YAKIMA CHERRIES and KIRSCH-FLAVORED WHIPPED CREAM
"Signature"

"Cooking with Erika"
Created and demonstrated this on local, weekly TV Segment, aired during year 2002.

Serves: 4

1 cup all-purpose, flour, plus extra for rolling out dough
3 tablespoons sugar
½ tablespoon baking powder
2 tablespoons almonds, finely ground
¼ cup chilled unsalted butter, cubed
¼ cup of chilled whole milk
1 small egg

Preheat oven to 400°F
Line a baking sheet with parchment paper, and spray parchment paper lightly with cooking spray.

Combine flour, sugar, and baking powder in a medium bowl and whisk to blend. Add butter and rub-in with fingertips until mixture resembles coarse meal. Mix-in almonds. Beat milk and egg in small bowl to blend.

Gradually add milk mixture to dry ingredients, tossing until dough comes together in moist clumps. Gather dough together, turnout onto a lightly floured surface and gently knead 5-turns to combine.

Gently shape into a 4-inch long log and cut cross-wise into 4-rounds and shape each into 2½ x ¾-inch round. Arrange rounds on prepared baking sheet. Bake shortcakes until bottoms are golden, about 15-minutes, and a tester inserted into center comes out clean. Cool on rack 15-minutes.

CHERRY SAUCE

1 pound of fresh Bing cherries, stemmed, pitted, halved
3 tablespoons sugar
1 tablespoon Kirsch (clear cherry brandy, avail. at Liquor Stores)
4 tablespoons Zinfandel Port Wine
2 teaspoons of cornstarch

Cherry Sauce instructions: Combine cherries, sugar and kirsch in a medium, non-stick saucepan. In a small bowl, combine port wine with cornstarch. Bring cherry mixture to a slow boil, whisk port wine mixture into cherry mixture and cook until slightly thickened, about 2-minutes- stirring constantly. Transfer to a glass bowl and let cool. Note: Can be prepared 1-day ahead, covered and refrigerated.

TOPPING

1 cup chilled whipping cream
1½ tablespoons confectioner sugar, plus extra for dusting
½ tablespoon Kirsch (cherry) Liqueur
Mint leaves for garnish

Beat cream, confectioner sugar and kirsch in a medium bowl until stiff peaks form. Cover and refrigerate until ready to use. Cut warm shortcakes horizontally in halves. Place bottom halves on serving plates, spoon ¼ cup cherry mixture over the bottom half and top each with ¼ cup cream, cover with the top half of shortcake, dust each with confectioner sugar, garnish with mint leaves and serve.   *Note:* Topping can be prepared 6-hours ahead, covered and refrigerated until ready to serve.

FRUIT TWIST PASTA
"Signature"

"Cooking with Erika"
Created and demonstrated this on local, weekly, local TV segment, aired March 3, 2003

Serves: 4-6

1 cup of heavy cream
½ cup mascarpone cheese
½ cup of sugar
1 tablespoon of fresh limejuice
1 tablespoon of lime Vodka or 1 tablespoon of fresh orange juice
1 tablespoon freshly grated orange zest
3 large ripe peaches, peeled, pitted and chopped
1/3 cup Amaretti cookies, finely ground
4-6 tablespoons of red currant jam, for garnish

Mint sprigs, for garnish

1 pound of spaghetti
1½ teaspoons sea salt

In a mixing bowl, beat cream and mascarpone until soft peaks form, and add sugar, limejuice, vodka or orange juice and orange zest. Beat until stiff peaks form.

Fold in peaches, refrigerate until ready to serve. Meanwhile, bring a large saucepan of salted water to boil and cook spaghetti according to package directions.

Drain well and divide among individual-large serving plates.

Spoon ¼ cup of peach mixture over pasta, sprinkle each with amaretti, garnish each with one tablespoon of red currant jam and mint sprigs.

Chef's note: quick, easy and tasty way to enjoy the seasonal fruits with a pasta twist the entire family will love!

APPLE TORTE with RUM and ALMONDS

Serves: 8-10

SHORTBREAD CRUST

¾ cup all-purpose flour
¼ cup confectioner sugar
4 tablespoons chilled unsalted butter, plus
extra for greasing cake pan

Preheat oven to 350°F
Butter a 9-inch spring-form pan

In a medium bowl, combine flour and confectioner sugar. Cut chilled butter into the flour-sugar mixture, and press the very loose dough into the prepared cake pan.

NUT LAYER

2 tablespoons unsalted butter
1/3 cup of sugar
2/3 cup blanched whole almonds, finely ground

Place butter, sugar and almonds into a food processor and process for 1-minute. Spread the nut layer on top of the shortbread crust and bake for 15-25 minutes. Remove from oven and set aside to cool.

APPLE FILLING

2 tablespoons unsalted butter
3 large golden delicious apples, or Pink Lady, peeled, cored and thinly sliced
1/3 cup of sugar
1¼ cups sweet dessert wine, such as late harvest Riesling or sweet Rebecca
3 tablespoons white rum

Heat a large skillet over medium heat to hold the apples in one layer.

Toss-in the butter (avoid browning), add apples then sprinkle apples evenly with sugar. Cook apples about 3-minutes, add half of the wine and evaporate it completely.

Repeat with remaining wine if the apples appear to be too firm. When apples have developed a caramel color, sprinkle them with rum. Cook apples one minute more. Transfer apples to a plate and let cool completely. Reserve any liquid.

CHOCOLATE FILLING

8 ounces semi-sweet chocolate, of good quality, chopped into small pieces
1¼ cups whipping cream
2 teaspoons confectioner sugar

Place an inch of water in a 2-quart double boiler and bring to a boil. Set chopped chocolate in the upper bowl over the boiling water. Turn-off heat and cover the bowl to melt chocolate in about 2 or 3 minutes.

Remove bowl from heat. Stir chocolate until it loses all heat. Whip 1-cup cream and confectioner sugar to a soft peak.

Fold 1/3 of cream into the cooled chocolate. Fold remaining cream into chocolate.

SAUCE

In a small saucepan over medium heat, add remaining ¼ cup of cream, stir-in reserved liquid and cook 2-minutes, and let cool slightly.

312

ASSEMBLE TORTE

Spoon chocolate cream over the cake crust in the spring-form pan, and spread evenly with a spatula. Carefully arrange the (cooled sautéed) apple slices with flat sides overlapping and fanned. Cover and refrigerate 2-3 hours. Remove 15-minutes before serving and remove from the spring-form pan, and place torte on a large cake plate. Cut torte into serving slices. Drizzle sauce on each serving plate, place a slice of torte on top of sauce, and enjoy with coffee or tea.

Chef's note: Using 2 medium-size skillets to avoid overcrowding apples is recommended.

SAUTÉED BANANA HALVES
With
CARAMEL and RASPBERRIES

Created for demonstrating on weekly local, TV segment, aired during year 2002

Serves: 4

1 tablespoon unsalted butter
1 tablespoon light brown sugar
1 tablespoon of fresh orange juice
4 ripe bananas, peeled, cut in half
2 cups vanilla ice cream
2 cups raspberries, rinsed and patted dry
6 tablespoons sugar
Mint leaves, for garnish
Confectioner sugar, for dusting

Melt butter in a large skillet over medium heat, add brown sugar, stir until melted, stir-in orange juice, turn heat to medium-high, add 4-banana halves, and sauté on both sides until golden – about 1-minute per side.

Transfer bananas to 4 warmed serving plates, repeat process with remaining bananas, drizzle juices from skillet over bananas, and top each with a scoop of vanilla ice cream and ¼ cup raspberries.

CARAMEL

Pour 6 tablespoons of sugar into an 8 or 10-inch frying pan over medium-high heat, shake and tilt pan often until sugar is melted and amber colored, about 2-3 minutes. At once, pour caramel slowly in thin streaks over desserts. Garnish with remaining raspberries, mint leaves and dust lightly with confectioner sugar, and enjoy!

AMARETTO PLUM-ALMOND CAKE
"Signature"

"Cooking with Erika"
Created and demonstrated this on local, weekly TV Segment, aired during 2001

Serves 14-16

1¾ cups all-purpose flour, plus extra for dusting pan
1 teaspoon of baking powder
4 tablespoons unsalted butter, melted, plus extra for greasing pan
2 large eggs
½ cup sugar plus 2 tablespoons
1 teaspoon of vanilla extract
1 teaspoon finely grated lemon zest
1 teaspoon finely grated orange zest
2 cups Italian plums, halved and pitted
4 teaspoons Amaretto liqueur (Avail. in liquor store)
1/3 cup of blanched almonds, finely chopped

Preheat oven to 350°F

Sift together flour and baking powder into a large bowl, add the butter, eggs, ½ cup sugar, vanilla extract, lemon and orange zests.

Work ingredients with a wooden spoon until dough is smooth and well blended, pat down the dough over the bottom of a buttered and floured 9 x 1-inch fluted tart pan, with removable bottom, to about 1-inch thickness.

Press plums lightly into the dough and sprinkle with the remaining 1-tablespoon of sugar.

Sprinkle plums with 2-teaspoons amaretto liqueur and almonds.

Bake for 40 minutes or until the crust is golden and the plums are soft.

Cool on a rack and serve at room temperature with a dollop of amaretto cream.

WHIPPING CREAM

1 cup whipping cream
1 tablespoon confectioner sugar
1 tablespoon Amaretto liqueur

In a small mixing bowl, whip cream until soft peaks form, fold-in confectioner sugar and tablespoon amaretto-whip until stiff peaks form. Refrigerate until ready to serve.

Chef's note: For variety, substitute plums with fresh peaches, pears, apples or blackberries.

BING (BLACK) CHERRY POUND CAKE
"Signature"

Serves: 12-14

2 cups all-purpose flour
½ cup of almond flour, (Avail. in supermarket baking section)
2 teaspoons baking powder
1 cup of unsalted butter, softened, plus extra for greasing cake pan
1½ cups superfine sugar, plus extra for dusting pan
4 large eggs
1/3 cup of fresh orange juice
1½ cups of fresh, sweet dark (Bing) cherries, pitted
Confectioner sugar, for dusting cake
Whipping cream, freshly whipped and sweetened, for garnish

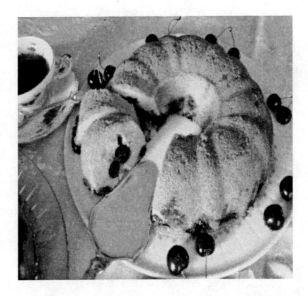

Preheat oven to 350°F
Lightly grease a large 10 to 12 cup nonstick bundt pan with butter and lightly dust with sugar

In a medium bowl, whisk together flour, almond flour and baking powder until well blended.

With an electric mixer, beat butter until very pale, add sugar and beat well until slightly fluffy – scrape sides of bowl well, add eggs, one at a time beating until well blended after each addition.
Add orange juice and flour mixture – mix on low speed until batter is well blended and smooth.

Switch from mixer to a stiff rubber spatula and gently fold-in the cherries.

Scrape batter into the prepared pan and bake in the center of oven until cake is golden brown, about 35-45 minutes or until a cake tester comes out clean when inserted into the center of cake.

Allow cake to cool for 15-minutes in the pan before turning out onto a wire rack.

Transfer cake to a large serving plate, dust lightly with confectioner sugar and serve with sweetened fresh whipped cream.

RED GOOSEBERRY COFFEE CAKE
"Signature"

Serves: 12-14

1 cup of unsalted butter, softened, plus extra for greasing cake pan
1½ cups of superfine sugar, plus extra for dusting cake pan
3 large eggs
1/3 cup of white rum
2½ cups all-purpose flour
2 teaspoons of baking powder
2 cups of fresh red gooseberries, trimmed-both ends (Avail. at Farmer's Market, when in season)
Confectioner sugar, for dusting cake
Whipping cream, freshly whipped & sweetened, for garnish

Preheat oven to 350°F
Lightly grease a 10-inch spring form pan with butter and lightly dust with sugar

In a large mixing bowl, cream butter, add sugar and beat mixture until light and fluffy.

Beat-in eggs one at a time – beat well after each addition. Add rum.

Sift together flour and baking powder and add to the egg mixture - mix on low speed until batter is well blended and smooth. Switch from mixer to a stiff rubber spatula and gently fold-in the gooseberries. Scrape batter into prepared pan and smooth out the top.

Bake on center rack until cake is golden brown, about 35-45 minutes or until a cake tester comes out clean when inserted into the center.

Let cake cool completely, about 1-hour in the pan, before loosening sides of pan and transferring cake to a large serving plate.

Dust cake with confectioner sugar and serve with sweetened fresh whipped cream.

The

GOOSEBERRY

Gooseberries, another tart, semi-sweet European berry, which eventually found its way into America in two predominant, green and red, varieties although there also are white and yellow varieties commonly found in European countries like England, France, Germany and Austria, to name a few - all of these countries are famous for creating excellent flavor in gooseberry cakes, tortes, flans and jams with least additives. Included also among those countries, is what British refer to as the "Gooseberry Fool" which consists of both cooked and puréed gooseberries folded into freshly whipped cream. You'll find more about this on the following pages.

When selecting fresh gooseberries plan to pick or shop for them during early to peak season in your area for the best choice. Look for fairly firm, berries with bright-shiny colors and the veins appear to be deep rather than nearest to the surface, which may indicate they were picked too early. More color generally means sweeter berries and dullness of color may mean they are old or picked too late. If you like gooseberries anytime of the year the prevailing green variety, either canned or

Comparatively though, the larger, more rounded gooseberries grown in Europe possess a consistent, slightly sweeter and subtly tangy flavor whereas the small, less rounded berries in America possess a more tart-sour flavor to varying degrees, depending on soil in which bushes are planted and weather conditions.

frozen, is usually available in supermarkets year round. Gooseberries, when methodically used, can deliver excellent to superior flavor regardless from where they came. Enjoy surprising flavor! _Shown above is Green Gooseberry-Apple Coffee cake, see recipe on next page._

317

GOOSEBERRY-APPLE COFFEE CAKE

Serves: 12-14

BATTER

1 cup unsalted butter, softened
1 teaspoon of vanilla
1 cup of sugar
4 large eggs
2½ cups all-purpose sugar
½ teaspoon baking powder

FILLING

2½ cups of fresh green gooseberries, trimmed at both ends (drain well if using frozen or canned gooseberries, although not recommended)
4 large apples, peeled, cored and thinly sliced, such as golden delicious
4 tablespoons of sugar (reduce to 2 tablespoons if using canned or frozen berries)
1 tablespoon of dark rum
¼ cup of almonds, finely ground

Preheat oven to 350°F
Spray a 10-inch spring form pan with cooking spray.

In a medium-size mixing bowl, cream the butter, vanilla sugar and sugar until light and fluffy. Add 1 egg at a time - beat well after each addition.

Sift flour and baking powder into the butter mixture and beat well, about 5-more minutes.

Spoon half of batter into the prepared pan, sprinkle gooseberries evenly over batter, top gooseberries with apples, sprinkle sugar and rum over fruit, spoon remaining batter over fruit, and sprinkle nuts over the batter.

Bake 35-40 minutes, or until a wooden pick inserted into the center of the cake comes out clean.

Cool cake completely. Remove sides of pan, place cake on cake plate and prepare glaze.

GLAZE

1 cup of confectioner sugar
1-2 tablespoons of rum or fresh lemon juice

In a small bowl, combine confectioner sugar with rum or fresh lemon juice to make a smooth paste, and drizzle over cake. Enjoy with a dollop or two of sweetened whipped cream.

MIXED - FRUIT FLAN

Serves 12-14

CAKE BATTER

9 tablespoons of all-purpose flour
9 tablespoons of sugar
½ teaspoon baking powder
4 tablespoons orange juice, freshly squeezed
9 tablespoons almond oil, available in supermarkets
5 large eggs, preferably organic

Preheat oven to 350°F

To prepare cake batter: Place all ingredients in a medium size mixing bowl and beat on high speed for 3-4 minutes. Spray bottom and sides of a 10-inch fluted flan pan with "no stick" cooking spray – preferably organic.

Pour batter into prepared pan, smooth out the top with a cake spatula and bake for 15-20 minutes or until light brown and firm to the touch.

Remove flan from oven, allow cake to rest for 10-minutes. Loosen cake from sides of pan with a knife and place the cake upside down on a 12-inch cake plate, cover with plastic wrap – set aside.

FRUIT FILLING

1 cup of fresh raspberries
1 cup ripe bing cherries, pitted and halved
1 cup of ripe red gooseberries
3 large, ripe peaches, peeled, pitted, and thinly sliced

Arrange a patterning of fruit in rows over the top of the flan. Prepare glazing, if desired.

GLAZING

1 cup of apricot jam
¼ cup apricot liqueur or fresh orange juice
2 tablespoons of water

In a small saucepan over medium-low heat, melt apricot jam with apricot liqueur or orange juice and water, while stirring. Remove from heat and force the mixture through a fine sieve into a clean bowl, spoon glaze over the fruit and serve with sweetened, freshly whipped cream, if desired.

BLACK MUSCAT-PORT WINE CHEESECAKE
With
RHUBARB-PORT SAUCE
"Signature"

Theme Recipe created as a featured dessert for the up and coming Washington State Fairground's 2002 "Grand Ole Wine Fest", Yakima Valley Wine Region, Yakima, Washington

Serves: 10-12

PASTRY CRUST
"Signature"

1 cup of all-purpose unbleached flour
¼ teaspoon baking powder
3 tablespoons unsweetened coco powder
¼ cup sugar, plus 2-tablespoons
¼ cup chilled unsalted butter, cut into small cubes
1 large egg, slightly beaten
1 tablespoon Black Muscat wine

Spray sides and bottom of a 10-inch spring-form pan with non-stick cooking spray.

Pastry Crust: In a medium bowl, sift together, flour, baking powder and coco powder. In a food processor, combine flour mixture and sugar. Blend 5-seconds.

Add butter using on/off turns until mixture resembles coarse meal. Add egg and Black Muscat wine. Blend until moist clumps form.

Form dough (crust) into a ball. Press crust over the bottom of prepared pan, sprinkle crust with remaining 2-tablespoons of sugar and set aside.

FILLING
"Signature"

2½ pounds of cream cheese, room temperature

1¾ cups sugar
4 large Eggs
2 tablespoons Port wine
2 tablespoons Black Muscat wine
3 tablespoons whipping cream
2½ tablespoons cornstarch

Filling: Using electric mixer, beat cream cheese in a large bowl until fluffy, about 6-minutes. Gradually add sugar and beat until smooth. Beat-in eggs one at a time, mix-in Port wine, Black Muscat wine, cream, and cornstarch. Beat 2 more minutes.

Preheat oven to 350°F

Spoon filling over crust and bake for 30-minutes. Reduce heat to 325°F and bake for 30-more minutes, or until cheesecake is set in center and beginning to brown. Transfer cheesecake to rack and cool completely. Place cheesecake in refrigerator and chill overnight. *Prepare ahead, the Rhubarb-Port Sauce on next Page.*

RHUBARB-PORT SAUCE
"Signature"

4 cups rhubarb, washed, trimmed, cut into
1-inch pieces
1½ cups sugar
1 cup Port wine
Mint leaves, for garnish

Sauce can be made ahead: Cook rhubarb and sugar in a wide 3-4 quart, heavy saucepan over moderately high heat – stirring constantly until rhubarb begins to give off juices. Reduce heat and simmer, stirring frequently, until rhubarb falls apart. Add Port wine and simmer for about 15-minutes. Transfer rhubarb to a heatproof glass bowl, and let cool to room temperature. Purée rhubarb in batches until smooth and transfer to a glass bowl, cover rhubarb with plastic wrap, and refrigerate until ready to use.

To serve: Run a small-sharp knife around pan-sides to loosen, release pan sides, place cheesecake on a large cake plate, cut into serving pieces, spoon Rhubarb-Port Sauce over each slice, and garnish servings with mint.

BROILED GRAPEFRUIT CUPS
With
MASCARPONE and AMARETTI
"Signature-1995"

Serves: 4

2 large pink, or white-grapefruit, cut in half
6 tablespoons mascarpone cheese
1 tablespoon superfine sugar
3 tablespoons whipping cream
6 amaretti cookies, crushed
1 large banana, chopped
2-3 tablespoons brown sugar
4 strawberry halves, for garnish

Preheat oven to broil

Scoop-out grapefruit flesh, remove pits, pith and chop grapefruit flesh. Fill each grapefruit cup evenly with chopped grapefruit flesh. Place grapefruit cups in a large ovenproof dish. In a small bowl, combine mascarpone cheese, sugar, cream and crushed amaretti cookies. Fold-in chopped bananas, spoon mascarpone mixture evenly on top of each grapefruit half. Sprinkle each prepared grapefruit with brown sugar. Place grapefruits under hot broiler, broil until golden brown on top, about 3-5 minutes. Transfer grapefruit cups to heatproof serving bowls, garnish with strawberry halves and serve as first course for breakfast. Enjoy!

Note: Mascarpone cheese is available in supermarket Deli sections. Amaretti cookies are available in specialty gourmet shops.

The ultimate MINIATURE CHEESECAKES
"Signature"

Makes 4 – 4-inch cheesecakes

½ pound of cream cheese (8 ounces), at room temperature
½ cup of whole milk ricotta cheese, drained overnight, refrigerated
1¼ cups of mascarpone cheese, preferably imported from Italy
1 large egg
½ cup of super fine sugar, plus extra for dusting cake pans
1 tablespoon orange liqueur
¼ cup of whipping cream
1 tablespoon of cornstarch
2 teaspoons of all-purpose flour

No-stick cooking spray, preferably organic
Confectioner sugar for dusting cheesecakes

CHEESECAKE GARNISHINGS

¼ cup ripe Bing cherries, pitted and halved
1 medium ripe peach, peeled, pit removed and thinly sliced, plus 1 teaspoon of fresh limejuice combined with one teaspoon of sugar for brushing peach slices
½ cup of fresh blueberries
½ cup of champagne currants or red currants

BLACK CURRANT SAUCE – see next page
(Sauce can be prepared ahead)

Preheat oven to 325°F

Lightly spray bottom and sides of 4, 4-inch spring form pans with a removable bottom, and lightly dust each with sugar and set aside

To prepare cheese filling: In a medium mixing bowl, beat together the cream cheese, drained ricotta and the mascarpone – add egg, sugar, orange liqueur and cream – beat 5-more minutes or until mixture is thick and creamy and stir-in the cornstarch and flour.

Divide cheese mixture into 4 prepared cake pans. Place cake pans in a large baking pan that has at least 2-inch sides, and add enough hot water to the baking pan to reach half way up the sides of the spring form pans. Bake cakes in the middle rack of oven for 35-45 minutes. Turn oven heat off and let cakes stand in the oven for 15-20-minutes, leaving the oven door closed.

Carefully transfer cheesecakes from the baking pan to a wire rack to cool completely - chill cheesecakes loosely covered for at least 2-3 hours before removing the cake pan sides and bottoms. Transfer cakes to serving plates, dust each lightly with confectioner sugar, garnish with Bing cherries, peach slices, blueberries and currants.

Spoon black currant sauce around each serving and garnish with mint sprigs and mint leaves. You really are in for an exquisite treat. *Enjoy!*

Note: Wrap the outside, bottom & sides, of cake pans with one layer of aluminum foil as a safeguard against leakage due to inadequate seal of pans.

BLACK CURRANT SAUCE
"Signature"

Makes about ½ cup

6 ½ tablespoons of sugar
6 ½ tablespoons of water
2 tablespoon untreated orange peel
4 ounces of black currants
1 tablespoon black currant liqueur
(Available at Liquor stores)

To prepare Black Currant Sauce:
Prepare syrup with the first 3 ingredients, (sugar, water and orange peel), - bring to a boil, then remove from heat and let syrup steep until completely cooled. Pass syrup through a fine sieve into a small saucepan, discard orange peel, add black currants and cook 4-5 minutes, then allowing it to cool completely. Add currant liqueur and transfer to a food processor - blend to a smooth purée and pass sauce through a fine sieve into a small bowl. Chill covered until ready to use. Recipe can be doubled. Sauce is excellent over pancakes, pound cakes or with ice creams and custards.

Clockwise from top - Individual Cheesecakes /
Center & center left - mixed Fruit Flans

BOWTIE PASTA with BANANA TWIST

Created and demonstrated this on weekly, local TV Segment, aired during April, 2003

Serves: 4

PASTA

1 pound of bowtie pasta
1½ teaspoons of sea salt
6 quarts of water
2 tablespoons of unsalted butter, melted

In a large saucepan, bring water to a boil, add salt and pasta, and cook for 12 minutes or until al dente.

Drain well, transfer to a large warm bowl, drizzle with melted butter and toss gently. Cover to keep warm.

BANANA TOPPING

2 tablespoons of unsalted butter
3 tablespoons of sugar
4 large bananas, peeled, cut into ½-inch rounds
1 tablespoon of fresh orange juice
¾ cup whipping cream
2 tablespoons confectioner sugar

2 tablespoons of orange liqueur or fresh orange juice
¼ cup shaved semi-sweet chocolate
Orange slices for garnish

Heat 2 tablespoons of butter in a large skillet over medium heat and add sugar.

Prepare banana: Cook until sugar is melted, about 1 minute stirring constantly. Add banana rounds and sauté quickly for 1-2 minutes. Stir in orange juice and keep warm

Topping: Whip cream with confectioner sugar, orange liqueur or orange juice until stiff peaks form. Divide pasta among 4 warm serving plates, spoon equal amounts of banana rounds over pasta, spoon dollops of cream on top of bananas and sprinkle each with chocolate. Garnish with orange slices and enjoy!

APRICOT CREAM DESSERT

1 pound of fresh apricot, halved and pitted
1 cup of low fat yogurt, drained overnight in the refrigerator
2 tablespoons orange honey (Avail. health food stores)
½ cup whipping cream
1 tablespoon of apricot liqueur or 1 tablespoon of fresh orange juice
2 tablespoon orange honey
Mint leaves, for garnish

Place apricots, yogurt and 2-tablespoons of honey in a blender to puree until smooth, transfer to medium bowl, and set aside. Whip cream in a medium bowl with a hand-mixer until stiff peaks form, fold in the apricot liqueur, or orange juice and the remaining 2-tablespoons of honey, whip 2 seconds. Carefully combine cream with the apricot purée, spoon into dessert glasses, let cool 2-hours, garnish with mint leaves, and enjoy. *Chef's note:* Add 1-2 tablespoons of honey to sweeten dessert, if preferred.

ORANGE LEMON SOUFFLÉ CAKES
With
MANGO-APRICOT SAUCE

Serves: 8

CAKE BATTER

1¼ cups whole milk
1 tablespoon finely grated lemon zest
1 tablespoon finely grated orange zest
5 tablespoons unsalted butter, room temperature
1 cup sugar, plus 2-tablespoons, plus extra for dusting ramekins
5 large eggs, separated
½ cup all-purpose flour, plus 2-tablespoons
1/3 cup of fresh lemon juice
1/3 cup of fresh orange juice
Orange slices, for garnish
Lemon slices, for garnish
Mint leaves, for garnish
Confectioner sugar, for dusting

Preheat oven to 350°F

Lightly spray eight 6-ounce ramekins with vegetable cooking spray, sprinkle each lightly with sugar, and arrange them in a large ovenproof glass dish.

In a small saucepan, combine milk with lemon and orange zest, and bring just to a simmer. Strain milk through a sieve Into a medium bowl, and let cool to room temperature. In a medium bowl, using an electric mixer, beat butter with 6-tablespoons of sugar at moderately high speed until light and fluffy, about 6-minutes. At medium speed, beat-in egg yolks one at a time until incorporated. Using a wooden spoon, stir-in flour, lemon and orange juice and the infused milk until combined.

In a large bowl using clean beaters, beat egg whites until soft peaks form. Add remaining ¾ cup of sugar, 1-tablespoon at a time – beating until the egg whites are firm and glossy. Working in batches, gently fold meringue into the batter just until combined, and spoon batter into prepared ramekins. Pour enough hot water into ovenproof glass pan to reach halfway to sides of the ramekins. Bake 35-40 minutes or until small cracks appear on top of each cake. Using tongs, transfer ramekins to a rack to cool.

MANGO-APRICOT SAUCE

1½ cup of apricot preserves, imported preferred
4 tablespoons fresh orange juice
2 large mangoes, peeled, chopped and puréed

Make sauce: In a food processor, purée apricot preserve with orange juice until smooth. Transfer to a glass bowl, stir-in mango purée, and set aside.

Prepare to enjoy: Run a blunt knife around each cake and invert onto dessert plates. Spoon mango- apricot sauce around each soufflé cake – garnish with orange slices, lemon slices, mint leaves, and dust each with confectioner sugar.

CARROT-ALMOND-MARZIPAN TORTE
"Signature Family Recipe"

Created during year 1981, and demonstrated this on weekly, local TV Segment "Cooking with Erika", aired during year 2002

Serves: 10-12

½ cup unsalted butter, softened, plus extra for greasing
1 cup of sugar
4 large eggs
6 ounces of marzipan (Almond paste), coarsely grated
2 tablespoons of Amaretto liqueur
1 teaspoon finely grated orange zest
1½ cups of all-purpose flour
2 teaspoons baking powder
1-1/3 cups blanched almonds, finely ground
1½ cups carrots, finely shredded

Preheat oven to 350°F

Butter a 10-inch spring-form pan and sprinkle bottom and side with 1/3 cup of ground almonds, set aside.

Cream the butter and sugar in a large bowl with electric mixer until pale and fluffy.

Beat-in 1-egg at a time, beat-in the marzipan, add Amaretto liqueur, and the orange zest.

Sift together the flour and baking powder and fold it into the batter, then fold-in 1-cup of ground almonds and the shredded carrots.

Transfer batter to prepared spring-form cake pan, place it on middle rack of oven and bake until golden or until a cake tester comes out clean when inserted into the center, 35-45-minutes.

Let cake cool completely in pan, remove sides of pan, and transfer to a cake plate.

ORANGE WHIPPED CREAM

2 cups whipping cream
2 tablespoons confectioner sugar
1 tablespoon orange liqueur
1 teaspoon finely grated orange zest

Whip cream with electric mixer until soft peaks form, add confectioner sugar, orange liqueur, orange zest, and continue whipping until stiff peaks form. Refrigerate until ready to use.

Slice carrot torte into serving pieces, top each with a dollop of Orange Whipped Cream and enjoy.

CHOCOLATE SOUFFLÉ CAKES
With
HAZELNUT-ORANGE-CREAM

Serves: 8

SOUFFLÉ

8 ounces good quality bittersweet chocolate, chopped
6 tablespoons unsalted butter, about ¾ stick
6 large eggs, separated
½ cup sugar
1/3 cup of water
2 ounces bittersweet or semi-sweet chocolate, cut into 8 equal pieces

Preheat oven to 375°F - butter and lightly flour 8, ¾ cup soufflé dishes.

Stir 8-ounces chopped chocolate and butter in heavy-medium saucepan over low heat until melted and smooth.

Pour into large bowl, whisk in yolks, set mixture aside.

Stir sugar and water in small saucepan over low heat until sugar dissolves. Increase heat and boil while stirring until candy thermometer registers 236°F, swirling pan occasionally, about 5 minutes. Let cool.

Meanwhile, beat egg whites in another large bowl until soft peaks form. Gradually beat syrup into whites in a slow, steady stream, continue beating until stiff, about 3 minutes. Fold whites into chocolate mixture in 3 additions.

Divide soufflé mixture among prepared dishes. Press 1-chocolate piece into the center of each soufflé until submerged, place soufflé dishes on a baking sheet and bake soufflé until slightly puffed and softly set, about 15-20 minutes.

HAZELNUT-ORANGE CREAM

8 tablespoons hazel nut liqueur
2 cups whipping cream
¼ cup fresh orange juice
4 tablespoons confectioner sugar
½ cup mascarpone cheese
Orange slices, for garnish
Confectioner sugar, for dusting

Using electric mixer, beat cream until soft peaks form, and add hazelnut liqueur, orange juice, confectioner sugar and mascarpone cheese. Continue beating until stiff peaks form.

Place soufflé dishes on top of large serving plates, spoon a dollop of hazelnut cream on top of each soufflé, and garnish each with a slice of orange and serve.

CHOCOLATE SOUFFLÉ
With
ORANGE CREAM
"Signature"

"Cooking with Erika"
Created and demonstrated this on local, weekly TV Segment, aired during year 2001

Serves: 8

CHOCOLATE SOUFFLÉ

10 ounces bitter sweet chocolate, chopped (not unsweetened or semi-sweet)
10 tablespoons (1¼sticks) unsalted butter, plus extra for greasing
1 cup of sugar
4 large eggs
4 large egg yolks
½ cup all-purpose flour, plus extra for dusting

Preheat oven to 400°F

Lightly butter and flour eight ¾ cup ramekins and set aside.

Melt chocolate and butter in medium bowl set over a pan of simmering water, stirring occasionally. Remove bowl from pan and cool chocolate mixture to lukewarm.

Using an electric mixer set at high speed, beat sugar, eggs and yolks in a large bowl until batter falls in heavy ribbon when beaters are lifted, about 6 minutes. Sift flour over egg mixture and fold-in. Gradually fold in the lukewarm chocolate mixture.

Divide even portions of mixture among prepared ramekins.

Place ramekins on a baking sheet, and bake soufflés until puffed and beginning to crack on top (center will still be soft), about 18-20 minutes. Serve warm.

Note: Soufflés can be prepared ahead. Cover individually with plastic wrap and refrigerate up to 1 day.

ORANGE CREAM

1 cup of whipping cream
2 tablespoons confectioner sugar
1 tablespoon of fresh orange juice
10 orange slices and mint sprigs, for garnish

Using electric mixer, at high speed, beat cream, confectioner sugar and orange juice until stiff peaks form.

To enjoy, place each warm ramekin on a serving plate, top each soufflé with orange cream, garnish with a slice of orange and mint.

CHERRY PANCAKES with VANILLA ICE CREAM

Serves: 6

BATTER

3 eggs
1 cup of whole milk
2 tablespoons of water
1 1/3 cups of all-purpose flour
¼ teaspoon of sea salt
6 tablespoons of unsalted butter
2-3 tablespoons of sugar, for sprinkling over pancakes

In a medium bowl beat together eggs, milk and water. Gradually beat in flour and salt. Let pancake batter stand 10 minutes.

TOPPING

1 tablespoon Kirsch or other cherry flavored liqueur
1¼ cups cold water
2 tablespoons of sugar
1 tablespoon of cornstarch
1½ pound cherries, pitted
Vanilla ice cream
Mint leaves, for garnishing

In a medium saucepan, combine kirsch liqueur, water, sugar and cornstarch. Cook over medium heat, stirring constantly, until thickened and clear, add cherries, cook 1- minute and keep warm.

In an omelet pan, heat 1 tablespoon of butter over medium heat, spoon in ¼ cup of batter to make the first pancake, tilting pan so batter spreads evenly.

Cook until lightly browned on one side, turn over, and cook 1 minute longer. Repeat procedure with remaining butter and batter.

To enjoy, place cooked pancakes on warm plates, spoon cherry mixture on half of each pancake, fold over other half to cover, sprinkle each pancake with sugar, top with vanilla ice cream, and garnish with mint leaves.

CHOCOLATE-AMORETTO-APRICOT TORTE
"Signature"

Serves: 14-16

½ cup unsalted butter
1 cup of white cake flour or all-purpose flour, plus 1 tablespoon
½ cup unsweetened coco powder
1 teaspoon of baking powder

6 large eggs
1 cup of sugar
1 tablespoon of amoretto liqueur

Preheat oven to 350°F
Line bottom of a 10-inch spring form pan with wax paper and set aside

Melt butter over low heat. With a spoon, skim off any foam that rises to the surface and discard foam. Keep butter slightly warm, but not hot. Sift flour, coco and baking powder 2 times and set aside.

Place eggs and sugar in a large heatproof bowl, set over a pan of hot water, and with an electric hand mixer, beat until mixture doubles its volume and becomes thick enough to leave a ribbon trail when the beaters are lifted, about 8-10 minutes - add liqueur. Sift over the dry ingredients in 3 batches, folding in carefully after each addition and fold-in the warm butter. Pour batter into prepared pan and bake for 25-30 minutes.

Note: Expect the cake to slightly pull away from pan while baking.

Transfer cake to a wire rack or heatproof surface to cool – when cool enough to handle, remove cake from the pan and peel off the wax paper – let cake cool completely before cutting it into 2 layers. Meanwhile, prepare "fillings" and "topping".

FILLINGS and TOPPING

¼ cup apricot jam of good imported quality
2 tablespoons amoretto liqueur

In a small bowl, combine apricot jam with 2 tablespoons amoretto liqueur and set aside.

¼ cup whipping cream
½ cup mascarpone cheese
3 teaspoons confectioner sugar
2 teaspoons amoretto liqueur

Fillings and toppings instructions: In a medium bowl, whip cream until soft peaks form. Add mascarpone, confectioner sugar and 2 teaspoons amoretto liqueur and beat until stiff peaks form. Refrigerate until ready to use

CHOCOLATE GLAZE

8 ounces of semi-sweet chocolate
6 tablespoons of whipping cream

In a small heavy saucepan, combine chocolate and whipping cream – stir over low heat until melted and smooth.

To assemble torte: Place the bottom layer, cut side down, on a platter or large cake plate. Spread with apricot mixture. Spread amoretto cream over apricot mixture, place the second layer – cut side down – on top of amoretto cream. Spread glaze over top and sides of torte and let it rest until set. *Do not refrigerate torte.* It is important to allow the glaze to completely harden.

Cutting procedure: Whether an electric knife (preferred) or cake knife is used to cut torte into wedges, *heat the*

knife blade under hot running water or dip the blade in a hot water bath before making each cut a clean cut. Cut torte once across to halve it. Turn torte - cut across again to quarter it. Turn torte – cut across again to get 6 wedges. Turn torte – cut across again to get 8 wedges - repeating this procedure should yield up to 14 to 16 servings, depending on how many more crosscuts made. See photo left, which illustrates cut lines. Before serving, any repairs to smooth out the chocolate glaze can be made using a spreader blade dipped in hot water or held under hot running water.

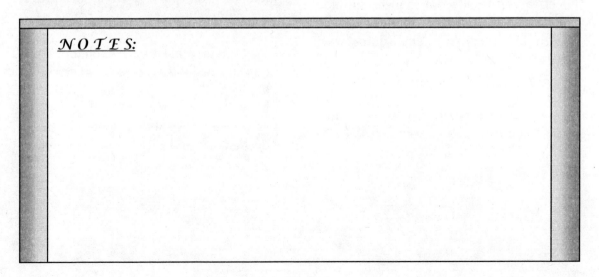

NOTES:

POTATO-APPLE-ALMOND CAKE

"Signature" – Original, among other identified recipes in this cookbook created for, and personally demonstrated for the Washington State Potato Seed Commission at the Washington State University Exploratory Laboratory, November 27, 2006.

Serves: 14-16

5-6 large golden delicious apples
Juice of 1 lemon
6 large eggs, at room temperature, separated, preferably organic eggs
¼ teaspoon sea salt
1¼ cups of sugar, preferably organic, plus extra for sprinkling apples
1 cup blanched almonds, finely ground
½ cup of golden raisins, soaked in 3-tablespoons of white rum and set aside
2 cups cooked, cooled and finely grated potatoes, such as Yukon gold, Yellow Finn or Butterball
Unsalted butter, for greasing cake pan

Preheat oven to 350°F
Lightly grease bottom and sides of a 10-inch spring form pan

¼ cup apricot jam
1 teaspoon of fresh orange juice

Peel, quarter and core apples; sprinkle them with lemon juice; thinly slice and gently toss them with lemon juice – set aside

In a large bowl, beat together egg yolks and 1 cup sugar until mixture is thick, pale and creamy, about 6-minutes. Fold-in almonds, the soaked raisins and potatoes.

Beat egg whites with salt in a large clean dry bowl until foamy, continuing to beat, adding ¼ cup of sugar, until stiff peaks form, gently fold-in egg whites in three batches. Pour batter into prepared pan.

Arrange apple slices in overlapping circles on top of batter, and sprinkle apple slices lightly with sugar as shown on photo, next page.

Bake 45-55 minutes or until apples are golden brown and cooked through. Place cake on a wire rack to cool completely. When cake has cooled, place apricot jam and orange juice in a small saucepan, bring to a boil, turn-off heat and strain into a small bowl. Using a pastry brush, lightly brush apples with jam to give apples a shine and prevent drying out.

<u>*Note:*</u> Cake must be completely cooled before brushing with jam, otherwise the apples will soak up the jam and the cake loses shine when cool. Serve with sweetened, freshly whipped cream, if desired.

YUKON GOLD POTATO APPLE CAKE
"Signature"

A, first of its kind, cake I created to present at the invitational potato tasting demonstration-conference held on November 17, 2006 and hosted by the Washington State Potato Commission and Science Division of the US Department of Agriculture.

Serves: 16

1 cup unsalted butter, plus extra, room temperature
1 cup of sugar
1½ teaspoons of dark rum
3 large eggs
2½ cups all-purpose flour, plus extra
2 teaspoons baking powder
½ teaspoon of sea salt
1½ cups of Yukon gold or butterball potatoes, cooked, cooled, peeled, and finely grated
4 large golden delicious apples, peeled, cored and thinly sliced
¾ cup golden raisins
2 tablespoons of fresh orange juice
½ teaspoon ground cinnamon
¼ cup of sugar
Confectioner sugar for dusting cake

Preheat oven to 345°F

Lightly grease and flour bottom and sides of a 10-inch spring form pan

In a large bowl, beat butter, sugar and rum until creamy. Add eggs 1 at a time, beating well after each addition.

In a sifter, combine flour, baking powder, salt, and gradually sift over sugar mixture folding in while sifting.

Fold-in potatoes and spoon half of batter into prepared pan - smooth out top.

In a large bowl toss apple slices with raisins, orange juice, cinnamon and sugar.

Arrange apple slices on top of batter, spoon remaining batter over apple smooth out top.

Bake 50-55 minutes or until a wooden pick inserted in center comes out clean.

Cool on a wire rack and let cool completely before removing cake from pan.

Dust cake lightly with confectioner sugar. Absolutely delicious and natural!

CINNAMON-BRANDY-CHOCOLATE-POTATO CAKE
"Signature"

An original, among other identified recipes in this cookbook created for, and personally demonstrated this recipe for the Washington State Potato Seed Commission at the Washington State University Exploratory Laboratory, November 17, 2006)

Serves: 12-14

2 cups all-purpose flour
¼ teaspoon sea salt
1½ teaspoons baking powder
1 tablespoon of ground cinnamon
¼ cup unsweetened coco powder, plus extra for dusting cake pan
¼ cup brandy or dark rum
3 chocolate squares, 1-ounce each, of good quality
1 cup unsalted butter (2-sticks), plus extra for greasing cake pan
1½ cups sugar, preferably organic
3 large eggs, preferably organic
½ cup cooked potatoes, finely grated, such as Yukon gold, Yellow Finn or Butterball
Confectioner sugar, for dusting cake

Preheat oven to 325°F

Grease a 3-quart bundt pan and dust lightly with coco powder and set aside

Sift flour, salt, baking powder, cinnamon and coco powder together and set aside.

Combine brandy or rum, chocolate and butter in the top of a double boiler and heat until chocolate and butter have melted and the mixture is smooth- stir occasionally.

Pour chocolate mixture into a large bowl, using an electric mixer on low speed, gradually beat-in the sugar continuing beating until sugar has dissolved - add eggs, one at a time – beat well after each addition - increase mixer speed to medium and add the sifted dry ingredients plus the grated potatoes, mix well.

Pour the batter in the prepared bundt pan – bake for 1-hour, 15-minutes or until a cake tester inserted in the cake comes out clean.

Let cake cool in the pan for 15-20 minutes before un-molding, and placing cake on a wire rack to cool completely.

When cake has cooled, dust it lightly with confectioner sugar, transfer cake to a large cake plate and serve with sweetened fresh whipped cream, if desired.

PANNA COTTA
With
FRESH YAKIMA PEACH COMPOTE
"Signature"

Serves: 4

PANNA COTTA

¼ cup of water
2½ teaspoons of unflavored gelatin
1¼ cup whipping cream
½ cup of sugar
1 teaspoon of vanilla extract

Pour ¼ cup water into a small bowl, sprinkle with gelatin and let stand 10 minutes.

Bring cream and sugar to simmer in a heavy-medium saucepan over medium heat, stirring until sugar dissolves. Remove from heat, add gelatin mixture and whisk until dissolved. Whisk in vanilla.

Divide mixture among four ¾-cup custard cups or gelatin molds. Cover and chill overnight.

Cut around edges of each panna cotta to loosen, and set each cup in a shallow bowl of hot water for 10-seconds, and immediately invert cups onto plate, lift off cups and top each serving with peach compote.

Note: Panna Cotta can be made 1-day ahead and kept refrigerated.

PEACH COMPOTE

Makes about 2 ½ cups

2 pounds fresh peaches, halved, pitted, peeled, and sliced, about 4 cups
2½ cups of water
¼ cups fresh orange juice
¼ cup orange liqueur
½ cup golden brown sugar

Place all ingredients in a medium non-stick saucepan and bring to a boil, turn heat to medium, stir until sugar dissolves.

Reduce heat to medium-low and simmer until fruit is tender, about 10 minutes.

Cover and chill overnight.

Enjoy chilled or at room temperature. Note: Peach Compote can be made 2-days ahead and kept refrigerated.

CHOCOLATE - EGGNOG - APPLE TORTE
"Signature"

Serves: 10-12

CAKE BATTER

6 large eggs, separated – organic preferred
3 tablespoons fresh orange juice or water
1 cup of sugar, organic preferred
1 cup of white cake flour or all-purpose flour
¼ cup unsweetened coco powder
2 teaspoons baking powder

APPLE FILLING

1¼ cup Late Harvest Riesling
2 teaspoons of fresh orange juice
½ cup of sugar, organic preferred
4 large apples, golden delicious or wine-sap, peeled, cored and thinly sliced
1 teaspoon of ginger root, freshly grated
4 teaspoons cornstarch

EGGNOG-CREAM FILLING

2 tablespoons cornstarch
1 cup of eggnog, organic preferred
2 tablespoons eggnog liqueur
2 cups whipping cream
2 tablespoons confectioner sugar
Chocolate cookie crumbs or chocolate sprinkles, for garnish
Small chocolate candies, for garnish

To make apple filling: Place 1 cup of wine, orange juice, sugar, apples and ginger root in a large saucepan. Cook over medium-low heat until apples are soft but not mushy, about 15-20 minutes. Turn heat to low, in a small bowl, blend cornstarch and ¼ cup remaining wine until smooth, slowly stir cornstarch mixture into apple mixture and cook over low heat, stirring until mixture is clear and thick, about 2-3 minutes. Transfer apple mixture to a heatproof glass bowl and let cool. Cover with plastic wrap and chill until cold. *Apple filling can be made 1-day ahead.*

To make eggnog-cream filling: In a small saucepan, combine cornstarch, eggnog and eggnog liqueur, stirring constantly. Cook over medium heat until mixture comes to a boil and thickens. Remove from heat, transfer to a medium heatproof bowl, press plastic wrap directly onto surface of eggnog and chill until cold. *Filling can be made 1-day ahead.*

Whip cream in a large chilled bowl until soft peaks form. Add confectioner sugar, beat until stiff peaks form - gently fold chilled eggnog filling into whipped cream. *Refrigerate until ready to use.*

Preheat oven to 350°F
Line the bottom of a 10-inch spring form pan with wax paper and set aside

To make cake batter: In a large mixing bowl, beat egg yolks and orange juice or water until foamy – beat in sugar until thick and pale. In a sifter, combine cake flour or all-purpose flour, coco powder and baking powder, gradually sift over egg yolks mixture, folding in while sifting, in a medium-size mixing bowl. Beat egg whites until stiff, but not dry, gently fold into batter. Pour batter into prepared pan, smooth out top.

Bake 30-35 minutes or until wooden pick inserted in center comes out clean. Cool in pan on wire rack 10-15 minutes. Remove from pan, peel off paper and let cake cool completely.

Cut cake into 2 layers, place bottom layer - cut side down, on a large cake plate or platter. Spread with ½ of chilled apple filling, spread 1-cup of eggnog-cream filling over apple filling, top with remaining cake layer. Spread remaining eggnog-cream filling over top and sides of cake and lightly sprinkle top and sides of cake with chocolate cookie crumbs or chocolate sprinkles. Spread remaining apple filling in a circle on top center of cake. Pipe swirls of remaining eggnog cream on top of cake. Decorate with chocolate candies if desired. Chill torte until ready to serve.

To make cookie crumbs: Crumbs from any dry, natural cookie can be used. Natural cake crumbs can also be used. To yield best, clean flavors, commercial cookies are not recommended because their saltiness, sugar content and chemical additives will adversely dilute intended natural benefits of this moist, delicate flavored torte. *See Index for cookies that can be used in lieu of commercial, processed cookies.*

Crushing cookies into crumbs: Break cookies into small pieces. Place small batches of broken cookies in a heavy-duty plastic bag and roll over them with a rolling pin. Or, finely grind them in a blender or food processor. Cookie crumbs will freeze well up to 2 months.

Enjoy the grand flavor of this Signature

Chocolate-Eggnog-Apple Torte

Make your own eggnog & enjoy this festive torte anytime of the year!

INDIVIDUAL LEMON-LIME-ORANGE CAKES
With
APRICOT SAUCE

Serves: 8

CAKES

1¾ cups whole milk
2 tablespoons lime zest, finely grated
5 tablespoons unsalted butter (room temperature)
1 cup sugar, plus 2-tablespoons
5 large eggs, separated
½ cup all-purpose flour, plus 2-tablespoons
¼ cup of fresh lemon juice
1 tablespoon finely grated orange zest

SAUCE

2-cups fresh-ripe apricots, halved, pits removed, or
1 8½ ounces can of apricot halves in syrup, drained
½ cup apricot preserves, of imported quality
3 tablespoons Apricot liqueur or water
2 teaspoons fresh orange juice
Orange slices for garnish
Mint leaves for garnish

Preheat oven to 325°F

Lightly spray eight 6-ounce ramekins with vegetable cooking spray and arrange them in a small roasting pan or in a heatproof oblong-large Pyrex dish.

Preparing cakes: Combine the milk and lime zest in a small saucepan and heat just to a simmer. Strain milk through a sieve into a medium bowl and let cool to room temperature. In a medium bowl, using an electric mixer, beat butter with 6-tablespoons of sugar at moderately high speed until light and fluffy, about 5-minutes. At medium speed, beat-in egg yolks one at a time until incorporated.

Using a wooden spoon, stir-in flour, lemon juice, and the infused-cooled milk until it's combined. In a large bowl, using clean beaters, and beat egg whites until soft peaks form. Add remaining ¾ cup of sugar, 1-tablespoon at a time, beating until egg whites are firm and glossy. Working in batches, gently fold the meringue into batter just until combined. Spoon the batter into prepared ramekins. Pour enough boiling water into the roasting pan to reach halfway up the sides of the ramekins. Bake 30-35 minutes, or until small cracks appear on top of each cake. Using tongs, transfer ramekins to a rack to cool.

Preparing sauce: In a food processor or blender, purée apricots with preserves, Liqueur or water, and orange juice until smooth. Run a blunt knife around each cake to loosen and invert onto a dessert plate. Spoon apricot sauce around each cake, and garnish with orange slices, and mint leaves.

LEMON CURD

Makes: about 2½ - 3 cups

2 tablespoons finely grated lemon zest
1 cup fresh lemon juice
1½ cups sugar
4 large eggs
1¾ sticks of unsalted butter, cut into
tablespoon size pieces

Whisk together zest, lemon juice, sugar and eggs in a 2-quart, heavy saucepan, and add butter all at once and cook over moderately low heat, whisking constantly until curd is thick enough to hold whisk marks and the first bubbles appear on substance surface, about 10 minutes. Immediately pour curd through a fine sieve into a bowl then chill, and cover with plastic wrap. *Note:* Lemon curd keeps, covered and chilled for about 1-week. *Excellent spread, or filling for cakes, tortes, scones and trifle.*

LEMON MOUSSE

Makes: about 2½ - 3 cups

1 cup chilled whipping cream
1 cup of lemon curd

Beat cream in a medium bowl with an electric mixer until it holds stiff peaks, and gently fold-in lemon curd. Excellent spread on muffins, scones, toast bread, or as a filling for sponge cakes, cake tarts and pound cakes.

LEMON CREAM

Makes about 1 cup

½ cup whipping cream
1 tablespoon of fresh lemon juice
¼ teaspoon finely grated lemon zest
2-3 tablespoons confectioner sugar

Place cream, lemon juice, zest and confectioner sugar in a small bowl, and beat with electric mixer until stiff peaks form — refrigerate until ready to use. Lemon cream is delicious spread over scones, muffins, and pound cakes.

LEMON LIQUEUR with COINTREAU
"Signature"

Makes about 1½ - 2-quarts

¾ cup, plus 1 tablespoon of fresh lemon juice
2 tablespoons of fresh lemon peel
2 tablespoons of fresh lime peel
1/3 cup, plus 1 tablespoon of water
¾ cup of sugar
3 tablespoons Cointreau
1 bottle of Vodka (750ml)

Combine lemon juice, lemon peel, lime peel, water and sugar in a medium saucepan, bring mixture to a full boil, turn heat to medium-low and cook for 5 minutes. Add Cointreau and let mixture cool. Add vodka, pour into 2 bottles with the lemon and lime peel, seal bottles, let stand in a cool place for one week. Shake well before pouring into Aperitif glasses. Refrigerate up to 2 months. Best served chilled.

POACHED PEARS with AMARETTO-CHOCOLATE SAUCE
"Signature"

Serves: 4

4 firm, but ripe pears, such as
Comice or Bartlett, carefully peeled leaving stems intact
Cold water
Juice of 1 lemon
4 tablespoons of sugar
2 cups of water
6 tablespoons amaretto liqueur
Peppermint leaves, for garnish
½ cup of almonds, sliced

1 cup of amaretto chocolate sauce, see recipe below

Place pears in a bowl of cold water acidulated with lemon juice. In a large saucepan, bring sugar and 2-cups of water to a boil. Place pears in a non-reactive saucepan on their sides, pour amaretto liqueur over them and simmer covered for about 20 minutes, turning once. *Note:* After 15 minutes of cooking, test pears with the point of a small paring knife for doneness. Pears should be tender throughout, but not mushy. Test pears frequently, cooking time will vary from 15, 30 or more minutes, depending on ripeness, size and variety of pear. Carefully remove pears from saucepan and arrange on serving dishes. Ladle juices from the saucepan over pears, let cool, cover and chill overnight to enhance flavor, before serving.

Drizzle or spoon warm Amaretto-Chocolate Sauce over pears and garnish with mint leaves and sliced almonds.

AMARETTO-CHOCOLATE SAUCE

Recipe can be doubled

8 ounces semisweet chocolate, cut into bits
½ cup of strong brewed coffee
2 teaspoons of amaretto liqueur

In the top of a double boiler over simmering water, melt chocolate with coffee and amaretto liqueur. Keep sauce warm until serving time. If sauce becomes too thick, add a small amount of coffee. Enjoy!

MASCARPONE GRATIN with RHUBARB COMPOTE

Serves: 6

GRATIN

1½ pounds of mascarpone cheese, imported from Italy -preferred
¼ cup whole milk
2 eggs, beaten
1 cup of sugar
1 teaspoon orange zest, freshly grated (preferably organic)
¼ cup farina (cream of wheat)
Unsalted butter for greasing dish

RHUBARB COMPOTE

4 cups rhubarb, washed, trimmed on both ends and cut into 1-inch pieces
1½ cups of sugar
¼ cup orange juice, freshly squeezed
2 tablespoons Crème de Cassis – A black currant liqueur (Avail. in liquor stores)

Preheat oven to 375°F

Butter a round 8½ x 1½ inch flame proof dish

Prepare mascarpone gratin: In a medium size mixing bowl, combine the first 6 ingredients and pour mixture into prepared dish -bake 30-40 minutes or until golden brown on top. Remove gratin from oven and let it cool for 5-minutes before serving. While gratin is baking, prepare rhubarb compote.

Prepare rhubarb compote: Combine rhubarb with sugar in a medium saucepan, add orange juice, crème de cassis, and bring to a boil and immediately turn heat down to a bare simmer. Cover with a lid and cook 5-10 minutes or until rhubarb is tender. Rhubarb should hold its shape - cook gently to avoid overcooking. Transfer to a heatproof glass bowl, let rhubarb cool slightly - serve warm, or prepare a day ahead – refrigerate until ready to use. Reheat gently to serve warm.

To serve: Spoon mascarpone gratin into 6-dessert plates or glass bowls, spoon ¼ cup of rhubarb around each gratin and enjoy.

NAPOLEONS
With
EGGNOG CUSTARD and CARAMELIZED APPLES
(One of my versions)

Serves: 8

EGGNOG-CUSTARD

1 cup of whole milk
½ cup of eggnog liqueur (Avail. at Liquor stores)
2 egg yolks
3 tablespoons of superfine sugar (Avail. in baking section of supermarkets)
4 tablespoons cornstarch
Confectioner sugar, for dusting eggnog

Bring milk and eggnog to a boil in a nonstick medium saucepan – turn heat to low.

In a medium bowl, beat egg yolks and sugar until creamy stir-in the cornstarch continuing to stir while pouring the hot milk mixture into the egg yolk mixture.

Now pour bowl contents into the same saucepan and carefully simmer on very low heat for 1-2 minutes stirring constantly – avoid boiling or burning.

Pour eggnog custard into a heatproof glass bowl and lightly dust with confectioner sugar or press a round piece of plastic wrap directly on surface of custard to prevent a film or crust forming on surface and refrigerate until chilled, about 3-4 hours, or make 1-day ahead.

CARAMELIZED APPLES

5 large apples, golden delicious or pink lady, peeled, cored and cut into ¼ inch thick slices
5 tablespoons unsalted butter
5 tablespoons superfine sugar
2 tablespoons of Calvados or Applejack (Avail. in Liquor stores)

Heat butter and sugar in a nonstick, large skillet, and cook over medium heat until mixture resembles light caramel, add apple slices and brown apple slices evenly on all sides, about 5-6 minutes.

Once apples are soft, add calvados or applejack, briefly flambé and remove from heat.

Note: If you prefer to forego the flambéing step, cook apples one more second to just incorporate alcohol into the apple mixture.

However, if you prefer to flambé, exercise extreme caution when doing so - not all kitchens are designed, or have enough clearance, for doing this. Keep a large enough lid handy to cover skillet if necessary, and a fire extinguisher nearby.

PUFF PASTRY

1 sheet frozen from a 17¾ ounce package of puff pastry thawed at room temperature, about 30-minutes
8 teaspoons of sugar
Confectioner sugar, for dusting Napoleons

Line 1-large baking sheet with parchment paper

Roll out pastry sheet on a lightly floured surface to 12-inch square. Cut pastry into four 5-inch squares, cut each square diagonally into triangles then transfer them to the prepared baking sheet, prick each triangle with a fork, sprinkle each with 1-teaspoon of sugar and refrigerate for 10-minutes.

Preheat oven to 400°F

Bake 15-20 minutes or until puffed and golden brown. Transfer pastry from the baking sheet to a wire rack to cool.

On a cutting board, cut each triangle lengthwise in half, place bottom halves on dessert plates, top each with 2-3 tablespoons of eggnog custard, top custard with apple slices and top apples with the other half of pastry, and dust each serving with confectioner sugar.

Arrange any remaining apple slices around the edges of each Napoleon along with a drizzling of caramel sauce and enjoy.

Napoleons with Eggnog Custard and Caramelized Apples

ORANGE CHEESECAKE
With
FRESH BERRY TOPPING
"Signature"

Makes: Two 9-inch cakes – each cake serves 8-10 generous slices

6 packages cream cheese (8-Ounces each), room temperature
2½ cups sugar
2 tablespoons Grand Marnier, or other orange liqueur, or orange juice
1½ cups mascarpone cheese
1/3 cup of whipping cream
6 tablespoons of cornstarch
2 large eggs
2 tablespoons of fresh orange juice
2 tablespoons finely grated orange zest
Butter for greasing cake pans
Sugar for dusting cake pans
2½ pints raspberries
2½ pints blackberries or blueberries
½ cup apricot preserve
3 tablespoons fresh orange juice

Preheat oven to 345°F

Generously butter the sides and bottoms of two 9-inch by 2¾-inches deep spring-form pans, and dust the bottom and sides of the pans with sugar, shakeout excess, and set pans aside.

Note: A 5-quart mixing bowl is needed to mix batter for two cheesecakes, otherwise, divide this recipe.

Using an electric mixer, beat cream cheese in a large bowl until thick and smooth, about 10-minutes, and add sugar, Grand Marnier, and beat until thoroughly combined.

Add mascarpone, cream and cornstarch, and beat 5-more minutes, add eggs one at a time beating well after each addition, and fold-in orange juice and the orange zest.

Divide batter between prepared pans, bake cheesecakes until outsides are set, but centers still move slightly when pans are shaken, about 1-hour and 15-minutes.

Transfer cheesecakes to racks to cool, cover with plastic wrap and refrigerate cheesecakes overnight. Run a small-sharp knife around pan sides to loosen cheesecakes if necessary to release pan sides.

Transfer cheesecakes to cake plates. Toss berries gently in a large bowl, and mound berries on cheesecakes leaving a 1-inch border.

Heat apricot preserves with 3-tablespoons orange juice in a small saucepan over medium heat, stirring until melted. Brush warm glaze over berries, cut cake into wedges, and enjoy.

PASTRY CREAM

Makes about ½ cup

½ cup whole milk
2 tablespoons sugar
1 teaspoon of vanilla extract
2 tablespoons cornstarch
2 large egg yolks
2 teaspoons unsalted butter

In a small saucepan, combine the milk, 1-tablespoon sugar and vanilla extract. Cook over medium heat for about 5-minutes stirring until the milk boils and sugar dissolves. Remove from heat.

Prepare pastry cream: In a small bowl, combine remaining tablespoon of sugar and the cornstarch. In another small bowl, lightly whisk egg yolks, add cornstarch mixture and whisk to mix.

Slowly, but constantly, whisk 2-3 tablespoons of hot milk mixture into the yolks to prevent eggs from curdling (a process called tempering).

Return saucepan to the stove over very low heat. Add tempered yolks to the saucepan, cook and gently stir for 4-6 minutes until hot and smooth, prevent curdling. Remove pastry cream from the heat and stir-in butter until incorporated.

Transfer pastry cream to a glass bowl, cover with plastic wrap and refrigerate until ready to use. Enjoy as a filling in sponge cakes, pancakes, or trifles.

PAPAYA PUDDING with CRÈME DE CASSIS
"Signature"

Serves: 4

1 large papaya
4 scoops vanilla ice cream
1 teaspoon of fresh limejuice
1 teaspoon of fresh orange juice
2 tablespoons mascarpone
2 tablespoons whipping cream
4 tablespoons of crème de cassis – (Black Currant liqueur, avail. at Liquor Stores)

Cut papaya lengthwise in half. Scoop-out seeds and discard, scoop out fruit flesh with spoon, place papaya into blender, add vanilla ice cream, lime juice, orange juice, mascarpone and cream to blend until mixture becomes smooth and very creamy.

Pour papaya pudding into stemmed glasses, chill 1-hour, and drizzle each with crème de cassis. _Enjoy_!

PAPAYA-ORANGE POUND CAKE
With
MANGO-COINTREAU MOUSSE
"Signature"

Serves: 12-14

POUND CAKE

2 sticks of unsalted butter, softened, plus extra for greasing
1¼ cups, plus 1-tablespoon of sugar
4 large eggs
2 tablespoons fresh orange juice
1 tablespoon finely grated orange zest
2¾ cups unbleached cake flour
2 teaspoons baking powder
2 ripe medium-size papaya, peeled, seeded and cut into small cubes
1 tablespoon of confectioner sugar

Preheat oven to 350°F

Lightly butter a fluted, 4-cups capacity ring mold and dust with 1-tablespoon of sugar

In a large mixing bowl, using an electric mixer, cream the butter. Add 1¼ cup of sugar a little at a time and beat the mixture until light and fluffy.

Beat-in eggs one at a time, and beat well after each addition. Add the orange juice and zest. Sift together the flour and baking powder and add to the egg mixture alternately with the papaya and beat the mixture until well combined.

Pour the batter into the prepared ring mold and smooth the top with a spatula.

Bake the cake in the middle of the oven for 45 minutes to 1-hour, or until a cake tester inserted in the center comes out clean.

Let the cake cool in the pan on a rack for 15 minutes, invert it onto the rack and let cool completely.

Before serving, sift the confectioner sugar over the cake and transfer the cake to a cake platter.

MOUSSE

2 ripe mangos, peeled, coarsely chopped and puréed with 2 tablespoons orange cointreau
1½ cups whipping cream
3 tablespoons confectioner sugar
1½ cups fresh blackberries, for garnish
Mint leaves, for garnish

In a chilled bowl, and using a hand-mixer, beat heavy cream and confectioner sugar until it holds soft peaks. Add the mango purée and beat the cream until it holds stiff peaks.

Place cake slices on serving plates, top with Mango-Cointreau Mousse, and garnish with blackberries and mint leaves. *Enjoy!*

PEACH TIRAMISU
"Signature"

Serves: 6

1½ pounds of mascarpone
½ cup sugar
1 cup of whipping cream
1 8-inch orange sponge cake *(see recipe in column, right)*, cut into cubes, or
1 box of store-bought Lady Fingers, imported from Italy
2 cups cold espresso or strong, cold coffee
3 large fresh peaches, halved, pits removed, peeled, sliced, or
2-15 ounces canned, sliced peaches, drained
¼ cup peach liqueur (Avail. in Liquor Stores)
½ teaspoon ground cinnamon
2 cups of fresh strawberries, stems removed and sliced
4 tablespoons sugar
2 tablespoons peach liqueur
Unsweetened cocoa powder for dusting

Place mascarpone and sugar in mixer bowl, and beat with an electric mixer at low speed for 5-minutes, add the cream, and beat at high speed until mixture is stiff. Keep refrigerated until ready to use.

Spread a thin layer of mascarpone cream in a 9 x 8-inch container and arrange cake cubes or ladyfingers on top of mascarpone cream, spoon espresso or coffee over cake cubes or ladyfingers.

In a small bowl, mix peach liqueur with cinnamon, arrange peaches on top of cake cubes or lady fingers, drizzle peaches with peach liqueur-cinnamon mixture, spread remaining mascarpone cream over peaches, cover and refrigerate.

Purée strawberries, sugar and 2-tablespoons peach liqueur in a food processor or blender until smooth. Cut tiramisu into 6-pieces placing each on dessert plates drizzled with strawberry purée and dust tiramisu with cocoa-powder.

ORANGE SPONGE CAKE

2 large eggs separated
¼ cup of sugar
1 cup of all-purpose flour
¼ teaspoon baking powder
3 tablespoons fresh orange juice

Preheat oven to 350°F

Line the bottom of an 8-inch spring form pan with wax paper

With an electric mixer, beat egg whites on high speed in a medium bowl, adding sugar a little at a time, until stiff peaks form, mix-in the yolks and sugar - sift the flour and baking powder together, and fold into the egg mixture. Add orange juice and spoon batter into the prepared pan. Bake 25-30 minutes. Let cake cool and remove wax paper.

PUMPKIN-MANGO CHEESECAKE
With
HUCKLEBERRY SAUCE
"Signature"

Created during 1991, at my former restaurant location in Tacoma, and demonstrated on local, weekly TV segment, aired during November 9, 2000 in "Yakima Valley Wine Country" Yakima, Washington

Serves: 10-12

PUMPKIN FILLING

2 cups of fresh pumpkin, peeled, seeded and cut into small cubes
¼ cup of fresh squeezed orange juice
¼ teaspoon of sea salt
2 tablespoons of sugar

Place pumpkin, orange juice and salt in a medium saucepan, and cook it until soft but not mushy, about 10-15 minutes.

Purée pumpkin, with 2 tablespoons of sugar and chill it. Puréed pumpkin should yield one cup, which can be made one day ahead and refrigerated until ready to use.

CRUMBLE

1 cup of all-purpose flour, plus extra for dusting cake pan
½ teaspoon baking powder
¼ cup of sugar
1 small egg
2 tablespoons unsalted butter, softened, plus extra for greasing cake pan
½ teaspoon finely grated orange zest

Grease and lightly flour a 10-inch spring form pan

Using a fork or pastry blender, combine the flour, baking powder, sugar, egg, butter, and orange zest until mixture is crumbly. Sprinkle crumble over bottom of prepared cake pan and set aside.

Preheat oven to 350°F

CHEESE FILLING

4 8-ounce packages cream cheese, softened
2 eggs, separated
1½ cups of sugar
3 tablespoons of mango purée (1-small ripe mango, peeled, chopped and puréed)
2 tablespoons orange liqueur
2 tablespoons whipping cream
4 tablespoons cornstarch

In a large mixing bowl, and using an electric mixer, beat together cream cheese, egg yolks, and sugar until thick and smooth, about 6 minutes. Add the mango purée, orange liqueur, and cream, beat 1-more minute. Then fold in the cornstarch and 1 cup of chilled pumpkin purée.

In a small mixing bowl, beat egg whites until stiff peaks form, fold beaten egg whites into cream cheese filling, and spoon filling over crumble and smooth surface.

Bake 45-55 minutes, or until cake tester comes out clean when inserted into the center of the cake, remove cake from oven. Let cheesecake cool completely, cover and refrigerate overnight. Prepare Huckleberry Sauce.

HUCKLEBERRIES

2 cups of fresh huckleberries
1 cup of sugar
4 tablespoons of port wine

Place huckleberries in a medium saucepan, add sugar, the Port wine, and cook over medium-low heat for 5-10 minutes. Chill before serving.

Run a small sharp knife around pan sides to loosen cake and release pan sides. Slide cake onto cake plate.

Cut cheesecake into serving pieces and spoon huckleberry sauce over each slice and enjoy!

ORANGE CUSTARD SAUCE
"Version two"

Excellent served with pound cake, fruit compotes, chocolate puddings, pancakes, poached apples and pears.

Makes: About 2 Cups

4 egg yolks
2 tablespoons vanilla sugar
¼ cup granulated sugar
1½ cups light cream, such as Half & Half, scalded
2 tablespoons Orange Liqueur
1 teaspoon finely grated orange zest

In a mixing bowl, beat egg-yolks with vanilla sugar and the granulated sugar until pale and thick. Pour-in the hot (scalded) cream, in a stream, stirring constantly. Transfer mixture to a medium saucepan, gently stir mixture with a wooden spoon over low heat for 10-15 minutes, or until custard coats the back of the spoon and mixture leaves a clear parting when a spoon is drawn across. Avoid boiling.

Remove pan from heat, stir-in liqueur and the orange zest, strain custard sauce into a heatproof glass bowl, cover sauce with a buttered round of wax paper positioned to directly touch the surface of sauce, and let cool. Refrigerate until ready to use.

PUFF PASTRY TARTS
With
STRAWBERRY SAUCE
"Signature"

"Cooking with Erika"
Created and demonstrated this on weekly, local TV segment, aired during year 2002

Serves: 6

1 sheet frozen puff pastry from a 17 1/4 oz. package, thawed at room temperature, about 30 minutes
6 teaspoons sugar
¼ cup confectioner sugar
2 cups of fresh strawberries, stems removed, plus 6-extra for garnish
½ cup crème de cassis, (Avail. at Liquor Stores)
1½ cups whipping cream
1 tablespoon orange liqueur
1 tablespoon of confectioner sugar
1/3 cup of mint leaves, chopped
6 mint sprigs for garnish

Preheat oven to 400°F

Unfold puff pastry sheet and gently roll out with a lightly floured rolling pin on a lightly floured surface, into a 12-inch square.

Trim edges with a sharp knife, and cut pastry into 6 rectangles – about 6 x 4-inches each.

Arrange rectangles 1-2 inches apart on un-greased baking sheet, prick them all over with a fork, sprinkle each with sugar, and bake in the middle of oven until pastry is puffed and golden, about 15 minutes. Cool pastry on baking sheet on a rack. Dust each evenly with confectioner sugar.

STRAWBERRY SAUCE

Place strawberries with cassis in a food processor and purée until smooth.

Transfer strawberry purée to a glass bowl. In a small mixing bowl, whip cream with orange liqueur and 1-tablespoon confectioner sugar until stiff peaks form.

Chef's note: Strawberry sauce and whipped cream can be made 1-day ahead and refrigerated until ready to use.

To enjoy, place pastry tarts on serving plates top each with a dollop of cream, sprinkle each with chopped mint, drizzle each serving with strawberry sauce, garnish with mint sprigs and remaining whole strawberries.

ALMOND PUDDING
With
RASPBERRY PURÉE

Serves: 8

1½ cups of blanched almonds, finely ground
2 cups of whole milk
½ cup sugar
1-2 drops almond extract
6 tablespoons Knox unflavored gelatin
4 tablespoons almond liqueur or fresh orange juice
1¾ cups whipping cream
1 tablespoon of confectioner sugar
1 pound fresh raspberries, plus 1-cup for garnish
2 tablespoons raspberry syrup or 2 tablespoons orange honey
1/3 cup of unsalted pistachios, chopped
Mint leaves, for garnish

In a medium-size bowl, combine almonds with milk, add sugar and transfer to a non-stick, medium saucepan. Bring to almost boiling, stirring constantly, turn-off heat and let stand on the hotplate for 15 minutes.

Stir-in almond extract, transfer to a large mixing bowl and refrigerate for one hour or until almost stiff.

In a small bowl dissolve gelatin with almond liqueur or orange juice. Let stand 10 minutes.

In a small saucepan, bring water to a simmer, place bowl with gelatin over simmering water, stir to dissolve gelatin. Remove bowl and let cool for about 1 minute. Remove the almond pudding mixture from the refrigerator, and with the mixer running, slowly pour cooled gelatin into pudding mixture, blend 2-3 seconds to combine.

Transfer pudding to a clean, large glass bowl, place in refrigerator and let cool completely, about 3-4 hours.

In a medium mixing bowl, whip cream with confectioner sugar until stiff peaks form. Add whipped cream to cooled pudding and blend to a smooth cream.

Rinse 8 small molds in cold water, tap out any excess water, spoon almond pudding into molds and chill for at least 5-hours, or until they are gelled enough to turn-out onto serving plates.

Purée raspberries with raspberry syrup or honey and spoon the raspberry purée onto dessert plates. Loosen pudding from molds with the point of a knife.

Dip mold bottoms quickly into hot water, turnout pudding onto raspberry purée, sprinkle with pistachios, and garnish with mint leaves and the remaining raspberries.

For sweeter raspberry purée, add more syrup or honey.

BLACK and WHITE RICE PUDDING
With
ORANGE CREAM and FRESH PEACHES
"Signature"

Serves: 4

BLACK RICE PUDDING

½ cup of black Thai rice, thoroughly rinsed
1/8 teaspoon of sea salt
¾ cup of water
¼ cup of whole milk
¼ cup of sugar
1 teaspoon orange zest, finely grated
2 teaspoons Orange Liqueur

In a medium nonstick saucepan, combine the black rice, salt and water and bring to a boil.

Cover and simmer over low heat until the water has been absorbed and the rice is almost tender, about 15 minutes. Add the milk, sugar, orange zest and orange liqueur, and simmer stirring occasionally, until the rice is tender and pudding-like, about 10 minutes. Let rice cool to room temperature.

WHITE RICE PUDDING

1 cup of basmati rice, thoroughly rinsed
2¼ cups of water
¼ teaspoon of sea salt
½ cup whole milk
¼ cup of sugar
1 teaspoon orange zest, finely grated
1/3 cup of fresh orange juice
2 cups of whipping cream
3 tablespoons of confectioner sugar

2 tablespoons orange zest, finely grated
5-6 medium peaches, halved, pitted, peeled and chopped, plus extra peach slices for garnish
½ cup orange marmalade

In a medium nonstick saucepan, combine basmati rice, water and salt, bring to a boil. Cover and simmer over low heat until the water is absorbed and the rice in tender, about 15 minutes.

Add milk, sugar, 1-teaspoon orange zest and orange juice. Simmer stirring occasionally until the rice is thickened, about 10-15 minutes. Let rice cool to room temperature.

Meanwhile, whip together the cream confectioner sugar and 2 tablespoons orange zest until stiff peaks form. In a small bowl, combine chopped peaches with orange marmalade.

To assemble: Layer the puddings among 4 tall glasses by alternating 2 layers of basmati rice topped with chopped peaches, 1/3 cup of cream and 2 layers of black Tai rice, finishing each with a layer of cream garnished with peach slices. Enjoy chilled or at room temperature.

PURPLE RICE PUDDING
With
ORANGE CUSTARD SAUCE
"Signature"

Serves: 4-6

1 cup purple Thai rice, soaked for 2 hours and drained
2 cups canned, unsweetened coconut milk
¼ teaspoon of sea salt
3 ounces of unsalted butter, plus extra for greasing casserole dish
½ cup sugar
2 eggs

In a medium saucepan, bring rice and coconut milk to a boil, turn heat to low and simmer 25 minutes stirring often.

Remove from heat, stir in salt and transfer to a large bowl to let cool.

Preheat oven to 350°F

In a small bowl with electric mixer, beat butter and sugar, then add eggs and continue beating for 2 more minutes.

Add to the cooled rice mixture. Butter a round casserole dish and pour the rice mixture into it.

Bake for 35 minutes and remove from oven to let stand 10-minutes.

ORANGE CUSTARD SAUCE

1½ cups of whole milk
2 tablespoons cornstarch
½ cup of sugar

1 tablespoon orange liqueur
Orange slices, for garnish
Mint leaves, for garnish

In a medium saucepan, combine milk with cornstarch, sugar and orange liqueur.

Bring to a slow boil, stirring constantly. Cook until thick, about 2 minutes.

Pour custard into a heatproof glass bowl, cover with plastic wrap and let cool slightly.

ORANGE CREAM

1 cup of whipping cream
2 tablespoons orange liqueur
1 tablespoon of confectioner sugar

Using an electric mixer, beat whipping cream in a medium bowl until soft peaks form, add orange liqueur and sugar, continue beating until stiff peaks form. Refrigerate until ready to use.

To enjoy, spoon 4 tablespoons of custard on each serving plate, spoon warm rice pudding on top of custard and top with a dollop of orange whipped cream. Garnish with orange slices and mint leaves.

CHOCOLATE PUDDING
With
STRAWBERRY PURÉE and SWEET CREAM
"Signature"

Serves: 4

1 cup of whipping cream
1 cup of whole milk
2 egg yolks, lightly beaten
½ cup baker's sugar, plus 2-tablespoons
2 tablespoons unsweetened coco powder
2½ tablespoons cornstarch
2 tablespoons unsalted butter, plus 1-teaspoon
3 ounces bittersweet chocolate, finely chopped
2 cups fresh strawberries, halved
½ cup of baker's sugar
2 tablespoons Grand Marnier
1 cup sweetened whipped cream, for serving
Mint leaves, for garnish

In a medium saucepan, whisk cream with milk and egg yolks. In a small bowl, combine ½ cup, plus 2-tablespoons of sugar with cocoa and cornstarch.

Add to the saucepan, and cook over very low heat, about 5 minutes, or until it begins to thicken whisking constantly. Strain the pudding into a medium bowl, stir-in the butter and chocolate until melted.

To cool pudding, pour into a large heatproof glass bowl.

Press the plastic wrap directly onto the surface of the pudding and refrigerate for 30-minutes or until chilled.

Spoon pudding into 4-glass bowls or parfait glasses, and keep refrigerated until ready to serve.

STRAWBERRY PURÉE

Place strawberries, the remaining ½ cup of sugar and the Grand Marnier in a blender and purée until smooth.

Top pudding with whipped cream, drizzle strawberry purée over whipped cream and pudding, garnish with mint leaves, and enjoy!

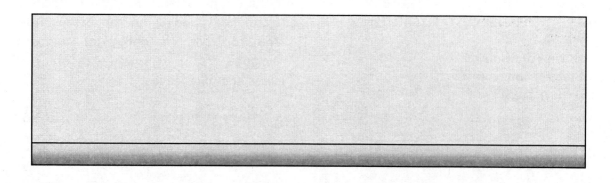

354

QUINOA-ORANGE-PEAR PUDDING
"Signature"

"Cooking with Erika"
Created and demonstrated this on weekly, local, TV segment, aired during year 2002

Serves: 4-6

1 cup of quinoa (pronounced "kinwa"), thoroughly rinsed
½ cup fresh orange juice, plus extra
½ cup Half & Half
½ cup water
½ cup whole milk
¼ teaspoon sea salt
2 medium pears or apples, peeled, cored and finely grated
6 tablespoons orange-honey
¼ teaspoon ground cinnamon
1 cup whipping cream
2 tablespoons confectioner sugar
Orange slices, for garnish

Place all 7 ingredients in a medium saucepan and bring to a boil.

Turn quinoa to simmer and cook until tender, about 15-20 minutes, stirring often.

Quinoa should be thick and creamy. You may add more orange juice at this time if pudding is too thick.

Add honey and cinnamon, cook 1-more minute. Transfer to a heatproof glass bowl, cool slightly.

Whip cream and confectioner sugar until stiff peaks form.

Spoon pudding into parfait glasses or serving bowls, top with sweetened, whipped cream, and enjoy this refreshing pudding garnished with orange slices.

<u>*Note:*</u> Quinoa is normally bitter in taste. To reduce bitterness, I recommend several changes of rinse water. Pudding is delicious served chilled or at room temperature. You may top pudding with other fruits, such as mango, strawberries, rhubarb, blueberries, or huckleberries.

RHUBARB-APPLE COBBLER
With
STRAWBERRY CREAM

Serves: 6-8

COBBLER

1½ cups of sugar
4 tablespoons of cornstarch
¼ teaspoon ground cinnamon
¼ teaspoon fresh ginger, minced
6 cups rhubarb, cooked and cooled
3 apples, peeled, cored and grated (Wine sap or Golden Delicious)
1 tablespoon white rum
2 teaspoons unsalted butter, for greasing dish

Preheat oven to 350°F - Butter one 13 x 9 x 2 inch glass baking dish.

½ cup (1-stick) unsalted butter, room temperature
1 cup sugar
1 large egg
1 teaspoon of vanilla extract
½ cup whole milk
1¼ cups of all-purpose flour
1 teaspoon of baking powder

Rhubarb: Trim both ends of rhubarb (3-4 pounds) and cut into 1-inch pieces. Cook rhubarb with 1 cup of sugar and 1/3 cup of fresh orange juice for 3-5 minutes, let cool and set aside.

Strawberry cream: Slice 1-cup of fresh strawberries, sweeten 2 cups of freshly whipped cream and fold strawberries into the whipped cream. Refrigerate until ready to use.

Fruit mixture: Whisk 1½-cups of sugar and next 3 ingredients in a large bowl to blend. Mix-in the cooked, cooled rhubarb, grated apples, the rum and transfer to prepared dish, bake for 20 minutes, remove the fruit mixture from the oven and keep oven heat on.

While fruit mixture is baking, cream the butter and remaining 1-cup of sugar in a medium-size bowl until light and fluffy. Beat-in egg, vanilla, milk, and sift flour and baking powder over the butter-egg mixture, beat until smooth. Drop batter by scant tablespoonfuls over hot fruit mixture – return cobbler to oven. Bake cobbler until topping is golden and filling is bubbling thickly, about 25-30 minutes, let cobbler rest 5-minutes. Spoon cobbler into heatproof bowls, spoon 1-dollop of strawberry cream on top of cobbler and enjoy warm.

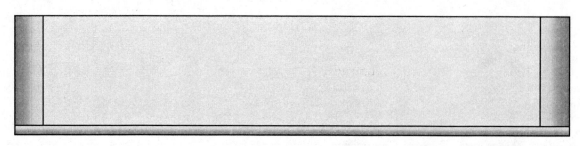

SWEET POLENTA
With
CHERRY-PORT WINE SAUCE
"Signature"

Created for the Washington Fruit Commission and performed the cooking demonstration taped by Taiwanese International Television crews on June 23, 2000 for showing in their home country.

Serves: 6

2 cups of whole milk
1 tablespoon of whipping cream
¼ teaspoon of sea salt
4 tablespoons orange honey
1 cup of polenta
2 tablespoons of unsalted butter, plus extra for greasing pots-de-crème
2 tablespoons grated white chocolate
½ cup slivered-blanched almonds

Preheat oven to 375°F

In a nonstick medium saucepan, bring milk, cream, salt and 2 tablespoons of honey to a boil. Reduce heat to medium low, stir in polenta, add one tablespoon of butter and cook, stirring often, for 10-15 minutes. Remove from heat, and let mixture stand for 10 minutes. Stir in the white chocolate.

Butter 6-6-ounces pots-de-crème or ramekins. Fill each ¾ full and arrange ramekins in a 2-inch deep metal, or glass, baking pan. Fill pan with hot water halfway up the sides of the ramekins. Cover with aluminum foil, situate pan in the middle of the oven and bake for 25-30 minutes.

Remove ramekins from pan and let cool until lukewarm. Run a thin knife blade around the inside edge of each ramekin to loosen the polenta and invert on serving plates.

ALMONDS

In a small heavy saucepan, heat remaining 1 tablespoon of butter and remaining 2 tablespoons of honey, stir in almonds, cook until golden, cool almonds on a large plate and chop them coarsely in a blender or food processor.

CHERRY-PORT WINE SAUCE

1½ cups of Port wine
1 tablespoon of cornstarch
2 tablespoons of sugar
1½ pounds of cherries, washed and pitted
Sweetened whipped cream and mint leaves for garnishing

In a medium saucepan, combine Port wine, cornstarch and sugar. Cook over medium heat, stirring constantly until thickened and clear. Add cherries and cook 1-more minute and keep warm. Note: Cherry Port wine sauce can be made ahead and reheated on low heat while polenta is baking. Spoon cherry port wine sauce over polenta and garnish with fresh whipped cream, or vanilla ice cream, mint leaves, and sprinkle with almond mixture. Enjoy!

WHITE RUM-BANANA-PEAR SMOOTHIE
"Signature"

Serves: 6

½ cup white rum
6 tablespoons sugar
2 bananas, peeled, cut into 1/8-inch pieces
4 pears, peeled, cored and grated
1½ cups fresh orange juice
2 cups ice cubes
Mint leaves for garnish

Blend ¼ cup of rum, 3-tablespoons sugar, 1-banana, 2-grated pears, ¾ cup of orange juice, 1-cup of ice in a blender until smooth. Divide among 3-parfait glasses. Repeat with remaining ingredients and divide among 3-more parfait glasses. Garnish with mint leaves and enjoy.

STRAWBERRY CREAM TART

Serves: 8-10

1¾ cups all-purpose flour, plus extra
1 cup of confectioner sugar
¾ cup (1½-sticks) of chilled unsalted butter, cut into ½- inch pieces, plus extra for greasing
1 large egg
1 package (8oz.) cream-cheese, softened
1 teaspoon of brandy
½ cup Mascarpone cheese
2 baskets (16oz.) strawberries, halved
½ cup raspberry or red currant jelly
1 tablespoon of brandy

Grease sides and bottom of a 9-inch spring-form pan, set aside.

Blend flour, ½ cup confectioner sugar in food processor, add butter and pulse until mixture resembles coarse meal, add the egg, and blend until moist clumps form. Gather dough into a ball, flatten into disk, wrap in plastic and chill 1-hour. Roll out dough on a lightly floured surface and shape it into a 14-inch round. Transfer to prepared pan, press into pan, trim edges to a ½-inch overhang, fold overhanging dough, and press in to form high-standing double-thick sides. Pierce all over with fork. Freeze 20-minutes.

Preheat oven to 350°F

Bake crust until golden, piercing with fork again if crust bubbles, about 20-minutes. Cool on rack. Beat cream cheese, brandy and remaining ½ cup confectioner sugar in medium bowl to blend, add the mascarpone and continue beating for 10-more minutes, or until light and fluffy. Spread filling into crust, and chill until firm, about 1-hour.

Remove pan sides from tart, place tart on cake plate, arrange strawberries on top of filling, melt jelly with brandy in a small saucepan over low heat, brush jelly mixture over berries and chill ½ hour. Slice, serve and enjoy.

HISTORY of the SANDCOOKIE

"Sandcookie" was so named because of its sandy-like texture and it's up close granular appearance, resembling sand.

Myth? Place of Origin, Normandy, France or Lüneburger Heide, Germany?

The 30-year war over the origin of this cookie rages on, but original circumstances have drastically changed over the years, since 1618-1648. The focus now is on a cookie, as to whether the original sand cookie is a, "Sable" or a "Lüneburger Heide" cookie, respectively? As far as the names are concerned, both are correct, except that the place of origin and recipes are slightly different. <u>Background:</u> The namesake of the Heide sand cookie derived from the story about the "thirty year" war "1618-1648", involving the Habsburgs, Denmark, Netherlands, Sweden and France. Resultantly, the war caused food shortages felt throughout Europe, including a shortage of flour, setting the stage for an ongoing debate over which of the two countries originated this "melt in mouth", delicious cookie.

It seems though, with the following scenario, Lüneburger Heide (Niedersachsen) had provided the most convincing evidence. It was there that, because of the scarcity of flour, some bakers had mixed milled sand in with flour to prolong on-hand supply level. The granules of sand gave the surface of the cookie an appearance resembling imbedded specks of sand. Needless to say, those bakers were identified and penalized. (The browned butter and sugar process gives the same visual affect as did sand.) In a declaration, the mayor of Lüneburg placed his seal and stamp on this cookie, thereby, establishing its origin and it's naming as the "Lüneburger Heidesand" Plätzchen.

Apart from the German and the French versions, there are other recipes that have been developed, which call for confectioner sugar and coarse salt that yield different than traditional results, certainly deflecting from the succulent flavor of the original – without sand, of course.

Contrastingly, the French claim the recipe originated in Normandy, France, so named, "Sable" petit gateau (cookie-biscuit). The English translation for "Sable" is "sand". In the French recipe, the butter <u>is not</u> browned, which is the process that gives the appearance of sand in that of the Lüneburger Heide version. Different also, is that the French add egg yolks and lemon rind, and the cookie dough is not rolled into logs as traditionally done in Lüneburg and elsewhere in Germany. Instead, the French roll out the dough and cut out cookies using a cookie cutter. Both of these versions are delectable!

SAND COOKIE

Aka "die Lüneburger Heidesand Plätzchen"

Makes about 36 cookies

1 cup, plus 1 tablespoon unsalted butter (See note, below)
1 cup of super fine white sugar or granulated white sugar, preferably organic
2 teaspoons vanilla sugar (See vanilla sugar instructions below)
Pinch of fine sea salt
2¼ cups all-purpose flour, sifted, plus extra
2 tablespoons whole milk, preferably organic

In a small, heavy saucepan, cook 1 cup of butter over moderate heat until hazelnut color. Transfer butter to a large mixing bowl and let cool completely, about 20-30 minutes. Using mixer paddle attachment, beat butter until creamy then add sugar, vanilla sugar and salt - beat another 2 minutes. On low speed, gradually add sifted flour and milk to blend until flour is incorporated - do not over-mix.

Divide dough in two halves and place each half on individual 12-inch long sheets of plastic wrap – dough will be quite soft at this point. Shape each half of dough into 1¼-inch thick rough logs, wrap plastic around dough and roll it to complete shaping of each half into smooth round logs. Twist ends of plastic wrap and tuck them under. Refrigerate logs for at least 3 hours or overnight – this hardens dough so it retains its shape during slicing.

Preheat oven to 350°F and position middle rack
Line 2 baking sheets with parchment paper

Retrieve, unwrap and crosscut logs into ¼ inch slices with a very sharp, thin blade knife and lay slices, spaced about 1-inch apart, on prepared baking sheets. Bake each sheet separately 12-15 minutes until golden on edges only –

turning baking sheets once after 5-7 minutes of baking. Remove sheet from oven and let cookies cool completely on wire racks or on a heatproof flat surface. Store the cookies in an airtight container. Flavor is best after 2-3 days.

These, melt in your mouth cookies, are storable airtight up to 30 days.

VANILLA SUGAR

2-3 cups superfine sugar
1-2 large vanilla pods
1 airtight container

Break the vanilla pod into several pieces. Put the sugar into the container. Put the pieces of vanilla in containerized sugar. Secure lid. Let set to infuse for a few days in a dry, cool place before using. Replenish sugar as needed in the container. Excellent flavoring for whipped cream, cake batters, custards, puddings and fruits.

Recommendations: To turn out authentic Heidesand Cookies, butter must first be browned cooled and creamed. Eggs should never be added and never should there be more than a pinch of salt in this cookie recipe.

To sustain authenticity for yielding best flavor and texture, I recommend using unsalted European butters, which have higher butterfat and lower moisture content, for richer, creamier cookies or like products.

Unsalted Danish and Irish butters are two European brands usually available in supermarkets. Bearre De Baratte with Normandy Cream and unsalted butter from Isigny, extra fine can be purchased from Internet supply sources.

If experiencing difficulty obtaining those butters, try substituting with widely available unsalted butter that's as close to organic as possible. Using any type of artificial sweeteners, butter substitutes, or margarine, will not yield expected results.

Notes

"WINE COINS"™
YAKIMA VALLEY WINE COUNTRY COOKIES™
"Signature"

Makes about 2 Dozen

½ cup of unsalted butter, at room
temperature
2 tablespoons of Late Harvest Riesling
Wine
½ cup of sugar
3 egg yolks
2 cups of all-purpose flour
Confectioner sugar, for dusting

To make cookie dough, mix butter and wine together at high speed until creamy. Add sugar and 1-egg yolk at a time beating well after each addition. Mix in flour, and beat 1-minute. Shape dough into a flat ball. Cover with plastic wrap and refrigerate 30-minutes.

Preheat oven to 350°F

On a lightly floured surface, roll out refrigerated dough to ¼ inch thickness, and flour a 2¾-inch smooth, round cookie cutter for cutting dough. Place cut dough 1-inch apart on un-greased baking sheets, bake 10-12 minutes or until edges are golden. Remove cookies from baking sheets to cool on wire racks. Sprinkle cookies with confectioner sugar and they're ready to enjoy!

"Wine Coins"™

<u>It may not be the wine.</u> Sometimes, our palate only needs a little priming. A swallow of water before tasting wine is always a good idea. This suggestion might sound odd, and impractical at times, but I've found it useful, when possible, to take a small bite of food served followed by two small sips of wine and another small bite of food and a sip of wine should clearly ascertain if it's a good pairing with the food or not. This makes any selection adjustments, if any, easy because you'll have determined flavor intensity level of the food (sauce) and that might call for either a Merlot with a softer finish or a bolder, full bodied Cabernet Sauvignon, you've got a perfect match. Advantageously though, if you are preparing the meal, you'll know off-hand the intensity of flavor in the finished food, and you'll probably be serving the same variety of wine used in your preparations thus an, likely on target, advantage when choosing wine varieties in balance with flavor(s) of your menu.

Let's say that dry Riesling was used as an ingredient in entrées, then quite possibly, a dry Riesling would pair well as would a Sémillon, a Sauvignon Blanc, or Pinot Grigio, especially if color is golden rather than pale white, medium dry to dry, respectively. Some Chardonnay's can be included, depending on the region from where grapes were harvested and whims of the winemaker, taking into account the finished flavor of each entrée. To venture a little further into the vast world of commonly known white wines, you may want to try Viognier, a dry white wine with low intensity flavor that normally wouldn't overpower

your preparation if the sauce, or preparation, is not very rich. Chardonnay can sometimes be a little tricky pairing with food - I say this because the strength level of oak in finish can vary from a hint of it to sometimes extreme, offering a wider range of applications. In view of this, I believe it's a good idea to pre-taste them and then decide. On the other hand, a known Chardonnay with a mild, buttery finish is least tricky pairing with food, which is why I listed it above among other white wines that are a bit more flexible because of their subtle finishes that oftentimes seemly give in to the flavor of the food enhancing both food and the wine. Red wines are most flexible, providing practically endless applications in flavoring food with a little less fuss, but again, their level of mildness to boldness, soft to hearty, fruity to tangy or spiciness, still needs to be taken into account in choosing wines to enjoy with food or just for sipping. The aforementioned only scratched a tiny surface, so, take a break and go wine tasting at your favorite Appellation wineries or adventurously visit wineries you've never before visited.

<u>*Displayed are few of many varietals of fine Yakima Valley wines*</u>

<u>*You may at times have asked yourself, why did the same wine I tasted and liked yesterday, taste less appealing the next day?*</u> *Rationalistically, it could have been that palate <u>conditions</u> the first day were different the second day! On a comparative note, our palate, like red wines so to speak, should be conditioned, or primed for tasting wine like the practice of exposing or interacting red wine with air - allowing it to breath - intensifying its flavor once the bottle is uncorked and maturing its flavor during the pouring into the glass and swirling the wine before the sniff and taste.*

<u>*The favorable conditions of the wine most likely didn't change the next day, but the condition of the taster's palate a day later quite easily could have and quite possibly did change.*</u>

The most likely cause may have been a lingering aftertaste of whatever food or drink consumed the first day that set up a more favorable palate condition ahead of the initial tasting compared to the changed condition of the palate the second day that led to the disappointing, or even surprising, results. Speculatively, perhaps those onion rings or the cola consumed the second day attributed to the unexpected results whereas the first day's light salad and mineral water setup better conditions for tasting. Tobacco products used before tasting will also render a false reading - producing a false impression of the wine's distinctive, truest flavor. To improve conditions, consider cleansing the palate. For example, a water rinse or a drink of water most likely will be all that's needed to neutralize the palate for tasting wine at home, or while on tasting tours. Once the palate has been favorably primed, or altered, with a swirl, sniff, sip and swish of wine to either discard or swallow you are ready for serious tasting and making better choices. Most wineries, if not all, will have a discard container(s) and a pitcher(s) of water readily available specifically for such purposes.

Discarding is a good idea when visiting several wineries during a tour, even more so if driving. It's also a good idea to allocate sufficient time touring a wine region spreading out visiting wineries over two plus days, rather than trying to visit them all in one day, or plan another trip to taste wines at wineries that weren't visited during the first trip. Be safe and designate a non-alcoholic drinking driver.

During tours of wineries, even some wines you've tasted, and rejected, could reveal great characteristics the next day when matched with the right conditions or food combination. This does happen, and more often that one might think! The following simplified guide was so well received in my second cookbook entitled A Touch of Europe® Cookbook - Bringing "Fresh" to the table – Naturally", I decided to repeat it in this cookbook. Consider:

1. The method-style of cooking, such as, roasted, broiled, baked, toasted, fried, sautéed, braised, deep-fried, or pan-fried;

2. Choice of meat, poultry, fowl, fish or seafood and their flavor strength in combination with 3 and 4, below;

3. The flavor of sauces, dark, medium or light: Beef, pork, chicken or fish/seafood stock, broth or gravy, domestic or wild-game ingredients, heavily spiced, buttery or oily substances used are some typical examples, or

4. Whether the finished preparation or entrée ends with a bitter, sweet, tangy, fruity, herby, oily, bland, burnt, woodiness of sorts, charcoal, spicy, soft, harsh, or sour finish.

Reminiscent return to Europe, singling out an experienced example, particularly with wines in Italy, may be an exception to what is generally considered the "white wine rule with fish and white meat" and the "red wine rule with red meat" because of herbal, delicate finishes in some Italian red (table) wines that seemed to blend extremely well with practically everything - even a light lasagna with a cheese- cream-mushroom sauce - except with some of Italy's many desserts like those fortified with liqueurs. Some discretion is needed in view of the latter, perhaps bolder red or most preferably a Port wine would be better choices. Rationalizing and using my lasagna episode in Udine, Italy, as an example, stems from the fact that those lasagna noodles were freshly handmade, the cream and cheese sauce was made fresh from whole-fat, and the fresh musty-woodsy flavor of the mushrooms was noticeable, but still in balance with all other ingredients – all of that with the restaurant's house made (non-labeled) soft, herby, light red wine contributed toward a terrific match. Mushrooms and cheeses were also component factors. When I asked questions

about the wine and asked if I could purchase a few bottles of it, they sold me only one bottle, and the proprietor kept the variety secret, except for saying that "it's a red table wine", the final answer to my question. Apparently, the blend is a house kept secret. Unsurprisingly, that response sounded like some of my responses when I'm asked for a recipe before I'm ready to release it. I could try guessing the variety, but it probably wouldn't do it justice, so I'll

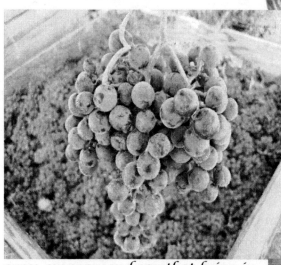

guess anyway and say that being in Northeast Italy at that time, it could have been one of Veneto Italy's respected Bordeau blends, or maybe a blend with Pinot Nero. Even so, we ordered, and equally enjoyed, another helping of lasagna before ending our journey traveling from Bibione, at the Adriatic Sea, to Udine (where we enjoyed the lasagna). After a stopover in Garmish-Partenkirchen, we proceeded to our home destination near Frankfurt, West Germany.

Germany, being the land of notable white wines, takes on a different, but original, role when it comes to food and wine. When I think about it, German cuisine is more suited to white wine varieties than with red because it is more a white wine producing country and "light meat" dishes like pork is favored, including fish, chicken, and veal. Of course, wild game, such as duck, venison, wild boar, hare and rabbit, are more suited with light red wine because German food is mostly mildly flavored-spiced, notwithstanding, hot and spicy food there exists in ethnic food but not predominantly. Components in sauces do make a difference, however. It would appear as though the type of cuisine was built around what was available in Germany to drink, such as mineral water, great beer and great white wine rather than in reverse. Except in certain appellations, such as in Rheingau and Sachsen, from there originates the Lemberger and Spätburgunder (Pinot Noir), respectively while white wines dominate most other wine grape growing appellations - a case in point only, and naturally there isn't deprivation of red wines, or white wines, anywhere in Germany, nor beer.

Traditional recipes and methods obtained from afar inspire modern day trends, which many times miss the mark on flavor. Experimenting is a good thing. I'm experimenting all the time, but I dearly hold true to my traditional ideal that "flavor is paramount." in anything I create. Embedded within me I guess, is my heritage, inducing traditional European flavors I grew up with and know very well, and not limiting my dishes to just German cuisine. Fusing, yes I do, but "flavor must be trump". Being the "refusenick" that I

am, I avoid venturing into the momentary arena of change or trends that seems to emphasize focus on unusual combinations or the use of one or more ingredients to dramatize a specific ingredient or components of concoctions rather than placing emphasis on producing scrumptious flavor resulting from those efforts. I'm certainly not indifferent to change it's just my sense of "production and results" ideals that are different.

What may be a choice by some, but many of the red varietals wouldn't be my choice paired with everything - but there are a few exceptions. Knowing what they are will make or break a pleasant experience. A white fish with a hearty, rich cream sauce may pair with red such as Pinot Noir, but with spicy sautéed prawns, I would recommend focusing on Pinot Gris. But I wouldn't rule out a Piedmont Nebbiolo D'alba, Pinot Noir or Sangiovese. Personally, I still enjoy a red wine depending on its boldness and flavor of sauces with red meats, such as lamb, beef, duck, foi gras and depending on spices used, paprika chicken may pair nicely with light red wines, and even with some salmon dishes, but these options still deserve some scrutinizing to be sure - that's why wine tasting is so enjoyable and favored.

Generally, I recommend dry to med-dry white wine with white fish. One example, cod or halibut sautéed in a natural herb sauce enhanced with white wine such as a dry Riesling or Sémillon, my focus would then be on either of those two varieties, including Sauvignon Blanc, Viognier or perhaps a Chenin Blanc. White fish with beer sauce deserves to be served with beer rather than with wine. Seafood posses a different scenario that may be challenging if a seafood dish or other dish has a mix of many herbs and strong spices, presenting a situation that may warrant a series of tasting events to find the right match. Oftentimes, the back label on wine bottles provide generic information beneficial toward that end After considering all of that and you still aren't sure, a glass of natural spring water may be just fine, then, regroup and plan another venture into wine country, even if it means conjuring up an excuse to do so. Cheers!

INDEX

A

B

C

D

E

F

G

T

NOTES

FOOD HANDLING TIPS

BASIC DECONTAMINATING - PRECAUTIONARY CONSIDERATIONS

After returning from food shopping, think twice about contaminating the refrigerator or storage unit before loading the refrigerator or placing purchases on countertops! Imagine the exposure of pre-packaged and raw foods to unimaginable potential contaminates (germs) after foods at processing plants are loaded onto conveyance vehicles; foods exposure to elements during transit; foods exposure during handling by destinations staff, and by shoppers before purchased.

Even so supermarket produce staff wash produce in a solution and have other procedures instituted to quash potential hazards, there is a certain amount of handling by shoppers before handled produce is purchased - a typical procedure when shoppers are browsing for fruits, tomatoes, and melons to name a few - just checking for ripeness. What isn't placed in the shopping cart is returned to the display counter – for the next shopper to check. What have those hands touched before then and what potential germy residue did they leave behind?

Some vegetables, like cauliflower and carrots displayed wrapped can be protected by covering original wrapping with new wrapping or preferably by replacing wrapping before storing in the refrigerator – do this in a sanitized, dry sink avoiding contact of wrapping exterior or hands with produce such as pre-wrapped cauliflower - slit sealed side of wrapping with a sharp knife, peel off wrapping and discard – (do not wash cauliflower until ready to use) - wash-dry hands, wrap cauliflower with clear plastic and store it in the refrigerator until ready to wash, process and use.

Loose vegetables should be washed and patted dry with paper towels before storing in crispers and then rinsed, patted dry with paper towels before using. Wash tomatoes, thoroughly dry them with paper towels and store them un-refrigerated in a dish, bowl or tray somewhere, most likely in the kitchen. Mushrooms - store refrigerated in a clean paper bag, rinse and pat them dry with paper towels before further processing and use.

Rather than using countertops for the decontaminating process, the sink is easiest to sanitize before and after, but if it isn't feasible to use the sink, I recommend covering an area of the countertop with wax paper or plastic wrap, which can be easily gathered and disposed of, or using a large stainless steel tray to set produce on while the sanitizing process of other produce takes place at the chosen work area. Habitual use of food handler's gloves combined with frequent changes is highly recommended.

ARE KITCHEN HABITS AND KITCHEN FUNCTIONALLY EFFICIENT?

I don't need a lot of clutter in my kitchen. After all, I grew up in Germany, where kitchen space was limited, and for the most part, still is. The more gadgets purchased, obviously meant more space was needed to store them and clean up, and they oftentimes end up being stored in the basement or stored in the garage in wait for the next yard sale to end the cluttered conditions.

If you aren't going from one end of the kitchen for something or other needed at least one time a day to complete your cooking endeavor, then your kitchen may already be efficiently organized, the biggest time saver is already implemented, and saving a lot of effort putting together meals.

But if it isn't, it generally only needs to be done once unless cooking habits surrounding schedules drastically change. Simply put, items such as; utensils, tools, pots, pans, lids, food, spices, oils, even wines and liqueurs used regularly or occasionally saves lots of time and effort when stored close by in cabinets, drawers, shelves and countertops, whichever least represents clutter and is within easy reach from the primary work station - whether it be the preparation counter, oven, stove top or other most frequently used kitchen area and appliances. Minimizing steps between two points is an obvious time and motion (effort) saver. Within an arm's reach is best whenever possible.

It also helps by storing infrequently used items separately from frequently used items. Store infrequently used items in a pantry or cabinet, for example, away from the most frequently used area in the kitchen, this eliminates clutter in an area most used and again saves time. But, it does help make projects much smoother to gather and pre-position infrequently used items in advance of planned use, such as, seasonal canning supplies, tools and pots. After completing that project, they're returned to the "infrequent use" storage area until next time. For items that haven't been used at all within a year, I ask myself if I really still need them, if not, they are destined to be in the hands of someone who does need them.

Helpful also is a spatula 10 feet away should be located to within an arm's reach when needed, and if a spatula is frequently needed at distant ends of the kitchen, consider duplicating and storing spatulas at more than one location. Another example, a 10-gallon stockpot used twice a year can be appropriately stored elsewhere until needed, including the long handled ladle. Accommodating routine use is highlighted here, secondly entertaining, if frequent or occasional entertaining is part of your lifestyle whether formal or informal for small or large gatherings - for relatives or friends, then formal and informal serving pieces, china, flatware, stemware, etc. are scenarios that warrant considering where these items should be stored. If you entertain guests in the dining room, store fine china, flatware and stemware etc. in the dining room, or nearest to it, *if possible and store the everyday (casual) china, flatware, glassware, etc. in the kitchenette if this is where everyday family dining occurs.*

I believe an organized kitchen instills confidence in anyone utilizing it, reduces frustration factors, eliminates delays looking for a needed item or utensil during the cooking process, so attention is focused on producing what you plan to produce - flavor and serving appreciative recipients of it. Simply put, tasks are easier to complete, and the saucepan on the stove isn't boiling over while looking for a tool needed at the moment. Pre-measuring ingredients reduced or eliminates potential delay factors, streamlining effort and saving time putting meals on the table. A kitchen doesn't have to be huge or contain the most expensive appliances to produce meals with great flavor, all that's needed are functional appliances, a little knowledge about cooking, "a good recipe", quality ingredients, an organized kitchen, and someone to cook for.

You may find other helpful information and tips in other pages of this cookbook, usually in the form of tips buried within recipes - ideas that may help organizing an efficient, simplified, yet gourmet kitchen , streamlining it to adapt to your movements - in concert with cooking habits and schedules - whether you cook meals once in a while; only on weekends; only on special occasions; only when entertaining friends, or a combination of any or all of those on a regular or irregular basis. Whichever type of kitchen set up you prefer or the type of occasion planned, preparing and cooking meals can be more easily and timely accomplished with precision in an organized kitchen.

SUGGESTED ESSENTIAL KITCHEN TOOLS-UTENSILS

*Start with the most affordable, highest quality of pots and pans. It's a plus if they are dishwasher safe with excellent performance ratings for braising meats, cooking vegetables, sautéing, frying, low-fat cooking, be oven safe up to 500°F and comes with a full defect replacement guarantee. High quality stainless steel and cookware with ceramic coating are my most preferred choices. I still use mine after 40 years of heavy use, they still perform as when new and they still look good. I personally am not very comfortable with some cookware with nonstick coating that may be susceptible to wearing off. If it wears off, what wore off must go somewhere and the most likely place would be in the food cooking in it. So,

*A 10-piece high quality (commercial rated) cookware set would be a good starter set, and for some families this size set may be all that is needed.

*A roasting pan with rack 16" long x 12" wide x 3.75" deep.

*A 10-piece glass bowl set, a set of 4 silicone spatulas, a chrome plated or stainless steel teakettle with nickel lining or copper teakettle with tin lining.

*A well balanced set of kitchen knives, including: A chef's knife for chopping, mincing, dicing and julienne.

*An 8-inch carving knife and metal skewers.

*At least one, 3-inch serrated paring knife for peeling and slicing small fruits and vegetables.

*At least one potato peeler, apple corer, zester, butter curler and channel knife for making citrus-peel twists.

*At least one of each, 3½ and 4½ inch paring knife with straight edge.

*At least one, 5 inch boning knife.

*One, 9-inch bread knife for slicing bread, which also effectively slices tomatoes and citrus.

*An electric knife sharpener or sharpening stone.

*Kitchen shears, a must have versatile tool, a nutcracker, lid lifter, jar and bottle opener, a can opener, and even a screwdriver and a pair of high quality pliers (for kitchen use only) are useful at times, such as removing hot skewers that held together rolled meats or fowl.

*A bottle opener, a jar opener and a cork puller.

*One reversible pounder with a smooth side for flattening and a ridged side for tenderizing.

*Disposable food handler gloves, very useful and sanitary.

*One dishwasher safe cutting board - marked for vegetables, herbs, etc. use only.

*One dishwasher safe cutting board - marked and reserved only for cutting meats, fowl, fish, etc.

*Thermometers designed for food testing, for refrigerator and for ovens.

*At least, one micro-plane grater, a fine-grater for citrus, and a ribbon-grater for hard cheeses and chocolate.

*Measuring cups: ¼ cup, 2 cups and 4 cups capacity. For durability and longevity, select measuring cups that are in one solid piece, rather than those with glued windows inserted in cutouts.

*At least two long and short handled slotted and non-slotted spoons and at least two long and short handled utility forks.

*At least two 12-inch long tweezers and at least one pancake turner.

*Strainers, fine mesh strainers for sifting cocoa, confectioner sugar, flour and smoothing lumps from sauces or gravies. 5.5", 6", 7" and 8" sizes are recommended.

*One salad/herb spinner.

*A food processor of sufficient size and capabilities to accommodate need.

*One each scale, measuring pitcher, measuring spoons, and wood spoons, toothpicks and wood (bamboo) or metal skewers.

*A multi-speed hand mixer for small jobs, like whipping cream, but powerful enough (220 watts) to cut through refrigerated butter.

*A counter-top (stand) mixer with beaters and dough hook plus any other capability of handling your style of use.

*Extra stainless steel and glass mixing bowls of various sizes.

*At least two cookie sheets: one 9" x 13" and one 14" x 16", and at least one 9, 10 or 12-inch spring-form pan with removable bottom.

*Cake boards, sable paint brushes, pastry brush and twirl for honey.

*Flat flexible blade (spatula), short and long, for smoothing out frostings.

*At least one 6 or 12 cup popover pan and muffin cups.

*Nonstick baking paper, parchment paper or wax paper and aluminum foil.

*Baking pans: A 10-cup bundt pan commercial weight – best are heavy walled cast aluminum.

*At least one dishwasher safe chrome plated or stainless steel cooling rack.

*A waffle iron, newer models are easier to use, a nice to have item.

*A quality filter/drip style coffee maker with a thermal carafe.

*Automatic yogurt maker, juice extractor.

MEASUREMENTS - CONVERSIONS TABLES

COMMON EQUIVALENTS – U.S.

1/8	teaspoon	=	1	dash
½	teaspoon	=	30	drops
1	teaspoon	=	1/3	tablespoon or 60 drops
3	teaspoons	=	1	tablespoon or ½ fluid ounce
½	tablespoon	=	1½	teaspoons
1	tablespoon	=	3	teaspoons or ½ fluid ounce
2	tablespoons	=	1	fluid ounce
3	tablespoons	=	1½	fluid ounces or 1 jigger
4	tablespoons	=	¼	cup or 2 fluid ounces
5½	tablespoons	=	1/3	cup or 5 tablespoons + 1 teaspoon
8	tablespoons	=	½	cup or 4 fluid ounces
12	tablespoons	=	¾	cup or 6 fluid ounces
16	tablespoons	=	1	cup or 8 fluid ounces or ½ pint
1/8	cup	=	2	tablespoons or 1 fluid ounce
¼	cup	=	4	tablespoons or 2 fluid ounces
1/3	cup	=	5	tablespoons + 1 teaspoon
3/8	cup	=	¼	cup + 2 tablespoons
½	cup	=	8	tablespoons or 4 fluid ounces or 1 gill
5/8	cup	=	½	cup + 2 tablespoons
¾	cup	=	12	tablespoons or 6 fluid ounces
7/8	cup	=	¾	cup + 2 tablespoons
1	cup	=	16	tablespoons or ½ pint or 8 fluid ounces
2	cups	=	1	pint or 16 fluid ounces
1	pint	=	2	2 cups or 16 fluid ounces
1	quart	=	2	pints or 4 cups or 32 fluid ounces
1	gallon	=	4	quarts or 8 pints or 16 cups or 128 fluid ounces
2	gallons	=	1	peck
4	pecks	=	1	bushel

QUICK REFERENCE MEASURES

1	ounce				=	30 grams
4	ounces				=	120 grams
8	ounces				=	125 grams
16	ounces	=	1	pound	=	450 grams
32	ounces	=	2	pounds	=	900 grams
36	ounces	=	2¼	pounds	=	1000 grams (1-kg.)
¼	teaspoon	=	1/24	ounce	=	1 ml
½	teaspoon	=	1/12	ounce	=	2 ml
1	teaspoon	=	1/6	ounce	=	5 ml
1	tablespoon	=	½	ounce	=	15 ml
1	cup	=	8	ounces	=	250 ml
2	cups (1 pint)	=	16	ounces	=	500 ml
4	cups (1 quart)	=	32	ounces	=	1 liter
4	quarts (1 gallon)	=	128	ounces	=	3.75 liter

32º	Fahrenheit	=	0º Centigrade (Celsius)
22º	Fahrenheit	=	50º Centigrade (Celsius)
212º	Fahrenheit	=	100º Centigrade (Celsius)

MOST COMMONLY USED METRIC EQUIVALENTS

Volume

¼	teaspoon	=	1/23	milliliters
½	teaspoon	=	2.46	milliliters
¾	teaspoon	=	3.7	milliliters
1	teaspoon	=	4.93	milliliters
1¼	teaspoons	=	6.16	milliliters
1½	teaspoons	=	7.39	milliliters
1¾	teaspoons	=	8.63	milliliters
2	teaspoons	=	9.86	milliliters
1	tablespoon	=	14.79	milliliters
1	fluid ounce	=	29.57	milliliters
2	tablespoons	=	29.57	milliliters
¼	cup	=	59.15	milliliters
½	cup	=	118.3	milliliters
1	cup	=	236.59	milliliters
2	cups or 1 pint	=	473.18	milliliters
3	cups	=	709.77	milliliters
4	cups (1 quart)	=	946.36	milliliters
4	quarts (1 gallon)	=	3.785	liters

WEIGHT

1	ounce	=	28.35	grams
8	ounces (½ pound)	=	226/8	grams
16	ounces (1-pound)	=	453.6	grams
2	pounds	=	910	grams
2	pounds	=	1	kilogram or
2	pounds	=	1000	grams

OVEN TEMPERATURES CONVERSION-FAHRENHEIT/CENTIGRADE

Fahrenheit	Centigrade	
225°F	110ºC	Very cool
250°F	130ºC	Very cool
275°F	140°C	Cool
300°F	150ºC	Slow
325°F	170ºC	Moderately slow
350°F	180ºC	Moderate
375°F	190ºC	Moderately hot
400°F	200ºC	Moderately hot
425°F	220ºC	Hot
450°F	230ºC	Hot
475°F	245ºC	Very hot
500°F	260°C	Very hot

Notes

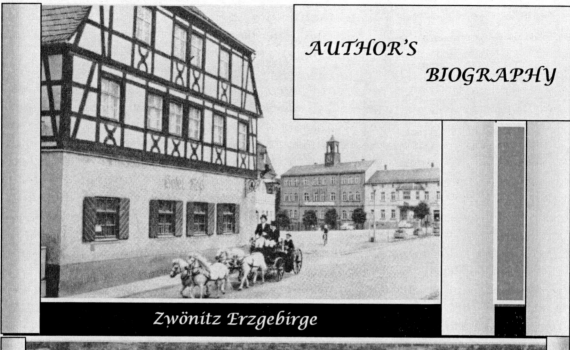

Zwönitz Erzgebirge

Spandau Campus before mission completely changed

ABOUT THE AUTHOR

Born in East Germany, raised in West Berlin and obtained culinary training regarding food, and restaurant and hospitality industries in residence at Spandau, West Berlin after WW II, and whose parents owned and operated hotel/restaurant "Lehngericht". Her father was a prominent businessman and her mother an accredited chef who previously apprenticed at the famous Ratskeller, West Berlin, Germany. Chef Erika, with over 30 years professional cooking, now shares experiences, tips, and eclectic recipes promoting her lifelong use of seasonal fresh, organic as possible, ingredients, spreading encouragement to those who wish to return to a healthier lifestyle by cooking from scratch. Through her culmination of experience at a, castle connected, 4-star restaurant in Dreieichenhain, West Germany named "Faselstall"; as a restaurateur, professional caterer, business owner in the food and hospitality industries and her travels through several European countries, other than her birth country, like Switzerland, Austria, France, Italy, Netherlands, Belgium and England assures essences of European flavors exist in all her creations, naturally.

Each week for nearly three years, chef Erika originated recipes specifically for demonstrating them on a local CBS affiliate TV station, "Cooking with Erika", some of which, are included and identified in this (third) cookbook and others were included in her second cookbook. She conducted cooking classes at the Pacific Lutheran University (PLU), and took top honors at culinary shows for her salmon and desserts masterpieces. Chef Erika's reputation was built on "flavor", the primary reason behind garnering "Best Chef" and "Best Evening Cuisine" Awards, USA and Canada, 2004 and 2005, respectively – within the top 15 participating. Chef Erika, and her husband, continue highlighting flavor in her prearranged signature 3-7 course dinners, including winemaker's dinners, served in her historic circa. 1889 Queen Anne Victorian, Bed & Breakfast-Fine Dining Establishment, in Yakima Valley wine country, Yakima, WA.

Chef Erika was featured in Canada's leading news source, Globe and Mail as well as in the Northwest Palate Magazine Article, "Spring Barrel Tasting-Asparagus Festival" and was selected for inclusion in NW Palate's recent 20th Anniversary edition – Best of the Northwest, Recipes & Wines, People & Places; Touring & Tasting "Wine-Food-Travel" Magazine Article, "Perfect Wine Tour Weekend-Yakima Valley"; featured in three articles in the Yakima Herald-Republic Newspaper, and most recently in the "2006" Winter edition of the Mid-Columbian magazine, a high quality publication featuring highlights of Eastern Washington people, places and attractions – a photo of her Establishment dominates it's front cover. "Uniquely, a chef-owned B&B".

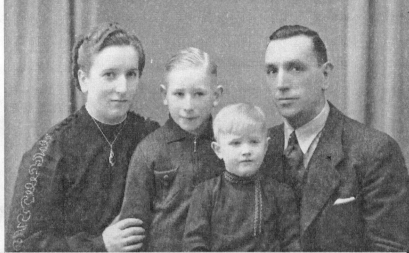

Above - Mother   ///   L - R Erika's Mother, Brother, Erika & Father

Zwönitz - Erika's Hometown - Market place at Christmas Time

Erzgebirge-Sachsen, Germany, translated means "Ore Mountains", a mountainous range along the Czech-German border, reaching its highest point of 4,080 feet in Kinovec, Leiberg, Germany located in the Czech Republic. Silver and iron mining are important industries, including manufacturing chemical, machinery and textile. Embroidering and toy making have long been traditional home industries. In 1938 the Czech part of the Erzgebirge was transferred to Germany by the Munich Pact, which was later restored to Czechoslovakia during 1945.

Summertime Historic Splendor

Wintertime Historic Splendor

Awards Winning Chef owned
A Touch of Europe® Bed & Breakfast-Fine Dining Establishment®
220 North 16ᵗʰ Avenue, Yakima, Washington 98902
www.winesnw.com/toucheuropeb&b.htm
www.atouchofeurope.info and www.cheferikagcenci.com

The Historic Charles Pollock Wilcox House, Circa. 1889
On the
National Historic Register
Home of
Author Erika G. Cenci's "A Touch of Europe®"
"Bed & Breakfast - Fine Dining Establishment"

NOTES